Inventing China Through History

SUNY series in
Chinese Philosophy and Culture

David L. Hall and Roger T. Ames, editors

Inventing China Through History

The May Fourth Approach to Historiography

Q. Edward Wang

STATE UNIVERSITY OF NEW YORK PRESS

Published by
State University of New York Press, Albany

Printed in the United States of America

For information, address State University of New York Press, Albany, NY
www.sunypress.edu

Production by Kristin Milavec
Marketing by Fran Keneston

Library of Congress Cataloging-in-Publication Data

Wang, Q. Edward, 1958–
Inventing China through history: the May Fourth Approach to historiography/Q. Edward Wang.
p. cm.—(SUNY series in Chinese philosophy and culture)
Includes bibliographical references and index.
ISBN 0-7914-4731-6 (alk. paper)—ISBN 0-7914-4732-4 (pbk.: alk. paper)
1. China—Historiography. 2. Historiography—China—History—20th century. I. Title. II. Series.
DS734.7.W33 2001
951'.007'2—dc21 00-020626

10 9 8 7 6 5 4 3 2 1

To GAO Ni

Contents

Acknowledgments

This project has developed over many years and has benefited from many people. My interest in historiography began in the early 1980s when I was pursuing my graduate work at East China Normal University in Shanghai, China, where I studied primarily with Professor Guo Shengming. Although Guo was considered an expert on the study of Western historiography in the PRC, in the 1930s he was a student of many of the historians—or the May Fourth scholars—studied in this book. Over the years, I also have had the pleasure to work with Professor Zhang Zhilian of Beijing University, who, along with Professor Guo, has given me both encouragement and advice. From Guo, Zhang, and many other Chinese intellectuals with a similar background I came to develop a personal "feel" of the May Fourth scholars in this book. In the initial stage of my research, I had an opportunity to interview Professor E-tu Zen Sun at Pennsylvania State University. A daughter of Chen Hengzhe (Sophia) and Ren Hongjun (Zen Hung-chün), close friends of Hu Shi, Professor Sun, like Guo and Zhang, graced me with her memory of the May Fourth generation, of which her parents and their friends were prominent figures.

I began my research on this subject in the aftermath of the 1989 Tiananmen Square incident. Although I was already in the United States at the time, I must say that the event has in many ways helped reorient the direction of my research and career. I am indebted to Professor Joseph M. Levine at Syracuse University and Professor Georg G. Iggers at SUNY Buffalo for their encouragement and understanding. In writing and completing my dissertation, which was the basis of this book, I have also benefited from the advice of Professor Norman A. Kutcher, a cultural historian of late-imperial and modern China at Syracuse. Professor Yu Ying-shih of Princeton University—whom I first consulted in 1989—also offered valuable advice that helped me define the scope of this project. I am grateful to all of them for their expertise in helping build my knowledge base on both Chinese and Western historical cultures and hope that this small volume can reflect some of their education. I would especially like to thank Georg Iggers for his warm friendship and strong support that I have cherished ever since 1984 when we first met. I am also indebted to Professor Arif Dirlik of Duke University who provided much needed critique for helping me reconceptualize the project at an early stage of its development.

In the summer of 1996, I participated in the NEH Summer Seminar on Chinese ethnicity and nationality organized by Prasenjit Duara and Dru Gladney at the East-West Center, Hawai'i. I benefited a good deal from the discussions in the seminar, particularly from my talks with Professor Duara, who had then just published his well-received book on historical narratives in modern China. At various stages when I prepared the manuscript for publication, I have benefited from the advice and help of the following people: Peter Bol, Paul A. Cohen, Ralph Croizier, D. W. Y. Kwok, Thomas H. C. Lee, Vera Schwarcz, Jeffrey Wasserstrom, Daniel Wolf, and Peter Zarrow. In the past several years, I have had several opportunities to present part of my work at the following institutions: Institute of History and Philology, Academia Sinica, Taiwan; Bielefeld University, Free University of Berlin, Germany; and at SUNY Buffalo. I am grateful to Wang Fan-sen, Jörn Rüsen, Mechthild Leutner, Thomas Burkman, and Roger Des Forges for their invitations and comments.

I would also like to thank German Academic Exchange Services (DAAD) for a short-term fellowship that allowed me to check out some necessary information in Germany in 1994. At the final stage of my revision, I was able to spend a semester at the Institute of History and Philology, Academia Sinica on a fellowship from the Center for Chinese Studies, National Library, Taiwan in 1999. I am indebted to Mr. Tu Cheng-sheng, the director of the Institute, for providing me with research facilities and allowing me to use the Fu Sinian (Fu Ssu-nien) Archives, housed in the Institute's library. My friendship with Ku Wei-ying, Wang Fan-sen, Huang Chün-chieh, Huang Chin-hsing, and others also made my stay in Taiwan a pleasant experience. Over the years, I have received funding from Rowan University, my home institution, which facilitated my research in general and my writing and revision of this book in particular. To my friends Linda Pirolli, Jim Rooney, Ken Hovey, and Minna Doskow, I owe my thanks for proofreading the manuscript and improving its prose. Some portions of chapter 2 were published in my article "History in Late-Imperial China," *Storia della Storiografia*, 22 (1992), pp. 3–22. I thank the journal editor Edoardo Tortarolo for his permission to reprint them here. I am also grateful to two reviewers of my manuscript for the press for their constructive and valuable comments. My thanks also go to my editors, Nancy Ellegate and Kristin Milavec, for their proficiency in producing this book. Yet it is I who is ultimately responsible for any remaining mistakes.

Last but not least, I would like to take the opportunity to thank my family for their love and support over the years: to my parents for teaching me the importance of education, even during the fierce years of the Cultural Revolution, and to my wife Ni for her patience and optimism. During the past decade, she has always believed in me and in the value of this project, for which I am particularly grateful. I would like to dedicate this book to her.

Chapter One

Introduction

> The past is always altered for motives that reflect present needs. We reshape our heritage to make it attractive in modern terms; we seek to make it part of ourselves, and ourselves part of it; we confirm it to our self-images and aspirations. Rendered grand or homely, magnified or tarnished, history is continually altered in our private interests or on behalf of our community or country.
>
> —David Lowenthal, *The Past Is a Foreign Country*

History connects past with present. This connection is established by and, generally, also for the present. Yet, the ways in which historians write history vary tremendously: History is and has been written differently for different purposes.[1] In order to cast light on present events, for example, one can simply collect and preserve any available information about the past. What prompted Herodotus (484–424? B.C.E.) to write his *Histories*, as he professed at its outset, was to prevent the memory of the Greeks about their glorious victory over the Persians from falling into oblivion. In China where historical writing has long been an integral part of its civilization, there is a well-known adage, "to know the future in the mirror of the past" *(jian wang zhi lai)*, that expresses a similar desire to remember past events for better understanding the present and successfully speculating upon the future. While interest in the past of this sort is shown in many historical cultures, contributing to the development of historical study, it by no means addresses fully the complex relationship between past and present. In fact, focusing on the past as a predictor shows a grain of naïveté in its implication that knowledge of the past can be directly applied to solving problems of the present, because such a focus presupposes the sameness of past and present and ignores the change of historical time.

Gordon Graham posits that a more ambitious way of linking past with present is, "to look beneath the surface of events and find their inner or ultimate significance."[2] In so doing, one examines the past from a teleological perspective and tries to search for meanings in the course of history as a whole, rather than in some individual historical events. Although this kind of historical understanding, or the construction of a historical metanarrative, had appeared before, it was seen more often in recent times, especially in the rise of modern nations. As shown in the histories of many countries, historical writing was an integral part of the nation-building project. This goal of making a modern nation compelled historians to look back at the country's past from a new, different perspective. Instead of regarding the past as a holistic entirety, for instance, they looked for multiplicity in the past and searched in tradition for elements useful to create a national history. In so doing, historians historicized the past against the change of historical time and differentiated the past—the subject of their study—from the present—their own time. Rather than a reservoir of knowledge, history now became a subject of study, or a mirror, that reflects not only the past for the present but also the present *in* the past. As a result, in the practice of nationalist historiography, there appeared an almost reversed relationship between past and present; the past was no longer viewed as a guidance but as a genesis of one's imaginary of a nation.

In China's long historiographical tradition, there existed many works written most definitely for the purpose of guiding the present. The most salient example was the writing of dynastic history, especially from the Tang Dynasty (618–907) onward, in which many historical events and figures, mostly in the arena of politics, were described in detail. By presenting these examples, which were considered precedents, dynastic historians hoped that the reigning dynasty could learn from past lessons and, by avoiding previous mistakes, would effect a long-lasting rule. However, in addition to these dynastic histories, which were considered by conventional wisdom the mainstay of Chinese historiography, there were instances suggesting that historians also attempted more ambitious approaches to historical explanation. In his magnum opus, *Records of the Grand Historian (Shiji)*, for instance, Sima Qian (145–86 B.C.E.) launched an investigation into the Heaven-Man correlation as manifested in history and sought out a comprehensive yet personal explanation. Over a thousand years later in the Northern Song Dynasty (960–1127), Sima Guang (1019–1086) in his *A Comprehensive Mirror of Aid for Government (Zizhi tongjian)* also tried to search for reasons beneath the rise and fall of dynasties and offered his perspective on the direction of Chinese political history for more than a thousand years, from 403 B.C.E. to 959 C.E.

A systematic attempt at constructing a historical metanarrative also appeared in late-nineteenth- and early-twentieth-century China. Influenced by the idea of nationalism, Chinese intellectuals came to reconfigure the past in order to build a nation-state, which was regarded by many as imperative for strengthening and reaffirming China's position in the modern world. In so doing, these intellectuals introduced changes to the tradition of Chinese historiography. These changes were manifested both in the idea and form of historical writing. In the following pages, I will describe and analyze the emergence of national history as a new historical consciousness in modern China.

In the first part of the twentieth century, there were three main schools of thought in Chinese historiography: the traditionalists; the liberals; and somewhat later, the Marxists. The traditionalists were not totally traditional in that they were not clones of ancient dynastic annalists. The liberals were not modernists intent on totally abandoning tradition. The Marxists were probably the purest of the three schools of thought, in that they sought to explain possible event in terms of class struggle. The protagonists in my book were one distinct group in the Chinese historical community, not only in terms of their educational background and career path but also in terms of their political inclination and ideologies. Having grown up in the late period of the Qing Dynasty (1644–1911), they all received a classical education when young. Yet at a later time, they all had the opportunity to study abroad, either in Europe or the United States. Their unique educational experience differentiated them from many of their cohorts who had little or no Western education. In the meantime, they also showed their disdain of the radical ideas of the Marxists who, while equally receptive to Western political ideology and nationalism, advocated the necessity of mounting a socialist revolution and establishing a proletarian dictatorship. By contrast, these historians preferred and practiced (whenever they could) the ideas of liberalism and constitutionalism. Working mostly in an academic setting, they produced works that represent a new direction in the history of Chinese historical writing. The above three-way division however does not do full justice to the complex development of modern Chinese intellectual history in general, and modern Chinese historiography in particular; for although they were attracted to Western political and cultural theories like the Marxists, these Western-educated intellectuals also showed a strong interest in reviving Chinese tradition, an agenda conventionally associated with the traditionalists.

This new direction was followed in the field of historiography, where two seemingly contrary interests came in to play at the same time. On the one hand, these liberal historians attempted to construct a historical narrative for the nation-state, which lent their historiography strong political overtones. On the other hand, they were intrigued by the idea of scientific history, exemplified in nineteenth-century Western historiography, which, in its ideal form, advocated "the attempt simply to arrive at an accurate account of past events based upon sufficient evidence, without regard to learning lessons, predicting the future course of events, or grasping the 'meaning' of human history as a whole."[3] To them, the practice of scientific history marked an important achievement by Western historians in modern times and was an essential component of the powerful, hence advanced, modern West, whose experience and success China should emulate and extend. Assisted and inspired by their knowledge of Western theories in historiography, these historians—such as Hu Shi (1891–1962), He Bingsong (1890–1946), Fu Sinian (1896–1950), Luo Jialun (1897–1969), Yao Congwu (1894–1970), as well as Chen Yinke (Chen Yinque, 1890–1969)[4]—most of whom were either the "teachers" or the "students" of the May Fourth/New Culture Movement of 1919, embarked on a series of projects, aiming to reform the writing of Chinese history based on the Western model. They introduced Western principles and methods in source criticism, established historical research institutes, translated Western history texts, and taught Western histories and historiography in colleges. Their interpretations of China's national history, therefore, were pursued at both ideological and methodological levels: the former refers to their sensitivity to nationalist concerns, the latter, to their adoption of the scientific approach to historical research. In other words, these historians were not only interested in forming a new connection between past and present from the perspective of nationalism, they were also concerned about the way in which this national history was to be written.

Pursuing a historiography that was both national and scientific led these historians to attempt a new form of historical writing that found its place not only "in the oppositions between tradition and modernity," as Prasenjit Duara suggests,[5] but also in the reconciliations between these two exaggerated cultural poles. To some postmodernists, the distinction between tradition and modernity is a reification. In their pursuit of a scientifically based national historiography, despite Western influences, these historians also constantly harkened back to Chinese cultural heritage. To be sure, they were very interested in Western and Japanese examples in scientific history and were eager to emulate them. But their main endeavor was focused on discovering similar scientific elements in the Chinese tradition. To that end, they critically examined Chinese literary culture, which made them appear to be iconoclasts. Their chief interest, however, was to search for traces of science in the Chinese tradition, to avoid the impulse to discredit and disregard the tradition in its entirety. Their endeavor contributed to the change of one's perception of the past in modern China. Out of their concern for the authenticity of source material, one of the primary requirements in studying scientific history, these historians revealed historicity, or anachronism, in China's literary tradition, which helped cast suspicion on the authority of the Past and demanded a new historical interpretation. This eventually led to the discovery of multiple Pasts, including a scientific past, and the construction, "invention," of a new tradition in China.[6]

This new phase of Chinese historiography, therefore, addressed two key issues in the study of modern Chinese history. In light of the fact that this scientific discovery of China's past is facilitated by the presence of modern science, this historiography acquires a transnational dimension, helping attest to the universal value (perceived at least at that time) of science. It suggests that in the formation of modern nation-states, especially in the experience of non-Western countries, there is always an intercultural, transnational dialogue that articulates and addresses the very idea of nationalism. In his study of nationalist movements in India and elsewhere, Partha Chatterjee acutely observes that in fighting Western imperialism, non-Western nationalists often adopted the nationalist discourse supplied by their Western precursors. Yet these Asian nationalists were also well aware of the cultural "difference" from the modular forms of Western experiences.[7] In the case of modern China, Chinese nationalist historians strove to understand science and scientific method against the backdrop of the Chinese cultural tradition and ground their nation-building project in foundations of the Chinese cultural heritage. Their interest in scientific history, while suggesting an intercultural development of modern historiography across the national boundary, was also pursued in juxtaposition with the intention to address distinct ethnic and/or national problems and even localized concerns. At the same time, we should note that although national history was a focus of attention of modern historians worldwide and was instrumental in defining national identity, it was presented and pursued in a transnational fashion readily identifiable in its methodological approach and its global attraction. In order to appreciate fully the process of the formation of the Chinese national identity, we must pay attention to both the transnational and national contexts in national history; we must examine not only why the modern Chinese were attracted to national history but also the way in which they constructed it, and how they modified the construction from time to time. Analyzing the development of modern Chinese historiography can help us perceive the complex history of modern China from yet another useful angle; it draws our attention to the interplay of foreign and native elements in shaping Chinese national culture, national and cultural identity, and Chinese modernity, hence inviting us to think more critically about what "Chineseness" means in the modern world.[8]

History and Modernity

Changes in the style and focus of Chinese historical writing in modern times have been examined by a few scholars from different angles. Joseph Levenson (1920–1969), for example, who began his career by producing an acclaimed monograph on Liang Qichao (1873–1929), examined extensively in his *Confucian China and Its Modern Fate* the changing attitude of modern Chinese intellectuals toward the past, from the late Qing to the founding of the People's Republic. Levenson stated that in response to Western cultural influence, radical intellectuals in China, especially those in the May Fourth movement in 1919, realized that tradition, or Confucianism in Levenson's definition, was not "absolute" any longer. Taking a relativist outlook on the Confucian tradition, these intellectuals claimed that the tradition merely had "historical significance," anachronistic to twentieth-century China. "Here was," Levenson explained, "an iconoclasm, then a bitter value-judgement, expressed as resentment of the absolute presentness of a past which should be relative—or, *historically* significant: let it be a subject of study but not a basis for present action." But their opponents, or the latter-day Confucians, soon found a new way to defend the legacy. Identifying tradition with Chinese history, they forced the iconoclasts into a defensive position. After all, one can deny one's tradition but not one's history. The iconoclasts could reject the value of the past to the present, Levenson found, but they could not disown the past to which they were emotionally attached. Nevertheless, the traditionalists also experienced some losses: once history was discovered in Confucianism, Confucianism no longer could hold onto its "absolute value" to the present. It eventually lost its moral and political applicability.[9]

Analyzing the complex role "history" played in modern China, Levenson revealed the intricate connection of the modern Chinese with their cultural tradition. He pointed out that Chinese history was a haven for both the traditionalists and antitraditionalists, as well as the Marxists. But unlike the traditionalists who uncovered the romantic "essence" of the history and the Marxists who placed the history in the Marxian scheme of world history, the antitraditionalists, or the liberals, were caught in a dilemma in which they could not simultaneously deny the value of the past and remain emotionally attached to it. In contrast to the "success" of the traditionalists and the Marxists, the antitraditionalists ultimately failed to achieve a tangible outcome, as did Chinese liberalism.[10]

Levenson's work has been useful for the study of historical consciousness in modern China. His powerful analysis of the antithesis of "history" and "value" helps illuminate the perplexing and multifaceted alliance between tradition and modernity shown in the cause of Chinese "liberalism." From the perspective of intellectual history, it also explains why it was the Communists who achieved an ultimate victory in China. But although he ingeniously discussed the ideological limits of the antitraditionalists, his conclusion seems simplistic. He appears to blame the "failure" of the antitraditionalists on their inability to sever their emotional ties with tradition. But the key issue, in my opinion, is not whether one is capable or incapable of breaking away from the past, but whether there is indeed an absolute dichotomy between tradition and modernity. Although there are some instances that suggest such a dichotomy, other examples show that tradition and modernity can supplement each other, especially in the writing of national history, where appropriation of the past is viewed as a matter of course.[11]

The complex issue involving the writing of national history was discussed by Laurence Schneider in his well-researched monograph on Gu Jiegang (Ku Chieh-kang, 1893–1980). Analyzing Gu's career against the background of the rising tide of Chinese nationalism, Schneider describes the "Ancient History Discussion" *(Gushibian)* of the late 1920s and the early 1930s, which Gu initiated, and assessed the impact of the discussion on changing the people's view of their past and on the construction of "new history" in modern China. He points out that Gu advocated source criticism in historical study and attempted a critical overhaul of Chinese historical culture. Gu's work was one in a host of examples of modern historical scholarship. But Gu also yielded to the authority of the present, that is, Chinese nationalism, and overlooked historical continuity. As a result, some of Gu's findings became "unhistorical."[12] Schneider has noted the painstaking effort made by Chinese historians in constructing national history; they had to negotiate between tradition and modernity. He has also acknowledged that nationalism was a major driving force for the movement of the National Studies *(guoxue)* of the 1920s, which was aimed at reconstructing the past on a scientific ground. However, swayed by Levenson's thesis, Schneider argues that this attempt at reconstruction was hardly successful. In his book, he describes in detail how Gu became anxious when the National Studies encountered problems in facing tradition and modernity. Hence he endorses Levenson's argument that the liberal antitraditionalists' approach to history failed to achieve sensible gains but was instead caught in limbo and contradictions.

Eager to join in the criticism of Chinese liberals for their presumably failed cause, therefore, Schneider seems to fall short of conducting a comprehensive in-depth critical analysis of Chinese nationalist historiography. This reflects on his limitations as much as on those of his subject. While an active member of the Chinese academic circle in the 1920s and the early 1930s, Gu Jiegang later developed a new interest in studying Chinese folklore. Consequently, he no longer played the leading role among historians from the 1940s onward as he had done in the earlier period. During World War II, known as the Anti-Japanese War in China, when Chinese nationalism reached its high tide, there was a wide spectrum of reactions as evidenced in the behavior of the scholars and intellectuals of Gu's generation. Many efforts were made to renew the linkage with the past in order to demonstrate the insurmountable vitality of the Chinese nation. However, many scholars also adopted different approaches to make this new connection; some went beyond the academic arena by joining the government. Gu, for example, was drawn more and more into his folklore study as well as into the study of historical geography, whereas his friends and schoolmates continued their pursuit of national history. In order to do full justice to the history of modern Chinese historiography, therefore, we must expand our research to include more figures from the Chinese historical community in Republican China.

As Schneider stresses the influence of nationalism in shaping the modern Chinese view of the past, Arif Dirlik analyzes the Marxist practice of history, using the "Social History Discussion" of the 1930s as an example. Echoing the opinions of his predecessors on the limits of the antitraditionalists in their approach to tradition, Dirlik states that "their contributions remained restricted to uncovering previously hidden or ignored facets of Chinese history or, as in the case of Ku, demolishing the claims of crucial Confucian traditions to empirical validity." But the Chinese Marxists, he writes, displaced the Confucian past and found a "new history." While acknowledging the fact that many Marxists ignored unsuitable data and manipulated historical sources in order to fit in with their new theory, Dirlik in general considers Chinese Marxist historiography a political success, because it effectively uses the past to illustrate a political agenda that fits, supposedly, with China's historical reality. For him, the success of Marxist historiography was twofold: One was its methodological breakthrough, seen in the Marxists' introduction of socioeconomic theory to the field of history; and the other was the Marxists' effort to establish an immediate connection between historical study and the social and political changes in modern China.[13] Marxist historians, consequently, carried away the palm that the liberals had failed to take.

Dirlik's analysis of the success of the Marxists and Schneider's work on Gu Jiegang have corroborated Levenson's thesis that liberal historians in China were bogged down by their intrinsic weakness: they were eager to seek inspirations beyond their own civilization but at the same time were sentimentally tied down to their own past. Legitimately, all three of them have analyzed the cause and development of modern Chinese historiography by drawing attention to the overarching impact of nationalism, namely the external forces. However they have overlooked a development within the discipline of historical scholarship in modern China and underestimated its significance. Liberal historians in the Republican period were criticized mainly because they failed to promote liberalism more successfully in China. That kind of teleological observation blamed Chinese intellectuals for a "failure" that had more to do with the extreme circumstances, that is, the Anti-Japanese War, than with any supposed "fallacy" in their political and academic pursuits. Consequently, it failed to give full credit to the role these intellectuals played in causing the transformation of historical study in China. As this study tries to show, it was largely due to the rise of national history that the status of history *(shi)* as a scholarly discipline was forever changed: It was transformed from a subject auxiliary to the study of Confucian classics *(jing)* to an autonomous discipline of modern scholarship.

Moreover, as an essential part of the modernization project in scholarship, the change of historical study reflects, perhaps better than in other cases, both the strong desire for modernity and the ensuing problems associated with it. In a recent study of the historical narratives in twentieth-century China, Prasenjit Duara offers a critical examination of the role history, that is, national history, played in the Chinese pursuit of modernity. He points out that the writing of national history, or History of the Enlightenment model that presented the past from a linear and teleological perspective, turned nation into a "moral and political force," overcoming "dynasties, aristocracies, and ruling priests and mandarins." As these forces (dynasties, aristocracies, and mandarins) became parts of history and lost their relevance to the present, national history helped the nation to become a "newly realized" and "collective historical subject poised to realize its destiny in a modern future." In other words, the writing of national history helped pave the way for China's modernization. His observation, which appears theoretical and abstract here, does not lack its backing from history. A few years prior to the fall of the Qing Dynasty, for example, revolutionaries like Zhang Taiyan (1869–1935), Liu Shipei (1884–1919), and others had launched the National Essence *(guocui)* movement. In their journal, *The National Essence Journal (Guocui xuebao)*, they published historical essays and attempted the writing of national history. Their enthusiasm for republicanism, along with their emphasis on the racial difference of the Manchu ruler of the Qing Dynasty, contributed to the downfall of the dynasty.[14] During the early twentieth century, as noticed by Duara, and demonstrated by Lydia Liu in her work, as the National Essence scholars pursued national history, a concept they imported from Japan, "a new vocabulary entered the Chinese language." The vocabulary of national history originated in the West but came to China by way of Japan. The adoption and appropriation of new ideas and concepts in changing historical discourse intertwined with the process of modernizing Chinese culture as a whole through the twentieth century.

"Indeed," observes Lydia Liu, "to draw a clear line between the indigenous Chinese and the exogenous Western" has become "almost an epistemological impossibility" by the late twentieth century.[15]

This kind of cultural and linguistic blend allows Duara to adopt a comparative approach to examining the historical narratives in modern China and India, as well as the modern West. However, as the title of his book suggests, what he intended in his book is not to celebrate this crosscultural prevalence of nationalism, but to expose and analyze its limit and propose an alternative that can transcend the nation-state imperative in historical writing. In place of a linear outlook on historical movement, which characterized the practice of national history, Duara presents a "bifurcated" conception of history, which shows that "the past is not only *transmitted* forward in a linear fashion, [but] its meanings are also *dispersed* in space and time."[16] That is, there have been a variety of ways for the historian to build, in his work, the bridge between past and present; the relationship between past and present is plural, not singular. It is temporal, contingent on the specificity of space and time. While an insightful and inspiring argument, it lacks substantive explications. In the second part of the book, Duara thoughtfully discusses four cases, ranging from religious campaigns and secret societies to feudalism and provincial politics, and considers these discourses as potential but ultimately unsuccessful to the nationalist discourse centering on the nation-state. It is however interesting to note that his discussion on the subject of historiography, which is the basis of his argument and is treated in the first part, remains relatively thin. In fact, the change of historical writing in modern China has a good deal to offer in substantiating his "bifurcated" thesis. The study of national history, which began as an attempt to adopt the evolutionary outlook on Chinese history, experienced many changes in its development and did not always, as Duara presumes, present history in a linear fashion. Rather, due to the change of the nationalist need in time and space, Chinese historians often presented a discursive relationship between past and present, in which the past—the inferior end according to the linear historical discourse—often assumed a worthwhile position comparable to that of the present.

In Xiaobing Tang's monograph on Liang Qichao's (1873–1929) historical thinking,[17] for example, we find that as one of the pioneers of national history, Liang's ideas of history as well as his perception of China's place in the modern world underwent significant changes in a period of twenty years. In Liang's *New Historiography (Xin-*

shixue), a seminal text in modern Chinese historiography that appeared first as a series of essays in the *New Citizen's Journal (Xinmin congbao)* in 1902, Liang presents himself as a committed national historian, drawn to the idea of evolutionism and determined to tie history together with nationalism. His three definitions of history, each contain the word "evolution" *(jinhua)*. History, therefore, was then viewed by Liang as a linear course of development. But in the early 1920s when Liang got another chance to ponder the nature of history again, he decided to eschew the term *jinhua* altogether.[18] Along with this change in his concept of history, Liang also adopted a new way of thinking about world history and world civilization and China's position in it and possible contribution to it. His new stance derived from a new conceptualization of history: History was now viewed, explains Tang, "as both 'movement' and 'dissimilarity,'"[19] in which difference was not only allowed but should also be taken for granted.

If what Liang Qichao arrived at in the end is the notion that one's search for modernity can be completed not necessarily at the expense of tradition, he was certainly not alone. In Lionel M. Jensen's *Manufacturing Confucianism*, we see an interesting case—Chinese modern scholars' reconstruction of the image of Confucius and his followers—in which the past has even been used as a convenient medium that supplies sources needed for legitimizing the changes in the present. By comparing Zhang Taiyan's and Hu Shi's interpretations of the term "confucians" *Ru*, as well as Jesuits' understanding of Confucianism, Jensen finds a great deal of fluidity and temporality in the Chinese view of their cultural heritage. As historical products, Jensen notes, *Ru* and Confucius were important to modern Chinese not because their meanings were fixed and stable, but because, as cultural metaphors of China's past, their significance "is generated from a delicate dialectic of ambiguity and invention."[20] In other words, ambiguity invites invention, which enables modern Chinese to imagine and construct "a suitable historic past."[21] Thus viewed, there is indeed a multifaceted and multidimensional relationship between past and present, which allows the historian to construct the past with different modes of narratives under the broad umbrella of national history. This is true of the changing views of Confucianism in modern China, and of the development of national historiography as well.

To understand the formation of historical narratives in modern China as an inventive and dialectic dialogue between past and present is not to deny and underrate the valiant endeavor of modern Chinese historians in "scientizing" historical study. One of the main motives for modern historians to reexamine and reconfigure the past came from their exposure to and interest in scientific history. To Liang Qichao, Hu Shi, and others, the attempt at national history required a scientific approach, exemplified in modern Western and Japanese historiography. This scientific approach involved efforts to search for lawlike generalizations in history and to conduct careful source analysis and criticism. If nation-building was modern historians' ultimate goal, scientific method was the indispensable means to that end; as the former defined their historiography, the latter characterized the way in which their historiography was presented. This interlocking between national and scientific history further suggests the complex interplay of both national and transnational forces driving the changes in modern Chinese historiography as well as in modern Chinese history.[22]

If we look at the worldwide development of modern science, we find that this interconnection between national and transnational is not unique to the Chinese experience. In fact, it has been identified in both the genesis and the growth of science in the modern world. On the one hand, scientific activities were based on a set of metaphysical assumptions that were shared by peoples across the world. On the other hand, however, as observed by Toby Huff, "The final breakthrough to modern science and its spread in Europe in the sixteenth and seventeenth centuries, paradoxically, occurred virtually simultaneously with the breakdown of linguistic unity, along with the rise of nationalism based on indigenous languages and local literary symbols."[23]

An example of the national/transnational experience is found in the course of development of modern European historiography. When European scholars began to examine their cultural heritage, especially the ancient classic Greek and Roman culture, they pursued it initially in Italy but soon searched in other parts of Europe. The Scientific Revolution, too, involved scientists all over Europe. The Scientific Revolution helped contribute to the decline of religious authority that had unified Europe by revealing the myth of the cosmos and changing people's faith in church doctrines about the correlation between heaven and earth. Consequently, it promoted religious agnosticism and historical Pyrrhonism. Ancient historical narratives were not considered trustworthy accounts of the past once they were scrutinized against scientific standards. European historians began to search for new ways in writing history.

During the Enlightenment the attempt to write scientific history acquired a new, philosophical aspect. Buoyed by the success of the Scientific Revolution, historians searched for laws in human history by analogy to the scientists' approach to uncovering the mysteries of nature. Historians believed in the idea of progress and regarded history as a meaningful and directional process that pointed to progress in the future of mankind. In the meantime, however, national histories, such as Voltaire's *The Age of Louis XIV*, thrived and juxtaposed the interest in universal history.[24]

By the nineteenth century, this Enlightenment historiography reached its peak. After centuries of search for a scientific method, historians became convinced that the success of scientific history depended on source collection and criticism, which helped them to describe laws in human history. Applying the scientific method, European historians began to write systematically national histories. In order to compose a factual history and overcome the naïveté of ancient historians in treating source material, nineteenth-century-European historians not only emphasized the use of original documentary sources but also sought archaeological and material evidence for writing history. Historical Pyrrhonism and the awareness of the distinction between primary and secondary sources contributed, according to Arnaldo Momigliano, to the rise of modern historical consciousness in the West.[25] Historians' critical use of source materials in writing history was then regarded as a new genre, known as "scientific history," exemplified in the work of German historian Leopold von Ranke (1795–1886). On the one hand, Ranke used philological methods to ensure the credibility of historical sources, which had a paradigmatic and international influence on the practice of historical writing in modern times. On the other hand, Ranke showed a great interest in writing national histories, especially the rise of modern nation-states in Europe. He penned histories for almost all major European nations, be they England, France, Italy, and (of course) Germany. It was not until the end of his life that he began to write a world history, which was left unfinished.[26]

The Rankean historiographical model faced challenges in the 1930s, especially in countries outside Germany. His critics, such as the New Historians at Columbia University in the United States in the "Progressive era" (whose practices inspired Chinese historians in the twentieth century), attempted a methodological revolution in historiography by seeking methodological inspirations in social sciences. As a manifesto of the New Historians, James H. Robinson's *The New History* called for broadening the use of historical sources and embracing the new scientific methods of the social sciences so that history could improve its didactic role in modern society. But

Ranke's interest in national histories was kept alive until much more recently when the French *Annales* school began tapping into regional history and "total" history from the 1960s onward. This new interest, which is now shared by historians across the world, in looking at the past beyond the national boundary will be, in my opinion, an interesting phenomenon as we enter the next century and the world becomes even more globalized.[27]

The Chinese Context

Changes in Chinese historical writing have provided us with a good opportunity to examine the transnational aspect in national history. Indeed, national history was introduced to China against a transnational background: China's military defeats shattered the Chinese confidence in believing that their country's status was the "Middle Kingdom" of the world thereby forcing the Chinese people to acknowledge not only the existence but also the strength of other civilizations. At that time, China's challengers included many European nations as well as its Asian neighbor Japan. To some extent, China's defeat by Japan in the Sino-Japanese War (1894–1895)—although occurring later—exerted a more traumatic impact on the minds of the people because Japan's victory alarmed them about their own slow pace in adjusting themselves to the changing world. In other words, China's national crisis in the late nineteenth and the early twentieth centuries occurred in a transnational context, beyond the China-West dichotomy. In coping with this crisis, Chinese historians pursued the writing of national history in order to promote national pride. Yet this national history, as this study will demonstrate, was written with inspirations from the Euro-American experience, the Japanese example, and the Chinese tradition.

In chapter 2, I describe the national crisis China experienced in the nineteenth and twentieth centuries and its sociopolitical impact. During this crisis, Chinese historians began to obtain knowledge about their Western and Asian adversaries. Wei Yuan (1794–1857), a historian at the time, defined their intent as "to use the way of the barbarians to fend off the barbarians" *(yi yi zhi yi)*. Wei's friend Lin Zexu (1785–1850), who served commissioner during the Opium War (1838–1842), also ordered that a historical account of the world be made—*Sizhou zhi* (A History of the Four Continents). Wei Yuan, along with Wang Tao (1828–1897), Huang Zunxian (1848–1905), and others, wrote histories of the West and

China's Asian neighbors, broadening the vision of traditional historians.[28]

Acknowledging the changes outside China, these historical accounts widened the worldview of the Chinese people. Some scholars, especially those in the PRC, have claimed that Wei's and others' works began a modern era in Chinese historiography. But a closer look at their historiography shows that while these authors wrote about China's close and distant neighbors, they did not change the conventional norm of historical writing. These historians did not attempt methodological innovations. Perhaps like most people at the time, these historians remained under the influence of the *ti-yong* dichotomy, a prevalent ideology in which Chinese tradition was "substance" *(ti)* and the knowledge of the West was "function" *(yong).* Historians seemed unable to understand that China's problems in associating with its neighbors, be they Western or Asian, were complicated by the expansion of the entire world, rather than caused by a simple China-West confrontation.[29] Viewing the Western merchants as pirates, for example, Wei Yuan produced a work on Qing military history, hoping to draw lessons from the successes of the early Qing rulers in shoring up the southern sea border. He hoped to offer historical wisdom to respond to the Western challenge at his time.

Significant changes in Chinese historiography did not occur until the turn of the twentieth century, known as the "transitional era,"[30] when Chinese historians consciously attempted methodological changes. They departed from the norm of traditional Chinese historiography—the writing of political/military history in an *annals-biographic* form—and pursued the writing of *scientific* history. Liang Qichao in his *New Historiography*, attacked the Chinese tradition of dynastic historiography, or the "standard histories" *(zhengshi)*, and waged a "historiographical revolution" *(shijie geming).* Inspired by the interest of Japanese historians in writing "histories of civilization" *(bummeishiron)*,[31] Liang pointed out that the main problem in the traditional practice of historical writing was its failure to acknowledge the role of the people and to foster a national awareness. At the outset of his *New Historiogrphy*, Liang stated that:

> In contrast to the subjects studied in Western countries today, history is the only one which has existed in China for a long time. History is the foundation of scholarship. It is also a mirror of people's nature and the origin of patriotism. The rise of nationalism in Europe and the growth of modern European

> countries are owing in part to the study of history. But how can one explain the fact that, despite this long tradition of historical study in China, the Chinese people are so disunited and China's social condition is so bad?[32]

Liang thus called for the writing of national history. What caused Liang to make this call was, as Xiaobing Tang points out, Liang's discovery of the spatial change in the world. In Tang's words, the influence of "spatiality, or a given mode of determining spatial organization and relationship" persuaded Liang to take a new approach to historiography. Xiaoging Tang argues that Liang's idea of history evolved together with the idea of the global space of the world, which allowed him eventually to perceive modernity in "a new global imaginary of difference."[33] Liang's global view of the world set him apart from his nineteenth-century predecessors.

Liang's history was novel in China not only because of its spatial view of the world but also because of its new view of the past. In his *New Historiography*, Liang posited that history shows human progress and its causes, or the change of time in history. This change of historical time entailed a search for new ways to present the past, in which current needs would dictate the direction of their historical outlook. Liang's historical thinking thus was based on his realization of the changes of both space and time in world history: The former helps shape his imagination of the new world, the latter exposes anachronism in history, making him consider the old world irrelevant.

This realization was indeed revolutionary in the Chinese tradition of historical writing. In imperial China, official history played the role of equating past with present. For instance, every dynasty, on its founding, embarked on the task of writing a history of its predecessor. This practice was based on the assumption that past experience was useful for the present. Information about the past thus was carefully preserved and became an important source of knowledge for historians. The writing of dynastic history, for example, was often based on the sources collected and bequeathed by the historians of the previous dynasty. Instead of searching for a new understanding of the past, historians simply annotated extant historical texts.[34] This historical interest derived from the notion that there was no essential difference between past and present.

Campaigning for the writing of national history, Liang attacked the historiographical tradition in his *New Historiography*. By the 1920s he saw that within the tradition, many masterpieces still shone with superb literary talent in historical presentation and high sensitivity for source examination. In other words, while Chinese historians' efforts to develop new interpretations of the past were thwarted by political oppression, they seemed quite advanced in historical methodology. In the late imperial period, Chinese historians expressed serious doubts about the validity of ancient histories and engaged in a meticulous textual exegesis of them. For example, the well-known "evidential" *(kaozheng)* scholars of the Qing Dynasty worked diligently to ascertain the authenticity of ancient texts through philological examination, which was used to verify historical sources.[35] Their work bore obvious resemblance of that of the antiquarians in seventeenth-century Europe.

Thus, as Liang Qichao and like-minded historians in the early twentieth century attempted to write a national history modeled on the work of Japanese historians, they were able to gain wisdom not only from their counterparts in the West and Japan but also from their own ancestors. Although their historiography served the seemingly narrow nationalist goal of making China rich and powerful *(fuqiang)*, their interest in writing history with empirical, scientific evidence was truly international. This international empiricism led them to communicate with historians of different nations as well as to engage in dialogues with their own predecessors.

Hu Shi, a leading advocate of such scientific historiography in China, believed that the success of modern science was based on its method, and therefore that methodological improvement was tantamount to the evolution of scholarship. At the outset of his dissertation on Chinese philosophy—completed at Columbia University—Hu declared: "That philosophy is conditioned by its method, and that the development of philosophy is dependent upon the development of the logical method, are facts which find abundant illustrations in the history of philosophy both of the West and of the East."[36]

Acting on this belief, young Hu Shi returned to China in 1917, ready to teach his compatriots the scientific method he deemed universal and quintessential in modern culture. Hu was not alone. In the late 1910s and early 1920s when Hu preached scientism, He Bingsong, a Princeton graduate and Hu's Beijing University *(Beida)* colleague, took on the translation of James Robinson's *The New History*, aiming to offer a concrete example of scientific history for his students and colleagues. Even the elder Liang Qichao was not immune to this enthusiasm for methodological experiment; Liang wrote the *Methods for the Study of Chinese History (Zhongguo lishi yanjiufa,* hereafter: *Historical Methods)* during this period.

In fact, this apparent zest for scientific method came to characterize the New Culture Movement of the 1920s. Under its influence, Fu Sinian, Luo Jialun, Yao Congwu, and Gu Jiegang (all Beida students) followed suit; they looked for methodological inspirations either from within—inside tradition—or from without—in Western culture, and supported the endeavor of their teachers in historiographical reform. While Gu Jiegang remained in the country, Fu Sinian, Luo Jialun, Yao Congwu, went to either Europe and/or America during this period to seek scientific knowledge. There they met Chen Yinke, a veteran student of Western scholarship and later a prominent historian in Tang history. While the length of their Western sojourns and the degree of their academic successes varied, their knowledge of scientific scholarship enabled them to pursue distinguished careers after returning to China. It was through their pursuit of scientific knowledge that a new history of China was written in the first half of the twentieth century.

For these historians, scientific history meant acquiring skills in textual and historical criticism, exemplified by the work of Western and Japanese precursors of scientific history as well as by the forerunners—for example, Qing evidential scholars—in the Chinese tradition. They emphasized the importance of differentiating primary and derivative sources and using reliable materials in historical writing. Accordingly, they introduced a new perspective on the past that allowed them to make distinctions between past and present, historical texts and historical reality, and the ancient and the modern. With these distinctions, Chinese historians were able to break away from an age-old tradition that extolled ancient wisdom and ignored the need to rewrite history. They could also display changes in history and accommodate new ideas in writing history.

Through the work of these Western-educated Chinese historians, the cause of modern historiography, centering on examining and rewriting China's past, gained momentum in the Republican era (1912–1949), as shown in chapters 3 and 4. In his teaching of Chinese philosophy at Beida, Hu Shi questioned the validity of ancient sources on China's high antiquity. By launching the project to "reorganize the national heritage" *(zhengli guogu)*, he conducted scientific investigation in almost every aspect of traditional Chinese scholarship, ranging from history and philosophy to religion and literature. In his research, Hu employed the scientific method which he himself summarized as no more than a "boldness in setting up hypotheses and a minuteness in seeking evidence" *(Dadan de jiashe, xiaoxin de qiuzheng)*. Inspired by Hu's exemplary work, Gu Jiegang, a student of Hu's at Beida, began to question the veracity of the historical literature on China's past. Gu's attempt resulted in a controversy known as the "Ancient History Discussion" *(Gushibian)*, as studied by Schneider and others.[37] Their efforts led to a new phase of Chinese historiography, in which historians used source criticism to verify the accuracy of ancient sources. During this reexamination of cultural tradition by differentiating past from present, historians came to understand the Chinese tradition from a new perspective.

Tradition and Identity

The May Fourth scholars' search of scientific knowledge constituted, according to Vera Schwarcz, the Chinese Enlightenment.[38] However, this Enlightenment was not a challenge to tradition, but was rather an attempt to re-create the past. Examining the old tradition led to the re-creation of a new tradition since tradition—perception of one's cultural origin—could never be totally discarded in any socio-cultural transformation. According to Hans-Georg Gadamer, this, too, was true to the Enlightenment in Europe. In contrast to the medieval tradition, the *philosophes* attempted to use reason, or the scientific method of natural science, to examine human affairs: they rejected the notion that one could accept anything on faith. But they did not completely cast tradition aside. "There is," analyzed Hans-Georg Gadamer, "no such unconditional antithesis between tradition and reason. . . . The fact is that tradition is constantly an element of freedom and of history itself. . . . Even where life changes violently, as in ages of revolution, far more of the old is preserved in the supposed transformation of everything than anyone knows, and combines with the new to create a new value."[39]

During the European and Chinese Enlightenments, scholars became better prepared to search for ways to construct a new linkage between past and present owing to their developing sensitivity to the distinction between past and present. In Europe, the Europeans tried to make a new connection with their tradition even before the Enlightenment. Both the Renaissance and the Reformation, for example, prompted the Europeans to look at the past from a new perspective. Analyzing these two social events, Anthony Kemp has concluded, "A sense of time is fundamental to human thought to the extent that the past must be invoked in order to establish any present ideology, even one that involves a discounting of the past. All ideologies are fundamentally descriptions not of a present state, but of a past history."[40]

In China, the May Fourth generation's critical overhaul of tradition was aimed at a historical reconstruction of China's past, as shown in chapter 4. The May Fourth scholars intended to transcend "old" tradition to look for "new" traditions that could help promote their new cultural cause. They returned to their national heritage in order to revive it with a new appearance and create a new identity. Their ties with tradition thus went far beyond emotional attachment. And their approach to the past, in a nutshell, was at once destructive and reconstructive. The title of the *New Tide (Xinchao)* magazine, a popular journal edited by the members of the New Tide Society (organized by Fu Sinian and Luo Jialun) on the Beida campus, best illustrated this intention. Buoyed by enthusiasm for Western learning, the members of the society decided to give an English subtitle to their magazine and chose the term "Renaissance." This subtitle suggests that the ultimate goal for these young radicals was to resuscitate Chinese culture, their own tradition. The term "renaissance" was later adopted to name a group of intellectuals whose activities, led by Hu Shi, focused on examining and organizing the Chinese tradition.[41] In order to make the renaissance of Chinese culture successful, these young intellectuals plunged themselves into the study of history. Not only did Gu Jiegang, a New Tide member, become a historian of ancient China, Fu Sinian and Luo Jialun also chose history as their careers.

The careers of these historians indicate that although they were interested in Western scientific learning, they focused their attention on Chinese culture and history and aimed to write a national history for China. Their project, thus, had two dimensions: Methodologically it was transnational and cross-cultural for their pursuit of scientific history that plunged them into a search for examples in the West and Japan and into a search for inspirations in tradition. Ideologically it was nationalistic, aimed at serving the goal of national salvation. The project responded to China's political crisis. In carrying out this project, these historians were facing a dilemma; a conflict between "imitation" and "identity."[42] Imitation was the imitation of Western scientific history. Identity was the Chinese cultural heritage, which was a source of strength in sustaining their identity and defining their nationalist aims. This choice between imitation and identity haunted the minds of these Chinese intellectuals. Comparing the European Enlightenment with the Chinese Enlightenment, Vera Schwarcz has made an important observation: "In the context of a nationalist revolution, . . . they [the Chinese] also faced an added charge: that of being 'un-Chinese.'"[43] To describe these historians' attempt to write a new history of China, we must pay attention to the conflict between imitation and identity and to how historians accommodated the methodological and the ideological, the transnational and the national. Thus viewed, as Yu Yingshih recently pointed out, neither *Enlightenment* nor *Renaissance*, both borrowed terms with Western culture-laden meanings of their own, seems adequate to describe their intellectual endeavor during the May Fourth era.[44]

Throughout the first half of the twentieth century, Chinese nationalism underwent many strong upsurges that affected the relationship between the transnational and national aspects of Chinese historiography. In the 1920s when the "renaissance" group advocated the use of scientific method in history, the scholars who associated with the journal *Critical Review (Xueheng)* emphasized the need to preserve China's cultural identity and tradition. The question of how to build modernity while keeping identity surfaced again in the debates on "Science versus life" *(kexue yu renshengguan)* and, more conspicuously, on "China-based cultural construction" *(zhongguo benwei wenhua jianshe)* versus "wholesale Westernization" *(quanpan xihua)* in the 1930s.[45]

Within the academic community, there were differences of opinions as to how much China needed to change for the modern world. But prior to World War II most Chinese historians thought it possible to work out an appropriate relationship between tradition and modernity and searched for comparable elements between them. Their interest in scientific methodology, or source criticism, in history reflected this belief. Comparing the traditions of source criticism in China and the West allowed historians not only to bridge Chinese tradition and Western culture, but also to revisit and reconstruct the former. Despite his strong criticism of traditional historiography in the *New Historiography*, for example, Liang used many examples from the Chinese historiographical tradition in writing the *Historical Methods*. Liang's renewed interest in the Chinese historiographical tradition arose in part from his trip to Europe after World War I. In that trip Liang had a chance to learn Western methods in historiography, which he quickly utilized in the framework of the *Historical Methods*. Moreover, he was thoroughly exposed to the devastating aftermath of the war. Having seen the disaster, he abandoned his desire for the "invincible" strength of Western civilization and turned back to China's past for inspiration. In other words, Liang gave up his early belief in the idea of progress, which placed nations in a hierarchic order along a unilateral time frame, and sought intercultural exchanges for a global "cultural history."[46]

Like Liang, Hu Shi, He Bingsong, Yao Congwu, and Fu Sinian all "returned" to China's past to search for scientific elements, as shown in chapter 4. Their "return" was not only because they intended to reorganize China's past but also because in their historical reconstruction, they were able to find an equivalence between Chinese and Western culture in historical methodology.

In searching for cross-cultural compatibilities, Hu Shi was a pioneering figure. Although he had questioned the authenticity of many Chinese sources in his study of ancient Chinese philosophy, he argued on many occasions that the Chinese, especially the Qing evidential scholars, had developed sophisticated methods in source criticism. He stated that the work of the Qing scholars showed a scientific spirit and that the significance of their scientific research of the texts was comparable to that of the Scientific Revolution taking place at the same time in Europe.[47] Additionally, in their teachings on historical methodology, He Bingsong and Yao Congwu attempted to compare Chinese methods with those of Europeans and Americans. Through this comparison, they demonstrated that Western science was not entirely "foreign" to the Chinese. Moreover, by creating a new image of the past, they have searched out—invented—a new tradition for the modern Chinese.

What makes their endeavor interesting and significant, therefore, is that their attempt at reconstructing China's past on a scientific basis helps us to see the interrelationship between tradition and modernity that was once considered antithetical. Believing in the efficacy of science, these historians resolved to replace the Confucian historiographical tradition with scientific history, or to replace tradition with modernity. But when they searched for modernity in the past, or attempted a scientific presentation of tradition, they also modified the tradition, for "tradition cannot be defined in terms of boundness, givenness, or essence. Rather, tradition refers to an interpretive process that embodies both continuity and discontinuity." That is to say, there is no absolute boundary dividing tradition from modernity, as anthropologists and ethnologists have discovered.[48] In these historians' attempt at reinterpreting history, tradition and modernity are not exclusive. They are rather mutually inclusive and reciprocal.

A tradition that connects past with present also sustains one's effort at creating a new cultural identity. In order to form this cultural identity on a scientific basis, these historians turned their attention to China's high antiquity, the origin of Chinese civilization. Applying modern techniques in historical criticism, Hu Shi and Gu Jiegang criticized the traditional historiography of the ancient ages, or the pre-Qin period (prior to 221 B.C.). They challenged in particular the stories of the "Three Kings" and "Five Emperors" *(sanhuang wudi)*, which were traditionally regarded as the ancestors of the Chinese people. As Hu and Gu conducted research on historical documents, their friend Fu Sinian looked for material evidence. Converted to positivism in his European sojourn, Fu believed that in order to unveil the myth of China's high antiquity, one had to rely on archaeological findings. Under his leadership, the Institute of History and Philology in the 1930s launched a series of excavations on the ruins of ancient dynasties. These excavations led to both new evidence (such as caches of valuable pottery and bronzeware) and new knowledge (such as inscriptions on oracle bones); both were helpful in attesting to the sophistication of ancient Chinese culture. These discoveries also helped to renew China's historical tradition and reinforce China's historical identity. So if the "Ancient History Discussion" launched by Hu Shi and Gu Jiegang had undermined China's antiquity, Fu's archaeological findings helped reconstruct it on a new ground.

Accordingly, this search for identity in history was bound up with the readily perceived influence of nationalism, which had encouraged historians to ascertain the validity of their national past, as shown in chapter 5. Identity emerged from "a relational interaction in which positioning and identification become necessary for defining and defending self-hood."[49] In this regard, Partha Chatterjee's analysis of Afro-Asian nationalism sheds some insight. Chatterjee points out that nationalist ideology usually operated in non-Western countries on two levels: problematic and thematic. The former refers to concrete statements on the social and historical possibilities of the ideology and the latter to a set of epistemological principles from which these statements derive.[50] Analyzing the nationalist influence on Chinese historiography on these two levels helps to explain why the enthusiasm of the May Fourth generation for Western science was soon translated into an effort at finding a new tradition in China. On the thematic level, Chinese intellectuals looked for inspirations in Western and other cultures that prompted them to urge political reform and cultural reorientation, yet on the problematic level when they searched for ways of expression, they adapted their work to the political structure of their society. To use elements from their cultural tradition for their undertaking, therefore, became a legitimate choice.

In the late 1930s and early 1940s, the "problematic" level, or the sociopolitical environment that sustained the exercise of the ideology, was dramatically changed as a result of the Japanese invasion. After losing Manchuria, China was caught up in an acute national crisis that traumatized the people, especially the intellectuals.[51] They now realized that their experiment with modern culture had become part of a political campaign for national salvation. Facing the danger of national subjugation, Fu Sinian, for example, made a passionate call: "What can a scholar do to save the nation?" He hastily immersed himself in the project of writing a history of Manchuria in order to prove that Manchuria had historically always been a part of China.

The goal of saving the nation also compelled He Bingsong to reorient his career. In promoting his theory of the construction of a China-based modern culture, he swiftly changed from his early position as an exponent of American historiography to a leading advocate of cultural preservation. He advised the people that although there was a need to learn from foreign culture, it was more important to maintain national culture. This led him to debate with Hu Shi and others. Hu Shi criticized He's position and argued that China still needed a "full exposure" to cultures of the world. Although disagreed with He, Hu showed no hesitation in joining the cause of national salvation. He and his friends published the journal *Independent Critique (Duli pinglun)* in order to voice their opinions in a political arena and offer historical advice to the government for dealing with the crisis. Working with other journals that appeared at the same time, the *Independent Critique* played a visible role in promoting a public forum or sphere in Chinese society and demonstrated an independent and liberal political stance. The willingness of the Chinese intellectual class to participate in Chinese politics resembled that of their European counterparts in the seventeenth and eighteenth centuries, when "the private people, come together to form a public, readied themselves to compel public authority to legitimate itself before public opinion."[52]

But this public opinion in China failed to achieve its goal of checking the power of political authority. It was instead smothered by the escalation of the war in 1937 when Japan invaded the whole country. The Chinese government consequently lost control of most of the land; people were forced to seek refuge by retreating to inland areas. This chaos made it practically impossible for the intellectuals to proceed with the public discussions they had just started. While the historians continued their scholarly pursuits in modern historiography, now characterized by more identifiable political inclinations, the momentum of their cause was lost. After its bitter victory over Japan in 1945, China erupted into a four-year civil war that resulted in the triumph of the Communist Revolution in 1949. From the 1950s onward, Chinese intellectuals were not only politically divided, but also physically scattered throughout Taiwan, Hong Kong, the United States, and Europe, as well as mainland China.

While their cause was interrupted by war and revolution, their accomplishment remains historically significant to the modern Chinese. It helped re-create China's past by rewriting its history, based on new methods and principles. What interests us most is not so much that their scientific presentation of the past can be more informative than Confucian historiography (perhaps it is!), but that their attempt to understand the past from a present perspective has turned Chinese historiography from a passive act of preservation into an active pursuit of historical consciousness, or a continuum of knowledge that constantly updates information of the past with new outlooks and new meanings. Thus, history becomes an interesting and intricate dialogue between past and present. In this dialogue, historians are not merely the agents of the past who deliver messages to the present. They also help generate interest in the past that reflects the concerns of the present.

Chapter Two

New Horizon, New Attitude

> Thus, new roads to power for Chinese, roads smoothed by western knowledge, had come to be dimly seen. A challenge was offered to the usefulness of Chinese thought, and when the question of its usefulness could be raised, the question of its truth came alive. Chinese thought, all schools of it, had a genuine, serious western rival.
>
> —Joseph R. Levenson, *Confucian China and Its Modern Fate*

In traditional China, history was an essential branch of scholarship and education. In the Western Han Dynasty (206 B.C.E.–23 C.E.) when Liu Xin (46 B.C.E.?–23 C.E.) first tried to categorize books in his *Seven Summaries (Qilue)* history was included in the category of the Classics.[1] Confucius (551?–479? B.C.E.) was believed to have composed the first history in China: *Spring and Autumn Annals, (Chunqiu)* which was also a Classic. The first attempt to divide books into four categories was seen in the beginning of the third century, in which history, ranked as the third, became a separate section, following the Classics and the works of ancient philosophers. This rank was changed after the Tang Dynasty (618–907) when Chinese bibliographers put "History" *(Shi)* in the second place, following "Classics" *(Jing)* and followed by "Philosophies" *(Zi)* and

"Literature" *(Ji)*. This order was maintained well into the late imperial period: the Ming and Qing Dynasties.[2]

In the Ming and Qing Dynasties, scholars also argued that all the Classics were de facto histories—"The Six Classics were histories" *(Liujing Jieshi)*. Their reason was that ancient people always used history to expound principles.[3] Zhang Xuecheng (1738–1801), a Qing historiographer whose name was well known to the historians in the twentieth century, noted that "As I see it, anything in the world that has anything to do with writing is historical scholarship. The six Classics are simply six kinds of histories used by the sages to transmit their teachings. The different schools of literary and philosophical writings all derive from history."[4] Zhang's argument was not completely original. Confucius had said: "If I wish to set forth my theoretical judgments, nothing is as good as illustrating them through the depth and clarity of past affairs."[5] For Confucius, history and Classics were two means that he used to express his ideas. The equivalence between history and Classics, as perceived by Ming and Qing scholars, suggests that in traditional China, history was not only a knowledge about the past, but also a repertoire of ancient wisdom readily available for the needs of the present. When China encountered the expansion of Western capitalism in Asia in the nineteenth century, Chinese mandarins, the ruling political and cultural elites in the society, again resorted to history for guidance and help. Historical study, therefore, was indispensable to the Chinese people when they entered the expanded world in modern times.

Past versus Present

In order to deal with the economic and political crisis caused by the Western intrusion, Chinese intellectuals, especially those reform-minded ones, realized that it was time for them to reconsider the value and relevancy of history. One of them was Gong Zizhen (1792–1841), a noted social thinker from a traditional scholar-official family. His grandfather, Duan Yucai, was an acclaimed evidential scholar *(kaoju jia)*. During his childhood, Gong received a good philological training in the studies of both history and the Classics. Yet after Gong grew up he became more interested in practical scholarship, or *Jingshi zhiyong*, and distanced himself from the evidential school for the latter's apathetic attitude toward social problems. He believed that historical study should reveal the *Dao* and that people should pay great respect to historical knowledge.[6]

In his "Explorations in Ancient History" *(Gushi Gouchen Lun)*, he emphasized the usefulness of historical study by drawing attention to the high status historians received in the Zhou Dynasty (1066–771 B.C.E.). Gong pointed out that in the Zhou the *shi* (historian, scribe) was a highly respected position in the royal court and was responsible for recording cultural activities. "There was no language without the *shi*, there was no writing without the *shi*, and there were no ethics and morals without the *shi*. *Shi* existed, so did the Zhou, *shi* disappeared, so did the Zhou."[7] For him historical knowledge thus played an essential role in the evolution of human history.

Interestingly, however, Gong did not view history as a catholicon for all the ills of his time. Acknowledging the change in history, he realized that there was no direct help one could obtain from China's past experience, for the Qing Dynasty was facing unprecedented social and political problems. In order to deal with these problems and respond to the imminent challenge from the West, Gong instead advocated a social and political reform *(bianfa)*, meaning to change the basic principles in running a country. In order to show the necessity of this reform, he again turned to history for illustration. "I read," he wrote, "many dynastic histories and various histories of the current Dynasty when I was young. [I find] that from antiquity to the present, there were no laws which remained unaltered, no conditions which did not result from accumulated [evils], no customs which did not change, no trends which did not shift."[8] Gong understood not only evolution but anachronism in history; the latter enabled him to see the difference and change in historical time, drawing a line between past and present, antiquity and the present.

Indeed, Gong seemed clearly aware of the epochal changes in history. Using the three-age theory *(sanshi shuo)* based on an interpretative reading of the *Spring and Autumn*, which described historical movement in three epochs—"decay and chaos" *(shuailuan)*, "rising peace" *(shengping)*, and "universal peace" *(taiping)*, Gong identified his own time with the age of "decay and chaos" and predicted its future development in the age of "rising peace." But the coming of the "rising peace" required the country to make more political changes and social adjustment.[9] Gong was attractive to this cyclical view of history because it emphasized the need for change and forecasted the coming of a new age. His use of this ancient Confucian theory proved to be very influential. A few reformers later followed his example. Kang Youwei (1858–1927), for instance, used the three-age theory to attest to the urgency of political reform. Kang argued that since Confucius intimated that theory in the *Spring and Autumn,* Confucius was not a nostalgic conservative, but a political reformer.[10] Interestingly, when these Qing intellectuals used the three-age theory, they often emphasized the importance and necessity of making the transition from a chaotic age to a better age through reform and change, and were less interested in the cyclical interpretation of historical movement per se.

From the 1820s onward when Western powers made an increasingly visible presence in Asia, Gong Zizhen decided to devote most of his time to the study of China's frontiers. He called it a "study of heaven and earth, east and west, and south and north." While his research resembled the work of evidential scholars, his interest stemmed from a practical concern. He hoped that the Qing rulers could fortify its norther border in order to ward off the Russian ambition. He also kept a vigilant eye on the English presence in the South China Sea. "The English," Gong noticed, "are indeed very cunning. [If we] refused their demand, they would knock on our door, if we agree with them, the consequence would bring harm to the entire country."[11] When Gong became aware that the Daoguang Emperor in 1838 finally decided to ban the opium trade and sent Lin Zexu to the Guangdong province, he applauded the decision and placed his high hope on Lin's mission. His death in 1841, however, prevented him from seeing the devastating outcome of Lin's assignment.

As an influential social critic, Gong shared his insights and thoughts with his compatriots to help them understand the severity of the problems China was facing at the time. In illustrating his ideas, he turned to history and made anew its sociopolitical function, which had a seminal effect on the direction of historical thinking in later years. He urged his fellow mandarins to broaden their worldview and study history for understanding the need of change. For many of his contemporaries, Gong Zizhen was the "social conscience" of his time. He revived the *jingshi zhiyong* idea and created a new intellectual atmosphere—scholars became more interested in pursuing practical knowledge for solving current problems and less interested in extracting meanings from ancient texts, as exemplified by the exegetic work of the *kaozheng* school. This connection between scholarship and politics encouraged historians to question the traditional practice of historiography.

Gong exerted his influence mainly through poetry, a form of literary writing favored by most mandarins in expressing their thoughts and feelings. Some of his friends, however, also attempted the writing of history. Wei Yuan, for example, was a very productive historian as well as a successful official in the late Qing. An important official in the provincial government of Zhejiang province, Wei participated in the Opium War (1838–1842) and witnessed Qing's defeat; during the war, he was in charge of the defense of the southeast coastline. His experience was reflected in his historical writings. In his later years, Wei was also involved in the campaign against the Taiping rebellion. Although his military career was hardly a glorious memory, from it Wei had learned a painful lesson: China needed a reform in order to strengthen its defense and overcome its weaknesses.

For Wei China needed a reform not only because of the present danger, but because China's past experience demanded it. Like Gong Zizhen, Wei Yuan believed in the idea of historical change and the three-age theory in Confucianism.[12] In fact, Wei regarded the three-age intimated in the *Spring and Autumn* as the origin of Chinese culture and a starting point of Chinese history. But unlike Gong, Wei seems not to believe the cyclical movement of history. He instead was interested in the later periods after the three ages and pointed out that history could outgrow the three ages. In comparing these later periods with the three ages, Wei argued that later ages had shown some progress and became more advanced and civilized than the ancient times at least in three areas. First, there was more leniency in punishment compared to the cruelty of the three ages. Second, the country was more and better unified than earlier when feudal division had been the social norm. Third, there was more openness in official recruitment process compared to the hereditary officialdom practiced earlier.[13] Since history changes and moves along a linear line, instead of a cycle, there is no need to return to the past. "It is imperative that one do not repeat the mode of high antiquity," Wei said.[14] Every age has its own mode. When the mode changes, so must history.

Wei's belief in historical change prepared him to understand the situation that faced his country in his time. He realized that the Qing Dynasty was meeting an unprecedented challenge. This new situation required historians to expand their knowledge both vertically and horizontally, namely to understand not only China's past but also the world. His historical writings fall indeed in both categories. The Qing Dynasty's inability to defend its territory prompted him to search for useful lessons in history. He wrote *The Military History of the Qing Dynasty (Shengwu ji)* which was started in the 1830s but finished in 1842 when the Qing signed the Treaty of Nanjing to end the War. Although Wei showed his anger and disappointment in its preface, he centered the text on showing the military successes of the early Qing, hoping to boost the morale of the people.

The *Military History* was an immediate success. In his prefaces to various editions (1842, 1844, 1846), Wei stated time and again that China's defeat in the Opium War was the biggest "national disgrace" *(guochi)* in history and that it was because of this defeat that he wrote this book. But viewing Qing military history in retrospect, Wei was not pessimistic. He instead placed his high hopes on the emperor and believed that the situation could improve if the emperor took initiatives for change. His confidence stemmed from his study of Qing military successes of earlier ages, which included, notably, its triumph over the Japanese pirates along China's coastline in the South China Sea. Considering the Western intrusion in Asia a new group of pirates, Wei thought it possible for the Qing to defend China's littoral in his time as well.

The popularity of the *Military History* suggests that Wei's optimism was widely shared by the intellectuals of his generation. To be sure, this optimism was not well grounded, for most of Chinese mandarins then had little sense of the magnitude of the Western challenge. But Wei had showed his eagerness to learn about the West and incorporate new information into his writing. He was very critical of traditional historiography, official and nonofficial, for it failed to pay adequate attention to China's neighboring countries. He pointed out that most official historians in the past had not known much about the West, nor had they showed any interest in doing research to obtain information. Those historians simply reiterated whatever had been previously written in their own accounts. As a result, simple facts like names of foreign peoples and places were often mistaken.[15]

Since traditional historiography failed to appeal to him, Wei in his *Military History* did not use the annals-biographic style, a standard form in dynastic history. Instead, Wei used the narrative form *(Jishi benmo)*, a relatively new style pioneered by Yuan Shu (1131–1205) in the Song Dynasty. As Peter Gay analyzes, the style change in history often indicates a cultural change.[16] In the case of Wei Yuan, the new style enabled him to narrate the stories from the beginning to the end, not to place them in difference places, hence improving the efficacy of the text. Also, the form allowed him to choose eye-catching headings for each chapter rather than to arrange his writing by following the chronological order of the emperors' reigns. In addition, Wei divided the book into two parts. The first part comprised ten chapters that described great campaigns in Qing military history. In the second part, which had four chapters, Wei shared his reflections on these successes with his reader. As the first part celebrated Qing rulers' military accomplishments, focusing in detail on their successes in subjugating their adversaries, the second part, in the form of historical treatises, explained the reasons for these victories and provided historical wisdom to the reader. While adopting Yuan Shu's form, Wei also made some modifications.

Although each part had its supposed role—one for historical narrative and the other for historical commentary—in the book, Wei however could not help making comments throughout the narrative. He had to use every possible chance to render history useful for the present situation. Consequently, not only was he selective in choosing most successful stories to celebrate the prowess of the Qing military force, he was also eager to present solutions for current problems drawing on past experiences. In addition to the four treatises in the second part, in which he analyzed the possibilities for the Qing to shore up its border, he frequently made remarks at the end of each story in the first part to share his thoughts with readers. In chapter 8, for example, where he describes Kangxi's (1654–1722) military victory in crushing the rebellion in Taiwan, he pointed out that Kangxi's success resulted in part from a stable domestic situation. Thus he suggested that if the Qing wanted to consolidate China's borders, it first needed to form a unity at home. He reiterated the same point in describing Jiaqing's (1760–1820) campaign and concluded that in order for any ruler to deal with challenges from the sea, he had first to settle its domestic problems and procure the necessary technology and armaments to strengthen its defense. "Previous history and recent events," he wrote, "are both recorded into documents. A good application of them can help thwart foreign offensive." However, although history was useful, it did not receive sufficient attention from the people of his time. Wei lamented that the early Qing rulers had used Dutch ships to launch their campaigns to attack Taiwan, but the governors in Guangdong turned down an offer from the English navy to help them deal with the Portuguese aggression in Macao.[17]

In order to use ingeniously the past experience, Wei thought it important to apply historical wisdom according to individual situations. Dogmatism could not do any good but harm, for there were no two identical situations in history. It was change that ultimately underscored the course of human history. The biggest change in Chinese history, in Wei's opinion, occurred as a result of the Western appearance in Asia. In his *History of the Opium War (Daoguang yangsou zhengfuji)*, Wei Yuan described the cause, process, and outcome of this new change. However, unlike his high enthusiasm in writing the *Military History*, which was composed mostly in the 1830s before the Opium War, in this work Wei seemed to have lost his optimism about the prospect of China's confrontation with the West. The main problem, in his opinion, was that China had not yet found an effective way to deal with the Western challenge. To be sure, Lin Zexu and other officials made a few crucial strategic mistakes in commanding the Chinese army in the war. But the major issue, Wei put bluntly, was that Chinese army did not have the same military equipment as the English. In order to respond effectively to the Western military aggression, China had to learn about Western military technology, or to "absorb entirely the advantageous foreign technology and transform it into our own." For that purpose, the government should continue banning the opium trade to stop silver outflow and then use the silver to purchase Western cannon and ships to build its navy.[18] Like the writing of the *Military History*, Wei wrote this book to search for practical lessons.

Although the idea seems simplistic, if not paradoxical (if China could succeed at banning the opium trade, then there would probably not be a problem in its defense), it was historically significant. Wei was probably the first Chinese who realized that it was time for China to learn from the West. In his other influential work, *Illustrated Treatise on the Sea Kingdoms (Haiguo tuzhi*; hereafter: *Sea Kingdoms)*, Wei summed up his idea in a famous dictum: "To learn about the advantageous skills of the barbarians in order to deal with them" *(Shi yi zhi changji yi zhi yi)*, or in a simpler form: "to learn from the barbarians for dealing with them" *(shiyi zhiyi)*. What made Wei known in history was his insight. But this insight also had its limitations. Wei, for example, did not think that there was anything worthwhile in the West besides military technology and weaponry. Unbalanced as it was, his suggestion had a great impact on shaping the Chinese perception of the Sino-Western relation in the modern era. For instance, the slogan "Chinese learning is the substance and Western learning the function" *(Zhongxue weiti, xixue weiyong)*, which became prevalent during the late nineteenth century, was clearly reminiscent of Wei's idea, in which China's relations with the West was defined somewhat in a China-West dichotomy.

Wei Yuan's interest in knowing about the world was shared by many others in his time. His writing of the *Sea Kingdoms*, for example, was inspired by Lin Zexu, who in his administration in Guangdong on the eve of the Opium War, sent out people to seek information about Britain. In 1839 Lin set up a translation bureau in Guangzhou, which was the first of its kind in China. Although Lin's knowledge of the world was rudimentary and superficial, he began the process in which the Chinese people embarked on the study of their neighbors in Asia as well as in the West. Lin and his assistants composed the *History of the Four Continents (Sizhou zhi)*, based on translations of Hugh Murray's *Encyclopedia of Geography*, which were produced in Lin's translation bureau.[19] When Lin was dismissed from his post and sent to exile in 1841, blamed for losing the Opium War, he asked his friend Wei Yuan to expand and revise the *History of the Four Continents*.[20] *Sea Kingdoms*, therefore, was based on Lin's work.

In the *Sea Kingdoms*, Wei Yuan traced the history of the Western intrusion into maritime Asia from the fourteenth century onward and provided a general geopolitical analysis of the Western maritime expansion. Wei maintained that the need to conduct such study was not only because China ought to know about the Western penetration into Asia after the Opium War, but also because the outcome of the War had indicated a changing tide of history since the Ming Dynasty. This was reminiscent of his earlier argument about the change of time in history. Since the change was caused by the expansion of the world, initiated by the West, the Chinese therefore had to learn about the West. In order to gain an authentic and genuine knowledge, one must use Western sources to write about the West. "This is," stated Wei, "how this book differentiates from those of the same kind in the past. That is: they described the West from Chinese sources, whereas this book uses Western sources to discuss the West."[21] Indeed, though translated Western works constituted only about twenty percent of its bibliography that includes a total of more than a hundred sources, Wei's *Sea Kingdoms* sets up a good example in using Western learning to describe the West, applying partially his *shiyi zhiyi* idea. Most of the Western sources Wei used were written by the missionaries such as Robert Morrison, D. B. McCartee, Richard Quarterman Way, Elijah Bridgman, and so on. The significance of his book, therefore, lies not only in the fact that his study probes the extent of Western power in Asia, but that it constituted a new experiment in Chinese historiography.

Insofar as Chinese historiography is concerned, Wei's decision to use Western sources reveals the limit of Chinese scholarship in history. In late imperial China, while historical geography was an important branch of scholarship, manifested in the work of the Qing evidential school, its focus was placed on Inner Asia, or on the land rather than on the sea, as shown in Gong Zizhen's works. This focus reflected the traditional concern of the Chinese government about its northern neighbors, be they Mongol, Jurchen, or Russian in a more recent period. Consequently, Qing scholars' knowledge about sea powers in the world was very limited.[22] This lack of knowledge was also shown in official historiography. Wei pointed out that the *Ming history (Mingshi)*, for example, even confused Europe with maritime Asia.[23] Therefore, in order to describe accurately the Western influence in maritime Asia, Wei had to use translated Western sources in his writing.

More important, Wei Yuan's decision to use Western sources shows a new understanding of time and history, suggesting a different conception of the world and its history. Wei realized that China was facing an unprecedented change, resulting from globalization. In writing the *Military History,* he suggested that the key to China's defense was to fortify its coastline supported by effective domestic policies, as exemplified by the early Qing rulers. In writing the *Sea Kingdoms,* he came to understand that it was more important to pry out the true ambition of the West in Asia. That is to say, he attempted to probe into the historical significance of the globalization introduced by capitalism.

In addition, to use Western sources seemed to be an exercise of Wei's own idea of "learning about the advantageous skills" of the West. "One can," Wei wrote, "decide if he wants to fight or negotiate when he knows the situation of himself and his enemy." In organizing his book, he not only arranged sections to demonstrate the menace of England and Russia in Asia, but offered brief descriptions of Europe as a whole, which, in his opinion, was responsible for the change in the world.[24] Thus, in Wei's account of the world, sea powers from the West obtained a central position, indicating a brand new conception of the world in which China was no longer the "central kingdom." In using Western sources, Wei brought a fundamental change to the Chinese worldview; the *Sea Kingdoms* covered a much expanded maritime world, including not only familiar Asian neighbors but also the unfamiliar, namely the newly arrived Western powers.[25]

Perceiving the West

If Wei Yuan expanded one's perception of the world, Wang Tao (1828–1897) actually stepped out of China and came to see the new world himself. Having spent a few years in Europe, Wang wrote about his sojourn and described in more detail, using his personal experience, the West for Chinese readers after his return. A frustrated young candidate who failed several attempts at the civil service examinations, Wang, at the age twenty, turned to the Western missionaries in Shanghai and Hong Kong to seek a career. He worked with James Legge (1814–1897), a Scottish missionary, in Hong Kong for a few years, assisting the latter in translating Confucian Classics into English. Because of their friendship, Legge invited Wang to Scotland in 1867. Wang thus became one of the few known Chinese who landed in Britain at the time. During his over-two-year sojourn in Europe, Wang witnessed the impact of the Industrial Revolution on European society and was considerably impressed with the achievement of modern technology. His trip exerted a great influence on his view of the West and the world and helped him to pursue a more successful career in China. Wang returned to Hong Kong in 1870 and began to write about his European trip and European history.[26]

For Wang Tao the study of Western history was not just for the purpose of learning about the "advantageous skills," as Wei Yuan put it, but also to learn about its social and political system. In his opinion, Wei's coverage of the West was myopic and inadequate, serving only an expedient purpose. In stressing the importance of learning from the West, Wang tried to explain why Wei Yuan's *Sea Kingdoms,* along with Xu Jiyu's (1795–1873) *Record of the Ocean Circuit (Yinghuan zhilue)* (1850) and Liang Tingnan's (1791–1861) *Four Essays on the Sea Kingdoms (Haiguo sishuo)* (1848), failed to provide an adequate, balanced knowledge. The failure resulted from a narrow understanding of the Western successes, believing that the West excelled only in military technology, hence overlooking other successful elements in Western society. "Military skills," as Wang put it metaphorically, were merely as "skin" and "hair" of a human body whereas other elements such as "politics" were its vital organs. Since Wei and like-minded historians in the mid-nineteenth century only intended to learn about the Western skill, their Western knowledge remained superficial.[27] In his writings, Wang utilized his eyewitness experience in Europe and some language skill to draw a more accurate and up-to-date picture of the West. In a depiction of the Prusso-France War of 1871, *Account of the Prusso-France War (Pufa zhanji)*, for example, he based the writing on many translated news coverages of the war and finished the work almost immediately after the war.

Indeed, for Chinese readers at the time, Wang's work had its exceptional value in perceiving and presenting the West. It was an advancement in historical writing with regard not only to its coverage but also to its idea of working exclusively on a contemporary event in the world; few scholars in the past made the same attempt. The *Prusso-France War* began with a description of the causes of the war, then proceeded to describing its process, and ended with the postwar negotiation and settlement. It provided a succinct yet comprehensive coverage of the war, which comprised detailed descriptions about the operations of the respective political systems, especially in Prussia, the military preparations of both sides, the reactions of the people (Wang even translated *La Marseillaise* into a traditional Chinese poem), and the diplomatic maneuvering.

Wang Tao's interest in current events paved the way for the development of new subjects of learning. Indeed, as Paul Cohen has noticed, Wang was also a pioneer in Chinese journalism.[28] In his writings, Wang converged history with journalism. His novel attempt was shown in what he wrote as well as how he wrote it. In writing *Prusso-France War*, for instance, Wang adopted a form that merges the chronicle and the biography. It allowed him to narrate the prosecution of the war with continuity. His style thus constituted a stark contrast to Sima Qian's *multiple narrative* style, to borrow Grant Hardy's term, which, in the so-called annals-biographic form, mentioned an event many times in various biographies.[29] The annals-biographic form, adopted by most dynastic historians, enabled one to focus on individuals' deeds. At the same time, it failed to present the wholeness in narration; descriptions of the same event were scattered in many places. By contrast, Wang Tao's narrative account allowed the reader to read the story in its entirety.

To some extent, Wang's style also differed from Yuan Shu's *jishi benmo* style, which, for example, was used by Wei Yuan in composing the *Military History*. Yuan Shu invented the style by rearranging the sections of Sima Guang's *Comprehensine Mirror* and provided a narrative for the events mentioned in Sima Guang's. However, his *The Narratives from the Beginning to the End in the Comprehensive Mirror of Aid for Government (Tongjian jishi benmo)* still followed biographic lines in structure. By comparison, Wang's style was rather event-oriented than individual-centered.[30] His adoption of the narrative style suggested the Western influence, indicating a change in historical thinking.

While receptive to Western influence, Wang Tao was not very impressed by the accomplishment of Western historiography. The narrative form, in Wang's opinion, prevented Western historians from offering reflections on historical change as well as detailed coverage of the specifics in history. Without anecdotes, Western histories lacked literary allure. "It is unfortunate," he remarked, "to see that in their histories there were no reflections on the rise and fall of political governments, there was no description on the change of territory in states, and there was no effort made to trace the origins of family history." By comparison, Wang pointed out that Chinese historians were interested in offering a comprehensive coverage of the past and attempted to record things in different categories and preserve the records. But their ambition to cover everything often resulted in problems in historical accuracy. As a conclusion, Wang stated that a good historian must overcome the deficiencies in both Chinese and Western historiography.[31]

Wang tried to become such a good historian. In writing the *General History of France (Faguo zhilue)*, he made an attempt to unite the two historiographical traditions. The first part of the *History of France* followed the form of chronology *(biao)* in the Chinese tradition to delineate the family line of the French royal house, particularly its dynastic succession, hence contouring the book's content. Then he focused in the second part on the French foreign expansions in the period, using the form similar to the "treatise" *(shu)*. Wang considered belligerence and militarism national characteristics of modern France. In the third part, Wang described political institutions, economic life, the war machine, and cultural activity in France in the form of "monograph" *(zhi)*. But in chapter eighteen, Wang created a new form, "broad narrative" *(guangshu)*, and used it to offer a comprehensive coverage of the evolution of French society.[32] This new form reflected his effort to incorporate Western historiographical styles in his writing.

As said earlier, the change of style in historical writing can be indicative of a change in historical thinking. In perceiving and presenting Western history, Wang shared his thought about the change of history and formulated a new understanding of the world. In his analysis of the Franco-Prussia War, for example, he tried to perceive its significance in a global context. Although he believed that Prussia's better preparation, advanced military technology, and effective tactics contributed to its victory over France, he pointed out that the war outcome suggested a new trend in world history. An important reason was that Prussia was a young country in incline whereas France was in decline and that the rise and fall of powers constituted the course of human history. Thus viewed, France's defeat became almost inevitable. Wang predicted that as a result of the Franco-Prussia War, European powers would lose their balance and the next dominant power could be Russia. Russia,

Wang warned, would either challenge the powers in western Europe or expand toward the east to attack China.[33]

Wang's forecast about Russia's future was based on his basic understanding of the movement of history. He maintained, analogous to Wei Yuan in this regard, that the competition among different states was the norm of history and that the situation in Europe was similar to that of the Spring and Autumn period (722–481, B.C.E.) in China. In this comparison, Russia was supposedly playing the role of the State of Qin, which, as happened in China two millennia earlier, would eventually take control of Europe and dominate the rest of the countries. Yet what really concerned Wang was the threat of this stronger and ambitious Russia to China. In analyzing the consequence of the Franco-Prussia War, Wang wasted no time to caution his readers about Russia's ambition in Asia. All these predictions were based on his theory that the Franco-Prussia War changed the balance of power that would affect both Europe and Asia. While the war was nothing but a single episode, it signaled the change of history in the world.[34]

What is interesting was that Wang formed his theory mainly with his knowledge of ancient Chinese history, rather than to base it on his observation of the Franco-Prussia War. Wang chose to work on a contemporary event in European history, which was unusual at his time, but he applied the principles that he drew from his readings of Chinese history in explaining both its cause and outcome. This kind of sinicization, of course, appeared to be ethnocentric; Wang regarded world events simply as replicas of the Chinese precedents. But by drawing comparisons between European and Chinese history, Wang was able to form his new worldview, which was essentially different from the traditional notion. If Wei Yuan had already distanced himself from the "central kingdom" myth, Wang went even further to explain why China was no longer the center and identify where the new centers of the world would emerge.

More important, Wang reached this worldview through his comparative studies of both European and Chinese history. Wang's ideas of history, especially his explanation for the change of history, seem to derive from a fundamental belief in historical recurrence, an ancient notion found in both China and the West. Wang intended to compare in his works Chinese and European history and stressed that historical events resembled one and another. He then formed a generalization to explain the histories of different regions in the world. In his *History of France* Wang asserted: "[All countries], when they reach the pinnacle of success, will begin to decline. Such change is governed by laws as constant as those which cause the sun to go down after reaching its zenith or the moon to darken by degrees after it has passed through its full phase."[35]

Wang's belief in the cyclical movement of history prepared him to perceive the role of the West in world history. For him there were laws in human history that remained essentially the same and never changed, such as the *gangchang*, or the basic relationship in human society. In the meantime, there were some social institutions that could and should transform themselves in response to the need of the present. This need for change arose primarily from the change of the times. Like Wei Yuan, Wang acknowledged that reform in China was necessary for the world had fundamentally changed. But in contrast to Wei who thought that the strength of the West lay primarily in some "advantageous skills," Wang perceived the West as a civilization, sustained by its own history and culture. In order to understand the rise of the West and comprehend the change of the world, one thus needed to discover what was beneath the military prowess of the West. His *An Inquiry into the Beginnings of Western Learning (Xixue yuanshi kao)*, for example, suggested his intention to address this need.

But since Wang believed that there were certain perpetual laws in a culture that could not only endure the change of history but could distinguish it from the other counterparts, he did not believe that the fundamentals of Chinese culture had become outdated, and he did not think what had worked for the West could also work for China. In his opinion, China was known for its study of metaphysics, whereas the West was known for its study of technology. This fundamental difference determined that the spiritual foundation, or Confucianism, of Chinese culture and politics was irreplaceable.[36] Wang did not formally use the substance *(ti)* and function *(yong)* dichotomy to define the relationship between Chinese and Western culture, but his line of thinking was similar. To Wang, as well as to Zhang Zhidong (1837–1909) who championed the *ti-yong* idea in the late Qing, China's quest for wealth and power could be achieved by combining Chinese and Western culture. In such a combination Chinese learning was the substance and Western learning was the function.[37]

In fact, not only were Wang Tao's ideas very much in vogue with the intellectual trend of the late Qing, he was also its influential spokesman, especially through his numerous publications in history and journalism. Indeed, in regard to the knowledge of the West, Wang was one of the most learned men of his time. As a prolific writer, he campaigned for the unity of the two cultures and experimented with it himself, shown in his new style history. In perceiving the world, he relied mainly on the traditional belief in the three-age theory, believing in historical recurrence and attempting to use it to explain the change of the world. But Wang was no conservative. Even if he resorted to past experience, he also understood quite well the present situation and pondered on the future of mankind. He maintained that histories of all nations would eventually converge into an age of universal peace *(taiping)*, in which the world would reach a great unity *(datong)*. In that unity Chinese Confucian culture would absorb Western technology into its own system, namely the *ti* would imbibe the *yong*.[38] Hence, although Wang witnessed many violent changes in the world and appreciated the strength of Western culture, he never lost his firm belief in the validity of the Chinese cultural tradition. Instead, as Paul Cohen puts it, "It could be argued that it was precisely the security afforded by this immersion in the past that permitted him to entertain certain highly untraditional notions without experiencing the shock of cultural dislocation."[39] This assessment proved quite insightful. Of course, in the early twentieth century when China experienced even deeper national crisis, not many intellectuals could feel the same "security" that Wang did by looking at the past. But like Wang Tao, they immersed themselves in the study of tradition, or history, to search for solutions (if not security). It was this strong bond to tradition that characterized the endeavors of Chinese intellectuals, even the iconoclasts, to seek modernity in China.

New Historiography

China's repeated losses in confronting the Western military challenge had forced historians in the nineteenth century to incorporate the Western world into Chinese historical narratives. But it was the outcome of the Sino-Japanese War of 1894–1895 that ultimately prompted Chinese intellectuals to search for a new understanding of tradition by rewriting Chinese history. As China's defeat to the Western powers had proved to them that China had lost its "central kingdom" position in the world, its further defeat by Japan taught them that China was no longer a leading nation in Asia. In 1898 when the news of the Treaty of Shimonosaki that had ended the Sino-Japanese War reached the capital Beijing, anxious students like Kang Youwei and Liang Qichao petitioned the court for reform and gained temporary endorsement from the young Emperor

Guangxu. Although the Reform of 1898 ended in a failure in slightly over a hundred days, Kang and Liang in their writings, *inter alia*, addressed the need to overhaul the tradition of Chinese culture, including its historiographical heritage.[40] In doing so, they continued the cause pioneered by Wei Yuan and Wang Tao to seek a better understanding of the West and the world.

Liang never learned any Western language. But he read many Western books in Japanese and Chinese translations.[41] Liang's first contact with Western books dated back to 1890 when he failed the metropolitan examination and on his way back to Guangdong, had a brief sojourn in Shanghai. He found several Chinese translations of Western books and learned for the first time that there were five continents in the world.[42] While leading the 1898 Reform, Liang associated closely with two European missionaries, Timothy Richard and Gilbert Reid; the latter formed the Christian Literature Society for China, which had been designed for introducing Western science and technology to China. During the Reform, the society played a visible role in China's political arena extending support to the reformers. Besides his contact with these missionaries, Liang at the same time befriended Yan Fu (1853–1921), a renowned translator and social thinker. Educated in nineteenth-century Britain, Yan translated Thomas Huxley's *Ethics and Evolution* in 1896, which exerted a revolutionary impact on the *Weltanschauungen* of Chinese intellectuals.[43] Liang also read Yan's other translations, sometimes in manuscript form. Ever since that time, social Darwinism seemed to have left a strong imprint on Liang's mind; he embraced the principle "survival of the fittest" and used it to argue for the need of political and cultural reform. He was convinced that only through social and political metamorphoses might China be able to resume its power in the world and fend off the aggression of foreign powers. This mixture of nationalism and social Darwinism characterized Liang's approach to historiography.[44]

Although Liang's interest in Western culture began in the reform years, it was after the reform that he had an opportunity to engage in a serious study of Western learning. His memoir tells us that in his exile in Japan Liang was able to study systematically different cultures and ideas in the world through Japanese translations. "After one year residence in Tokyo, I can read Japanese and my thoughts have changed accordingly."[45] Following the Japanese example in adopting Western ideas of history, he began his search for a new history. Like his Japanese counterparts, his interest in new history led him to depart sharply from the tradition of dynastic historiography.

Exposed to Western influence, some Japanese historians launched a reform in the mid-nineteenth century to rid themselves of the influence of traditional historiography patterned on the Chinese model. Inspired by the example of H. T. Buckle's *History of Civilization in England*, and F. Guizot's *General History of Civilization in Europe*, two of the earliest Japanese translations of Western historical books, Japanese historians attempted the writing of a new history known as "histories of civilization" *(bummeishiron)*. The main exponent of the *bummeishiron* was Fukuzawa Yukichi (1835–1901), an influential intellectual in Meiji Japan. Fukuzawa criticized the traditional approach to historiography for its emphasis on moral education and on the feats of a few "great men." Looking for an alternative, he advocated a history of civilization that was to include the lives of ordinary people; common people, Fukuzawa believed, played a major role in making history.[46] Fukuzawa's ideas of history and the *bummeishiron* school provided a new perspective for Liang to understand China's historical past.[47]

Liang's interest in historiographical issues was closely related to his ideas of political reform, or the nation-building project he and others were involved in. During the period when Liang was in Japan, he published a revolutionary paper called *Journal of Disinterested Criticism (Qingyi bao)*. According to Liang, the paper should serve the following goals:

1. to promote human rights;
2. to study (Western) philosophy;
3. to purify government;
4. to emphasize national humiliation.

All these goals were aimed at building a modern Chinese nation.

In order to build such a nation-state, Liang embarked on the task of citizenship education. His main contribution to the *Journal of Disinterested Criticism* consisted a series of essays he wrote based on his readings of Western political philosophy. In addition to the social Darwinist theory with which Liang had been familiar, other theories that appeared in modern Europe caught his attention as well, such as the works of Hobbes, Spinoza, Rousseau, Bacon, Descartes, Darwin, Montesquieu, Bentham, and Kant. To promote citizenship education, he edited another newspaper called *New Citizen Journal (Xinmin congbao)* in 1902, in which he proposed the idea of educating "new citizens" for China with selected Western political ideals and values.

To be sure, the term *xinmin* (new people) appeared originally in the Confucian classic *Great Learning (Daxue)*, but Liang borrowed it to introduce the idea of citizenship, based on his understanding of Western liberalism. In discussing the concept of the new citizen, Liang quoted extensively passages found in the works of Jeremy Bentham and John S. Mill. He was especially impressed with Bentham's principle of "the greatest happiness of the greatest number," which was quoted most frequently by him at the time.[48] Liang's political ideal, therefore, was colored strongly by the idea of modern nation-states, as formulated by the thinkers of social Darwinism, utilitarianism, and liberalism. In his attempt to construct a modern Chinese nation, he came to discover history. In 1902, the same year he launched the *New Citizen Journal*, Liang penned an important text in modern Chinese historiography, the *New Historiography*, which was serialized in the journal.[49]

Thus, although the *New Historiography* was one of Liang's earliest historical publications, it was an integral part of Liang's nationalist search for a modern China.[50] It pioneered and exemplified the nationalist approach to the writing of history in China, hence ushering in a new phase of Chinese historiography. From this nationalist perspective, Liang launched his attack on the official historiographical tradition in China. He stated that though about sixty to seventy percent of Chinese books were historical works, including dynastic histories, chronologies, bibliographical books, biographies, and local gazetteers, almost none of these books could offer any help to the country and its people. Traditional Chinese historiography had perilous fallacies which, Liang claimed, constituted obstacles to China's search of wealth and power *(fuqiang)* in modern times.[51]

The first problem was that Chinese court historians only paid attention to events that happened in or were related to the royal court. Mistakenly identifying the royal family with the entire country, they failed to understand the concept of nation. As a result, the twenty-four dynastic histories were just twenty-four genealogies of royal families. Since history was written to provide lessons for the ruler and help prolong his reign, court historians showed little interest in the lives of the ordinary people.

Court historians also centered their attention on a few prominent figures in their historical accounts; their individual-oriented approach amounted to the second problem in Chinese historiography. Liang believed that when great attention was paid to a few individuals, historians would not be able to see the people as a group, let alone the nation. Thus, Liang challenged the age-old annals-biographical form in official historiography. He explained that the form presented history as an assembly of various biographies of heroic figures, including the biographies of every reigning emperor. It did not present the history of the Chinese people.

The third problem, Liang found in Chinese historiography, was its emphasis on ancient times. As a result, the earlier the history was, the more writings were done about it. Few historians wrote histories of their own age for they were afraid that the ruler might consider their writings harmful to his reign. Because of the political risk, historians felt safer to write a history of ancient times. This focus on the past rendered Chinese historiography irrelevant to the people's lives at the present.

The fourth and the last problem in Chinese historiography, according to Liang, was its lack of theoretical contemplations on the nature and movement of history. Liang was particularly concerned with the fact that most traditional Chinese historians did not study historical causality in their research; they merely accumulated and scrutinized facts. Historical knowledge preserved in their accounts thus offered no real help for the need of the present.

Due to these problems, traditional historiography was bogged down by two major fallacies:

1. There was only description but not novelty.
2. There was only conventionality but not creativity.

These two problems had made history unaccessible to ordinary people. First of all, readers were intimidated by the enormous quantity of historical works. Second, though historical writing in imperial China experienced several changes in its form and methodology, few histories were interesting enough to attract common readers. In fact, because of an almost nonexistent demand, few copies of those multivolume dynastic histories were printed after their completion. Third, because of their repetitious content, people usually found it difficult to draw any useful and inspiring thoughts from reading history. All of this renders traditional historical scholarship an impractical form of learning.[52]

If traditional historiography was impractical as a knowledge, hence inadequate for helping the nation-building goal, what kind of a new history was Liang looking for in the *New Historiography*? Like his Japanese counterparts, Liang was interested in a people's history, which, in his opinion, should be responsive to the need of the present. For him history should serve the interest of the present society, especially the interest of the people. On this score, Liang's *New Historiography* was largely patterned on the works of the Japanese *bummeishiron* historians.[53]

Liang's interest in updating and improving the method of history also made his *New Historiography* comparable to James H. Robinson's same-titled *The New History*, written ten years later. Indeed, Liang and Robinson had much in common in challenging the heritage of traditional historiography in their culture. For example, they were both very critical of the elite-centered approach in historical writing and campaigned for expanding the scope of historical study and making history relevant to everyday life.[54] In addition, both Robinson and Liang showed a great interest in introducing new methods, although they pursued their interest in a different context. Liang's main concern was how to learn from his Western and Japanese counterparts; his *New Historiography* was thus regarded as a landmark in the practice of scientific history in China.[55] In the 1920s when Liang had a chance to teach history, he continued his search for methodological innovation and produced *Historical Methods*, a major work in studying the method of history in modern China.[56]

In writing the *New Historiography* Liang also extended his criticism of traditional historiography to some specific issues. One of these was the "legitimacy theory" *(Zhengtonglun)*, which involved the legitimacy question in dynastic succession[57] and therefore related to the moral function of traditional historiography. Historians pronounced morality by adopting a certain "writing style" *(bifa)* in their writings. As shown in the *Spring and Autumn* the author, who was thought to be Confucius, passed his judgment on historical events through different descriptions, hence the *"Chunqiu bifa"* (the writing style of the *Spring and Autumn Annals*). For example, if a legitimate prince was murdered by his minister, the historian would find a way to tell his readers that the death was abnormal; say, using the verb *assassinate* instead of the verb *kill* to emphasize his moral disapproval. Following the example of the *Spring and Autumn*, most people in imperial China regarded maintaining morality in historical writing as a paramount duty for a historian.[58] However, Liang did not think making moral comments a crucial issue in historiography. For him upholding morality in historiography was rather trivial in comparison with the attempt to write national history, which entailed a broad understanding of history. Without such a grand vision, Liang argued, the historians' moral concern could be misplaced.

Despite his limited understanding of the Western tradition in historiography, Liang, in his *New Historiography*, attempted to make comparisons and use Western examples to illustrate his points. In his opinion, Plutarch's *Parallel Lives of Illustrious Greeks and Romans* and Edward Gibbon's *The Decline and Fall of the Roman Empire* were great examples. What attracted Liang were Plutarch's comparative approach and Gibbon's success in general history.[59] In Chinese dynastic historiography, to be sure, both approaches were not emphasized, although Sima Qian's *Records of the Grand Historian* could be an exception for its attempt at a general history.

But what is useful for Liang on the one hand can be detrimental to his argument on the other. Liang originally cited these two Western history texts to stress the importance of delinking morality and history. However, Plutarch and Gibbon were not helpful in this regard for both had strong moral concerns, nor were their foci on political and military history supportive of Liang's advocacy of a new, people's history. In fact, Plutarch's purpose in writing the *Parallel* was not different from that of Chinese historians': recording heroic historical figures to promote moral education for Roman citizens. Gibbon, however, was concerned with the spread of Christianity in the Roman Empire, which he believed was a principal reason for the Empire's downfall in the fifth century.

Despite his awkwardness in explaining the Western examples, Liang made a valiant effort to take a comparative approach to campaigning for his "historiographical revolution" *(shijie geming)*. Compared to his predecessors like Wei Yuan and Wang Tao, Liang expanded the process of learning from the West. If Wei introduced the idea of adopting new military technology, Wang included the political and cultural, and now Liang added history. This suggested that by the early twentieth century, some Chinese intellectuals had begun to regard Western civilization as a holistic entity; its military power was sustained by factors that, as James Pusey puts it, ran "far deeper, in men's mind. The Westerner's secret was in their attitude, their philosophy."[60]

Buoyed by this enthusiasm for Western culture and history, in the *New Historiography*, Liang came to redefine history from the nineteenth-century Western perspectives on nationalism, Darwinism, and modernism. Following the idea of progress and evolution, he considered history, or History in Hegelian philosophy, a process of linear development. In his understanding, the concept of history had three aspects or dimensions. In its first dimension, history described the phenomenon of human evolution or progress, which was comparable to biological evolution for they both grew or evolved according to a certain order or phase. From this perspective, he rejected the cyclical interpretation of historical process, which, exemplified by the "three-age theory," was prevalent in Confucian historiography.

Since evolution was the law in human history as well as the natural world, history acquired its second dimension, that was to describe the process of human evolution. Liang stated that social transformation, such as the development from tribes to societies, suggested the advancement of mankind as a whole, although this advancement was not necessarily shown in individual intelligence—ancient sages were often more insightful than we were. But individual intelligence, Liang stressed, should not prevent one from seeing progress in history. Chinese historians in the past failed to expound on the idea of history because of their ancestor worship. A new historian, following Liang's logic, who writes a people's history, should be able to understand and describe social evolution.

Indeed, Liang believed that historians were able to delineate the course of history by discovering its law, which was the third dimension of history. In making this argument, Liang adopted a dualistic view of the world. He perceived the world as a composition of the objective *(keguan)* and the subjective *(zhuguan)*; the former referred to the world outside one's mind and the other referred to the epistemology of that world. The goal of research thus was to seek a congruity between these two. As scientists looked for lawlike generalizations in their research of nature, historians sought for general interpretations of history and pondered on the philosophy of history.[61]

Apparently, in writing the *New Historiography*, Liang basically followed the example of modern Western historiography to define history, or History, as a directional, teleological process. From that perspective, he campaigned for a new history, stressing the necessity of expanding the scope of history and introducing new methodology, and challenged both the form, style, and principle of historiography in traditional Chinese culture. Thus, Liang's *New Historiography* marked a new beginning in Chinese historical thinking and the rise of nationalist historiography. Liang initiated this nationalist discourse on history out of his concern for the problems in his country; he hoped that a new, nation-oriented historiography could help address the deficiency—anachronism—in the Chinese cultural tradition. In the meantime, however, this nationalist discourse is also transnational, at least in two aspects. First, the idea of writing national history was directly related to China's international experience in the nineteenth century, namely its defeats by the West and Japan, and to the spatial reconfiguration of the global world. Second, Liang's conceptualization of national history, as shown in the *New Historiography*, was inspired by his counterparts in Japan as well as the West. In the following chapters, we will see how the native and the foreign interacted with each other and how this interaction, as a form of historical consciousness, affected the construction of history in modern China and the shaping of Chinese identity in the twentieth century.

Chapter Three

Scientific Inquiry

History saw the gradual development of a new spirit and a new method based on doubt and the resolution of doubt. The spirit was the moral courage to doubt even on questions touching sacred matters, and the insistence on the importance of an open mind and impartial and dispassionate search for truth. The method was the method of evidential thinking and evidential investigation *(Kao-chu* and *Kao-cheng)*.

—Hu Shi, "The Scientific Spirit and Method in Chinese Philosophy"

We are not book readers. We go all the way to Heaven above and Yellow Spring below, using our hands and feet, to look for things.

—Fu Sinian, "An Introduction to the Work of the Institute of History and Philology"

Liang advocated a new history because he perceived the spatial change of the world, marked by the arrival of Western powers and the rise of Japan.[1] In the meantime, he also realized the times had changed. He criticized the tradition of official historiography not only because it was confined by an ill-conceived spatial arrangement of the world, in which all continents outside Asia were ignored, but because it failed to acknowledge the idea of anachronism, or the concept of historical time that differentiated past and present, and therefore the need to update one's knowledge of history. Thus viewed, Liang's *New Historiography* introduced a new phase of historical thinking in China.

As said earlier, this new history addresses a nationalist concern in a transnational age. It is national because, like his predecessors, Liang called for a new history out of his strong concern for the weakness of his country in the modern age. But unlike his predecessors, Liang realized that due to the change of historical time, it has to depart from the past experience. In other words, he understood that this nationalist historiography must involve the "other," despite its aim is for a stronger China. This "otherness," or transnationalism, shown in the *New Historiography* by Liang's enthusiasm for Japanese and Western historiography, becomes an integral part of the new historiography for reasons that are true to nationalist historiography in general, and Chinese historiography in particular.

As many have noticed, nationalist ideology is bound up with transnational factors; not only is the demarcation of nations possible only if there exists a transnational context but the formulation (political as well as ideological) of nation usually bears transnational similarities. Nationalist historiography thus is noted for a few features shared by experiences of many countries, such as the emphasis on the rise of nation-state and the role of statesmen. Since Chinese nationalist historiography is by and large a new phenomenon that results from the global expansion of capitalism, it also has acquired its distinct features. On the one hand, Chinese nationalism is characterized by its intense radicalism, due to the fact that it was introduced after China's shattering defeats by both the West and Japan. Liang's eagerness to learn from others and his attack on the Chinese historiographical tradition are a good example. On the other hand, China's long, rich and diverse cultural tradition, while being sharply criticized initially, readily sets a stage for the presentation of this new historiography. Although Liang was extremely interested in examples found in the Western historiographical tradition, he could not and would not cast aside his own cultural background, including the tradition of historical writing. In creating national history, historians often need to utilize elements from the past.

This intricate connection between change and continuity—the former suggested a desire for modernity and the latter represented an attempt to make use of tradition—proved to be the experience of modern Chinese historiography. In this chapter we will describe how

Liang's yearning for a new history led Chinese historians to attempt the writing of scientific history and how this project on scientizing history led them to examine China's past and search for scientific elements in the Chinese tradition.

Innovation or Renovation?

To describe this scientific orientation in Chinese historiography, we need to look at the May Fourth generation, for it was during the May Fourth era (ca. 1915–1925) that science was first put on a pedestal in China. Among the May Fourth historians, Hu Shi was an outstanding figure. Compared with Liang Qichao, Hu Shi belongs to a younger generation. When Liang became widely known as a political reformer and published his *New Historiography*, Hu had not yet reached his teens. Hu was born into a scholar-official family in Anhui Province. His father was a poet and geographer and served as a county magistrate in Taiwan when Hu was born, and died in 1895 when Hu was only four years old. Hu's early education was thus mainly monitored by his mother who arranged for him to study with one of the relatives of his father's generation.

Although Hu's mother herself did not have much education, she requested that her son have a rigorous training in classical education including, of course, history. To warrant the quality of his son's education, as Hu later recalled, she gave the teacher six times the usual tuition.[2] What was arranged for Hu in history was, as it happened probably to almost every child at the time, to read Sima Guang's *Comprehensive Mirror*.[3] That was in 1901, the year when Liang published his *Introduction to Chinese History (Zhongguoshi xulun)*, the very first chapter of his new yet never completed survey of Chinese history, and began pondering the issues that were to be discussed in the *New Historiography*. Hu's early education attested to the fact that prior to the publication of *New Historiography* in 1902, few had realized the necessity of cultural reform. As civil service examination was still held triennially in Beijing, traditional texts remained attractive to people, especially to families like the Hu's who lived in Anhui, a province away from the coast and therefore the impact of the Western intrusion.

Although seemingly anachronistic, Hu's early education in Chinese learning was not irrelevant to his career. In fact it provided him with the necessary background knowledge for his later attempt to "reorganize the national heritage," or "*zhengli guogu*," with a scientific approach. Hu's intention was first inspired by Liang Qichao.

In 1905 when he was only fifteen, he was fascinated with Liang's new approach to the evolution of scholarship in ancient China, which appeared as a series of articles in the *New Citizen Journal*. When Liang discontinued the series, Hu became very disappointed and had an ambition to complete the project himself. His ambition led him to read more of the Classics that eventually laid the foundation for his writing of the *An Outline History of Chinese Philosophy (Zhongguo zhexueshi dagang)*.[4] From his college diary written at Cornell University in the period of 1910–1915, one discerns that in his busy college life, Hu's interest in Chinese learning never waned, nor did he forget his ambition. He read many Chinese Classics and wrote poems on various occasions, emulating the style of traditional literati. In the meantime, he became interested in scientific method and read a few books in the area.[5] Hu's fondness for Chinese poetry as well as his study of Western science helped him to launch the well-known "literary revolution" *(wenxue geming)*.

Hu's revolution began when he tried to incorporate colloquial phrases and vernacular language in his "prose diction" poems. His attempt, known as "Revolution in Poetry" *(shijie geming)*, initiated the first phase of the May Fourth/New Culture Movement. It also paved way for the introduction of Western culture into China, for what Hu attempted was a breakdown of the "Latin" dominance, or literary Chinese, and the promotion of the local vernaculars in China, modeled on the Europeans in the early modern period. But in the beginning, few supported Hu's "revolution" at home; among Hu's staunch critics were some of his fellow students in the United States.[6] However, rather than succumbing himself to criticisms and ridicules, Hu extended his experiment from poetry to all written Chinese, aiming to replace the classical literary Chinese with a new vernacular language. His perseverance eventually paid off when Chen Duxiu (1879–1942), dean of the humanities in Beijing University (Beida) and editor of the successful *New Youth (Xin qingnian)* journal, enthusiastically endorsed Hu's brief proposal submitted to the journal, lending his name to Hu's experiment with the language reform. Prior to his return to China in 1917, through Chen's introduction, Hu had already become a well-known figure in the Chinese intellectual community. After his return, Hu joined Chen to teach philosophy at Beijing University. His contributions to the *New Youth* journal and his association with such like-minded colleagues as Chen Duxiu and Li Dazhao (1889–1927) turned him into a luminary during the May Fourth era; together with their followers and cohorts from a few campuses in Beijing, they made up the main body of the so-called May Fourth generation of Chinese intellectuals.[7]

As a "new" scholar who received an advanced degree in Western education, Hu Shi's contribution to the New Culture Movement went far beyond literary exertions. For him, "literature is my enjoyment, philosophy my career, and history my training." Although Hu had been too young to follow Liang's advocacy of a new history in 1901–1902, during the 1920s he helped Liang to pursue a scientific approach to history in writing the *Historical Methods*. As John Dewey's graduate student at Columbia University, Hu Shi became the chief spokesman for Western science in China (we will discuss Liang's work in chapter 5). Hu preached Deweyan pragmatism and translated it into "experimentalism" *(shiyan zhuyi)*. He believed that Dewey's theory presented the essence of scientific method, which consisted of five steps or phases:

1. the process of thinking begins with suspicion, which offers the problem awaiting resolution;
2. determining where the problem lies;
3. identifying possible methods in solving the problem;
4. determining which method is most effective;
5. verification.[8]

These five steps were, Hu claimed, a synopsis of Deweyan philosophy which was both an art and technique. "In its essence," as Hu remarked,

> [it] consists of a boldness in suggesting hypotheses coupled with a solicitous regard for control and verification. . . . This laboratory technique of thinking deserves the name of Creative Intelligence because it is truly creative in the exercise of imagination and ingenuity in seeking evidence, and devising experiment, and in the satisfactory results that flow from the successful fruition of thinking.[9]

For Hu Shi, the main attraction of Deweyan pragmatism was that it succinctly summarizes the way of human thinking and helped create a methodology that was applicable to studies of other cultures. Whether or not this is true of Deweyan pragmatism (it is doubtful considering Dewey's deep roots in American philosophical and political tradition), Hu appropriated it out of his belief in the transnational nature of science. To attest to this belief, Hu arranged Dewey for a two-year lecture itinerary in China during 1919 and 1920. He himself not only accompanied Dewey to most of the places where Dewey gave a speech, he also interpreted Dewey's lectures for the audience. Dewey's personal appearance in China lent support to the ongoing cultural reform during the May Fourth era and fueled the science craving on many college campuses.[10] In response to such enthusiasm, Hu wrote a series of articles explicating Deweyan philosophy.

But in the meantime, as most of his students turned to the West for scientific inspirations, Hu himself turned inward and searched the Chinese tradition for traces of science. Since Hu believed that Dewey's scientific theory was transnational, he tried to locate scientific elements in his own culture. In 1921, Hu wrote on the evidential scholarship of Qing scholars and examined this phase of Chinese learning from the scientific perspective. His study confirmed his belief that scientific method was not confined to any particular culture. It was nothing more than a "boldness in setting up hypotheses and a minuteness in seeking evidence" *(dadan de jiashe, xiaoxin de qiuzheng).*[11] Through this reduction, Hu transcended the national and cultural confinement of Deweyan philosophy and raised it to a transnational level. As a result, he succeeded in turning Deweyism into something universal. His "hypothesis-evidence" phrase also became a trademark of his scholarship.

Hu proceeded to apply science to examining the Chinese literary tradition. His *History of Chinese Philosophy*, published in 1919, was his first scientific project. Although its content derives from his doctoral dissertation at Columbia—*Development of Logical Method in Ancient China*,[12] it was not published by Hu simply for fulfilling the Ph.D. requirement of the university (following the German tradition, most American universities at the time required Ph.D. recipients to publish their dissertations); and it was not for the purpose of teaching at Beida. Hu's revision of his dissertation showed his preparation for fulfilling his ambition of reviewing the Chinese cultural tradition.

The *History of Chinese Philosophy* is a scientific experiment because in writing the book, Hu seems more interested in showing how the history of philosophy should be studied, rather than what has been accomplished by ancient Chinese philosophers. Unlike previous books on ancient Chinese philosophy that chronicled its development from China's remote past to the modern age, Hu began his book by educating the students about the importance of source verification. He stated that although the goal of students of Chinese philosophy was to discuss the ideas of various philosophical schools and discover a successive relationship among them, they should base their studies only on reliable sources and valid information. To this end, one should employ scientific method to examine carefully the source material. In Hu's opinion, previous records were often contradictory and incorrect. Thus in his introduction, he discussed in detail the nature of historical sources and the method in working with them. For example, Hu stated that sources were usually divided into two categories: primary and derivative. The former referred to philosophers' own works, the latter to the works about them.[13] One should not confuse one with the other and ignore their differences.

Considering philosophical study a scientific inquiry, Hu further argued that possessing sources has not completed the preparation for research. A more important step was to examine them, namely to go from observation to experimentation. Hu enumerated five necessary preparations for historians to conduct source criticism:

1. content;
2. language;
3. style;
4. ideas;
5. comparison with contemporary works.

These aspects helped a student to verify the validity of a text. For instance, if the text's style and language were anachronistic; or if its content was contradictory and its ideas inconsistent, then it was likely that the text was a forgery.[14]

Apparently, Hu was indebted to Dewey in forming his scientific approach to the history of Chinese philosophy. But there was evidence that he was also influenced by others. In writing the part on source criticism, for example, Hu borrowed ideas from Langlois and Seignobos' *Introduction to the Study of History*. Wilhelm Windelband's *History of Ancient Philosophy*, too, inspired him in determining the objectives for the study of the history of philosophy. Windelband, for instance, defined in his preface the task of the historian of philosophy as follows: "In the first regard the history of philosophy is purely an historical science. As such, it must without any predilection proceed, by a careful examination of the tradition, to establish with philological exactness the content of the philosophic doctrines." Hu Shi's understanding of scientific research was clearly along these lines.[15]

Hu's scientific approach to philosophical study was influenced by his Western counterparts; he was critical of the Chinese tradition and was interested in putting it through a rigorous scrutiny. But he did not think what he intended to do was unprecedented. On the contrary, Hu believed that Chinese scholars in the past, especially the Qing evidential scholars, had demonstrated a readily perceptible sensitivity in regard to the authenticity of ancient texts and developed adequate skills in source criticism. To him, there was thus a long and identifiable tradition of textual criticism inherent in Chinese culture. He claimed that Qing evidential scholars' philological and phonological methods were effective in practice and scientific in kind. Because of this tradition, he was able to see Chinese philosophy in conjuncture with the Western scientific tradition and make sensible comparisons between them. At the time when he wrote his doctoral dissertation, he had already noticed that every development in philosophy, both in China and the West, could be attributed to the development of the logical method.[16] In turning his dissertation into the book, Hu cited many antecedents from the Chinese tradition to illustrate the way in which modern scholars conducted research.[17]

Pioneering a new approach, Hu Shi's scientific experiment with ancient Chinese philosophy was an immediate success at his time. Despite some harsh criticisms about its content, most of them from the conservative camp of tradition-bond scholars, it received enthusiastic endorsement from open-minded scholars like Cai Yuanpei (1868–1948), then the Beida chancellor. Offering a forward to Hu's book, Cai congratulated Hu for his success in introducing a new way of thinking. This kind of praise was what Hu needed the most; Cai as a *jinshi* confirmed Hu's ability to take on a subject—Chinese philosophy—that was at the core of Chinese classical learning. Like Cai, Liang Qichao was also impressed by Hu's novel approach. Though he had some reservations about the book, Liang cited it as a good example for source criticism in his own study of the methods in studying history.[18]

What really turned Hu into a doyen of scientific scholars in modern China was his students. But they initially also had some doubts. Gu Jiegang, for example, recalled that, "Most of my fellow students, including myself, were rather dubious of his (Hu Shi's) abilities in Chinese scholarship, with the result that our first estimates of him ran somewhat as follows: 'He is just a returned student from America, without real qualification for taking the chair of

Chinese philosophy in the Peking National University.'" The students were much surprised, as Gu related, at the fact that Hu omitted all references to the dynasties before the Zhou and began his class directly from the ninth century B.C.E. For Hu Shi, the reason was simple; he had no way to verify the sources before the Zhou. Yet for his students, this omission was a big shock because they had been accustomed to accepting the lore of the Three Kings and the Five Emperors in Chinese antiquity. However, Hu later convinced his students with his new approach. Gu Jiegang seemed to be the first one with whom Hu had the success. After a few classes, Gu told his classmates, "Although his (Hu Shi's) lectures do not show the wide reading of our other teachers, his powers of judgment are such as to place him in a position of independence."[19]

Although Hu never had a chance to finish the second volume, he himself was fully aware of the significance of the *History of Chinese Philosophy*, or the *Zhongguo gudai zhexueshi* as appeared in later editions. He declared that with this book, he had become the "father/founder" *(kaishanzu)* in the study of Chinese philosophy in China,[20] for the book introduced the methodological revolution that paved the way for his students and colleagues to pursue scholarship in a modern/scientific fashion. To him, the development of philosophy, or for that matter, the establishment of modern scientific culture, entailed a methodological innovation. This methodological progress was displayed in source criticism, a tradition found both in Chinese and Western learning to which Hu had nearly equal exposures.

Thus, Hu Shi's attempt at uniting Western and Chinese culture served the chief impetus for launching this methodological revolution. In his scientific study of Chinese philosophy, he sought not only an innovative approach, attributed to his American education and his conversion to Deweyan philosophy, but a renovation of the Chinese tradition. On various occasions, he posited that methodological breakthroughs also took place in premodern China. His binary aim at innovation and renovation, as he admitted in his dissertation, was at once pedagogical and cultural; he hoped to help his fellow people understand that the Western (scientific) method was not totally alien to the Chinese mind but an intercultural element. Scientific method, he proclaimed, was "the instrument by means of which and in the light of which much of the lost treasures of Chinese philosophy can be recovered."[21]

Due to his keen interest in methodological change, Hu seemed less concerned, in writing both the dissertation and subsequently the *History of Chinese Philosophy*, about offering a comprehensive coverage of the subject; he was more interested in searching for valuable traces from the Chinese tradition for scientific comparison. For instance, Hu's dissertation was supposed to trace the development of logical method in ancient Chinese philosophy, however, it lacked sufficient discussion of the development of the history of Chinese philosophy needed even for background knowledge. Perhaps, later Hu himself also realized this problem. When he rewrote the dissertation in Chinese and turned it into a book, he left out the term "logical method" from its title.

All the same, the dissertation is important for Hu's career development. In its introduction, he briefly discussed the methods used by Neo-Confucians such as Zhu Xi (1130–1200) and Wang Yangming (1472–1528). In his opinion, the former emphasized the investigation of reason in things and the latter held that reason could only be achieved by bringing forth the intuitive knowledge of the mind.[22] By emphasizing the methodological progress from the Neo-Confucians like Zhu and Wang to Qing evidential scholars, Hu traced the development of scientific culture in Chinese scholarship. While sketchy in Hu's description, this scientific development represented a linear progress, covering a long time span. It originated from the formative years of Chinese cultural tradition in the pre-Qin period, developed through Neo-Confucianism in the middle imperial period, and culminated in Qing evidential scholarship.

Hu's entire career was centered on examining and analyzing this scientific tradition. After publishing his *History of Chinese Philosophy*, he wrote a few articles explaining the linear progress of the Chinese scientific culture. In 1919–1921, for example, Hu wrote an article discussing Qing scholars' methodology and tracing it back to Zhu Xi and Wang Yangming. Zhu Xi's interest in investigation manifested, Hu argued, a scientific spirit. However, the investigation did not apply scientific method, for it lacked hypotheses.[23] Hu stated that a scientific method had to consist of two things: hypothesis and experiment. Without hypothesis, one loses one's target for investigation. Yet because Zhu Xi's method encouraged induction, it paved the way for Qing scholars' scientific research. In Hu's opinion, Qing scholarship *(puxue)* originated from Han scholarship around the first century and consisted of four parts: philology, phonology, textual criticism, and higher criticism or evidential research. The major difference between Zhu Xi's and the Qing scientific investigation was that the latter used hypotheses. To confirm their hypotheses, Qing scholars used both inductive and deductive methods. They developed certain rules in examining ancient books and employed the inductive method to ensure their authenticity. A combination of the deductive and inductive methods was shown in Qing evidential scholarship that covered all these four areas.[24]

How do hypotheses and evidence work together in scientific research? Hu maintained that they form a dichotomous relationship. On the one hand, one ought to be bold enough to come up with hypotheses, using an unbounded imagination; on the other hand, once one has a hypothesis that person must be meticulous in searching for evidence to either prove or disprove it; hence Hu's well-known maxim: "A boldness in setting up hypotheses and a minuteness in seeking evidence." While his précis is not immune to reductionist thinking, Hu truly believes that it has simplified the five steps in Deweyan experimentalism, for a bold hypothesis entails skepticism and a careful search for evidence embodies the essence of the scientific method. For him, a scientific method is nothing more than a kind of "respect for facts and evidence." Hu maintained this belief throughout his life.[25]

When Hu Shi gave his definition of the scientific method, he also answered the question of what science is. Apparently, Hu Shi had an empirical understanding of the concept of science, referring to a systematic knowledge based on observation and experience. It championed the need for observation, hypothesis, experimentation, and the return to observation. From this perception, Hu argued that though Chinese scholars were not involved in the study of nature in the sixteenth and seventeenth centuries during which modern science acquired its original form, they established a scientific scholarship in the humanities. "In all these fields of work," Hu wrote, "Chinese scholars found themselves quite at home, and the scientific spirit which had failed of application in the study of things in nature began to produce remarkable results in the study of words and texts." Again, Hu traced this scientific study in Neo-Confucianism of the Song Dynasty. More important, this new critical scholarship was carried on in late imperial China, namely the Qing Dynasty, and reached its maturity in the works of Gu Yanwu (1613–1682), Yan Ruojü (1636–1704), and other Qing evidential scholars. Hu concluded, "Galileo, Kepler, Boyle, Harvey, and Newton worked with the objects of nature, with stars, balls, inclining planes, telescopes, microscopes, prisms, chemicals, numbers and astronomical tables. And their Chinese contemporaries worked with books, words, and documentary evidence. The latter created three hundred years of scientific book learning, the former created a new science and a new world."[26]

It is impossible for us to engage a full-length discussion here on the definition of science and the question of whether China had science before the nineteenth century. But we can at least look at three books that are directly relevant to the subject. One is Joseph Needham's multivolume magnum opus *Science and Civilization in China*, which traces, as the title suggests, the development of science, or more exactly, applied science in traditional China. Needless to say, Needham believes that China had science before the West. Yet he acknowledges the difference between modern science and the science in the premodern period.[27] He also thinks that in contrast to Western "mechanistic" cosmology, China had its "organic" view of nature.[28]

The other book is written by Charlotte Furth, in which she furthers Needham's point. Integrating the physical and spiritual worlds, the "organic" approach to the cosmos differed, argues Furth, from modern natural science. She tries to gauge the extent of the influence of Western science on the New Culture Movement by focusing her study on Ding Wenjiang (Ting Wen-chiang, 1887–1936), a close friend of Hu Shi and a leading scientist of the age. In doing so, Furth emphasizes the dissimilarity between the two cultures and seems to disagree with Hu Shi's evaluation of the achievement of the Qing "empiricists."[29]

The third book is Daniel Kwok's *Scientism in Chinese Thought, 1900–1950*, in which the author not only discusses Hu Shi's understanding of science, but also the concept of science in general, describing it as "scientism." According to Kwok, scientism came to China in two forms: one was empirical and the other materialistic. And Hu was a leader of empirical scientism because he emphasized observation, hypothesis, experimentation, and the return to observation, a heritage that derived from Francis Bacon and was developed by American pragmatists from whom Hu obtained his education. Dewey taught Hu the importance of skepticism and a specific method of inquiry, or, in a simplified term, "the respect for facts and evidence." It was from this simplification, Kwok states, that Hu extended Western scientism to ancient China.[30]

While our brief review of the previous scholarship seems helpful for our discussion, we need also return to Hu's own writings to see how he considered the extent and nature of scientific culture in China. What we have found, interestingly, is that Hu never used directly the term "science" in describing Chinese culture. Instead he used the terms "scientific" *(kexue de)* or "scientific spirit" to refer to certain elements in the Chinese tradition. By "scientific" Hu meant a systematic approach to learning.

So, in his deep mind, Hu Shi indeed believed that scientific method was traceable in Chinese tradition. He warned his students in the New Tide Society that their radical departure from tradition served little purpose. In response to Mao Zishui's (1893–1992) argument that Chinese traditional culture offered no help for the pursuit of scientific knowledge, Hu wrote that it was still necessary for young students to study Chinese culture because it contained scientific elements.[31] In his essay, "On the Significance of New Thinking," Hu further explained that the reason for them (Hu and the New Culture advocates) to emphasize the use of scientific method was not to throw out tradition, but to reorganize it with a critical attitude in order to "recreate civilization" *(zaizao wenming)*. These two approaches, to "reorganize tradition" *(zhengli guogu)* and "recreate civilization," underscored the goals of the New Culture Movement.[32]

To reach these goals, Hu pioneered the National Studies Movement in the 1920s. Its emphasis and scope suggested that it was an extension of Hu's scientific project on traditional Chinese culture. As a pragmatist believing in experimentation, Hu intended to winnow out the scientific element from the past and attest to the efficacy of science as a crosscultural research method. To him, in humanities studies, scientific method amounted to a high level of textual criticism. The movement thus was focused on applying source criticism to evaluating critically all written texts.

The center of the National Studies Movement was in Beijing. But its influence reached many corners of the country. As a result, Hu Shi, along with his student Gu Jiegang, and his Beida colleague Qian Xuantong (1887–1939) became well-known figures in China for their controversial roles in challenging and questioning traditional notions and ideas. What made them famous was their discussions on the ancient history of China. Inspired by Hu Shi's study of traditional learning and his new empirical method, Gu Jiegang began his research on finding forgeries in the Chinese literary/historiographical tradition. In the process, he corresponded regularly with Hu Shi and Qian Xuantong. The correspondence among the three, as well as a few others, was later published in the journal *Critiques of Ancient Histories (Gushibian)*, edited by Gu Jiegang.

The publication of the journal *Critiques of Ancient Histories* represented a high point of the National Studies Movement. It caused a controversy in the Chinese intellectual community for its critical assessment of the Chinese historiographical tradition. In the discussion, Gu and others argued that China's high antiquity, namely the "Three Dynasties" (Xia, Shang, and Zhou) prior to the eleventh century B.C.E., only represented a legendary past; there was not much credible evidence for their existence. Gu posited that people at various times had gained a tendency to forge and/or embellish texts in order to create a past that extended the glory of their ancestors and the longevity of Chinese history.[33] Consequently, Gu concluded, China's high antiquity was not real but a fabrication.

Due to his rejection of ancient Chinese history, Gu was regarded as a leading figure of the "Doubting Antiquity School" *(yigu pai)*. But the spiritual leader of this school was Hu Shi. Hu hired Gu as his research assistant after Gu's graduation. On Hu's request Gu came to know Yao Jiheng's (1647–1715?) book on forgery. On reading Yao's book, as well as Cui Shu's (1740–1816) critique of ancient histories, Gu began to disbelieve the entire literature on China's antiquity. Yao and Cui taught Gu that there were a number of forgeries in the Chinese literary tradition.[34] In order to identify them, Gu first decided to make a complete bibliography of forged books. Then an idea came to his mind: If many books on ancient China were forged in a later age, how could one trust the veracity of Chinese antiquity? Encouraged by Qian Xuntong, Gu embarked on the project to cleanse the historiographical tradition of Chinese antiquity. His skepticism of ancient historical records eventually led him to question the validity of over three thousand years of ancient Chinese history. If Hu in his teaching had shortened the history of Chinese philosophy, Gu now shortened the course of Chinese history from five thousand years to a little over two thousand years.[35]

Hu Shi also helped acquaint Gu with a scientific approach to research. In his long self-preface to the first volume of the *Critiques of Ancient Histories*, Gu recalled that though he had suspected the authenticity of many ancient texts, he did not doubt the historical tradition, and he did not know how to analyze the process whereby the forgeries were fabricated through the ages. It was from Hu Shi's course on the history of Chinese philosophy, especially Hu's call for a critical attitude toward ancient tradition, that Gu learned how to apply a historicist, or "genetic" in Hu's term, approach to looking at ancient texts and tracing their origins.[36] Gu came to understand that he not only needed a skeptical attitude toward ancient texts, but a method that could help him identify and explain who interpolated them, when, and why. This discovery opened up a new world for Gu. In the self-preface, he developed a long list of research topics that he planned to work on, which covered the time span between eighth century B.C.E. and the third century C.E. and ranged from political systems, religious rituals, ancestor worship, to the position of Confucius and the relationship between intellectuals and non-intellectuals.[37] Like Hu, thus Gu intended to reorganize the entire Chinese cultural tradition.

Meanwhile, Gu's research benefited from his own interest in folklore drama. He discovered that though most folklore dramas were based originally on simple stories, they were elaborated from time to time with new additions of dramatized plots, figures, and events. Drawing on this folklore tradition, Gu argued that similar embellishments also occurred in the Chinese literary tradition. Many texts, histories, and Classics, were either interpolated, intentionally or unintentionally, or forged.[38] Thus there were isomorphic problems in both traditions: many texts underwent a continual process of ornamentation and glorification.

For most of the cultural conservatives, Gu's doubts on China's high antiquity was an assault on Chinese history and therefore very detrimental to the modern understanding of the validity of Chinese culture. For instance, Liu Yizheng (1879–1956), a historian who had vigorously opposed Hu Shi's "literary revolution," wrote to Gu and lectured him that in order to study ancient histories, one had first to understand traditional scholarship in both the Han and Qing Dynasties. Yet to Gu, both Han and Qing scholars also demonstrated for him how unreliable ancient history was. The difference lay in their attitudes toward traditional scholarship and it was as much scholarly as political.[39]

While Gu's doubts on antiquity earned him the title of destroyer of tradition, actually he was not interested in casting it aside. Rather, he intended to rebuild it on a new ground. In his prefaces to the subsequent volumes of the *Critiques of Ancient Histories*, he said time and again that "destruction is for construction. They are two sides of one coin, not far apart." Defending his earlier work, he explained, "How could I not know that writing new history is more constructive than criticising old history?" He went on to say that he wanted to study anthropology, sociology, and historical materialism in order to construct the history of ancient China, but he simply could not do all of them at once. Later on, Gu indeed developed a research plan, despite his complaint about the time constraint. His plan for teaching ancient history at Yenching University included three parts:

1. ancient history in an old system;
2. comparative critique of old and new historical sources;
3. ancient history in a new system.

These parts highlighted the major components of his future scholarly career, namely to compare the ways in which ancient history was and should be studied.[40] The plan also was a clear indication of his real intention in the National Studies Movement, which was to "reorganize the national heritage."

To Hu Shi, Gu Jiegang's editorship of the *Critiques of Ancient Histories* journal achieved more than he had expected in launching the movement.[41] Through the discussion on ancient Chinese history, the movement gained its high momentum. Despite his hectic social life, Hu Shi himself wasted no time joining the movement and pursuing his research project.[42] During the 1920s and the early 1930s, he concentrated his study on some famous Ming and Qing fictions, including the *The Dream of the Red Chamber (Honglou meng)*. In his study, Hu focused primarily on two things: authorship and text authenticity. In other words, he did not treat these novels merely as literary works. Rather, he took them as objects of his scientific research. His goal was to provide a reliable account as well as correct information about the author for readers. In doing so, Hu departed from the focus of previous scholarship, which was placed more on finding political implications. For example, in studying the *The Dream of the Red Chamber*, previous scholars were mainly interested in knowing whether the author intended to ridicule the Qing rulers and how much his family fortune was linked to the rise and fall of a certain prominent figure in the Qing regime. But Hu contended that the first and foremost task in studying these works, or any existing works, was to examine them with a critical method.[43] By studying these widely circulated novels, he extended his scientific approach from the study of philosophy to that of literature, leaving a great influence on modern Chinese scholarship as a whole. Indeed, Hu Shi's accomplishment was cross-disciplinary. For many of his cohorts, his scientific approach cut across the boundaries of many disciplines and demonstrated a modern research model.[44]

To a great extent, Hu's appropriation of Western science and his scientific research established the parameters of the New Culture Movement. His belief in the interculturality and transnationality of scientific method inspired many others, such as Gu Jiegang and Qian Xuantong, to examine critically the Chinese tradition. Throughout his life, he never changed this belief. In the 1930s, when Zhang Junmai (Carsun Chang, 1886–1969) and others doubted the value of scientific approach, he, along with his friend Ding Wenjiang, defended the necessity in acknowledging the interculturality of science.[45] In order to construct modern Chinese culture—Hu argued in an article published at the end of his life—the Chinese had to maintain exposure to the world, not to be confined by their own cultural and national boundary.[46] Hu's advocacy of science led others to believe that he campaigned for "wholesale Westernization" (*quanpan xihua*). While he did not object completely the term, he stated that what he really wanted was "complete globalization" (*chongfen shijiehua*).[47] His choice revealed the dialectic connection between the indigenous and the exogenous in the New Culture Movement. In other words, as the movement was clearly driven by a strong nationalist impulse, resulting from China's military defeats and diplomatic humiliation, it involved efforts to pursue it at a transnational level, given its strong methodological interest in science.

The American Model

Hu Shi's scientific belief was shared by many others, especially those who had a similar educational background. He Bingsong, for example, was Hu's Beida colleague who taught courses on Western civilization and historical methods. Hu and He shared the same intellectual origin in the United States, shaped by the campus culture of Columbia University in the 1910s. As the Columbia philosophy professors John Dewey and F. J. E. Woodbridge (1867–1940) inspired Hu Shi, the Columbia historians, known as the New Historians in the United States, enabled He Bingsong, and later Luo Jialun, to gain a knowledge about the theory and practice of modern historiography. Indeed, promoted by John Dewey's China itinerary in 1919–1921, there was a "Columbia fad" in early twentieth-century China. Of the most famous Columbia graduates were Hu Shi, Gu Weijun, Jiang Tingfu, and Feng Youlan; all of them were prominent figures in modern China. Between 1909 and 1920, according to Barry Keenan, the number of Chinese students on the Columbia campus increased rapidly from 24 to 123.[48] Luo Jialun's case was quite revealing. Admitted first by Princeton, he transferred to Columbia in the second year. Luo acknowledged that among the attractions at Columbia were the historians like Carlton J. H. Hayes, William Dunning, and James Shotwell—members of the New History school headed by James H. Robinson—in addition to Dewey and Woodbridge (we will discuss Luo in chapters 5 and 6).[49]

Yet even the fact that Luo first entered Princeton was not without a reason. It was where He Bingsong received his education, from whose adoption of Robinson's *The New History* as the textbook in the historical methods course at Beida, Luo had gained his first impression of the New History School. Indeed, if Hu Shi was the Chinese exponent of American pragmatism, He Bingsong was an advocate of American progressive historiography.[50] Circulated in the campus for a few years, *The New History* became formally published in Chinese in 1924, making it one of the most influential texts in modern Chinese historiography. Tan Qixiang (1911–1992), an acclaimed Chinese historian, recalled that when he entered university in 1927, he read the book and admired both the author and the translator. Tan's recollection attested to the popular influence of *The New History* among Chinese history students at the time.[51] In addition to Robinson's book, He Bingsong also translated many other works from the same school, as well as Woodbridge's famous pamphlet *The Purpose of History*, which was to have a great impact on Luo's perception of history.[52]

As stated above, interestingly, He Bingsong was not a Columbia alumnus. Having received a B.A. from University of Wisconsin at Madison and an M.A. in political science from Princeton in 1916, He had no academic connection with Columbia. His interest in the historical school arose mainly from his friendship with Hu Shi; the two had frequent contacts between Princeton and New York in 1915 and 1916, after Hu transferred from Cornell and He from Madison.

Born in Jinhua, Zhejiang Province, on October 18, 1890, He Bingsong was one year older than his friend. Having failed to pursue an official post through the civil service examination system, his father became a clan schoolteacher throughout his life. Yet an intellectual tradition remained well traceable in He's family history; many of He's ancestors were acclaimed scholar-officials. He Bingsong's father was known for his fondness of Neo-Confucianism, which also influenced his son. If Hu Shi's mother had to pay the teacher extra money in order to give her son a good education, He Bingsong had a teacher available at home. But Bingsong at first did not show much incentive for study, although he was taught to read at the age of five. As a punishment, he was sent to a private tutor's house for intensive study. However, He became ill on the third day and returned home. After that incident, He was educated by his father until age fourteen.[53] In 1903 He participated in a primary level examination held in the county and his performance impressed his peers.[54] Apparently, He's early family education was successful at last.

After that examination, however, He's education took a noticeable turn because of the abolition of the civil service examination in

1905, but he adjusted to it very well. At both middle and high schools in Jinhua and Hangzhou, he excelled in his study and, on graduation, was chosen to study in the United States with a full scholarship from the provincial government. Before his departure, He taught English briefly in a middle school in Jinhua, suggesting his proficiency in the language. He arrived in the United States at the beginning of 1913, enrolled in the University of California at Berkeley, taking French, political science, and economics courses. For some unknown reason, however, He left Berkeley a few days later.[55] In that summer, he entered the University of Wisconsin instead, majoring in history and political science. At Wisconsin, while an undergraduate, He was offered to participate in a research project by helping collect data on Sino-Japanese relations, which probably nurtured his interest in history. After graduation, He entered the graduate program at Princeton, working on his thesis on interstate relations in ancient China.

He Bingsong's contact with Hu Shi began when he became an editor of the *Chinese Students' Monthly* in 1915, a journal founded and published by Chinese students studying in the United States. Through correspondence, he and Hu developed a friendship.[56] After his graduation from Wisconsin, he spent a summer in New York City where he met Hu Shi. They kept in touch afterward as He studied at Princeton, Hu worked on his doctoral dissertation at Columbia. It was likely that through Hu Shi, He Bingsong got to know the New Historians' works at Columbia.

Unlike Hu Shi, however, He Bingsong did not pursue a doctoral degree. In the summer of 1916, he completed his master's thesis on the interstate diplomatic relations in the Warring States period (403–221, B.C.).[57] Some of his research was published in *Chinese Student's Monthly*, describing the origins of political factions and parties in China.[58] No sooner did He complete his master's program than he returned to China, on the request of his aging parents. Had he stayed, he might have pursued his Ph.D. at Columbia.

After a brief service in the provincial government after his return, He received two appointments from Beijing Normal College and Beijing University respectively in March and August of 1917, teaching Western Civilization and English. He left for Beijing in September to begin his teaching career. In the same month, Hu Shi too arrived in Beijing after a month long trip from the United States. From 1917 to 1922, He Bingsong taught at these two colleges for five years and was promoted from lecturer to professor at Beida in 1919. His most important accomplishment during the period, as mentioned earlier, was his translation of James Robinson's *The New History*. Both Hu Shi and Zhu Xizu (1879–1944), then the chairman of the History Department at Beida encouraged him to embark on the translation. With the help of his student assistant, He finished it in a few months.[59]

He's translation of Robinson's *The New History* helped turned him into a leading exponent of the American New History School.[60] If Liang Qichao's *New Historiography* had drawn attention to anachronistic factors in traditional historiography, Robinson's work opened a window for the history students to peek into modern historical scholarship in the West. To be sure, despite the sameness in the titles of their works, Liang and Robinson had very different concerns and purposes. But they shared much in common in one area: their criticisms of the "old history." Robinson was unsatisfied with nineteenth-century Rankean historiography for its emphasis on political and diplomatic history, just as Liang was discontent with Chinese official/court historiography for its excessive (in Liang's opinion) coverage of emperors and ministers.

In 1922, He Bingsong wrote "An Introduction to *The New History*," summarizing the major points of the book for the perspective Chinese readers. He wrote that what concerned Robinson the most was the narrow vision of traditional historians in perceiving the scope of history. Robinson's criticism of the European tradition thus helped one see the problem in Chinese historiography. In He's opinion, Robinson's *New History* was useful because it urged historians to look beyond political history and gear their studies toward a goal beyond the chronological arrangement of the dynasties. Historical study did not need to pursue a didactic purpose, for human history was not cyclical; past events might not repeat again in the present. History was rather an expansion of one's memory, which assisted him to understand the current situation, but would not guide him in the present. Every age needs a new history.[61]

He's interpretation of Robinson's work reinforced Liang Qichao's argument that historians should have a broader vision, looking beyond the scope of political history. He also used Robinson's work to challenge the traditional, cyclical belief in historical movement, a theoretical foundation of dynastic historiography. His criticism of cyclical interpretation of history undermined the age-old notion that the future could be mirrored in the past, or *jianwang zhilai*. If the future was not reflected in the past, what then would be the goal of historical study? For He Bingsong, the answer to this question draws the fundamental difference between the old and new history. If the old history was for a didactic, moral purpose, the new history should be a scientific history, aimed to enhance one's scientific understanding and knowledge. For that purpose, He drew attention to Robinson's advocacy of the alliance between history and the social sciences. He argued that scientific history was a corollary of the evolution of European historiography. From the sixteenth century onward, many changes occurred in European historiography. Having experienced with these changes, European historians by the mid-nineteenth century reached a consensus about modern historiography that consisted of:

1. source criticism;
2. objectivity;
3. focusing on the common people;
4. the disillusionment of the past.

These four were based on two changes shown in perceptions of history and historiography: one was the belief in progress and the other the scientific approach to depicting the progress in history. The development of modern science and its consequential impact on human society enabled European historians to realize and demonstrate the superiority of the present over the past. In the meantime, their use of scientific method improved the understanding and writing of history.

These two conceptual changes also broadened the vision of the historian. In his translation, He drew attention to Robinson's definition of historical time in *The New History*, in which Robinson argued that one should envisage the course of human history against the long evolution of the natural world. Once this broad perspective was introduced, the historian would rethink the conventional terms like "ancient" and "modern." Situated in the long existence of natural history, human history became shorter and more integrated. Ancient peoples could well become their contemporaries. This new understanding, He wrote, had helped Western historians to shed the antiquarian worship.[62] The success of the Chinese new historians, therefore, also depended on a new historical thinking.

After *The New History*, He continued his translations of American historians' works. In 1922, he translated Henry Johnson's book *The Teaching of History in Elementary and Secondary Schools*; Johnson was then a professor at Teachers College of Columbia University. In 1929, he and Guo Bingjia published their translation of James Shotwell's *An Introduction to the History of History*, another

Columbia professor's work.[63] He's new teaching responsibilities at Beida and Beijing Normal College, which now included upper-level courses on medieval and modern European history, also prompted him to translate more history textbooks from the United States. Most of the textbooks he chose, again, were written by the historians of the Columbia New History School. For example, he used and translated James H. Robinson's *An Introduction to the History of Western Europe* and Robinson's and Charles A. Beard's *An Outline of European History* and *History of Europe: Our Own Time*. It is therefore not an exaggeration to say that it was through He's translations and interpretations of the New History School that Chinese history students gained a knowledge of the practice and theory of history in the West.

A convert to modern American historiography, He's receptiveness to its influence was well perceived in his own works during the period. Let us take a look at a few examples. In 1920 when he was elected the editor of the *The Journal of History and Geography (Shidi congkan)* at Beijing Normal College, He wrote an introduction to promote this newly founded journal. He wrote that the title of the journal suggested that it was based on a legitimate foundation, for history and geography were closely linked and equally important in understanding the past. It was, he explained, in his studies of geography and biology that Charles Darwin formed the evolutionary theory that eventually altered our understanding of the past. Applying the theory to human history, historians began to develop the idea of progress in history. Consequently, historians gave up their antiquarian worship and geared historical study to the need of the present.[64]

He's emphasis on the importance of gearing history toward the needs of the present was reminiscent of the New History School. As noticed by John Higham, Robinson and his colleagues promoted a presentist approach to the study of history, taking the pragmatic outlook of the Progressive era.[65] Indeed, when He Bingsong wrote the article, his mind probably remained occupied with memories of his American education. He mentioned Henry Johnson's *The Teaching of History in Elementary and Secondary Schools*, a book he translated earlier, and stated that in American schools, history and geography were often merged into one course in the curriculum, indicating their natural affinity.[66]

This natural alliance between history and geography lay in the fact that, found He, the two applied similar methods in studying culture. There was only a minor difference between the two: history usually focused on the past culture whereas geography dealt with contemporary culture. Since culture involved activities of human beings in response to nature, history and geography studied the same subject. Second, history and geography were similar because as scientific disciplines, they were designed to seek truth. In search of truth, history and geography employed scientific method, which consisted of two basic elements: objectivity and observation. Drawing on Western theories, He Bingsong thus redefined both the goal and method of historical study.

But He Bingsong was also aware of the limitation in the application of science to the study of history. In fact, he was not sure if history could become a bona fide science. He said that in employing scientific method, the historian often encountered difficulties, for he had to "observe" the past through limited records. Moreover, these historical records were often obscured by people's bias and subjectivity. As a result, he conceded, history in a sense was not a pure science.[67] He's concession indicated that, perhaps, he was aware of the famous debate between John Bury and George M. Trevelyan in the early twentieth century about the nature of history. As Trevelyan challenged the notion of scientific history, Bury responded with a famous statement that history was a science, "no less and no more."[68]

Although He Bingsong was not as confident as John Bury, He still contended that source criticism, or the scientific method in historical writing, could offset such limits and repair the scientific status of history. Holding a critical approach to historical sources, historians could examine and verify the validity of sources and maintain objectivity in history. As long as historians could keep this objective attitude toward historical writing, history could be likened to geography and other social sciences.[69]

Despite his prudence and caution, He shared Liang Qichao's enthusiasm for and Hu Shi's confidence in modern science. His knowledge of Western historiography enabled him to explain both its successes and problems to his students and readers. But like the other two, He was no less eager to apply science to solving the problems in Chinese culture; his use of Robinson's *The New History* to challenge the Chinese historiographical tradition is a good example. As we shall see in the next chapter, He also tried to sinicize science by incorporating it in the Chinese tradition.

History and Philology

In different ways, Liang Qichao, Hu Shi, and He Bingsong all contributed to the project on constructing a new, modern culture through history. Many have noticed that in their pursuit of the project, they promoted an antitraditionalism that prevailed in the New Culture/May Fourth Movement, especially among the young college students and faculty.[70] But what was less noticed was that even during this iconoclastic period, tradition still maintained its appeal, both to the modernists who aspired to modernize it and the traditionalists who rejected the need for change. Having started their teaching careers at Beida at twenty-seven and twenty-eight respectively, both Hu Shi and He Bingsong, for example, had to prove to their students and colleagues not only the necessity for cultural reform but also their own qualifications for undertaking the task. For Hu Shi this was especially difficult, for what he taught at Beida was Chinese philosophy, one of the core subjects in classical learning. Moreover, his students were mostly his cohorts and before entering the university, they already had received a solid training in Chinese Classics.[71] Luckily, Hu's new approach won over his students without encountering much resistance. Although Gu Jiegang, who became Hu's protégé later on, credited Hu's success to his positive remarks on Hu's teaching, he also acknowledged that it was his roommate Fu Sinian who ultimately cleared up their peers' doubts on Hu's scholarship in Chinese learning (Fu's attendance of Hu's lecture was encouraged by Gu Jiegang).[72]

In modern Chinese history, Fu's name was associated with the May Fourth Movement for his iconoclastic stance and student radicalism. But before his meeting with Hu Shi, Fu had been a devout student of classical learning. Among his peers, Fu's knowledge in classical literature was proverbial; he once even pointed out his teacher's mistakes in class.[73] It was thus not fortuitous that Fu used to be a favorite student of Huang Kan (1886–1936), a disciple of the learned Zhang Taiyan. While Hu Shi's colleague at Beida, Huang disdained Hu's novel approach and opposed vehemently the New Culture Movement. Because of this, Fu was not initially trusted by Hu's other friends, even after he was won over by Hu Shi and became Hu's close follower. When Fu organized the New Tide *(Xinchao)* society at Beida, Chen Duxiu and Zhou Zuoren, Hu's colleagues and friends, were quite suspicious of his motive.[74]

But Fu was sincere. Five years junior to his teacher, Fu later became Hu's life-long friend and colleague. Hu also cherished Fu's friendship and support. On Fu's death in 1951, Hu sent a telegram to Fu's wife in English, which read: "In Mengchen's (Fu Sinian's courtesy name) death China lost her most gifted patriot, and I, my best friend, critic and defender." The telegram was cited again in Hu's letter to Fu's wife on January 6, 1951. In that letter, Hu further acknowledged, out of modesty, that Fu actually read more of the

Classics than he did and that Fu was more knowledgeable about classical culture.[75] As Hu's protégé and defender, Fu also cared about Hu's scholarly reputation. In his letter to Hu on January 8, 1920 from his European sojourn, Fu earnestly suggested that Hu focus on his research rather than become a social celebrity.[76]

To be sure, Fu's support of Hu's teaching of Chinese philosophy was important to Hu's career; Hu was now endorsed by his students to take on the task of reforming the Chinese tradition. But the fact that Fu, then a promising young student of Chinese Classics, could lend his name to Hu's teaching and scholarship suggested that on the Beida campus, classical education was still very well appreciated, as was the literati tradition. Indeed, even a scholar interested in or trained by new/Western culture needed to demonstrate his knowledge of traditional learning as well. Therefore, tradition naturally became a point of departure for any constructive cultural activity in modern China. The New Culture Movement received such a wide attention because its appraisal and reform of the Chinese tradition were pertinent to the concerns of every student at the time. To a great extent, its success depended as much on introducing a new knowledge as on reviving the tradition, hence integrating modern and traditional scholarship. In modern China, many well-known "new" scholars too were well versed in classical learning.

Luo Jialun, a cofounder of the New Tide Society, was an advocate of Western science and culture and a noted student leader in the May Fourth Movement. But in his recollections of his friendship with Fu, Luo openly expressed his admiration for Fu's erudition in classical texts.[77] How could Fu Sinian, then a twenty-something college student, receive so much respect from his peers and teachers? To answer this question we must probe into Fu's family history and his early education. Fu's family in the late Ming and early Qing Dynasties produced quite a few successful mandarins; some of them held high positions in the Qing central and local governments. Fu was born on March 26, 1896 in Liaocheng, a relatively isolated small city in the Shandong Province. While his father held a *Juren* degree and had been a teacher in an academy, Fu did not remember much of his father. Like Hu Shi's father who died when Hu was a child, Fu's father died when Fu was only nine years old. But since the age of five, Fu had been educated at home by his grandfather. Later his father's protégé, Hou Yanshuang, who earned a *Jinshi* degree, took over Fu's education when he returned to Liaocheng. Indebted to Fu's father for the assistance in his education, Hou taught Fu and Fu's younger brother wholeheartedly. Pledging at the tomb of Fu's father,

Hou vowed to take full responsibility for Fu's and his brother's upbringing.[78] Under the instruction of Fu's grandfather and Hou, Fu read and remembered most of the Classics. It was said that Fu finished the thirteen Classics at the age of eleven, which was unusual even at that time.[79]

Hou's influence on Fu went beyond providing him with a solid education in classical learning. While a seasoned classical scholar, he was well aware of the educational changes in the big cities, resulting from China's contacts with the Western world. He first introduced Fu to some new knowledge that had already been taught at city schools at the time. Later, when Fu reached the age of fourteen, Hou encouraged Fu to attend a middle school in Tianjin, a large port-city near Beijing. He went with Fu to give some necessary advice. In that "new" school, Fu was first exposed to a new host of subjects he never studied before: geometry, algebra, geography, biology, as well as foreign languages.

In 1914, Fu entered the preparatory school of the Beijing University. Two years later, he became a student in the Department of Chinese Literature at Beida. His schoolmates were Gu Jiegang, Mao Zishui, and Luo Jialun; the first two were also his classmates at the preparatory school. Although he often missed classes because of his poor health and extracurricular activities, Fu always managed to be number one in his class, according to Mao Zishui.[80] Since he was from Shandong and erudite in Confucian Classics, Fu was nicknamed by his classmates as the "heir of Confucius."[81] Fu's decision to major in Chinese literature and language after the preparatory school stemmed from his understanding that linguistic study was the key to understanding ancient Classics, a key notion found at the core of Qing scholarship and advocated at that time by Zhang Taiyan and Huang Kan, Zhang's favorite pupil and Beida professor of literature and philology.[82]

Zhang was a propagandist in the 1911 Revolution who had eloquently attributed China's weakness to the Manchu rule and called for a revolution. Spurred by this racial sentiment, he advocated the renovation of a pure Chinese culture, National Essence *(Guocui)*, through a philological probe of ancient works.[83] Zhang's evidential study revealed the fact that many ancient works were actually forgeries. His research was utilized later by May Fourth scholars to launch assaults on traditional Chinese culture as a whole. But Zhang had no intention to criticize Chinese culture per se. His strong faith in the value of Chinese tradition later distanced himself and his pupils from many May Fourth leaders. Fu worked with Huang Kan for some time on Zhang's scholarship, only to leave him after meeting Hu Shi. But Zhang's influence was still traceable in Fu's thoughts.[84]

As a student who had immersed himself in classical learning and kept that interest well into his college life, Fu's sudden conversion to new culture had an extraordinary significance to the May Fourth Movement. According to Mao Zishui, when Hu Shi came to the university, advocating the vernacular Chinese in the "literary revolution," most students followed him because they could not write literary Chinese well. Only a few among Hu Shi's followers also mastered classical Chinese. Fu was indeed one of those exceptional few. It is thus not surprising why Hu Shi so highly valued Fu's support and friendship.[85]

Fu and Hu became closer during the New Culture Movement. Following the *New Youth* journal edited by Chen Duxiu, Hu Shi, and Li Dazhao, Fu's own journal, the *New Tide*, came out in 1918. Hu Shi was invited to be the chief adviser. Meanwhile, Fu and Luo Jialun, the associate editor, consulted Lu Xun (1881–1936) and other Beida professors.[86] The journal became exceedingly popular on and off campus; some of its earlier issues exceeded 10,000 copies. Fu wrote the forward to the journal and many articles, critiquing the status quo of Chinese scholarship. In his forward, Fu proclaims that the member of their society intended to pursue four goals:

1. to integrate Chinese learning with world intellectual trends;
2. to reform Chinese society and criticize dishonorable social behavior;
3. to promote a commitment to scholarly study;
4. to discuss the ideal type of the new youth.[87]

What they wrote actually falls in two areas: one was to introduce Western culture; the other to compare it with Chinese culture to introduce cultural reform.

Fu's writings covered a variety of topics, ranging from history, literary history, drama, to linguistics, suggesting his broad interest. While Fu's interest in Western culture was evident, his main concern was about the problems in Chinese culture. In order to revive the Chinese tradition, Fu and his friends compared many aspects of Chinese and Western culture to search for a solution. Their intention was well indicated in the title of their journal. They chose "New Tide" for the title in Chinese and *Renaissance* in English, and were pleased by this correspondence. Apparently, they tried to produce new tides in Chinese culture. They hoped that a new cultural tide waged by their introduction of Western science could lead to the rebirth, or the renaissance, of Chinese culture.

Why was it necessary? Fu explained that compared with scholarly developments in the West, Chinese scholarship had seven basic failings. First of all, Chinese scholars lacked an individualist and relativist approach to their subjects. As a result, many of them were both pompous about themselves and ignorant of different opinions. In addition, Chinese scholars often overstate two things: one was practical scholarship, the other comprehensive understanding. As the former resulted in superficiality, the latter trapped them in frivolousness. Yet what disappointed Fu the most was the fact that, in traditional education, scholars did not seek logical argumentation. Instead, they were indulged in speculation, which hindered methodological improvement. Consequently, in conducting their research, scholars were often complacent about advancement in form, but not in content.[88]

To overcome these fallacies in Chinese traditional scholarship, Fu stated, required a change of attitude toward and cognizance of modern scholarship, which meant that Chinese scholars needed to fully understand the essence and spirit of Western culture. Fu regretted that because Chinese scholars tended to be interested only in form rather than in content, what had been imported from the West to China in the past was merely military technology. But military technology per se was not sufficient to help resuscitate the Chinese culture that had been seriously ill. A better approach was, Fu believed, to recognize fully the fundamental difference between Chinese and Western culture and re-evaluate the Chinese cultural legacy by Western standards. Only with this radical approach could China survive the fierce competition in the modern world. Only by wiping away obstacles in traditional learning would China be able to create a new culture.[89]

Western theories were thus brought in for the purpose of dealing with problems in China. In Fu Sinian's essay on Chinese history and historiography, we can see how he used the Western concept of periodization to discuss the evolution of Chinese history. To justify the necessity of using the Western concept, Fu first attacked dynastic historiography. When history was broken into various dynasties, Fu complained, historical change and distinction were blurred. But while he supported the idea that Chinese history use the Western periodization of ancient, medieval, and modern to indicate periodic changes, transcending the fall and rise of dynasties, he opposed the division made by some Japanese historians to Chinese history as seen at the time. For him, their attempts were shallow and superficial. In his opinion, what the Japanese did was simply merge a few dynasties together to make a historical period. Their division failed to show the fundamental transformations in Chinese history. A tenable periodization of Chinese history, Fu contended, should reflect a scholarly understanding based on studies of the trend of Chinese history. Because Chinese history was fraught with wars between "barbarian" peoples and the Han Chinese people—both of them established dynasties in China—he suggested that such periodization reveal these struggles and the interaction and blend of "foreign" and "native" cultures.[90] In other words, Fu proposed to use the growth and decline of Han Chinese culture as barometers in studying Chinese history.

For him, this ebb and flow of Han Chinese culture could first be seen in the fifth century, for none of the subsequent dynasties were able to fortify its governance after the fall of the Han Dynasty. The rise of the Sui and Tang Dynasties in the sixth century did not represent a true revival of Han culture, but the opposite, because both dynasties were founded by non-Han peoples. After a long period of recovery, Han Chinese culture finally reached an age of prosperity in the Song Dynasty of the tenth century, only to be subdued again by the Mongols in the thirteenth century. It was not until the Ming Dynasty, founded in 1368, that Han Chinese culture regained its position. Nevertheless, it only lasted three hundred years and lost again to the Manchus in 1644. In order to emphasize the Chinese people's struggle in maintaining their culture, Fu rearranged the three-stage division seen in the Japanese works. He also subdivided historical periods by breaking down the dynastic division to illuminate the changes in history.[91]

Fu shows his originality in understanding Chinese history. Written in 1918, his work also became one of the earliest attempts made by a Chinese historian to address theoretical issues in Chinese historiography. Noticeably, in periodizing Chinese history, Fu adopted a multi-ethnic approach to understanding the historical evolution in China. His interpretation thus differed fundamentally from many old and new theories seen at the time, including the revolutionary approach advanced by Zhang Taiyan for overthrowing the Qing Dynasty. Zhang Taiyan had adopted a racial approach to explaining the change in Chinese history. He and his comrades in the Revolutionary Alliance had argued that the Manchu rulers in the Qing did not represent Han Chinese culture. The "barbarian" rule of the Qing Dynasty caused many problems, including China's defeat by the West. Viewed in this regard, Fu's distinction between Han and non-Han peoples was reminiscent of Zhang's focus on racial and cultural differences between the Han and the non-Hans. But he departed from Zhang by pointing out that before the Manchus, Han Chinese culture had already encountered many up and down turns. He implied that there was no "pure" Chinese culture before the Manchu invasion in the seventeenth century. In his discussion, he also reminded his readers that in the past, non-Han Chinese peoples too had performed commendable feats. Historians should base their explanations on facts, rather than on emotions.[92]

While Fu's interpretation of Chinese history was not agreed to by all in his time, his attempt to break down the dominance of dynastic division in Chinese historiography proved significant and influential. His theory inspired, for example, his Beida schoolmate Yao Congwu to form his interpretation of the interactions between Han and non-Han Chinese people in history.[93] Fu Sinian himself also used a similar approach to periodizing the history of Chinese literature. Instead of discussing different literary genres that flourished along the dynastic lines, he tried to look at Chinese literature as a whole and portrayed its evolution by discussing the changing trends of different historical periods.[94]

Fu Sinian's effort to use Western theories to reform Chinese culture thus extended well into other areas in the humanities. As Hu Shi's close follower, for instance, Fu supported Hu's literary revolution, which aimed to unite written and spoken Chinese and adopt the vernacular in writing. Yet in his own analysis of the Chinese language, Fu went much further and argued that a thorough and successful literary revolution depended on a total abandonment of the written literary Chinese so that one could use Western/foreign terms directly.[95] In his own writings, he often used English terms for precise expression. On one occasion, he even went so far as to argue that the true solution to the Chinese language was to abandon the ideographs and replace them with the Roman alphabet.[96] This radical iconoclasm suggests Fu's strong bias in favor of Western culture. But again, one may notice that his emphasis on the change of language for cultural reform is reminiscent of the Qing evidential scholarship, as evidenced by the work of Zhang Taiyan at that time.

While a highly noted student leader of the May Fourth Movement, Fu Sinian himself also experienced an intellectual transformation through the movement. Before the May Fourth Movement, he was a "Confucius' successor," admired and appreciated by his peers and teachers for his classical knowledge. But after the May Fourth Movement, he became a committed cultural reformer, most noted for his radical iconoclasm and scientific conviction. To account for this drastic change, Hu Shi's influence was crucial. Although Fu sometimes turned out to be even more radical than Hu Shi, he was obviously indebted to his teacher for many of his ideas. In the May Fourth Movement, Fu and his friends often spent their weekends at Hu's to exchange ideas. Fu's interest in science sprang from these meetings and conversations. Luo Jialun later recalled that although New Tide members came from different departments, they shared a common interest in reading Western books. For example, Fu Sinian was in the Department of Chinese Literature whereas Luo in the Department of English, they however paired together to search for English books. Buying and reading English books thus became Fu's life-long habit on which he often spent all his money.[97]

Fu's enthusiasm for Western learning was indeed emblematic of the entire May Fourth "student" generation. It was this kind of enthusiasm that prompted Fu and many of his cohorts to seek opportunities to receive a Western education, following the footsteps of their teachers like Hu Shi and He Bingsong. While many Chinese students of that generation became quite "Westernized" in both their conceptual outlook and lifestyle, hence alienating themselves from the Chinese society,[98] there were still many more who remained committed to the cause of Chinese cultural reform. Members of the New Tide society seemed to be good examples in this respect. Buoyed by antitraditionalist ideas, as mentioned earlier, Fu once suggested romanizing the Chinese language and believed that only by so doing could the reform make headway. But his suggestion actually reflected the influence of Qing evidential scholarship.[99] Interestingly enough, Fu was never really able to rid himself of the influence. When he returned from Europe to China in 1927, he proposed to establish the Institute of History and Philology, one of the earliest modern research institutes in China. To some, Fu's decision to pair history off with philology suggested the German humanist influence, to which he was exposed while studying in Germany. But, as we shall see in the next chapter, it is equally legitimate to say that his decision, too, evinced the Qing evidential focus on linguistic studies.

Thus, it seems that even the most radical iconoclasts in the May Fourth Movement were tradition-bond in both their outlook and approach, despite their avowed antitraditional claims. On surface, there was an obvious contrast between tradition (Chinese culture) and modernity (Western science) as perceived and presented by the participants in the movement. But these cultural reformers never eschewed tradition in their cultural pursuit. Indeed, as analyzed by Edward Shils, constructive intellectual pursuit usually began by working with an existing tradition. The purpose of their criticism of tradition was to help re-create it, which required a scrutiny. In fact, according to Shils, real intellectuals always take a critical attitude toward tradition; they "create works which extend and change their traditions."[100]

The May Fourth intellectuals' re-creation of tradition also underscores their firm political commitment to Chinese nationalism. In addition to China's repeated military losses from the mid-nineteenth century onward, the country met a diplomatic defeat at the Versailles conference in 1919. This increasingly deepened political crisis called students into action. The leadership role Fu Sinian, Luo Jialun, and other New Tide members played in the movement clearly indicated that the May Fourth Movement was not only a cultural experiment, but also a political campaign. When students made their first rally on Beida campus, Fu was elected the marshal and led the demonstration onto the streets, whereas Luo Jialun drafted their manifesto. Fu, his brother, and other fellow students also broke into Cao Rulin's house and set it on fire, because Cao was an alleged pro-Japanese minister and had fled his home by the time students got there.[101]

After this momentous action, Fu graduated from Beida and prepared to study abroad. On his graduation, he reflected on his experience at Beida, especially his involvement in the New Tide Society and the journal, with a sense of fulfillment. Before his departure, he wrote an article concluding the activities of the New Tide Society. He stated: "I believe that the purest, deepest, most durable feelings are those based on a shared mind-set. These far surpass religious or familial alliances. Those of us who came together did not have previous contact."

Apparently, this "shared mind-set" was based on their nationalist concern for the country and their commitment to its cultural revival.[102] Their interest in science, hence Western culture, is juxtaposed with their concern for the nation. This juxtaposition, therefore, characterized the binary dimensions of the May Fourth Movement: one showed a strong nationalist impulse and the other a transnational interest in science. These two merged together in their pursuit of scientific history—like their teachers, Fu Sinian, Gu Jiegang, and Luo Jialun all became historians. On the content level, this scientific history was nationalistic, aimed to portray China's past from a nationalist perspective. Yet on the methodological level, this history was pursued on a conviction in the universal value of scientific method that united Chinese tradition with modern culture.

Fu Sinian arrived in England in January 1920 and was enrolled in the University of London. In spite of his earlier training in the humanities, Fu decided to pursue a degree in science. He took courses in biology, psychology, and mathematics at the university and tried to earn an M.A. in experimental psychology.[103] It seems that after his dramatic conversion to "new culture" at Beida, Fu Sinian was ready to make another big change in his life. To Fu, this change was quite rational, based on his understanding of the need of China's cultural reform and his interest in Western scientific culture. Luo Jialun, his close friend, later provided a good explanation in his memoir:

> In order to understand Fu's decision [to major in science], we must understand the psychological background of the May Fourth scholars. At that time, we all worshiped [Western] natural science. We wanted not only to learn the trustworthy knowledge provided by the study of natural sciences, but also to obtain its methodological training. We thought that the method of natural science was applicable to all subjects.[104]

Luo's words revealed that for Fu and his friends at that time, the advance of Western learning lay principally in its methodological improvement. It was very likely that they obtained that idea from John Dewey's lectures at Beida, in which Dewey stressed that modern science manifested "the methodological importance of testing hypotheses with verifying evidence."[105] Fu's decision to study science reflected this belief, to which he had been converted before his departure for England. In other words, while enthusiastic about modern education, he was not really interested in becoming an expert in any specific field. Rather, he was interested in pursuing "real learning" in order to solve "big problems."[106] Here the "real learning" meant the scientific method, which, in Fu's belief, enabled him to solve all kinds of problems, be they social, political, or academic.

Fu's understanding of science, therefore, was positivist. He strongly believed that a scientific approach could be used to explain all riddles in life and give it a meaning. In 1918, he wrote an essay for the *New Tide* discussing the meaning of life with his knowledge of social sciences. He stated that in order to appreciate fully the real meaning of life, one had to look beyond the discussion of human life per se and take a glimpse at how human life was being studied by biology, psychology, and sociology, because those studies provided answers to the questions of what the position of human beings was in nature, how the composition, function, behavior, and will of human beings were shaped, and how individuals were associated with each other in a society.[107]

Therefore, Fu had begun showing interest in methodological questions before going abroad. Influenced probably by Hu Shi, he did some studies on logic, especially Western theories on the subject, such as W. Stanley Jevons's *The Principles of Science: A Treatise on Logic and Scientific Method*, and F. C. S. Schiller's *Formal Logic: A Scientific and Social Problem*, which he reviewed for the *New Tide*. Unlike Hu, however, he was not sure if the study of logic constituted a major interest among traditional Chinese scholars. Fu's interest in methodology also led him to take notice of Freud's theory of psychoanalysis. From his study, he concluded that "philosophy is inseparable from science; it is rather a synthesis of science."[108] Thus viewed, Fu's study of science in England extended his long interest in scientific method. To him, scientific method was probably somewhat of a magic finger that could turn dross into treasure by a single touch.

Needless to say, Fu was ambitious, but he was also earnest. In a letter written to Hu Shi from England on January 8, 1920, he told Hu that he found himself interested in the study of science and regretted the fact that he had been a student of literature at Beida. He also stated that the reason for him not to take any philosophy courses in England was that he thought it necessary to have some knowledge in natural and social sciences before attempting any philosophical contemplation.[109] To that end, as shown in his book collection, Fu bought and read a variety of books while in Europe, whose subjects ranged from physics, biology, and geology to philosophy, history, and linguistics.[110]

Fu did not act alone; his idea was shared by many of his cohorts. In Europe, many of the students of the May Fourth generation were inclined to seek a versatile education, tapping into every subject that seemed interesting and potentially useful. Their purpose was, according to Luo Jialun, to seek a general understanding of modern scholarship, especially the linkage of natural science, social sciences, and humanities. Among Fu's friends, Mao Zishui, later known as a Chinese philologist, was a mathematics student at Beijing University. But after graduation, he took part in the examination for studying history in Germany and he, together with Yao

Congwu, succeeded in it. While in Germany, Mao took courses in geography and Greek. Their friend Yu Dawei (1897–1972), who later became the Minister of Defense in Taiwan, had even a more versatile interest. In Germany, Yu studied mathematics, mathematical logic, Western classics, music, and finally ballistics and military strategy. Compared with his friends, Luo was relatively focused on philosophy, history, and education, namely the study of the humanities. While likening the May Fourth Movement to the Enlightenment in Europe, Luo declared that their behavior was comparable to that of the French Encyclopedists. He even compared Fu with Voltaire.[111] The only exception among them was probably the nerdy student Yao Congwu, who confined his study in Germany to history. But before going to Germany, Yao had also been interested in geography.

Of course, Luo was very proud of his friends. While praising their enthusiasm for modern education, his remarks also revealed a paradox in this scientific pursuit. Apparently, what drove them to study in the West was the desire to learn how to overcome the deficiencies in Chinese learning. One of these deficiencies was its comprehensiveness, as Fu had acutely observed in his critique. In other words, traditional scholars rarely tried to specialize their study and confine their interest. While critical of the Chinese tradition, these May Fourth scholars were not immune to this tradition in their pursuit of Western knowledge. In his influential study of the May Fourth antitraditionalism, Lin Yu-sheng has observed this problem, albeit from a different perspective. He argues that the totalistic, or comprehensive, rejection of tradition, as shown in the work of these intellectuals, reflected the traditional influence. Namely, their indiscriminating, "either-or," approach showed a traditional line of thinking.[112] Lin has ingeniously shown us the traditional nexus of the May Fourth Movement, which was also well present during this period when these young radicals furthered their interest and education abroad.

Indeed, the comprehensive approach adopted by the May Fourth scholars to scientific learning extended their activities in the New Tide Society. As the end of the society was to promote cultural reform, an important issue concerning the majority of the students on campus, the society attracted members across the departments. Its journal also published essays written by authors from many departments, not necessarily by the humanities students. For example, Mao Zishui, a mathematics major, wrote an important essay discussing the possibility of applying science to the study of traditional Chinese culture. It was received so well that Fu Sinian, one of the "authorities" from the society on such subjects, admitted that there was no need for him to elaborate on the same subject.[113] Likewise, Fu also attempted to learn about other subjects. Luo Jialun recalled that, though Fu majored in Chinese literature, he often took English courses in Luo's department. The two, too, shared courses with Gu Jiegang in the Department of Philosophy.[114] Thus viewed, Fu's decision to study psychology was not a spur-of-the-moment action, but underscored a shared mind-set of his generation in understanding the potency of science and in response to the need of cultural reform.

While a worthwhile plan designed after careful thinking, Fu's study of science in England was anything but smooth. First of all, he arrived a bit late, failing to catch the beginning of the spring semester in 1920 at the University College of London University, where he was registered in the Department of Psychology, chaired by Professor Charles Spearman. Moreover, no sooner did Fu arrive in London than Yu Pingbo, his friend and a New Tide member at Beida, decided to go back to China. Fu chased Yu from England to France and tried to persuade Yu not to quit, but to no avail. As a result, he had to enroll in the fall semester.[115] In the interim, he took some time off for preparation.[116]

During this interval, Fu seemed unable to resist the temptation, his old habit, of reading literary works, although he was supposed to prepare for becoming a psychology major. Fu read widely in English literature, particularly poems, and history. According to Luo Jialun, Fu finished all the works of Bernard Shaw during his brief English sojourn. From Shaw's works, Fu gained some knowledge of modern European literature and learned for the first time the term *Ibsenism*.[117] Although later on, Fu became quite critical of Shaw, considering his ideas unoriginal in both literature and politics.[118]

Despite the distractions, Fu was able to complete his undergraduate program in London in two years and was also admitted into the graduate program. However, Fu later decided to forsake his pursuit of a master's degree in psychology in England, either because of financial or academic difficulty.[119] In 1923 he left England for Germany, entering the University of Berlin. While maintaining his interest in science, he seemed to have decided to stay away from psychology permanently—he indeed never reverted to it throughout his life. He became attracted to the breakthrough of modern physics made by the German physicists Max Planck and Albert Einstein. But what really interested him was positivist theorists, such as Ernst Mach (1838–1916). He was engrossed by Mach's *Analyse der Empfindungen* and *Mechanik*, on which he spent most of his leisure time.[120]

More interestingly, encouraged by his friends Chen Yinke and Yu Dawei, Fu began to resume his interest in the humanities, attending classes in history and comparative philology. He was enchanted with the German historiographical and philological achievement. Besides the German achievement in physics, he and his friends considered German historiography to be another contribution to the modern world. Fu was excited about the idea that with that philological method, he could reorganize his classical knowledge and thereby find a new horizon in the study of Chinese antiquity.[121] No sooner had he returned to China in 1926 than Fu practiced his idea by founding the Institute of Philology and History at Sun Yat-sen University.

Thus it was in Germany that Fu's later career began to take its shape. Out of his conviction in positivism, Fu took pains to integrate the study of natural science with his humanistic interests. He adopted a liberal approach to his study in Germany, taking whatever courses he liked. Exhorted by Chen Yinke, for example, he attended history and philology classes; accompanied by Yu Dawei, he studied physics and other sciences. His ambitious plan was not particularly successful, but it allowed him to gain a broad knowledge base and later helped him to become an effective academic administrator in designing research plans for the Institute of Philology and History.[122]

But Fu was not yet ready to become a historian; he still tried to become a scientist. When he heard about the National Studies Movement, especially the "Ancient History Discussion," led by his former roommate Gu Jiegang and his mentor Hu Shi, he became very excited about it and closely followed its progress. He looked for Gu's article on Xia and Yu in Germany, two legendary emperors in ancient China, and showed it to Chen Yinke with great enthusiasm and excitement. On Gu's request, he wrote a long letter back to Gu, which was published in the journal of Sun Yat-sen University in January 1928, entitled "A Letter to Gu Jiegang about Ancient Historical Books."[123] In his letter, he praised Gu's achievement, calling him the "king of historiography." In the meantime, however, he said that having spent so many years in the West pursuing a scientific knowledge, he himself was no longer a student of the humanities.[124]

Fu's final return to the field of humanities did not occur until he received an appointment from China. At the end of 1926, he went back to China to become the dean of the School of Humanities in Sun Yat-sen University. From that time on, it is hard for anyone to find visible traces of his scientific exertions in Europe, or his training in psychology which he had studied full-time in England.[125] What appeared instead was his favorable comments on the achievement of modern German historiography, in which Leopold von Ranke and Theodor Mommsen (1817–1903) were deemed as key figures.[126] As his scientific fervor gradually cooled down, Fu became convinced that the very basis of modern historical scholarship was its source criticism, as exemplified by the works of the Rankean school and some Chinese historians, especially Qing evidential scholars. Taking a different route, Fu reached at last the same conclusion as did his Beida teachers Hu Shi and He Bingsong.[127]

Though his interest shifted from science to history, Fu remained a modern scholar to many of his colleagues and friends.[128] He was expected to play a leading role in making this newly founded university a center of new culture. In Sun Yat-sen University, Fu chaired two Departments: History and Literature. Besides teaching in the two Departments, Fu proposed to strengthen the university by alluring young and like-minded scholars to the faculty.[129] Gu Jiegang, therefore, became his natural choice, who joined Sun Yat-sen University in 1927. While they eventually ended their friendship with a quarrel, at least in the beginning, Fu fully supported Gu for his continual effort at examining the literature on Chinese history. He also secured resources to push the movement further. He stated in a letter that "I am determined to wipe out backward cultural elements from the tradition," echoing Hu Shi's slogan of "chasing the devils and beating the ghosts."[130]

Through the use of the method of philology in source criticism, Fu believed, one could not only write a scientific history of China's past but bridge the German philological scholarship in history with the Chinese philological tradition. His decision to found the Institute of History and Philology reflected this belief. Applying philological methods to examining historical sources, Fu now joined his friends and teachers to carry out the project on scientific history in China. In this pursuit, Fu also found his own niche in career growth that satisfied both his early interest in history and philology and his enthusiasm for science. Thus viewed, his seven-year search for "true learning" in Europe was fruitful at last. In the next chapter, we shall see more closely the role Fu Sinian and his Institute played in this scientific endeavor.

Viewed in retrospect, Fu's participation in the project is not fortuitous at all. In explaining the success of the New Tide Society, Fu mentioned that there was a "shared mind-set" among its members. This explanation can also be used here to explain why many May Fourth scholars, students and teachers alike, became historians and, moreover, why scientific history—a discovery of China's past from the perspective of science—became an integral part of the New Culture Movement. This "shared mind-set" was shown not only by these scholars' common interest in cultural reform, but was supported by the relative uniformity of their educational background that provided a common ground of knowledge. The May Fourth generation grew up at the turn of twentieth century. As a result, most of them were schooled more or less by Chinese classical learning. Regardless of their academic interests, their early exposures to classical education enabled them to see its problems and discuss them together as a group. In other words, they were a transitional group caught in the conjuncture of tradition and modernity. Their unique position in Chinese history, therefore, allowed them to play a role similar to the *philosophes* in the Enlightenment, hence the Chinese Enlightenment, coined by Vera Schwarcz.[131] Although some have now questioned their seemingly overzealous quest for scientific culture,[132] it is important for us to recognize that as a group they played a significant role in pioneering a way in which both tradition and modernity were not only united but each acquired a new meaning in this union.

Rankean Historiography

Compared to his flamboyant and charismatic schoolmate Fu Sinian, Yao Congwu (Shi'ao) was modest about his goals and a bit slow in response to changes. While a cohort to most of the New Tide members, he did nothing exciting in his student years and was quite unnoticeable on the Beida campus. Despite the fact that the May Fourth Movement was such an eye-catching movement and the Beida students were its vanguard, Yao remained largely an outsider. If Mao Zishui was somehow afraid to join his fellow students, Yao Congwu seemed almost indifferent to their movement; when his schoolmates were roaring in the Beijing streets, crying for the sovereignty of the country, he probably still immersed himself in the newly bought complete paperback dynastic histories.[133] It was not until in Germany, when he and his former Beida classmates Fu Sinian, Luo Jialun, and others were studying at the University of Berlin, that he began to befriend them. Still, different from his friends, Yao remained a plain and "pure" scholar, as one of his students and colleagues put it.[134] Fu Sinian later earned a reputation as the "academic hegemon" *(xueba)* for his leadership role in the Institute of History and Philology. Luo Jialun became a close friend to Chiang Kai-shek (1888–1975) in the Guomindang (GMD) party and held a few high-profile positions in both the party and the government. By contrast to their successes, Yao never held any official position in his life long enough to gain him political prestige, nor did his voice become influential and distinct in public or among scholars.

But it was this "pure scholar" who became an authority in German historiography for the Chinese—a position both Fu and Luo were unable to hold or challenge. Although Fu was very proud of his German education and impressed by the scientific rigor of modern German historiography, it was Yao who expounded the German historical method through his teaching and research. If He Bingsong was an advocate of the American New History school, Yao was the spokesman for European/German historiography. To be sure, what they recommended represented two different stages in the history of Western historiography—the New History school actually challenged the Rankean influence—but this "age difference" was not so important to the Chinese historians. In fact, both were appropriated for the Chinese cause, advocating the need to broaden the vision of the historian on the one hand and his use of the philological method, *Quellenkritik* in German and *Xungu* in Chinese, on the other.

Yao Congwu was born into a literati family on October 7, 1894, in Henan, the central province in China. Although his ancestors used to be high-ranking officials, Yao's father did not hold any position in officialdom. Yao was educated at home in his early childhood and later at Henan No. 2 High School. In 1917, Yao entered Beijing University to study history. His devotion to learning did not allow him to take interest in any extracurricular activities. What made Yao proud of his three-year undergraduate study at Beida was his detailed class notes. While diligent, he also appeared to be aloof. Mao Zishui recalled: "Although we both graduated from the university in 1920, I did not know Yao in the school until the fall of 1922 when we both passed the examination for studying history in Germany."[135]

After his graduation from Beida, Yao entered a graduate program at the National Studies Institute of Beijing University and stayed in Beijing until 1923 before leaving for Germany. At Beida, Yao developed an interest in historical geography and was considered by his teacher as one of the best students in the class.[136] He furthered this interest in his graduate study and became the editor of the *Journal of Geography (Dixue zazhi)*, to which he often made contributions as well. His works that appeared in the journal centered on the impact of geographical environment on human society and culture, including articles and translations. For example, he translated selectively Ellsworth Huntington's introduction to *Civilization and Climate* for the journal.[137] Yao later discontinued his study of historical geography, but from his research on Mongolian history and the history of the Chinese frontier, one can still discern his long-term interest in the geographical influence in human history. In his historical study, he noticed the geographical influence, especially the changing climate, on the behaviors of the nomadic peoples along the borders of ancient China and discovered that their incessant migrations were often a result of that influence.[138]

Yao Congwu spent a total of eleven years in Germany, from 1923 to 1934. German education was thus a determinant factor in his research and characterized his scholarly career.[139] When he was in Germany, Yao belonged to a close-knit group of Chinese students, which included Fu Sinian, Chen Yinke, Mao Zishui, Yu Dawei, and Luo Jialun. But of the group, few stayed in Germany as long as he did. Luo barely stayed a year and left for France in 1925. Chen had been to Europe earlier, but left earlier too in 1925. Fu Sinian was next to Yao in respect to the duration of their German education. Having arrived in the fall of 1923, Fu remained in Germany until the end of 1926. Insofar as their studies were concerned, Chen, Fu, and Yao appeared quite serious, whereas Yao was not only focused but also persistent.

Yao's interest in an academic life was unusual at the time among many Chinese students. Of course, not many Chinese students had the chance to study abroad, but those who had seemed not to appreciate the opportunity very much. Studying abroad was almost like following a fashion to them; they spent a couple of years in the West in order to polish their résumés and then go back home to bargain for a better position.[140] A few contemporary publications showed us that though there were a fairly large number of Chinese students in Germany at the time, their academic records were generally not impressive. Most Chinese students were attracted to Germany because of the favorable exchange rate due its hyperinflation. As a result, Berlin in 1924 gathered about a thousand Chinese students. However, not many of them were officially registered in universities; the rest "preferred to spend their time outside the schools and lecture halls." When the inflation ended, three fourth of them left Germany. Luo Jialun's brief sojourn in Germany was a good example in this respect. Luo recalled that because of the favorable exchange rate, he was better off than most Germans at the time. He frequented concerts and enjoyed going to the opera.[141]

Thus, the fact that Yao spent substantial years in Germany was enough to earn him respect from his students and colleagues. When Yao returned to China and took a position as history professor at Beida, he was received in a meeting chaired by Hu Shi, then the dean of the School of Arts. In his introductory remarks, Hu mentioned to students and colleagues that Yao had received a long and solid German historical training, which left a strong impression on the audience.[142] From that time on, Yao was regarded as an expert on Rankean historiography in China.

While in Germany, Yao Congwu studied with two historians at the University of Berlin: Otto Franke (1863–1946) and Erich Haenisch (1880–1966).[143] Otto Franke was an acclaimed historian in Chinese history in Germany, whose *Geschichte des Chinesischen Reiches* was hailed by his colleagues as a milestone in the field. In this five-volume book, Franke divided Chinese history into eight periods; his division was based not only on the rise and fall of dynasties but on the ebb and flow of Confucianism. However, Franke did not complete his survey of Chinese history; his work stopped in 1911. The volume on Republican China was provided by his son Wolfgang Franke (b. 1912), a sinology professor at the University of Hamburg.[144]

According to Yao, Otto Franke had a superb knowledge of Chinese culture and language. From 1888 to 1901, Franke lived in Beijing, Shanghai, and Xiamen (Amoy). After he returned to Germany, he became a secretary in China's embassy in Berlin for three years (1903–1906). Franke not only mastered Chinese, but also experienced many momentous events that happened in or were related to China. Franke's first work was *Studien zur Geschichte des konfuzian* which had already suggested his interest in Chinese Confucian culture. Moreover, Otto Franke was a student of Johann Droysen (1804–1884) and Wilhelm Wattenbach (1819–1897),[145] both were leading historians in nineteenth-century Germany. Droysen was more important to Franke's career because, as a student of Leopold von Ranke, he provided Franke a Rankean training in history. Greatly impressed with German historiography, Yao used it to outline and design his historical methodology course at Beida.[146] In his article about Franke's achievement in the study of Chinese history, Yao noted emphatically that "because Franke was a student of Droysen, he could grasp the historical method of the Prussian school. He knew the importance of comparing what appeared in the

Chinese Standard Histories with contemporary sources."[147] He insisted that Franke's treatment of sources was superior to that of other Western sinologists because of his rigorous training in Rankean historiography.

Erich Haenisch was an authority on Mongolian history in Germany. With him Yao studied Mongolian history and the language, which left a discernible trace in his later career.[148] In Germany, Yao translated Haenisch's introduction to Mongolian history into Chinese and published it in the *Journal of Furen University (Furen xuezhi)* in China in September of 1929. To assess the impact of the Mongol conquest on Europe, he also made trips to Hungary, Austria, and Czechoslovakia, to search for reminiscences of the Mongols.[149] In 1934, Haenisch and Yao worked hand in hand in annotating two source books of Mongolian history, which became a foundation for a complete translation in the 1980s.[150]

By working with these German professors, Yao developed a broad interest in examining China's cultural relations with its neighbors in Asia and other continents. For example, he explored the transmission of paper-making technology from China to Europe, which became a major scholarly publication in his career.[151] Yao provided written and material evidence to describe the process how the Arabs first learned it from the Chinese and gradually passed it on to the Europeans. At the end, he argued that the paper-making technology facilitated the Reformation in Europe, suggesting his motive for researching the subject.

But when Yao sent his manuscript home to be published in the *Journal of Furen University*, his conclusion caused a controversy. Since the university was founded by Catholic missionaries, the journal editor added a note and stated that Yao's argument lacked evidence and was thus unfounded.[152] Interestingly enough, some thirty years later in 1966, Yao decided to publish the article again in Taiwan and restated his position.[153] This episode shows that while a "pure" scholar, Yao was quite willing to render his research useful for nationalist historiography, in which elements from the past were discovered and used to enhance the national pride.

Yao's interest in cultural transaction reflected the influence of his another German professor, Kurt Breysig (1866–1914), a well-known cultural historian at the University of Berlin. Together with Karl Lamprecht (1856–1915), Breysig challenged the Rankean historiographical tradition for its emphasis on political and diplomatic history. Breysig advocated instead the study of cultural history, focusing on the evolution of civilization. Moreover, he was interested in describing the phasic development of the evolution and the major characteristics, or *Zeitgeist*, of each phase. In Yao's study of the relationship between the Han Chinese and border/nomadic peoples, he also drew attention to the phasic differences in their interactions. The same approach, too, was taken by him to analyze the development of Confucianism in Chinese history. We will describe these works in detail in chapter 6.[154]

Except for his article on the paper-making technology, Yao's early publications were centered around European scholarship in sinology, such as Otto Franke's accomplishment in Chinese history.[155] In 1930, he published a review article: "European Scholars' Work on the Huns," discussing European scholarship on the Xiongnu (Huns), an ancient nomadic people on the northern border of China. Yao reviewed the works of three leading European sinologists in the field: J. Deguignes (1721–1800), F. Hirth (1845–1926), and J. J. M. De Groot (1845–1921). But at the end, he did not forget to mention that defeated by the Han Dynasty, the Huns gradually moved westward and reached Europe around the first century, contributing to the Great Migration and the fall of the Roman Empire.[156] This observation shows again a nationalist connotation in Yao's research; his article was aimed to discover the past glory of the Chinese empire: he carefully presented a triangular relation—the Chinese, the Huns, and the Romans—in which the Chinese were the most superior.

In another publication during the period, we find that Yao also applied German historical method to the study of Chinese history. In 1933 he wrote an article in German, entitled "Ein Kurzer Beitrag zur Qullenkritik der Kin-und Yuan-Dynastie" (A brief introduction to source criticism of the Jin and Yuan Dynasties), which was published in *Asia Major*, a prominent journal in sinological studies. What makes this article important is twofold. First, it indicates that Yao's research interest was focused on non-Han dynasties in middle imperial China; he later indeed became an authority in that area. Second, it shows that his research method was based on source criticism, or *Qullenkritik*, a similar interest found in the careers of his many friends in their search for scientific history.

Besides doing research, Yao also held a few teaching positions while in Germany. In 1929, for example, Yao was appointed a lecturer at the Oriental Study Institute of the University of Bonn to teach the Chinese language and linguistics. In 1931, he transferred to the University of Berlin to teach similar courses.[157] Besides these teaching obligations, he worked with Erich Haenisch as a research assistant. However, despite his eleven year stay in Germany, Yao did not receive any degree from a German university. There is no clear explanation for this, although it is always possible that he failed his course work. But another possibility must be considered: He might not have been interested in obtaining a degree from a German institution, particularly given the examples of Fu Sinian and Chen Yinke and many others.

After his return to China, Yao continued his research on Mongolian history and other non-Han dynasties in Song China. However, to his many students, of all the courses Yao taught, it was the "Historical Methods" *(lishi fangfa lun)* that was most memorable.[158] Du Weiyun, Yao's student at National Taiwan University, stated that "Historical Methods" was a trademark of Yao's forty-year teaching career. In his teaching of the course, Du recalled, Yao usually spent more than half of the time discussing the works of German historians from Ranke to Bernheim. He often got excited when he mentioned Ranke's name; his voice became louder and his face shined. Like most historians in the West, Yao considered the publication of Ranke's *Geschichte der Romanischen und Germanischen Volker, von 1498 bis 1535* in 1824 a breakthrough in modern historiography, because in its epilogue, Ranke used the critical method to judge the works of Renaissance historians and pointed to the new direction of modern historiography. In addition, Yao also translated some chapters of Ernst Bernheim's *Lehrbuch der historischen Method und der Geschichtsphilosophie* for class handouts.[159]

In teaching the methods course, Yao came to define the meaning of history and discuss its relation to other disciplines. In his opinion, history was different from historiography, because "History is the process of many influential events, whereas historical writing is the record of those influential events and their changes over a certain course." Ideally, historical writings should correspond to actual history. Using a term borrowed from the Chinese tradition, he called this kind historiography "conscientious history" *(xinshi)*. However, for various reasons, he conceded, the real *xinshi* was hard to attain. Historical methods thus were developed to overcome any discrepancies between historiography and history. History became a form of learning because it provided a way in which one understood the causes of historical events, interpreted fairly and plausibly their meanings, and described them in a good style.[160]

Like his friends Yao considered methodological improvement crucial to the growth of history as a modern discipline. In his opinion, historical methodology had two aspects: one dealt with general questions, the other with specific subjects. The former provided answers to questions such as: What knowledge and language were usually useful for a historian? How could ideas and methods be borrowed from other related disciplines to discover new questions and topics in history? How should one distinguish primary and secondary sources and verify the validity of a historical source? The latter guided a historian to work on a specific topic, helping him to find a perspective, design his research, and conduct an investigation of historical events. The focus of his course, however, seems not to be on theories. Yao advised his students to take an empirical approach. In order to learn how to ride a horse or swim in a river, he said, one needed to get on the horseback and jump into the river. In other words, historical methodology was not a subject to discuss, but a subject to practice.[161] Like Hu Shi, therefore, Yao also regarded historical study as a scientific experimentation.

Indeed, Yao's method in history was not theoretical. He was fully aware of the difference between history and philosophy, which reminds us of Ranke's contempt for Hegelian philosophy. For Yao history was essentially different from both literature and philosophy for historians pursued a different "vocation" *(shiming)*. Unlike his friends, who pursued a versatile interest in Western learning, Yao believed that specialization and professionalization were two important developments in modern scholarship. From the perspective of the "vocation," he stated that, on the one hand philosophers were interested in the aesthetic question of how to understand ultimate beauty and goodness; they were less interested in the actual existence of beauty or goodness. Literary writers, on the other hand, created images in their stories with inspiration and imagination; like the philosophers, they were not concerned about real facts. By contrast, historians worked primarily with three things: "what happened in the past," "well-grounded records," and "remainders of the past—antique substances." Historians, thus viewed, were not supposed to indulge themselves in speculations.

From this empiricist perspective, Yao questioned Georg Hegel's (1770–1831) philosophy of history. Hegel believed that everything occurred in history was *Vernunftig* (reasonable)—"*was geschien ist, ist Vernunftig*." Yao disliked this conclusion. For him, not everything in history was reasonable, such as Japan's invasion of Manchuria, nor did it have to happen. As a practicing historian, Yao believed that the duty of the historian was to investigate an event and provide an explanation. In doing so, one had first to discard any prior ideas or beliefs and present truth *(zhenxiang)* with evidence *(zhengju)*.[162] In refuting Hegel, Yao reiterated Ranke's position regarding the difference between history and philosophy.[163]

Yao remained loyal to the ideas of Rankean historiography throughout his life. A few months before his death in 1970, he published an article tracing the origins of modern historical methods in Europe, in which he credited the tradition of German historiography and praised nineteenth-century German historians for their accomplishment in philological criticism. Following Ernst Bernheim, whose *Lehrbuch der historischen Method und der Geschichtsphilosophie* was the required text for his teaching of the methods course, and Eduard Fueter, who wrote *Geschichte der neuren Historiographie*, a definitive text on European historiography before G. P. Gooch's *History and Historians in the Nineteenth Century*, Yao regarded Ranke and his predecessor Niebuhr as "revolutionary" figures in the history of modern historiography.

Drawing on Fueter's book, Yao concluded five principles in source criticism from Rankean historiography. First, whenever possible, always use primary sources. Second, take a critical attitude toward source materials and check them before use. Third, use reliable secondary/derivative sources if primary ones are not available, although in terms of their value, secondary sources are no equal to primary sources. Fourth, a source becomes primary because it provides direct information for the event, not because of its style or format. And fifth, be careful about the author's intention and attitude.[164]

Receptive to the German influence notwithstanding, Yao took pains to search for examples in the Chinese tradition for illustration. For example, he used Sima Qian's *Records of the Grand Historian* to explain why it is necessary and sometimes difficult to distinguish a primary source from a secondary one. First of all, it is hard to determine which sections in the work were actually written by Sima Qian, since he lived over two thousand years ago. How can you, Yao asked, be sure that the *Records of the Grand Historian* was not interpolated and altered by others? Second, that some sections were actually written by Sima does not mean they can be considered primary sources. For instance, Sima Qian's "Biographies of the Huns" *(Xiongnu liezhuan)* provided valuable information about the Huns. But, Yao pointed out, it ought not be regarded as a primary source in the study of the history of Huns because it was written by a Han Chinese, not a Hun.[165] Through Yao's explanation, not only did the Western theory become applicable to the study of Chinese history, but the latter also acquired a new perspective in the Chinese context, presenting the reciprocal relationship of tradition and modernity.

Yao took the same approach to the question of historical interpretation. If source selection and differentiation were the first step in historical research, interpretation of sources was the second. While drawing on Bernheim's book to define source interpretation, he provided Chinese examples to explain why it was necessary. In the Western tradition, Yao found, source interpretation meant a study of *Hermeneutik*, or hermeneutics in English, meaning "explanations or illustrations of a text," or the study of *xungu* (explanations of words in ancient text through philology and phonetics) in the Chinese tradition.[166] From this perspective, Yao analyzed various needs for source interpretation:

1. the philological need that stemmed from the change of word meanings;
2. the logical need for understanding a text in its own historical context;
3. the psychological need that resulted from the difference between one's attitude toward a person, an event, etc. and that of the past;
4. the technical need for understanding some historical terms and phrases;
5. the cultural need that resulted from the change of cultural customs and social habits.

For example, quite a few Chinese words changed their meanings through the years. The word *zhongri* (a whole day) meant something quite different in ancient times. Yao mentioned three cases in which the word did not mean "a day" but "after a while" *(liangjiu)*. Also, people often changed their attitude/opinion about someone in the past. Famous historical figures like Qinshihuang, Emperor Wu of the Han Dynasty, and Wang Anshi received divergent evaluations at different times. Thus the information on them often varied tremendously and required explanation.[167]

Yao's effort to enmesh German ideas with Chinese cases too is found in his analysis of the methods in historical interpretation. He stated that there were five methods, as discussed by Bernheim. They were:

1. induction, or *Schluss-folgerung vom Besonderen aufs Allgemeine* (to seek a general rule from the particulars);

2. deduction, which was the opposite of induction;
3. analogy;
4. comparison;
5. counterevidence or reduction.

To explicate the use of these methods, he again supplied Chinese examples. For instance, in discussing the methods of analogy and comparison, he asked students to compare the wars between the Han and non-Han Chinese in the Han and Song Dynasties. The outcome of these wars—the Han was the winner whereas the Song was the loser—was often determined by horse raising. Horse raising caught the attention of the Emperor Wu of the Han. The Han therefore built its cavalry force, with which it defeated the non-Han horse riders from the north. By contrast, Song emperors paid little attention to horse raising, thus the Song army appeared very ineffective in defending its territory from the invasion of skillful horse riders of northern nomads. An analogy of horse raising in the Han and the Song, therefore, was useful for historical interpretation.[168]

In sum, as a devout exponent of Rankean historiography, Yao played a crucial role in applying the Western experience to the study of Chinese history. His expertise was well received by his cohorts and students not only because he expounded the German model of modern historiography, which, by itself, was an important addition to the transnational aspect of scientific history in modern China, but because in demonstrating this knowledge, Yao, like Hu Shi and others, explored the way in which Chinese and Western historical traditions could form a reciprocal relationship, benefiting each other. That is to say, Yao's interest in historical methodology highlighted what drove his friends in their pursuit of modern scientific history: through the study of methodology they were building a bridge that allowed them to (re)visit China's past world as well as the world outside China.

Chapter Four

Equivalences and Differences

> Galileo, Kepler, Boyle, Harvey, and Newton worked with the objects of nature, with stars, balls, inclining planes, telescopes, microscopes, prisms, chemicals, and numbers and astronomical tables. And their Chinese contemporaries worked with books, words, and documentary evidences. The latter created three hundred years of scientific book learning; the former created a new science and a new world.
>
> —Hu Shi, *The Chinese Renaissance*

What we have discussed in the previous chapter shows that May Fourth scholars shared a common interest in scientific method and that they pursued it with a general understanding of its crosscultural value. Though their scientific educations were not identical, they developed a consensus in perceiving the way in which scientific method was to be applied to the study of history, or scientific history. They all seemed to agree that the key to the success of scientific history was the exercise of source criticism, in which historians carefully examined their source materials through applications of philological method and the methods of social sciences. To the May Fourth scholars source criticism provided the basis as well as the main feature of scientific history.

To account for this understanding and practice of scientific history, we need to consider the integration of both the traditional and modern elements in modern Chinese historiography. What prompted the Chinese to search for scientific history arose from their interest in national history; Liang Qichao's case was particularly salient on this score while others' were similarly revealing. In the meantime, their understanding of scientific history reflected an international consensus in the nineteenth and the early-twentieth centuries; among historians in the world, especially those in the West, source criticism then was considered a cornerstone of modern historiography. The reason that Rankean historiography was treated, or mistreated, as a good example of "scientific history" was due as much to Ranke's use of archival sources (he was by no means the first one) as to his well-known phrase *wie es eigentlich gewesen* (what really happened), a motto for most historians when they aspired to the writing of history at the time.[1]

The national factor, which was similarly important if not more so, provided the sociopolitical context in which the Chinese received the knowledge of science. As analyzed by Edward Shils, "The productive intellectual acts within the framework of intellectual traditions. . . . He also incorporates into his image of the world and responds to his preintellectual and extraintellectual experience in society."[2] This "preintellectual and extraintellectual experience" was China's sociopolitical crisis in the nineteenth and the early twentieth centuries. The Chinese pursuit of scientific history that occurred at that time was not coincidental when we consider the nationalist impulse behind the New Culture/May Fourth Movement.

While both were important to the growth of scientific history in China, the national and transnational elements could cause some friction if they were not united in source criticism. As analyzed by Joseph Levenson, the May Fourth intellectuals were eager to apply science to carrying out the reform of Chinese culture. But they also realized that it was through the work of Western scientists that the method of science gained its credence and potency. In other words, as the intellectuals recognized the "value" of science, they also clung to the "history" of Chinese tradition; hence the dichotomy between "value" and "history."[3]

But the May Fourth intellectuals also tried to overcome this dichotomy. Their solution was to sinicize science before employing it in studying history. Their definition of scientific history as an exercise of source criticism constituted such an attempt. Through this sinicization, they revived the Chinese historical culture and reviewed the experience of their predecessors in textual criticism.

Thus viewed, Chinese scientific history became as much a reform of the Chinese tradition as a Chinese reform of modern science. Chinese modernity was not sought in a borrowed culture but embedded deeply in a remodeled Chinese tradition.

Methodological Attempt (A)

Let us begin with Liang Qichao, the founder of scientific history in China.[4] Shortly after writing the *New Historiography* in his exile in Japan, Liang was able to return to China and was drawn again to various political responsibilities. It was not until the 1920s that he had a chance to study history again while teaching and researching at Qinghua University.

After World War I, Liang got an opportunity to visit Europe, which turned out to be an eye-opening experience for him. He not only witnessed the horrible aftermath of the war but learned about Western historical methodology through the Chinese students in Europe.[5] Li Zongtong, a historian who studied in Paris at the time, recalled that Liang had asked him and other Chinese students about different kinds of Western learning, including history.[6] A few years after his return, he began to write the *Historical Methods*. An influential text in modern Chinese historiography, however, the *Historical Methods* was written for a different purpose. If the *New Historiography* was aimed at wiping out obstacles and paving the way for writing a new history, the *Historical Methods* could be regarded as a brick Liang contributed to this edifice.

In building such an edifice, Liang was continuously inspired by Western historians. His definition of historical methodology, his perception of its importance to historical writing, and his understanding of history's relations with other subjects all seemed to have followed the conventional definitions developed by Western historians at the time. Much as he liked Western historiography, Liang began to appreciate the Chinese tradition. In writing the *Historical Methods* and (especially) its sequel, *Supplement to the Methods for the Study of Chinese History (Zhongguo lishi yanjiufa bubian*; hereafter *Historical Methods 2)*,[7] Liang showed a modified attitude toward both the Western experience and the Chinese tradition in historiography.

In his *New Historiography*, for example, Liang had angrily charged that Chinese historians only concentrated their work on writing biographies of emperors and ministers but not people's history. In the *Historical Methods 2*, however, he spent half of the space on discussing the methods in composing biography, giving, quite willingly, biography a central position in historical writing. Moreover, Liang accepted all traditional classifications in biographies, including the *liezhuan* (biography), the most widely used biographical form in Chinese dynastic historiography. He even recommended that modern historians rewrite the biographies of emperors, because the ones written earlier were incomplete.

What accounts for these changes had something to do with his trip to Europe, where he found, much to his surprise, that Western civilization had lost much of its vigor, due to the disastrous effect of the Great War, as known to the people of that time. As many Western intellectuals became pessimistic about the fate of their own culture, Liang realized that there was no need for the Chinese to admire the West any longer. He became more and more conscientious about his Chinese identity and interested in whether Chinese culture could contribute to the world.[8]

In his introduction to the *Historical Methods*, for example, he modified his position in regard to the role of history, no longer considering it important to convey the idea of progress.[9] He assigned a new task to Chinese historians and argued that they should pay particular attention to the relationship between the Chinese and non-Chinese in making Chinese history and relate Chinese history to other parts of the world. He asked: "What was the contribution the Chinese people made in the past to world civilization as a whole?" "What was the place of Chinese history in world history?" He hoped that once Chinese historians addressed these issues, they could help readers realize their responsibility to the world.[10] China, according to Liang, was no longer a receiver of world culture, but a participant in its making.

Having redefined the role of history, Liang began to search for the valuables in Chinese culture. In the second chapter, "Old Chinese Historiography," he praised rather than criticized the Chinese tradition in historiography. He declared that in ancient times, due to the establishment of Historiographical Office *(bianshiguan)* in the royal court, historical writings in China reached its highest level, towering above that of other cultures. As historians were given official positions in the government, they had convenient access to historical records and government documents. Moreover, the Office provided a good place for many established scholars to conduct their writings and research.[11] In a word, the Historiographical Office was not a place where rulers exercised censorship and interference, but a supportive agency nourishing the historical enterprise in imperial China.

Liang's praise of the Historiographical Office was not only untrue, but constituted a sharp contrast to the assessment he made earlier in the *New Historiography*. First of all, even in the Chinese tradition, none of the histories produced by the Historiographical Office could compete with Sima Qian's *Records of the Grand Historian* and Sima Guang's *Comprehensive Mirror*, both of which were started as individual projects, in terms of their historical and literary value. Moreover, Liang ignored the fact that the Office received many criticisms from scholars and historians and was not always an ideal place for a historian to conduct his research and writing. For example, at the time when the Office was just introduced, Liu Zhiji (661–721), the famous historiographer in the Tang, expressed strong suspicions about its role. Of his many criticisms, Liu considered the Office to be primarily a hindrance to creative thinking and free expression that disrupted the work of the historian.[12]

The change Liang made in regard to the Historiographical Office only signaled what he planned to accomplish with the *Historical Methods*. By devoting the book to the study of historical methodology, he intended to bridge the perceived gap between Chinese and Western experiences. Following the definition of the May Fourth scholars, he regarded source collection and criticism as two cornerstones of historiography in ancient as well as modern times. He also stated that both Chinese and Western historians made great contributions to the development of these two. His book became at once a useful source book for students of Chinese history and an attempt to bring up the traditional methods to the level of modern historiography.[13] He declared, for example, that all the methods he discussed in the book were not entirely unseen before—they had been used by Qing evidential scholars and others. In his opinion, the Qing scholars' methods in textual criticism were particularly similar to the Western inductive/scientific method. In fact, Liang asserted, Zhao Yi's (1727–1814) comparative approach to his annotation of dynastic histories amounted to a practice of scientific method.[14]

Liang's *Historical Methods*, therefore, was a comparative study of historical methodology. While Liang was indebted to his Western counterparts for theories and concepts, he mainly supplied Chinese examples for explanation. For example, in the chapter entitled "The Transformation of Historiography," Liang discussed the transition of historical writing from ancient to modern times. What differentiated the two, Liang believed, was the focus of attention among historians. The former was placed on the elites whereas the latter on common people, reminding us of his call for a people's history as well as the teaching of the New History School in the United States.

In the same vein, Liang stressed that modern history should serve the interest of the commoners and the present, not the nobility and the dead past. Once historians broadened their vision of history and divorced history from morality, they would be able to write it in a more balanced, objective manner. Scientific history was an ideal of modern historiography.[15]

From Liang's discussion on historical methods, we also find traces of his European trip, especially the influence of Ch. V. Langlois and Ch. Seignobos' *Introduction to the Study of History*, then a widely circulated college history textbook in France to which he probably was exposed while in Europe. Liang classified historical sources in two categories: material sources, and written records. He then divided the "material sources" into three subcategories: extant relics; oral testimonies; and archaeological excavations. He did the same to the "written records," dividing it into several subcategories. In these subcategories, dynastic histories came first in the tradition of Chinese historiography. Although dynastic histories mainly focused on political figures, Liang explained, they still provided ample information about social and cultural events for modern historians.

Once the historian obtained a basic knowledge of the scope of historical sources, he then needed to set out to look for them. In Liang's opinion, source collection should be as exhaustive as possible. Using an example provided by Langlois and Seignobos, he described Hubert H. Bancroft's (1832–1918) writing of *History of the Pacific States* in this respect.[16] Before embarking on his writing, Bancroft, a rich American businessman, used his financial resources to search for every possible source, ranging from family and company account books, bills, checks, to oral testimonies and interviews.[17] Echoing the praise given by his French counterparts, Liang regarded Bancroft's case as a great example in source collection. In addition to the example of Bancroft, Liang provided a bibliography of books in Western language on this subject.[18] However, his attempt to cite Western examples also resulted in mistakes. For example, he confused Herodotus for Homer, as noted by Hu Shi.[19]

According to Liang, historical sources were not only divided by kind, they were also divided by their usefulness. For instance, sources could be seen as "active" *(jiji de)* and "passive" *(xiaoji de)*, according to their pertinence to a subject. As active sources were directly relevant to historical events, passive sources became useful when the historian used them to help confirm a certain knowledge. Nevertheless, as passive sources tended to offer general information, they could be particularly valuable for the historian to fathom general trends in historical movement.[20] In addition, historical sources could be "abstract" *(chouxiang)* and "concrete" *(juti)*, according to the type of information they provided. Abstract sources often depicted demographic changes, inflation, education levels, and/or similar general phenomena, whereas concrete sources offered specific information on a person's life, career, and so forth.[21]

If understanding the nature of different kinds of sources was the first step of the work of the historian, source examination was the second. Before the historian used his sources, he first had to put them through a careful scrutiny. For whereas credible sources were of only one kind, unreliable sources were two: false *(wu)* and forged *(wei)*. In Liang's opinion, probably from his own experience in dealing with Chinese historical materials, the most effective way to tell forged or false sources was through the use of counterevidence. Influenced by Hu Shi and Gu Jiegang's "Discussion on Ancient History," Liang admitted that there existed many forgeries in the Chinese tradition; the earlier the age was, the more forgeries about it were fabricated—the same conclusion was drawn by Gu Jiegang.

Accordingly, historians should always maintain a skeptical attitude toward their sources. To exercise this skepticism against forgeries, the historian should follow twelve principles, such as: if there was no mention of the book in contemporary or previous sources, or it was mentioned that the book had been missing; if events recorded in the books contradicted those in other reliable books; if it used a new style unseen at the time; if it used concepts and described certain customs out of their historical context. Moreover, a reputable book too was not immune to alterations and interpolations. Like Yao Congwu, Liang pointed out that certain sections of Sima Qian's *Records of the Grand Historian* were quite suspicious, probably written by others in a later age. In other words, while one should first use primary sources he should also understand that not all primary sources are reliable.[22]

In the *Historical Methods*, Liang explained in great detail the methods in historical study. His discussion showed a basic understanding of modern critical history as well as a rich knowledge of Chinese historiography. Combining the two together, Liang provided a valuable text, the first of its kind on historical methods, for his students and readers. Although China had a rich legacy in historical criticism, few in the past had attempted to evaluate such a legacy as Liang did at the time. Thus what he accomplished became an important addition to Chinese historiography. In the Chinese tradition, it seems that there were only two scholars, in parallel to

Liang, who had attempted the study of historiography. One was Liu Zhiji, a Tang historian who, in his *Perspectives on History (Shitong)*, discussed the forms and styles in the historiographical tradition in China. The other was Zhang Xuecheng in the Qing Dynasty, who analyzed the meaning of history and its affiliations with other studies in his *General Meanings of History and Literature (Wenshi tongyi)*. But neither Liu nor Zhang had paid such an exclusive attention to the question of methodology and had understood the importance of source criticism.[23]

Indeed, Liang's *Historical Methods* was an original contribution to the development of Chinese historiography. For example, although scholars in the past used material sources, for example, bronze inscriptions *(jinwen)* and tablet inscriptions *(beiwen)*, in writing history, given the availability of a large quantity of written texts from the Chinese tradition, few acknowledged their great importance. During the 1920s, Wang Guowei (1877–1927) and Luo Zhenyu (1866–1940), two scholars who had some training in Japan, began to notice the inscriptions on oracle bones and tortoise shells found in the ruins of the Shang capital. Their research opened up a new horizon to the study of ancient Chinese history. Yet it was through Liang's inclusion of the "material sources" in his classification of historical sources that Chinese historians began to understand that material relics were equally valuable to written sources and that in the study of ancient cultures they were even more valuable.

In a similar vein, Liang's discussion on the difference between "abstract" and "concrete" as well as "active" and "passive" sources expanded one's understanding of history. As pointed out by Liang, traditional historians failed to appreciate the value of the "abstract" and "passive" sources because they were neither interested in social and cultural aspects, nor in general trends in historical movement. However, by employing these "hidden" sources, historians could enrich their understandings of the past. For instance, noticed Liang, Friedrich Hirth, a German/American sinologist, had used both the conventional source materials in dynastic historiography and other kinds of contemporary texts in his writing of the *Ancient History in China*; the latter helped Hirth to describe culture and society in ancient China.[24] Thus, the use of different kinds of sources could reflect a new understanding of history.

Writing the *Historical Methods* and its sequel showed Liang's effort to conceptualize history. And this conceptualization went through a few changes. At the beginning, he thought what made history useful was its analysis and description of the causal relations of events *(yinguo guanxi)*. Although by the time he wrote the books, as mentioned in chapter 1, he already eschewed the term *jinhua* (evolution) from his definition of history, he remained attracted to the idea of progress. For him, events were interrelated through historical causality. In writing history, historians needed to identify this causality, through which he could point out the future tendency in history.[25] However, this was quite difficult, Liang admitted, for causal relations often took various forms. Sometimes there were several causes for one event whereas other times one event led to several consequences. There were still times that one had trouble distinguishing one cause from another in establishing the causal relationship.

Needless to say, what made Liang emphasize historical causality was his interest in science; he intended to compare the study of history with that of natural science. But he soon realized their essential differences. In his opinion, scientists dealt with factors that were repeatable and determinable. By contrast, historical events were unique and singular. Also, matters in natural science were beyond time and space, whereas in history, events were always conditioned by time and space. That is to say, an event that took place twice might have very different meanings in history. The historical uniqueness—there was only one Confucius—made the work of the historian incompatible with that of the scientist.[26]

Some time after he published his *Historical Methods*, Liang had a chance to read Heinrich Rickert's (1863–1936) work.[27] A Neo-Kantian philosopher whose work espoused the ideas of German historicism *(Historismus)*, Rickert challenged the positivist position by emphasizing the difference between natural science *(Naturwissenschaften)* and humanities *(Geisteswissenschaften)*. Having discovered Rickert's thesis, Liang must have felt a great relief in modifying his position about historical causality. He stated that since history was different from natural science, it should not base itself on causal relations. In an article written shortly after the publication of the *Historical Methods*, Liang even apologized to his readers for confusing them with his own ambivalence: acknowledging the differences between natural sciences and history on the one hand but insisting on finding causal relations in history on the other. This confusion was his own, he confessed: due to his zest for science he thought it necessary to emphasize causality in historical study. Drawing on Rickert's theory, now he could regard history simply as a study of people's willful actions in the past,[28] namely, he no longer viewed historical progress as a linear progress wherein each period in the past was considered inferior, while contributing to the general progression, to the present. Instead, drawn to German historicism, he began to realize the value of past periods in their own terms.[29]

Having eschewed causality, Liang came to challenge the effectiveness of the inductive method in historical study. While a good scientific method, he found, it was however inadequate for the historian other than as an aid in collecting and examining sources. Considering historiography a form of culture, Liang became more and more interested in its humanities side, namely its function as a philosophical discourse on the past.[30] Since history was now a discourse, there was no need for the historian to describe the linear course of development in history, as expounded by the idea of progress. Instead, the historian should consider the unique worthiness of every historical figure. According to Liang, it would be absurd to compare Confucius with Buddha, or Dante with Shakespeare and/or Homer. In the development of culture, there was no definite and tangible progress.[31]

Liang's new position in understanding history allows Xiaobing Tang to offer a postcolonial reading of Liang's historical thinking. Tang states that Liang's cultural approach represented a new development of his thinking of history, in which China and the West were now regarded as equals.[32] Considering Liang's negative impression of Europe, or Western civilization, after World War I, it is understandable why he thought it was time for his country to play some role, if not regain its "central" position, in the world. On various occasions Liang admitted that he was prepared to challenge the "old me" *(jiuwo)* for a "new me" *(xinwo)*. That is to say, Liang changed his position in scientific history not only because he discovered Rickert, or German historicism, but because he developed a new outlook on world history, in which China was no longer a "sick man in the East," but a valuable, equal participant.

Since Chinese culture was now an equal to Western culture, so was the Chinese historiographical tradition. Liang began to find values in that tradition and attempted a new evaluation. For example, in the *New Historiography* he had angrily attacked dynastic historians for using the form of biography in writing history and taking an elitist approach. In the *Historical Methods*, he came to acknowledge the methodological value of these biographies, In the *Historical Methods 2*, he went further: biographical writing came to be the focus of his discussion on historical methodology.[33] Liang was even willing to make room for morality to play a role in history. In analyzing good qualities of a historian, he chose to follow the ideas of Liu Zhiji and Zhang Xuecheng and used their terms: "intelligence, knowledge, insight, and integrity *(cai, xue, shi, de)*" for an explanation, despite their obvious moral connotation in Confucian culture.[34] Thus viewed, Liang adopted an appreciative attitude toward the Chinese legacy in historiography.[35]

In the 1920s, the last decade of his life, Liang experienced a dramatic change both in his career and his thinking. It was during that period, after several failed attempts in politics, that Liang finally settled down to become a serious scholar, devoting his time to historical research and teaching at the National Studies Institute *(Guoxue yanjiusuo)*, a research institute staffed with leading scholars like Wang Guowei and Chen Yinke, at Qinghua University until his death in 1929. Besides the *Historical Methods*, he produced many valuable texts on Chinese intellectual history, centering on the Ming and Qing Dynasties, especially the evidential scholars. From his research interest, we can easily discern Hu Shi's influence of the National Studies Movement. It is interesting that in the 1900s Hu had been inspired by Liang in his novel approach to scholarship; now it was Hu's turn to influence Liang.

Yet Liang remained much needed for Hu's cause. With the *Historical Methods*, Liang offered a useful example for Hu's attempt to "reorganize the nation's past." In the book, one could not only find Liang's wide knowledge of the Chinese historical tradition and his receptiveness to foreign influences, but also enjoy his lucid and expressive style that was proverbial at the time. It was not surprising that the *Historical Methods* became an influential text, selling in the thousands through the 1940s.[36] More significantly, like his *New Historiography*, Liang's *Historical Methods* played a notable role in introducing a new historical thinking, despite the fact that the two were written in different times and with somewhat divergent approaches. If the *New Historiography* introduced the concept of historical time by emphasizing the difference between past and present, the *Historical Methods* urged one to construct a new linkage to bridge between the two. By eschewing the idea of progress in the latter, Liang no longer viewed historical development as following a hierarchical structure, for example, China being inferior to the West. Rather, he considered China an equal partner in the global community and provided evidence for a cultural equivalence between China and the West in historical writing.

Methodological Attempt (B)

Liang's effort to seek equivalencies between China and the West proved inspirational to others. While an exponent of the

American New History School, He Bingsong, too, attempted a new understanding of China's past by drawing analogies between China and the West. He's study of Chinese historiography, especially historical methodology, reflected both his early training in traditional Chinese learning and his interest in Western theories in historical writing.

He Bingsong's first project was a study of Zhang Xuecheng, a Qing historiographer from the Zhejiang Province, the same province that He came from. His interest in Zhang coincided with many others, such as Liang Qichao's (as shown earlier) and Hu Shi's. As colleagues at Beida, Hu Shi and He Bingsong exchanged ideas about Zhang Xuecheng's scholarship. According to Paul Demiéville, the French sinologist, before Zhang was "discovered" by these modern scholars, he had been a lesser-known figure. Demiéville even likened Zhang's position to Vico's, for both were relatively unappreciated in their own times.[37] Of course, Zhang was not entirely unknown to people who were well versed in the Chinese tradition, such as Liang Qichao and He Bingsong's father. It was probably from his father that He Bingsong first gained some knowledge about the Eastern Zhejiang School *(Zhedong xuepai)*, of which Zhang was the last but perhaps most important figure.

But to a great extent, Zhang Xuecheng was indeed "discovered" by modern scholars, or more precisely, by Naito Konan (1855–1934) in Japan and Hu Shi and He Bingsong in China.[38] From their studies of Zhang Xuecheng, Hu Shi and He Bingsong produced two different kinds of work. They were drawn to Zhang because Zhang in his *General Meanings of History and Literature* discussed issues in theories of history and historiography, something not commonly seen among traditional Chinese scholars. Since Zhang was not appreciated by his contemporaries, Hu Shi decided to compile a chronological biography of Zhang, introducing Zhang to his cohorts. He pieced together a well-researched biography, showing his painstaking labor in source criticism. Hu hoped that by doing so he could exemplify the use of scientific method.

He Bingsong, however, concentrated on Zhang's ideas of history. He wrote two articles and a long introduction to Hu's biography of Zhang.[39] His main argument, or discovery, about Zhang Xuecheng was that Zhang's many ideas were comparable to those of modern historians. Of course, by "modern historians," He really meant the New History School of the United States, with whom he had been familiar. In other words, He Bingsong's study of Zhang Xuecheng was aimed at presenting an equivalence in historical thinking between China and the West.

For example, He stated, Zhang Xuecheng had an intention to look for meanings in history *(shiyi)*. On many places, Zhang emphasized that the most important task for a historian was to discover a meaning in history. In so doing, the historian had to acquire a perspective when he wrote history. But this search for historical meaning had to be based on actual facts, not on speculations and imaginations. In fact, Zhang did not encourage people to discuss morals without first looking into real historical facts. Thus viewed, Zhang Xuecheng appeared like someone from the New History School who disapproved the antiquarian approach in history.

Not only did Zhang understand the importance of historical sources, he also intended to broaden its scope to include as many kinds as possible; another idea that made Zhang comparable to his modern counterparts. In Zhang's opinion, historical sources encompassed everything, ranging from the Classics, genealogies, and local gazetteers to tablet and bronze inscriptions.[40] Before using the sources, historians had to examine them. What made Zhang particularly comparable to a modern historian, He found, was that he even suggested that a history text should provide footnotes to indicate its citations, an original idea never put forth before. With his emphasis on source criticism and his idea of footnotes, He argued, Zhang was really a "modern" historian; his many ideas were practical and immediately useful, similar to those of an "empirical philosopher" in the West. However, due to his unstable financial situation, Zhang failed to implement his remarkable ideas in his writing of history, hence receiving little attention at his time.[41]

Yet what was really remarkable in Zhang, in He's opinion, was his belief in the idea of progress in history. Zhang argued that all institutions and cultures were in fact created to meet the particular need of a particular time period; people of later generations should not put a blind faith in them simply because they had been introduced by their ancestors. Instead, Zhang suggested that historians focus their study on modern times rather than on ancient events and people. For He Bingsong, what Zhang said implied the idea of progress—the present was better than the past. This argument turned Zhang into a Chinese counterpart of the New History School, adopting the same presentist approach to historical study. And this approach had a similar effect in challenging antiquarianism in both China and the West.[42] Thus, Zhang was a "modern" historian. In fact, he became almost like a modern professional historian when he separated history from literature (in the Chinese tradition the two were regarded as being naturally bound together) and supplied the method of history, source criticism, to historians.

In this modern interpretation of Zhang Xuecheng's historiography, there was definitely something missing: for example, Zhang's emphasis on morality. Zhang asked people to look for meanings in history because he was concerned about the morality question and hoped that history could expound moral principles with concrete examples, an intention not so dissimilar to that of a Confucian scholar in the Chinese tradition. In discussing the qualification for a good historian, Zhang followed Liu Zhiji's three criteria: knowledge, intelligence, and insight. But he also added his own, "integrity" *(de)*, as the fourth and deemed it the most important.[43]

However, while offering a modern interpretation of Zhang, He Bingsong had no intention of saying that since there were "modern" elements in the Chinese tradition, there would be no need to learn about the moderns. He was more interested in comparing the two, rather than pitting one against the other. In his preface to Hu Shi's biography of Zhang, he actually warned his fellow historians to watch for a "Zhang Xuecheng fever." In his opinion, this "fever" undermined the ongoing New Culture Movement and engendered a narrow-minded nationalism. Any overstatement of the value of traditional culture, He emphasized, prevented one from understanding the importance for the Chinese to learn from the others in the world, which, for the time being, should be the top priority of cultural construction in modern China.[44]

Thus viewed, He Bingsong's interest in Zhang Xuecheng was different from Hu Shi's. Of course, Hu Shi, too, was attracted to Zhang for his ideas of historiography. But due to his interest in experimentalism, his study of Zhang was more like an experiment with scientific method; Hu intended to demonstrate its efficacy through the work of source collection and criticism. Yet He Bingsong, through his comparative approach, discovered and analyzed Zhang's ideas. If Hu Shi's study demonstrated the applicability of scientific method in the study of Chinese history, He Bingsong's interpretation presented the compatibility of the ideas of historiography between the Chinese and Western traditions. Since He was interested in both the methods and theories in historical writing, he looked for a slightly different goal in the National Studies Movement of the 1920s. In He's opinion, Zhang Xuecheng definitely was a great historiographer. But there were not as many like Zhang in the Chinese tradition as in the Western tradition. Thus, there was a need to learn from the West.

In 1929 He published an essay, questioning many practices of the National Studies Movement, especially its ambitious goal and its comprehensive approach. He pointed out that the Movement had a few potential problems. First of all, it lacked a clear boundary and objective. It encouraged young people to take a wholesome approach to the study of Chinese culture, departing from the modern, scientific trend of specialization. Second, given the fact that it emphasized studying China, or the Chinese tradition, it could promote a narrow-minded nationalism and undermine the cause of the New Culture Movement. Third, by drawing attention to the Chinese tradition, it created the false impression on the general public that traditional Chinese culture still maintained its great attraction and value, thus distracting attention from cultural reform. What bothered He the most seemed to be the movement's wholesome approach, as its name "national studies" *(guoxue)* entailed. Why not the study of history, or literature, or philosophy, He asked? To him, this approach bucked the trend of modern scholarship.[45]

A year later, He published a new work, *A New Perspective on General History (Tongshi xinyi)*, showing his continuous interest in historiography, his chosen field. While drawing on Ch. Seignobos's *La Méthode Historique Applique aux Sciences Sociales*, He in the book discussed problems in the Chinese practice of modern historical writing. For him Chinese scholars at the time still had problems conceptualizing the difference between traditional and modern historiography. One of such that confused them was the concept of "general history" *(tongshi)*, as shown in the book title. Thus writing this book amounted to an effort to demonstrate the need for the Chinese to remain interested in Western culture, as He advocated earlier.[46]

He felt he was somehow responsible for this misunderstanding. Not only did he translate most of the Western histories, in his study of Zhang Xuecheng he also mentioned that Zhang's favoring of general history was a modern trait of his historiography. Writing the *General History* provided an opportunity for him to correct this misunderstanding. According to him, although historiographical form did make a difference, a good history depended on its use of sources. Like his peers, He Bingsong emphasized that source criticism differentiated the work of the historian from scholars of other disciplines. While other methods used in statistics, biology, and economics were useful for historians, source criticism was the foundation of historical study.[47]

Thus, He devoted the first part of the *General History* to espousing source criticism in history. Drawing on Seignobos's book, he discussed different kinds of methods in source collection, criticism, organization, and analysis. In the second part, from the same methodological perspective, he came to discuss the relationship between history and other sciences. He pointed out that while no other method could displace source criticism in historical study, it would be beneficial for a historian if he learned from others. For example, the methods of archaeology, biology, anthropology, and economics could help the historian observe social, economic, cultural, and customs changes in the past. In particular, psychological analysis was very helpful to a historian, for it analyzed and explained the minds and ideas of the people. Explaining these ideas could shed light on the ultimate cause of historical change.[48]

Advocating an alliance between history and social sciences, on the one hand, the *General History* reflected the influence of the New History School. However, on the other hand, He's emphasis on source criticism as the method of history suggested that he was also attracted to critical history, or Rankean historiography, the very target of criticism of the New History School. The New Historians aligned history with social sciences, reminding us of the practice of positivism,[49] about which He Bingsong now had some reservations. While he was interested in borrowing methods from other disciplines, he was not willing to go so far as considering history on a par with social sciences.

Indeed, He Bingsong's other writings showed that in his study of historical methodology, he began to depart from the American model and eschewed the positivist approach. Around the time when He published the *General History*, He was invited to give a series of lectures on historical methods at a few college campuses in Shanghai. His approach was anything but positivist. For He Bingsong, the term "history" had two meanings: one was the human activities in the past and the other the records of these activities. Historical study aimed to provide a truthful account of the human past. However, He hastened to add, there were three differences between history and natural science:

1. "point of observation" *(guancha dian)*—as historians looked for differences among facts, scientists were interested in the similarities;
2. kind of research objectives—historians had to study many sides of a fact or many facts in order to get a general knowledge, whereas scientists often focused on a specific subject among many others, for their knowledge was very specialized;

3. different process—scientists reached their conclusion through observation and experiment, whereas historians could not conduct experiment in history because they could not go back to the past.

In a word, history was a subjective knowledge *(zhuguan de xuewen)* and science was a objective knowledge *(keguan de xuewen)*.[50]

Due to these differences, historians should not seek causal relations in history. Like Liang Qichao, He Bingsong considered the attempt to look for causal relations in history a meaningless undertaking. It would accomplish nothing but show a lack of understanding of the nature of history. However, He argued, history remained a science because the word *science* referred to "a systematic knowledge" *(you tiaoli de zhishi)*. From that perspective, history was a science because it stood for a systematic knowledge. Like other sciences, history aimed to discover truth and advocated a scientific attitude. Scientific history was based on its methodology, which consisted of three major steps: source collection, analysis, and synthesis. For He there were two kinds of historical sources: material relics transmitted cultural remains, both written and oral. In terms of their relations with a subject,. historical sources fell into two kinds: primary and secondary.[51] Apparently, in defining the nature of science, here He Bingsong chose to use the German word *Wissenschaft*, referring to a system of knowledge, rather than the English word *science*, which more or less had a positivist connotation.

He's departure from positivism enabled him to revive the Chinese tradition. By considering scientific history an application of critical method, he discovered many similar practices of traditional historians. In the area of source collection and examination, for instance, Sima Guang's writing of the *Comprehensive Mirror* stood for a good example, for Sima made an admirable effort to exhaust all available sources before embarking on the writing. In writing his work, Sima also followed a meticulous procedure: he first categorized these sources and checked their validity. He then provided explanations for his criteria and research results. According to He Bingsong, this seriousness in source collection and criticism was equivalent to the ideal practice of modern historical methodology, as advanced by Western scholars.[52]

An important question in source criticism, He believed, was how to distinguish forgeries from credible accounts. To this end, historians needed to hold a skeptical attitude toward their sources. The last thing they should do was fail to understand the difference between historical sources *(lishi de cailiao)* and history. In other words, while ancient texts provided information about the past, they were not tantamount to the past per se. By the same token, even if something was attributed to Confucius, Sima Qian, or any great figures in history, its validity still should not be taken for granted, for it could have been tampered with by someone in a later time. In He's opinion, good examples in historical skepticism were abundant in the Chinese tradition. Modern historians should follow the examples of Wang Chong (27–97?), Liu Zhiji, Cui Shu, and Qing evidential scholars in dealing with sources.[53]

By drawing attention to source criticism, He Bingsong redefined the meaning of historical methodology *(shifa)* in the Chinese tradition. The term *shifa* used to mean the methods of passing moral judgment on historical events or personages, namely the so-called style of the *Spring and Autumn (Chunqiu bifa)*, in which historians chose different expressions to indicate his approval or disapproval of something that happened in the past. In the meantime, He pointed out, the study of source criticism in history also differed from the practice of "historical critique" *(shiping)* in the past for the latter usually comprised historians' casual remarks and personal reflection. Source criticism, by contrast, was a serious pursuit of scientific research. It allowed modern scholars to understand the nature of historical study from a new perspective.[54]

He's emphasis on source criticism, especially his mentions of the Chinese antecedents in that respect, was aimed at uplifting traditional Chinese historiography to the standard of scientific history. At the same time as he redefined historical methodology, he also redefined the study of history, hence providing a new perspective on the Chinese historical tradition. To complete this methodological modernization of Chinese historiography, he suggested two things. One was to add footnotes and the other to create indices for the sources in Chinese history, such as the twenty-four dynastic histories. On the one hand, by adding the footnotes, the historian could show the origins of his sources and his indebtedness to his predecessors and/or fellow historians. Indices, on the other hand, helped anyone who was interested in studying history. With these two additions, historical study in China could become a modern profession.[55]

He Bingsong's lecture notes were edited into a book and published in 1927, entitled *Historical Methodology (Lishi yanjiufa)*. In writing this book, as he admitted in the preface, He relied mainly on the works of European historians, rather than those of the American New Historians. His main sources were two: Langlois and

Seignobos's *Introduction aux Études Historiques* and Ernst Bernhein's *Lehrbuch der historischen Methode und Geschichtsphilosophie.*[56] His book thus bore resemblance to Liang Qichao's *Historical Methods*, although their titles were slightly different. If Liang's book was intended to apply modern historical methods to the study of Chinese history, He's was a discussion of methodological questions in historical study in general, reflecting his continual interest in theoretical issues in modern historiography.

Like Liang Qichao, however, He Bingsong was equally interested in combining the traditions of Chinese and Western historiography through source criticism. For that purpose, he reiterated his position that while history was a science, it differed from others, for it was not guided by the interest in finding causal relations in historical events.[57] From this emphasis on source criticism, He Bingsong reevaluated the role of the Historiographical Office in the Chinese tradition. He stated that while the Office had some problems, it represented a systematic and collective effort to record and preserve valuable sources. Its establishment made the Chinese tradition comparable to that of the modern West, He pointed out, for projects on collecting and editing official and/or semi-official projects were part of the practice of modern historiography in the West; modern nations like Germany, Britain, and France all made similar efforts in this regard, as shown by the *Monumenta Germaniae Historica*, the *Rolls Series*, and the *Collection de Documents Inedits sur l'Histoire de France.*[58]

The Chinese tradition was comparable, if not superior, to that of the West also because, contrary to the conventional notion of many people, traditional Chinese scholars were very much concerned about improving the methods of history. In every important field relevant to history, traditional China had its representative figures. These fields ranged from historical Pyrrhonism, source criticism, paleography, historical rhetoric, to historiography. Moreover, in terms of sophistication, He found, the works produced by these representative scholars were not inferior to their Western parallels.[59]

From the translation of *The New History* to the writing of the *Historical Methodology*, He Bingsong gradually changed his role in the Chinese pursuit of scientific history. If in the earlier years he was an exponent of modern American historiography, now he became more and more interested in finding equivalencies between China and the West. Although he disagreed with Hu Shi in regard to the goal of the National Studies Movement, he joined his friends to examine and interpret the Chinese tradition from the nationalist perspective. In so doing, as indicated by his studies of Zhang

Xuecheng and historical methodology, He reached new interpretations not only of the Chinese tradition but also scientific history.

When He published his *Historical Methodology*, he had left his teaching positions at Beida and Beijing Normal College and worked as an editor at the Commercial Press in Shanghai. In 1922 he left Beijing University to take on the position of president of Zhejiang No. 1 Normal College in Hangzhou.[60] He had been reluctant at first but was eventually persuaded by his friends to accept the job. He later explained that he left for Zhejiang because that was his home province; he owed a great deal (i.e., having been awarded a scholarship to study in the United States) to the people and teachers there and could not decline their earnest offer. However, his administration was soon wrecked by a terrible tragedy: twenty-two students and two employees died of food poisoning in March 1923. Though he somehow sensed that this incident was motivated by a conspiracy against his appointment, he had to take full responsibility for the tragedy.[61] In 1924, after the incident, he left Hangzhou for Shanghai and took the job at the Commercial Press whereby he could resume his interest in translating Western works in history. He published his lecture notes on medieval and modern Europe respectively in 1924 and 1925. His other translations also came out at the time, including Shotwell's *An Introduction to the History of History* and Johnson's *The Teaching of History in Elementary and Secondary Schools*.[62] In addition, his moving to Shanghai gave him a chance to teach a historical methodology course at universities in Shanghai.[63] These lecture notes became the basis of his writing of the *Historical Methodology*.

From Beijing to Shanghai, He changed his career from a professor to a publisher, which broadened his scholarly interest. Although he continued his translation projects, He became more and more enticed by the work of European historians in historical methodology, as shown in the *Historical Methodology*. In the meantime, he began his research on the Eastern Zhejiang School that resulted in two books *A History of the Eastern Zhejiang School (Zhedong xuepai suyuan)* and *Differences between Zhu Xi and Cheng Yi (Chengzhu bianyi)*.[64] In writing these two books, He Bingsong relied on Western theories to conceptualize his subject and weave into strands his research findings, but he also learned a great deal from his predecessors in understanding the nature of history and the method of history. He found, for example, the Eastern Zhejiang School, also known as the "historical school," took a historical approach to studying the Classics and a practical approach to understanding the function of history. His intention to offer a modern interpretation of Zhang Xuecheng's ideas of history, as well as his study of scientific method in history, seemed to have followed that tradition.

When He Bingsong became more interested in the Chinese historiographical tradition, he also noticed the "deficiency" in the New History School, which failed to pay sufficient attention to epistemological questions in historical methodology.[65] As mentioned earlier, He Bingsong was interested in theoretical issues in history. By contrast, the New Historians' interest was not centered on improving the method of history per se. To Robinson, history "should not be regarded as a stationary subject which can only progress by refining its methods and accumulating, criticizing, and assimilating new material."[66] Rather, they tried to align history with social sciences by adopting the latter's methods. This interest, however, did not appeal to He Bingsong any more. Like his peers, particularly Liang Qichao, He instead chose to appropriate source criticism from both the Chinese and Western/European historiography and present it as an equivalence between Chinese and Western historiography.

In Discovery of Ancient China

If historical methodology is an area where Liang Qichao and He Bingsong searched for equivalencies and differences in Chinese and Western historiography, Fu Sinian attempted to apply such methods to solving problems in history, especially the history of ancient China where many questions were raised in regard to its credibility during the National Studies Movement.

Fu shared the belief with his friends and teachers that source criticism, or the use of philological methods in history, was the key to modern historiography, hence his establishment of the Institute of History and Philology in 1927. On its founding, Fu wrote a long introduction explaining the goal of the institute. He stated that in order to become a modern historian, one had to learn to use scientific method, namely to base his writing on the philological examination of source materials. Insofar as the importance of source criticism was concerned, Fu was willing to go as far as to argue that historical study was de facto a study of historical sources and that the study of historical sources depended on the method of philology. He said:

> History and philology prospered in Europe only recently. Historical study was different from historical writing; the latter

> was more or less an ancient and medieval undertaking. Ancient historians looked for moral examples and literary fame in writing history. But modern historiography is essentially different; it is nothing but the study of historical sources, in which historians use scientific method to collect and criticize all accessible source materials in their study.[67]

Fu then pointed out that like history, philological study in Europe experienced tremendous progress and facilitated the emergence of modern nations. However, by comparison, the status quo of historical-philological study in China was disappointing. Echoing Hu Shi's assessment, Fu conceded that philological study in the Qing achieved great progress. But in his day, few scholars were able to carry on that tradition and make real contributions to the field. In fact, he lamented, philological study in China not only lacked improvement, it also degenerated, beginning in the later nineteenth century when scholars gradually lost their interest in methodology. Zhang Taiyan's and others' works on philology, in Fu's opinion, were not original; they were a mere replica of early Qing scholarship.[68]

In order to revive historical-philological study in China, Fu suggested that one find not only new ways to improve methods in source criticism, but also new sources outside the written tradition. In his opinion, modern "progressive" scholarship depended on the work on sources and was characterized by three features:

1. basing a study directly on sources, not on previous works or theories;
2. expanding the source materials in research;
3. continuing to search for new methods.

In these three areas, however, Chinese scholars had not done much. Most of their studies still depended on previous works and took no interest in finding new sources, especially material ones. By contrast, European scholars not only broadened the scope of historical sources, but also applied methods of natural science to studying history, such as those of archaeology, geology, geography, biology, and astronomy.

For Fu Sinian, to expand the use of sources was crucial to the development of modern scholarship. To this end, he divided the history branch of the institute into five programs: textual criticism, source collection, archaeology, anthropology and folklore, and comparative art history; only the first dealt primarily with written sources. In the philology branch, he emphasized a comparative approach in which the study of minority languages received a status equal to the study of Mandarin.[69] Fu's arrangement reflected his positivist approach. In his mind, history is not so different from such sciences as biology and geology, for they all deal with sources.[70]

Compared to most positivists who looked for analogies in the studies of nature and human society, Fu followed a reductionist approach to appropriating modern science. He first attributed the achievement of natural science to a breakthrough in methodology. He then equated this breakthrough with the study of source materials. As a historian, Fu was well known in China for his aphorism: "No historical sources, no history" *(wu shiliao jiwu shixue)*.[71] In fact, he believed that all modern disciplines depend on the study of sources. What makes one subject different from another is due to the different sources it uses in research. This however should not cloud the fact, which Fu believed most strongly, that all scientific disciplines need to adopt basically the same method in working with sources. Thus this method, or scientific method, is indeed universal across all disciplines.[72]

Since all scientific pursuits begin with sources, the way in which sources are used, examined, and analyzed becomes, for Fu, a line of demarcation between traditional and modern scholarship. In the study of history, whether or not the historian uses material sources in his writing marks this distinction. Traditional historians, Fu asserted, mainly worked with texts whereas modern historians used both written and material sources. He shared He Bingsong's doubts on the ongoing National Studies Movement for the movement was centered on textual criticism. Yet he went even further by stating that due to this narrow focus, the movement was tantamount to a surrender to tradition, because serious, modern scholarship should start from source collection and examination. From this empirical, positivist perspective, Fu, too, eschewed theoretical discussion, which he deemed nothing but an excuse for the scholars' laziness in working with sources. His Institute, by contrast, would only encourage scholars to work with sources.[73] He declared: "We are not book readers. We go all the way to Heaven above and Yellow Spring below, using our hands and feet, to look for things."[74]

Interestingly, while Fu's positivist approach differed from Hu Shi's in the National Studies Movement, it actually helped the latter to continue and extend the discussion on the credibility of ancient Chinese history. Indeed, it helped lead the discussion into a new direction. Fu's interest in scientific learning, which he had pursued wholeheartedly while in Europe, led him to conclude, as shown in one of his unpublished manuscript titled "Ancient Chinese History and Archaeology" *(Zhongguo shanggushi yu kaoguxue),* that the only solution to the mystery of China's high antiquity lay outside the written tradition.[75] While he credited with appreciation Gu Jiegang's achievement in bringing down the myth of the longevity of Chinese history through textual criticism, he did not believe that one could gain a real knowledge of China's past from reading and critiquing texts. Rather, a true understanding of ancient history depended on expanding the use of sources into material remains. That is to say, whether or not China had a long history could only be answered by an archaeological finding. In Fu Sinian's words, "The study of ancient China from now on should concentrate on reconstructing ancient history outside the legends, which depends mainly on archaeological excavation, supplemented by the reading of the Classics."[76]

Thus, the Institute of History and Philology became the first institution in modern China that attempted a new approach to the study of Chinese history. Although founded originally at Sun Yat-sen University in Guangzhou, Fu Sinian later moved it to Beijing, turning it into a national institute. The relocation of the institute owed much to Cai Yuanpei for his support. After GMD's success in the Northern Expedition, Cai was invited by Chiang Kai-shek to take charge of education and research for the new government. He asked Fu to come to Beijing to attend the preparatory meeting for establishing the Academia Sinica and hoped that Fu would help found a psychology institute, considering Fu's training in Britain. But Fu instead urged Cai and other participants to take the Institute of History and Philology as one of the founding institutes of the Academia Sinica, which was eventually realized in April 1928.[77] After its relocation from Guangzhou to Beijing in June 1929, Fu reorganized the Institute and divided it into three programs: history, philology, archaeology and anthropology, headed by Chen Yinke, Zhao Yuanren (1892–1982), and Li Ji (1896–1979), respectively. A scholar from a well-known mandarin family, Chen was also the brother of Fu's Beida schoolmate and a friend of his in Germany. Zhao was Hu Shi's friend who, though he studied physics in the United States, later became a well-known Chinese linguist. Li Ji was a Harvard trained anthropologist, although he was better known in China as an archaeologist.

The relocation of the Institute of History and Philology paved the way for its later successes and earning it a nationwide recognition. Fu's effective leadership was indispensable. As a well-known student leader of the May Fourth Movement and a Western trained scholar, Fu boasted excellent credentials and extensive connections both in the government and among the academics. Although Cai Yuanpei's relationship with Chiang Kai-shek later deteriorated, he had helped Fu secure necessary funding for the Institute at its outset. More important, while an academic institute, it had a clear nationalist agenda. Fu stated explicitly that his Institute intended to obtain and maintain an authoritative position in Chinese studies in the world. This was because, he emphasized, sinologists from the West, due to their experiences in using scientific method, already began to sneer at the work of Chinese scholars. He had to raise the level of Chinese scholarship to the modern scientific standard.[78]

Thus to Fu Sinian, scholarship was part of the nationalist cause: whether or not Chinese scholars could scientifically interpret their history would also affect China's position in the world. For if Chinese historians fail to achieve a scientific understanding of Chinese history, foreign scholars of scientific training would do that. Likewise, if Chinese scholars do not collect sources, written and/or material, foreign scholars would get their hands on them. Once foreign scholars possess the sources, Fu worried, they would interpret Chinese history and "re-create" China's past for the Chinese. Had this happened, it would cause the biggest disgrace to the Chinese nation.[79] In Fu's mind, therefore, to collect and control sources was the first and foremost step for a new interpretation of Chinese history, crucial to the success of a nationalist historiography.

Many projects initiated by the Institute reflected this nationalist concern. Fu, for example, ordered the Institute to purchase and preserve the Inner Chancery archives of the Ming and Qing Dynasties. The archives were priceless, containing ministers' memorials and emperors' comments and edicts, most of which had not been seen before. After the founding of the Republic, however, these archives were in a hazardous situation; many were lost, stolen, and destroyed. Individual scholars were unable to preserve them because of the enormous quantity whereas the warlord governments were indifferent to their value. Having made a successful plea to the Academia Sinica, relating the project to the national reputation, the Institute secured a fund and began to take charge of these documents.[80] A year later, in 1930, the Institute published the first ten volumes of these archives, entitled *Ming and Qing Archives (Ming Qing shiliao)*, in order to meet, Fu said, the scholars' pressing need for scientific research. These volumes were only a small part of the entire archive.[81] In fact, the whole project was not completed in 1949 when the Institute retreated to Taiwan, partly because of the Japanese invasion in World War II and partly because of the enormous quantity of these documents.[82]

The preservation of Ming and Qing archives was the first project managed by the history program. The philology program of the Institute began its research by establishing a modern linguistic laboratory. Fu hoped that through comparative studies of languages, he would come to a better understanding of the origins of Chinese civilization. The linguistic laboratory received praise from Bernhard Karlgren, a leading sinologist and linguist from Sweden, when he came to visit the Institute while in Beijing.[83] Karlgren's visit was of course one of the few the Institute received at the time. But receiving a positive remark from Karlgren must have been enjoyable for Fu, given his intention to make the Institute competitive to the work of Western sinologists. Fu kept his contact with Karlgren through the late 1940s, when Karlgren paid him a visit in New Haven, Connecticut, where Fu resided temporarily for medical treatment.[84]

Although the history and philology programs both had their initial successes, it was the archaeology program that received Fu Sinian's focal attention in running the Institute.[85] As mentioned earlier, he believed that the use of material sources was the threshold to modern scholarship. Both the history and philology programs worked on excavated sources, especially Buddhist sutras discovered in Dunhuang caves and the bamboo slips of the Han Dynasty. In the wake of the "Discussion on Ancient History" in 1928, Fu sent a team to Anyang, known as a capital of the Shang Dynasty (ca. 1600–1066 B.C.E.), to excavate and examine archaeological remains. From the late Qing Dynasty, many oracle bone inscriptions surfaced from the site and caused much curiosity. Yet Fu's aim was not just to check out the origin of these oracle bones; he hoped that new findings from the excavation could help settle once and for all the debate on China's high antiquity.

While his hopes ran high, the outcome did not come until 1934. It was however a sweet success. Paul Pelliot, the famous French sinologist wrote enthusiastically praising the achievement as "the most spectacular discovery made in the field of Asiatic Studies in recent years."[86] In his report, Li Ji, the archaeologist who was in charge of the project, stated that while the excavation did not find as many oracle bones as it had planned, it proved their authenticity as Shang remains, refuting the claims of some well-known scholars, such as Zhang Taiyan, that these bones were faked by the locals for profit. More important, many remains discovered from the site, such as the pottery, the tools, the soil, and the site itself, helped them to present an ancient culture that was more sophisticated and well developed than anyone had thought.[87] In other words, the excavation proved with hard material evidence that China indeed had a history tracing back to the second millennium B.C.E.

The excavation, too, literally put an end to the "Discussion on Ancient History." While Gu Jiegang and some others did not yet give up their position, it persuaded Hu Shi, the leader of the National Studies Movement, to withdraw his earlier support of Gu for the latter's doubts on the existence of China's high antiquity. Hu instead encouraged Fu Sinian to continue his scientific discovery of China's past.[88] Through the excavation, Fu also changed his position. Although he and Gu Jiegang had ended their long friendship while in Guangzhou, before the excavation, Fu by and large shared Gu's doubts on the validity of the Chinese written tradition in history. But with the archaeological discovery, he was able to piece together a history on a new ground. That is to say, while a well-known May Fourth iconoclast, Fu was now poised to reconstruct a new tradition.

This new tradition, needless to say, was no longer based on written texts. Through a series of archaeological projects, Fu and his colleagues at the Institute recreated the history of Chinese antiquity on artifacts and other material objects, which were used to either support or refute certain facts drawn originally on extant literature. For example, they used archaeological evidence to buttress the theory, concluded by earlier studies on comparative linguistics and history, that Chinese civilization had a plural, and possibly, multi-ethnic origin. Archaeology also led them to probe the territory of ancient China.[89] In a word, Fu's interest in material sources, as he hoped, opened a new horizon for Chinese scholars to understand the past and undertake the study of history. In reinterpreting history, scholars also found an effective way to execute the combined project on scientism and nationalism in the May Fourth Movement.

By pioneering a new approach to studying history, Fu Sinian was well received and viewed by his peers as a model scientific historian.[90] His expectation of himself also changed: he now considered himself as a historian, albeit a new, scientific kind. If in the 1920s while in Europe, he had regretted that he was trained as a man of letters, rather than a scientist, he no longer had the same feeling by now. We can attribute this change to several reasons. The first and foremost reason was probably his belief in positivism. Since Fu regarded all scientific subjects as basically the same in so far as their methodology was concerned, he could well take the same method to deal with historical sources. The second reason had something to do with his early education. While he developed an interest in science in college and pursued it in Europe, as discussed earlier, Fu was never very successful at becoming a good scientist, partly due to his lack of concentration and partly due to his poor training; he was much more comfortable with the study of the humanities. The third reason seemed to be related to his friendship with Gu Jiegang. As noticed by Wang Fansen, when Fu learned about Gu's successes in launching the "Discussion on Ancient History," he was both happy for and envious of his old college friend. While calling Gu "a king of Chinese historiography," he hastened to add that he himself had long forsaken his interest in history.[91] But what happened after his return to China, being first appointed as the chair of the department of history and literature at Sun Yat-sen University, seemed to have forced Fu to renew his early interest in the humanities. But he did not give up his scientific pursuit, as indicated by his insistency on not being a book reader and his interest in archaeology. It was the excavation at Anyang that made Fu finally decide to return himself to the study of history. It seemed as if he stumbled on a career because of his new interest in science. In fact, Fu was returning home to become someone he was cut out for. Viewed in this light, Fu Sinian's career in history, as well as his friends' and teachers', was a good example of the integration of tradition and modernity among modern Chinese intellectuals.

Fu's career best illustrated this integration. While a committed "scientist" in leading the Institute, Fu did most of his research in the realm of the humanities. In the 1930s, Fu published a few works, centering on the origins of ancient Chinese civilization. Contrary to his advocacy, he based his research on textual analysis rather than on material sources. By comparing available texts, he worked on the ethnic make-up of the ancient Chinese people and the origins of Chinese civilization. Fu planned to wrote a book entitled "*Nations and Ancient Chinese History*" *(Minzu yu gudai Zhongguo shi)*, but was never able to complete it. One of its chapters, *East and West theory of Yi and Xia (yixia dongxi shuo)* however was published independently in 1934 and received glowing reviews. Together with his *On the Greater and Smaller Eastern China (Dadong xiaodong shuo)* and other essays, Fu developed a pluralist interpretation of Chinese civilization and believed that many ethnic groups/"nations" contributed to the growth of ancient China and the formation of Chinese culture.[92] Fu's research owed to his early training in his first two years at Beida, where he learned skills in philological study *(xiaoxue)*. He usually began his study by comparing and examining the pronunciation and etymology of a few words and terms, an approach that bore a great resemblance to that of a Qing scholar, such as Zhang Taiyan's, whom Fu rebelled against and despised in the May Fourth Movement. Of course, Fu could justify his use of this method by pointing out the similarity of philological studies in China and the West.

Like his friends and teachers, Fu took a comparative approach to the study of historical methodology and believed that scientific method cut across cultures. When the Institute moved to Beijing in 1929, Fu taught the course Introduction to Historical Methodology at Beida (Yao Congwu succeeded him to teach the same course after his return from Germany),[93] in which he preached the positivist idea that all scientific pursuits were basically the same in so far as their methods were concerned. For example, he posited that like geology and biology, modern historiography was a form of objective learning. It was based on the study of sources, not on its alignment with philosophy, ethics, and/or literature.

Thus considered, modern historiography followed only one method: understanding the differences of sources and using them accordingly. In Fu's opinion, historical sources could be paired together: direct or indirect, official or individual, domestic or foreign, contemporary or later, with or without purpose, metaphoric or straightforward, and oral or written. Each kind had its distinct value, depending on how it was used. For example, on the one hand, though historians should use direct/primary sources to conduct their research, they also need indirect sources to conceptualize a general context of the subject. On the other hand, while most primary sources are relatively dependable, they, especially archaeological artifacts, are also fragmented and disorganized.

In order to organize his sources together really well, historians should have a good knowledge of the subject of their research. Han bamboo slips, Fu pointed out, were first discovered and used by Western sinologists. However, due to their limited reading of Chinese written history, the Western scholars failed to incorporate effectively the slips in their study. By comparison, once Wang Guowei saw the same bamboo slips, he instantly realized their tremendous historic value, for Wang boasted a broad knowledge in Chinese history and knew how to use them to supplement the written texts in his study. But Western scholars were not the only ones who failed in this respect, Fu added. Chinese scholars had long known how to use excavated materials such as bronze inscriptions *(jinwen)* to help their study, but a real meaningful comparison of written sources and material sources was not seen until quite recently.[94]

Likewise, one needs to adopt a similarly comparative approach to treating other kinds of sources. As official sources tend to contain accurate records of big events, they can be nebulous or even distorted when describing political struggles, scandals, and coups within the royal court. Conversely, while individual writers are inclined to indulge themselves in gossip and anecdotes—sometime they even fabricate details to embellish their accounts—their records often have good supplementary value. By the same token, while domestic records are more likely to offer better descriptions, foreign records can offer some insightful perspectives that are hard to find in domestic records; native historians tend to take certain things for granted and hence fail to realize their significance.[95]

In sum, Fu Sinian played a distinguished role in modern Chinese historiography. His advocacy of scientific history, seen both in his teaching and leadership of the Institute of History and Philology, was indispensable to the nationalist interpretation of Chinese history. On the one hand, his positivist belief lent support to his friends and teachers in their endeavor at bridging the gap between the Chinese and Western traditions in historiography by reinforcing the transnational understanding of scientific method. On the other hand, by launching the excavation in Anyang, he exemplified the use of scientific method in constructing history, which left a definitive imprint in the Chinese perception of the past.

In Search of Modern History

In the May Fourth Movement when Beida students took on the streets, Fu Sinian was elected the marshal and his friend Luo Jialun, the New Tide cofounder, was chosen to write its manifesto. Luo declared in the "Manifesto of All Beijing Students" that "China's territory may be conquered, but it cannot be given away; the Chinese people may be massacred, but they will not surrender."[96] Even the term "May Fourth Movement" was coined by Luo in an article he wrote two weeks after the event. In publishing this article, Luo used the pen-name *Yi* (resolute) to show his determination.[97] Luo Jialun's name was thus on a par with Fu Sinian in respect to their leadership of the student movement. When Fu later changed his life goal and decided to devote himself to the pursuit of scientific scholarship (he even made an oath not to be involved in politics after his return from Europe), Luo kept this political enthusiasm alive after his college years. Throughout his life, he pursued actively a political career, while maintaining his interest in history.

Luo Jialun's political activism could be traced to his youth. Born into an official family in Jinxian county, Jiangxi province on December 21, 1897 where his father was the county magistrate, Luo began his education at three when his mother began to teach him how to read and write. His father also told him stories based on history and asked him to recite poems. After the founding of the Republic of China in 1911, Luo was sent to a high school in Shanghai. Reading many newly published magazines, Luo was attracted to novel ideas in cultural criticism, disseminated at the time by Japan-educated students like Chen Duxiu and Liang Qichao. His long essay "New Students in Twentieth Century China," appeared then in the school journal, *Fudan Miscellanies (Fudan zazhi)*, reflected his interest, in which he discussed the responsibility of young students for contributing to a new culture. It was well received at the time and was reprinted in Shanghai newspapers.[98] Luo's radical ideas led him to contact some veterans of the 1911 Chinese revolution. One of them was Huang Xing (1874–1916), one of founding fathers of the Republic. When Huang died in Shanghai, Luo was the first to go to the house to express his condolences. Luo's earlier contacts with the Chinese nationalists sparked his interest in politics.

In 1917 Luo passed the entrance examination to enter Beida, majoring in English literature. Among his schoolmates were Fu Sinian, Gu Jiegang, and Mao Zishui. Because of his lucid style, Luo received the nickname "Confucius" from his class.[99] But what made him a student leader on campus was his involvement in cofounding the New Tide Society and his associate editorship of the *New Tide* journal. Not only was Luo the first person with whom Fu Sinian discussed the idea of organizing the society, he also suggested that the new society be called New Tide, in order to match its English subtitle *Renaissance*.[100] When Fu went to Europe in late 1919, Luo succeeded Fu's position both as the head of the society and the journal until he himself left for the United States in 1920, on a scholarship designated for Beida student leaders by the wealthy businessman, Mo Ouchu (1876–1943), who himself had studied in the United States.

As a student leader, Luo's student activism reflected the spirit of the May Fourth Movement. Chen Duxiu, the *New Youth* editor and a leader of the May Fourth Movement, placed his hope on China's youth and encouraged young people to untie themselves from the Confucian tradition, hence the journal title *New Youth*.

Luo responded enthusiastically to Chen's call. In 1918 he published an article "Young Students" in Chen's *New Youth* and called on his peers to become a model of "new youth" who ought to be "not feeble, not self-indulgent, not conservative." Drawing on his earlier essay written in Shanghai, Luo's article emphasized the need for young people to engage themselves in the New Culture construction. He expected his fellow college students to set a good example for their peers in the country, hence sharing Chen's belief in the Chinese young generation. In his summary of the May Fourth Movement, Luo applauded the students' patriotic action in saving China:

> This movement shows the spirit of sacrifice of the students. Chinese students used to be eloquent in speech and extravagant in writing, but whenever they had to act, they would be overly cautious. . . . This time, and only this time, they struggled barehanded with the forces of reaction. . . . The students' defiant spirit overcame the lethargy of society. Their spirit of autonomy can never be wiped out again. This is the spirit which will be needed for China to be reborn.[101]

It seems that Luo Jialun was the one who was excited more than anybody else by this spirit. Compared to his fellow Beida students of a similar educational background, Luo distinguished himself by showing his unfailing interest in politics. Indeed, after returning to China from Europe in the late 1920s, Luo had quite a few chances to pursue a promising career in history. But he was unable to resist the temptation of working with the government once an offer came. Hence, he could never stay long in an academic position. His incessant academic excursions, however, left a visible trace in modern Chinese historiography. In fact, this was somewhat related to his political experience. His deep involvement in the GMD's struggle against the warlords in the late 1920s and the Communists in the 1930s and the 1940s led him to take an interest in contemporary events. As a result, he pioneered the study of modern Chinese history. Compared to his close friend Fu Sinian, therefore, Luo played a different yet comparably important role for making the changes in Chinese historiography. If Fu opened a new horizon for the study of ancient Chinese history, Luo helped map out the terrain for a history of modern China.

From 1920 to 1926, Luo spent six years in America and Europe, taking courses in the humanities and social sciences. As mentioned earlier, Luo's decision to come to the United States was influenced by his teachers. Like He Bingsong, Luo entered Princeton University. A year later, he transferred to Columbia in order to work with John Dewey and Frederick J. Woodbridge as well as Carlton J. H. Hayes, William A. Dunning, and James T. Shotwell, all members of the New History School.[102] Luo had met John Dewey at Beida. When Dewey gave his talk, Luo had been asked to be a rapporteur.[103] Now he had the chance to work with Dewey personally. He studied at Columbia until the end of 1923 before he went to Germany. During this period, which lasted about a year, Luo was able to concentrate on his course work. He focused his interest on the study of the philosophy of history, taking courses with John Dewey and Frederick J. Woodbridge. In a letter sent to Hu Shi back in China during that period, Luo reported to his former teacher that though he was a bit disappointed by his absence from China's politics, he felt generally satisfied with his study at Columbia:

> This year, I was satisfied with my progress in study. At the end of last year, I participated in the convention of the AHA and presented a paper which was received pretty well. At present, I am concentrating on the study of the philosophy of history, which was quite encouraged by Woodbridge and Dewey. I have not written much recently. I feel frustrated that we cannot do much to help our country at this point. To study well is, therefore, the way in which we can put down our worries and distresses.[104]

His letter suggested that although Luo was happy with the progress he made academically during the period, he felt uneasy about being away from political action back in China. Luo was to be torn between the two—his interest in academics and his self-imposed political obligation—for the rest of his life.

Luo's study at both Princeton and Columbia did not earn him any degree, but he was deeply influenced by the works of the American New Historians. Following He Bingsong, Luo became an ardent convert to the New History School and tried to implement the ideas of New History in studying Chinese history. From the New History School, Luo learned the idea that modern history, or contemporary history, was more meaningful than ancient history, for it was closer and more pertinent to the present.

Of course, the idea was not entirely original. In introducing the New History School, He Bingsong mentioned its presentist approach. Wang Tao, in an earlier time, had also pioneered the writing of contemporary history, merging it with journalism. However, neither of them could be given the credit for establishing the field of modern Chinese history.[105] It was Luo Jialun who implemented the idea. Although Luo lacked a commitment to becoming a serious scholar, as an action-oriented man, he took the early initiatives for establishing it as a field that paved the way for the success of others. At first, Luo discussed his idea with Jiang Tingfu (1895–1965), his fellow student at Columbia, who was then working on his dissertation with Carlton J. H. Hayes, and encouraged Jiang to work with him on the subject.[106] Jiang later indeed became one of the forerunners in the field, specializing in modern Chinese diplomatic history.

Although attracted to the study of modern Chinese history, Luo was not yet ready to make himself a historian. Like his friend Fu Sinian, Luo Jialun did not become a history student while in the West. If Fu pursued a versatile interest in scientific learning, Luo was excited by political actions. In 1921, Luo plunged himself into an action to support the Chinese effort to reclaim Qingdao from Germany at the Washington Conference, a follow-up meeting after the Versailles Conference held in 1919. Luo and his friends formed the "Supporting Society of Chinese Students in the United States for the Washington Conference," in which Luo served as the secretary. Their main aim was to support the Chinese delegates and to make sure that Qingdao would be returned to China this time, a task they deemed unfulfilled by the May Fourth Movement. Although it distracted him from his study, it was also legitimate for Luo to take a leadership role in it for his active involvement in the May Fourth Movement.[107] The Washington Conference was ended in February of 1922, and at the conference, Qingdao was finally, officially returned to China. Afterward the "Supporting Society" was dismissed. Luo Jialun returned to his study, but he was also ready to leave Columbia.

In 1923 Luo went to Germany and enrolled himself at the University of Berlin. In Germany, Luo was again involved in extracurricular activities. Instead of going to classes, he worked independently in revising his translation of J. B. Bury's *History of Freedom of Thought*, a project he had started in 1919.[108] Because of the 1924 inflation, Luo led a relatively good life in Germany on the higher exchange rate for his scholarship sent from China. This was probably one of the reasons that he went to Germany—as did most of other Chinese students. In Berlin Luo met a few new friends such as Chen Yinke, Yu Dawei, and Zhu Jiahua (1893–1963), but his fellow Beida students remained at the core of his circle: Fu Sinian, Yao Congwu, Mao Zishui, and their former chancellor Cai Yuanpei.[109] In the meantime, he also courted Zhang Youyi, who was just abandoned by Xu Zhimo (1896–1931), Luo's Beida schoolmate and one of China's most famous poets.[110] This favorable exchange rate, however, did not last very long. As a result, the financial situation of these friends became worsened, as shown in a few newly discovered letters written by Fu Sinian to Luo Jialun during 1923 and 1926.[111] But Luo in 1925 already enrolled himself in the University of Paris. In Europe, his main interest remained in history and philosophy. But he pursued his interest more like a visiting scholar than a full-time student.

Taking few courses, Luo spent most of time on his translation and his research in library to search for valuable sources. He went to England a few times during that period to look for materials in the British Museum at London and Oxford University Library. For the same purpose, he also visited the Archives Nationales in Paris. He was struck by the fact that in the English and French libraries, there were a great number of valuable materials on modern Chinese history. He could not help copying them, even though he was not sure whether or not he could pursue his interest later on. Among the materials Luo copied from the libraries, many were related to the Taiping Rebellion (1851–1868), including a few impotant documents describing the administrative policies of the *Taiping Tianguo* (the Heavenly Kingdom of Great Peace, 1851–1864). Through the arrangement of his friends, Luo also visited the archive collection of the French Ministry of Foreign Affairs to review some of the archives dated before 1860, which were opened just recently.[112]

Yet there was another reason for Luo Jialun to travel between England and France: he was, again, involved in student activities. On March 30, 1925, a young worker called Gu Zhenghong (1905–1925), who worked in a Japanese joint-venture textile factory in Shanghai, was shot to death because of his alleged role in inciting a strike. Students in Shanghai organized rallies and demonstrations protesting the Japanese brutality. However, when the students marched in the streets of the British Concession of the city, they encountered the British police. In the clash, the English police opened fire killing four students. The news soon spread all over the country and caused larger student demonstrations. As soon as Luo and his friends heard the news from foreign presses in Paris, they formed the Chinese Information Bureau in England in June 1925, protesting British policy in China and seeking international support for their fellow students back home. Luo rushed to England to take the leadership of the bureau. He dedicated two entire months to the agency in London until it was dismissed in August, due to financial difficulties. Luo returned to Paris afterward. After this episode, he decided to return to China.

On leaving, Luo wrote a long letter to his Beida friend, New Tide member Gu Jiegang, discussing his job opportunities and his ideas about the study of modern Chinese history. On returning, as we mentioned earlier, Luo's friend Fu Sinian did the same thing. In other words, Gu Jiegang was Fu's and Luo's connection back in China. It was also somehow because of Gu that they all became historians, attesting to the "shared mind-set" of these three former New Tide members and their common interest in a scientific interpretation of Chinese history. Written on September 8, 1926, Luo's letter pointed to the future direction of Luo's interest in modern history, reminding us of his attraction to the New History School. At the center of his letter was a proposal for establishing a research center for modern history. Based on Luo's impression of the *Monumenta Germaniae Historica* and other similar projects in European countries, this proposal showed Luo's belief that source collection and criticism were key preparations for historical study. Like the historians we mentioned earlier, Luo believed that modern historiography was predicated on a scientific scrutiny of sources, or source criticism.[113]

When Luo wrote to his friend, Gu Jiegang was then teaching at Xiamen (Amoy) University, founded by a wealthy overseas Chinese merchant, Chen Jiageng (1874–1961), in 1921. Luo asked Gu whether Xiamen University could grant his proposal for the study of modern history; namely to establish a source collection center, the first of its kind in China. There were, Luo suggested, six kinds of sources that were necessary and worth collecting:

1. Primary sources, especially original documents (Luo told Gu that in Europe, he had purchased some Qing government documents).
2. The primary sources, which he could not purchase but could be copied or photographed. For example, the Qing archives and documents on the Taiping rebellion currently held in English and French libraries. However, if the Chinese did not act quickly, Luo warned, these documents could be dispersed in the future.
3. Rare books in Western languages that were available at the time, but were not in print any longer, such as missionary works, journalists' correspondence about China, works about the Opium War, etc.

4. Recent publications in Western languages about modern China. In his letter, Luo mentioned Alfred Waldersee's (1832–1904) memoir, *Denkwuerdigkeiten de Grafen von Waldersee*, which described his experience in battling the Boxers in 1900 as commander-in-chief of the allied forces from Germany, England, France, Russia, Italy, America, Japan, and Austria. Memoirs of this kind, Luo stated, were indispensable to the study of China's foreign relations.

5. Rare Chinese books on modern history that were no longer in print.

6. New Chinese publications related to the study.[114]

Luo believed that if the university could grant his proposal and establish the center, it would turn Xiamen University into a leading institution in China, given the importance of modern history study for the country. However, in the event that the university could not support the proposal at the time, given the political uncertainty and financial instability in 1930s China, Luo also proposed a substitute proposal. He requested 20,000 Chinese *yuan* each year as a seed fund to start the source collection process. With that amount of money, Luo stated that he could begin to implement part of the plan. If the project could be continued for ten years, he believed, it would have a fruitful and meaningful outcome.

Provided the university supported his idea, Luo then made three requests:

1. to study the Qing archives in Beijing with the title of a "Traveling Research Professor or Fellow" (Luo's own words), offered by the university;

2. that Chen Dengke, his Beida friend and Chen Yinke's younger brother, join him to help hand copy important Qing archives;

3. that the university buy Li Xiucheng's (1823–1864) Confession, which was then in the hands of Zeng Guofan's (1811–1872) descendants—but given the family's financial situation, Luo stated, they would probably sell it in a near future.[115]

Like Fu Sinian, who believed that founding the Institute of History and Philology would enable Chinese scholars to compete with Western sinologists, Luo stated that his goal in setting up this source collection center was to allow Chinese historians to rival their Japanese counterparts in the study of China. To tap the nationalist feeling, Luo cited the Morrisen Oriental Museum in Japan as an example. Of course, he conceded, the Japanese museum had already collected a large number of sources in Asian history. But "If we cannot compete with the Japanese museum in quantity of sources, we can compete with them in quality. Taken from the vantage point of our Chinese sources, we may even surpass it."[116] He emphasized: "The Japanese had long noticed the importance of the job, whereas in China, this kind of thing has not even started yet. What a shame! What a shame! If Chen Jiageng [the president of the university] can support this, our Chinese may stand up before the Japanese."[117] However, Luo's nationalist plea did not help him at that time. Due to the political uncertainty and the university's precarious financial situation, neither Luo's proposal nor his requests were granted by the university, in spite of Gu's presumed help on Luo's behalf.

Although Luo's proposal was unsuccessful, his letter constituted a valiant attempt to draw attention to the study of modern Chinese history. This attempt combined the traditional practice with a modern approach. In imperial China source collection was considered a high priority among official historians, although few of them attempted the writing of contemporary history. As a standard practice in dynastic historiography, the sources collected were to be used by later historians, often from the succeeding dynasty. But Luo's intention was different from that of traditional historians. He called for the study of modern history because it was important and immediately related to the nationalist cause. In other words, he wanted to collect the sources in order to develop a new perspective on China's recent, hence more relevant, past, not to preserve them merely for the convenience of future historians. In his letter, Luo also admitted that he made the suggestion because he was inspired by the antecedents in the West, such as the *Monumenta Germaniae Historica* and the *Rolls Series*.

On returning to China, Luo accepted a teaching position in the History Department of Southeastern University in Nanjing. Although the main campus of the university was located in Nanjing, about 200 miles away from Shanghai, its School of Management was then in Shanghai. Luo explained to Gu in his letter that he accepted the professorship because he planned to use the libraries in Shanghai for his study of modern Chinese history.[118] Luo of course had developed a habit of traveling around in Europe. But obviously, he seemed too optimistic about his ability to commute back and forth between Nanjing and Shanghai. This helps explain why he soon left the university.

Although the job was not ideal, Luo got a chance to implement his idea in studying modern history. In fact, at Southeastern University he not only taught the history he liked, he also found his protégé, Guo Tingyi (1903–1975), who later carried on his idea in pioneering the field of modern Chinese history. The two courses he taught seemed to be survey courses: Chinese History in the Last One Hundred Years and Western History in the Last One Hundred Years. But his new emphasis (on modern period) and new approach (using foreign sources) left a strong impression on the students, including Guo Tingyi. In 1955, about thirty years later and in the late years of Luo's life, Guo finally succeeded in founding the Institute of Modern History at the Academia Sinica in Taiwan, fulfilling Luo's plan for establishing a research center in the study of modern China.[119]

Despite his popularity among students, Luo however seemed unfulfilled at the time with his political ambition. When the GMD, led by Chiang Kai-shek, launched the Northern Expedition (1926–1927), Luo left the university and joined Chiang's National Revolutionary Army. Chiang appointed Luo as his secretary and the two developed a long friendship. In Chiang's campaign against the warlords, Wu Peifu (1874–1939) and Sun Chuanfang (1885–1935), he further appointed Luo as Chairman of the Editorial Board for the General Headquarters in charge of military propaganda and documents. Luo's involvement in the Northern Expedition and his friendship with Chiang Kai-shek enabled him to pursue higher government positions after the war. In the meantime, he also used his positions to promote the study of modern history.

Luo's many positions in the GMD party and government were related to the administration of education, which allowed him to pursue his interest in history. He was, for example, the vice-provost of the newly founded GMD Party Cadre School in late 1926. In that position Luo, helped by Guo Tingyi who had followed him to work for the GMD, embarked on an ambitious plan to compose a multivolume source book of modern history.[120] In 1928 when the GMD government decided to change the Qinghua School *(Qinghua liumei yubei xuexiao)*, a preparatory school for sending students to America, to Qinghua University, Luo was appointed by Chiang Kaishek as its first president to execute the plan. A year later, Luo was elected an alternate deputy member to the Central Committee of the GMD in its third national convention in Nanjing. In a few years after his return from Europe, Luo, still in his early thirties, emerged as a leading GMD party official in education. While following a different path, like his Beida friend Fu Sinian, Luo Jialun was now on his way to become one of the new leaders in the Chinese intellectual community.

However, Luo's tenure at Qinghua University did not last long. In May and October of 1930, Luo resigned his position twice and left the university the second time in October. In his administration, Luo pursued four goals: scholarship, democracy, discipline, and military quality.[121] To raise the level of scholarship, he was successful at purchasing better equipment and recruiting quality professors, among them his fellow Columbia alumnus Jiang Tingfu who was offered to teach modern history. Emphasizing discipline and military quality, however, Luo also tried to gear the administration and curriculum of the university toward the requirements of the GMD party, or "partification" *(danghua)*, turning Qinghua into a GMD training school.[122] Thus, he contradicted himself with his second goal of promoting democracy and alienated the faculty and the board of trustees. His call for a swift and sweeping change also caused resistance and apprehension among students. In the face of opposition, Luo resorted to extreme measures: he used resignations as a weapon to coerce his opponents to accept the reform. However, he only succeeded the first time, not the second.[123]

Luo's administration at Qinghua turned out to be unpleasant. But one of the speeches he gave in January 1929, entitled "A Necessary Understanding of the Importance of Modern Chinese History", merits our attention. It was one of the earliest discussions that defined the scope and nature of modern Chinese history. Rebutting the notion that modern history was too close to the present to be worth any scholarly attention, Luo argued that modern history study was important because it was closely relevant to the present, more so than the study of ancient history. Chinese scholars needed to pay a particular attention to the study of modern history because during the recent years, China experienced tremendous changes, resulting from the Western intrusion. The breadth and depth of the Western impact made modern Chinese history considerably different from the history of imperial China, when China's contacts with foreign cultures were rare.

From the viewpoint of China's foreign relations, Luo came to periodize modern Chinese history. He said that since 1834 China had witnessed four major historical periods:

1. 1834–1860, the age of confrontation;
2. 1861–1895, the age of submission;
3. 1896–1919, the age of entreaty;
4. 1920 to his time, the age of revolution.

During these four periods, Luo emphasized, it was China's relationship with foreign countries that highlighted the course of modern Chinese history. Toward the end of his speech, Luo did not forget to end his historical overview with an optimistic note. Having gone through various defeats and humiliations in the first three periods, he declared, China finally began to move in the right direction after the May Fourth Movement of 1919. The May Fourth Movement, thus, was a revolutionary event that ushered China into a new era.[124]

While a sketchy discussion, Luo's periodization of modern Chinese history left a far-reaching impact on future scholars in the field. In his periodization, Luo emphasized two turning points, one was the Opium War and the other the May Fourth Movement. Both of them were well accepted. For a long time, most textbooks, both in the PRC and Taiwan, began the course of modern Chinese history with the Opium War. Echoing Luo's emphasis on the importance of the May Fourth Movement, the People's Republic of China (PRC) historians also used it to divide the history into two periods, namely the so-called modern history *(jindaishi)*, from 1840 to 1919, and contemporary history *(xiandaishi)* from 1919 to 1949.[125]

Luo's interpretation of Chinese history is based on his basic understanding of the nature of historical study, which was shaped in part by his education at Columbia. To Luo, there is an essential difference between actual history and written history, a notion stressed emphatically by the American historian Charles Beard of the New History School.[126] Luo's letter to Hu Shi from the United States in 1923 told us that he was engrossed with the study of the philosophy of history while at Columbia.[127] It is, thus, not surprising that his idea of history reminds us of Beard's. To Luo, actual history is different from written history because the former is only selectively studied by and reflected in the latter.

To analyze the difference between actual and written history, Luo drew on the work of Frederick J. Woodbridge, the dean of the graduate school during the years when Luo was at Columbia.[128] Woodbridge was a prominent philosopher whose interest was not confined to the philosophy of history. But his popular pamphlet *The*

Purpose of History (1916), translated into Chinese by He Bingsong, seemed to have exerted a noticeable influence in shaping the pragmatic interpretation of history, on which Luo Jialun built his own thesis. Moreover, Woodbridge had studied in late nineteenth-century Germany and was exposed to "the German tradition of careful historical scholarship,"[129] which also attracted Luo. In *The Purpose of History*, Woodbridge articulated a progressive and pragmatist view of history:

> The truth of history is a progressive truth to which the ages as they continue contribute. The truth for one time is not the truth for another, so that historical truth is something which lives and grows rather than something fixed to be ascertained once and for all. To remember what has happened, and to understand it, carries us thus to the recognition that the writing of history is itself an historical process. It, too, is something "evolved and acted."[130]

These words explain why to the New Historians, historical works are not identical to real history. Historical writing reflects the viewpoints of the historians. Elsewhere, Woodbridge reiterated his position in stressing the difference between written and actual history. "History may be written in many different ways and our philosophies of life are individually characterized by the type of history we prefer." Therefore, "We are writing no *actual* history, but establishing a new historical tradition, . . . the essential point is that the writing of history is an over-simplification and a process of selection."[131] When Luo pointed out the difference between actual and written history, he was restating the position held by his Columbia professors.

Due to the difference between history and historiography, Luo writes, the historian must examine carefully and critically his sources, for the sources are the medium for him to know about the past, or the actual history. He shares the view of his friends that source criticism is the key to the success of historiography. Moreover, he intends to discuss its importance at a philosophical level. Like his Columbia professors, who challenged Rankean historiography for its belief in the historian's ability to retell the past, Luo asks his students to beware of the fact that no matter how historical a text is, it is only a written history, not actual history. This understanding has a positive effect on the May Fourth scholars' project in modernizing Chinese historiography: once historical texts are treated as sources, not real history, it paves the way for modern historians to search for new interpretations of the past. Thus considered, Luo's philosophical pondering supplies a theoretical justification for the endeavor at rewriting history, ancient and modern.

Despite his many political engagements, Luo Jialun never gave up his opportunity to share his ideas of history with others. During the 1930s and 1940s, Luo delivered a few speeches on roughly the same topic on various occasions. Luo gave his first recorded talk on Western philosophy of history in 1930 when he was teaching at Wuhan University, in which he divided Western philosophy of history into ten "schools," led by Georg Hegel, Karl Marx, St. Augustine, Charles Darwin, Thomas Carlyle, Henry Buckle, J. G. Herder, Wilfred Trotter, Jean-Gabriel Tarde, and Sigmund Freud, respectively.[132] In describing and discussing these "schools," Luo took an eclectic and subjective approach, emphasizing more their distinct ideas than their chronological sequence and ideological inheritance. For instance, as we can see, the extent to which these "schools" (some were hardly a school) influenced the thinking of history in the West varied greatly, but in Luo's treatment, they possessed an almost equally important position.[133] In his other speeches, while maintaining that there have been ten "schools" of the philosophy of history in the West, he often changed their order and sometimes replaced Henry Buckle with Auguste Comte or H. Tylor.[134]

All the same, in forming his philosophy, Luo had his preferences. Like the New Historians, he was interested in the positivist approach to the study of history and the alliance between history and social sciences. From that perspective, Luo explained the difference between historiography and the philosophy of history, as well as the nature of historical study, its function, and its relation with other disciplines. According to Luo, all the disciplines of social sciences, including history, are by their nature "sciences," because they are all aimed at description, whereas philosophy is aimed at explanation. "Science is," he claimed, "to place all things in their proper positions so that they can be organized into a system. The end of science is to clarify intricacies among things and seek a law in order to show how they change."[135] While description was the primary goal in scientific study, people from time to time also sought explanations. In natural science, Luo stated, Albert Einstein and Max Planck had intended to create a theory to explain the changes in the physical world, whereas Bertrand Russell and Alfred Whitehead tried to form a philosophy based on mathematics. As philosophers of natural science provided explanations for changes in the natural world, philosophers of history explained the evolution of human society. Thus the philosophy of history, Luo proclaimed, aimed to answer questions such as what the relationship between human beings and the universe is, what the relationship between individual and society is, in what direction society moved, whether there is any designated purpose of a society, and so forth.[136] In a word, "The philosophy of history," as a simple definition, "is a science which explains the nature and evolution of history based on historical facts."[137]

For Luo, because history aims at description and the philosophy of history at explanation, the two work at two different levels; the philosophy of history is at a higher level. But they must work together to provide a tenable explanation, for any plausible explanation is predicated on scientific scrutiny of historical facts. However, this scientific cooperation between history and the philosophy of history does not always produce identical outcomes. That is to say, there can be more than one interpretation based on the same kind of work with historical facts. While there is only one way to deal with historical sources, meaning source criticism, there can be many ways to construe the meaning of history based on these sources. Luo stressed that any attempt to offer one interpretation of history will always face an impasse.[138] By stating this, Luo reiterated his earlier emphasis on the discrepancy between written and actual history.

From Luo's discussion on the philosophy of history, the antitheses between historiography and the philosophy of history, actual and written history, and mind and nature, we can discern, again, the influence of F. Woodbridge, especially the latter's dualist approach to the understanding of epistemology, which argues that mind is a realm of nature. Drawing on the legacies of Aristotle, Locke, and Spinoza, Woodbridge constructed a metaphysics that stresses an active interaction between mind and nature. "If effective ideas," he described, "are really acquired through experience, an analysis of these ideas should reveal something about the world in which that experience occurs; and the chief revelations seem to be a limiting structure or structures for all events and a genuinely productive activity within these limits. The structure determines what is possible and the activity determines what exists."[139] Woodbridge here argued that experience is the source of ideas, or, nature is the source of mind, for experience is structured in nature. He thus implied that mind is able to apprehend nature, although with limits. By emphasizing mind as one of the products of nature, Woodbridge intended to improve one's understanding of the mind-nature dualism of modern philosophy.[140] Luo Jialun appropriated Woodbridge's theory of epistemology to form his ideas of history. To Luo, the historian's mind could provide a variety of interpretations of history, based on the human experiences in the past. But no single interpretation was ever final.

The plethora of historical interpretations reveal, to Luo, that no written history can be the same as actual history. Luo's adoption of Western ideas and concepts—he often used English terms directly in his speeches and writings—allowed him to espouse the importance of source collection in historical study, for sources here represented pieces of actual history. Luo also used this philosophy to illustrate the importance of the study of modern history. When Luo left Qinghua, he accepted the professorship of history at Wuhan University, where he published a research paper, entitled "The Meaning and Method of the Study of Modern Chinese History" in the journal of Wuhan University in 1931.[141] Before explaining the importance of modern Chinese history, he first defined what history is. Luo claimed that the object of historical study should be history itself, not historical books. "Historical works," he explained, "are merely historians' records of human history. They are selectively written according to historians' assessments and judgments." He further argued that there exist many histories, and human history is just one of them. But all histories are similar because they are composed of events that are interrelated. As events make all histories, human history is an "axis" that at once cuts across and ties together all the events and histories. Because of its unique role, Luo wrote, human history becomes most important to the present. Yet if history in general is important to the present society, modern history is even more so because of its still perceivable impacts on the present.[142]

To illustrate his thesis, Luo used two concepts: "continuity" *(lianxu xing)* and "interconnectedness" *(jiaohu xing)* and believed that these two concepts explained the nature of history, especially its horizontal and vertical effects on the present. What is indicated by the vertical effect of history is "historical continuity." Luo explained, although modern European history was usually believed to have begun with the French Revolution, the revolution did not change European society overnight. Likewise, although modern Chinese history started with the Opium War, in the ages before, China had made exchanges with foreign countries. To understand historical integration required an understanding of the horizontal interconnectedness among histories of different regions. The best way to observe this effect, Luo believed, is through the study of modern Chinese history, for China at that time was, willy-nilly, closely tied to the great chain of world politics. For example, China's conflicts with England and France between 1856 and 1860 were interrupted by the Indian Rebellion in 1859. For about a year, England had to pause its action in the war with China and send an army from China to India to reinforce its military force. Chinese, Indian, and English histories were therefore integrated during that period.

Both "historical continuity" and "historical interconnectedness" attest to the significance of modern Chinese history. The former explains why one should study modern Chinese history and the latter helps define its broad scope, through which one can see China's relation with the world. "Historical interconnectedness" thus differentiates the study of modern Chinese history from the study of ancient history and renders the subject more interesting and significant. To strengthen his argument, Luo also contended that to be a modern Chinese historian neither necessarily suggested inferior scholarship, nor indicated that the research would have more distortions from the historian's personal interest in and relation with the events and figures he described. Although Herodotus focused his work on recording things in the past, Luo, following many Western commentators, believed that his book was not regarded as highly as Thucydides', who wrote a contemporary history. Thus, the success of a historian is not dependent on the subject matter, but on the use of reliable sources. Moreover, according to Luo, both ancient and modern historians need to rewrite history, because new sources surface continuously, either through archaeological excavation or through the disclosure of the government.[143]

Thus, Luo's philosophical analysis helped him to emphasize source criticism in the work of the historian. On this matter, he commended G. P. Gooch's work on British diplomatic history because Gooch ably used the documents of the Ministry of Foreign Affairs in England. He also drew attention to H. B. Morse's *The International Relations of the Chinese Empire* because it contained information on the Opium War from the documents of the English government. These examples helped Luo to emphasize the importance of source collection, which, he pointed out, should also include contemporary newspapers and memoirs as well as government documents, for all of them were important for the work of a modern historian. A good historian should learn the method of *Heuristik*—he borrowed from Langlois and Seignobos' *Introduction to the Study of History*—meaning the way in which historians collected their sources.[144] In addition to his stress on primary sources, Luo divided sources in the field of modern Chinese history into three categories.

The first was Chinese materials. The second was foreign language materials. And the third was monographs of modern scholars on the subject, for these monographs demonstrated original research based on scrutinized sources.[145]

Luo's article revealed that while following a slightly different route, like his friends, Luo also reached the same conclusion that source criticism was the key to the success of scientific history. His interest in philosophy helped him explain its importance to historical study in general, and the study of modern history in particular. In explaining his position, Luo appropriated ideas from the New History School and used them for a different purpose. As the New Historians, such as Charles Beard, conceptualized the difference between "actual" and "written" history and used it to challenge Ranke's emphasis on source criticism, Luo turned Beard's conceptualization around to reinforce the foundation of Rankean historiography, hoping to bridge the difference through source criticism. In so doing, he also revived the traditional interest in source collection via government sponsorship. Like his friends, Luo in his study of modern Chinese history merged tradition and modernity in the work on historical sources.

But Luo was not able to execute his plan of source collection for a long time. Before his article appeared in the journal of Wuhan University in 1931, he had already been appointed president of the newly founded Central Political Institute, a school designed by and for the party.[146] It was not until he was fifty-four (1951), when the GMD retreated to Taiwan, that Luo obtained a chance while serving as the chairman of the editorial board of GMD history *(dangshihui)*. At that position, he launched a few ambitious plans to compose source books for modern Chinese history and wrote prefaces to most of them. His seemingly excessive enthusiasm, coupled with his noted status as a GMD veteran, incurred suspicions and criticisms of professional historians.[147] But the outcomes were no less remarkable. Under his general editorship, the board published two multivolume source books on Sun Yat-sen: *The Complete Works of Sun Yat-sen (Guofu quanji)* and *A Chronology of Sun Yat-sen (Guofu nianpu)*, in addition to many others of a similar kind for the rest of the revolutionary veterans. Because of Luo Jialun's leadership, this board became a center for the study of modern Chinese history in Taiwan.[148] During the same period, he also encouraged Guo Tingyi to found the Institute of Modern History at the Academia Sinica.

Besides collecting sources on modern history, especially the GMD history, Luo also resumed his own research. In 1960 he published an article describing in detail his investigation of the diary of Yuan Shikai (1859–1916) during the 1898 Reform. As a former Qing general and an alleged supporter of Empress Dowager Cixi (1835–1908) in suppressing the Reform, Yuan's diary of the Reform was a firsthand document and crucial to the study of the Reform. But it was not believed as true until Luo verified it with his research. In his article, Luo confessed that he did not believe its authenticity when he first saw it. But after a serious and careful examination, he concluded that except for some interpolations, the diary was authentic. Although genuine, however, it was not immune to its author's own modification, Luo added. Yuan allowed his diary to be circulated after the death of the Empress Dowager and the fall of the Qing Dynasty because, Luo explained, he wanted to use it to clear his name for his dishonorable role in persecuting the reformers. While a valuable primary source, therefore, it contained the author's strong bias.[149] Luo's assessment is shared by Dai Yi, a leading Qing historian in the PRC, in the latter's most recent analysis of Yuan's diary. Dai also notices that Yuan's decision to publish it after Ci Xi's death is for, while unsuccessfully, courting the reformers and revolutionaries who had gained by then an upper hand in power struggle.[150]

Toward the end of his life, Luo Jialun finally settled down to pursue his academic interest. As a scholar, he was not very successful; except for a few articles, most of his publications, amounting to ten volumes in toto, were written for other purposes than history. Thus viewed, Luo was like a modern mandarin; he used his education, combining both the Chinese and Western, to advance his political career for most of his life. It was not until later in his life, when he retired from politics, that he returned to scholarship. To be sure, his life was different from other May Fourth veterans—some chose to stay away from politics in order to concentrate on scholarship—but it was not totally unattractive to others. As we shall see in the next chapter, many of his friends chose to be involved in politics as well when China was drawn into a deeper national crisis.

Chapter Five

Seeking China's National Identity

> History—in all but a few, rather esoteric, senses of the term—is public time. This is, it is time experienced by the individual as public being, conscious of a framework of public institutions in and through which events, processes and changes happened to the society of which he perceives himself to be part. . . . To say that "history is public time," therefore, is to say that individuals who see themselves as public beings see society as organized into and by a number of frameworks, both institutional and conceptual, in and through which they apprehend things as happening to society and themselves, and which provide them with means of differentiating and organizing the things they apprehend as happening.
>
> —J. G. A. Pocock, *Virtue, Commerce, and History*

To China and its people, the coming of the 1930s brought nothing but sorrow, anger, and shame. In September 1931, the Japanese created the Mukden incident and began conquering Manchuria. Chiang Kai-shek, who just defeated the warlords and unified China proper, decided not to fight Japan. The loss of Manchuria, which occurred so suddenly and easily, angered and frustrated many intellectuals. If World War I led European intellectuals to cast doubts on the future of Western civilization, the loss of Manchuria caused a similar trauma to the Chinese. In the eyes of Chinese nationalists, Japan's occupation of Manchuria, China's northeastern region, threatened the very existence of Chinese civilization. It was like Damocles' sword hanging around the neck of the Chinese nation. Their worry was very legitimate. A few years later, Japan launched a nationwide invasion in China, starting World War II in Asia.

In modern Chinese history, China's relations with Japan often exerted a crucial impact on the direction of its movement. As the Sino-Japanese War of 1895 led Chinese intellectuals to campaign for political reform, Japan's invasion of Manchuria, and subsequently the whole of China, in the 1930s, forced them to reconsider the focus of China's cultural reform. This reconsideration was clearly reflected in the practice of historical study. If in the 1920s, the May Fourth historians evoked the past to reconcile tradition and modernity, negotiating between China and the West, now they were more interested in using the past to fortify and foreground the Chinese national identity. Consequently, foreign cultures, whether from the West or Japan, changed its role as the "other" in this process of identity construction; it was viewed more as an antagonistic "other" than as a comparable, supplementary "other."

This change was reflected very distinctly in the career orientation of Chinese intellectuals. The loss of Manchuria and the imminent danger of more invasions from Japan created a serious national crisis. In the face of the crisis, these scholars were no longer able to sit complacently in their ivory tower, continuing their research. One after another they were drawn to political actions. Some chose to accept offers from the GMD to join its government, others formed political forums to take part in the discussion on national defense. If in the 1920s, Luo Jialun was somewhat of an exception among his friends, he now became an example in uniting politics with scholarship. Fu Sinian, for example, who had vowed not to be involved in politics earlier, now challenged his peers with an emotional question, "What can a scholar do to save the nation?" Fu's own answer was, as shown by his actions at the time, to come out of their studies and classrooms and rally behind the government, preparing to contribute their wisdom and knowledge to the cause of national salvation.

In the study of Chinese intellectual history, many have argued that there was a perceptible antithesis between enlightenment and nationalism, the former referred to the May Fourth enthusiasm for science and free thinking and the latter to the nationalist impulse, which from time to time urged intellectuals to modify their goals in the former.[1] However, as we have shown earlier, the relationship between enlightenment and nationalism was not always antithetical. Rather, in the pursuit of a scientific approach to history, they appeared reciprocal: By appropriating elements from both Chinese and Wester culture, May Fourth historians re-created a past that was suitable to China's national needs. In fact, we can go as far as to argue that it was this reciprocity, rather than the antithesis, between enlightenment and nationalism that supplied the very basis for constructing modern Chinese culture. Once the reciprocity was replaced by antithesis, the culture itself would also lose its momentum.

During the wartime, the endeavor of Chinese historians at reconstructing Chinese history faced a new challenge, which required them to develop a new approach that could, on the one hand, address the urgent need of national salvation and the importance of national identity and, on the other hand, maintain an openness for foreign cultural influences. While some of the historians seemed to have retained this openness, some faltered, recanting their previous position; still others who, while remaining committed to an academic career, simply had to change the style and subject of their research in order to cope with the treacherous war situation. This wide spectrum of reactions seen in the behaviors of these intellectuals, rather normal as it seems given the impact of the war, nevertheless undermined their cause; they were no longer able to pursue a collective project in which they could share their common concern and interest.

If in the course of modern Chinese history, there could be a three-way grouping of intellectuals it would be traditionalists, Marxists, and liberals. The liberals during the wartime became widely divided, if not disintegrated. By contrast, the other two groups grew at the loss of the liberals; as more and more young students turned to Marxism, there also appeared an apparent attraction of traditional culture, as shown in the popularity of Feng Youlan's new interpretation of Confucianism and Qian Mu's (1895–1990) comprehensive and thoughtful narration of Chinese history.[2] The Anti-Japanese War, therefore, contributed to the polarization, or "radicalization" according to Yu Ying-shih,[3] of Chinese intellectual history, which not only determined to a great extent the fate of Chinese liberalism but also delineated the future course of modern Chinese history in the second half of the twentieth century.

China-Based Modern Culture

For He Bingsong, the Japanese invasion was immediate and devastating. When Chinese and Japanese armies fought in Shanghai in January 1932, the Commercial Press, where he worked as the director of the translation department, was heavily bombed and destroyed by the Japanese air force, including its Oriental Library.[4] Though He stayed on his job until 1935, this catastrophic incident decisively changed his career orientation.[5] He curtailed an ongoing large project which was originally planned to translate a series of Western history works. In its place, he proposed a new series, entitled "National Rejuvenation" *(Minzu fuxing congshu)*, to which he contributed his study on Chinese folklore in a pamphlet called *A Study of Chinese Folklore (Zhongguo minsu zhi yanjiu)*.[6] In fact, from the late 1930s to his death in 1946, He did not publish anything on Western history, except two high school textbooks.[7]

This change is particularly conspicuous in He because in the 1920s he was an ardent advocate of the importation of Western learning. His study of Zhang Xuecheng, as shown earlier, espoused the need for comparative studies in historiography, emphasizing the relevancy of the Western experience. But he now decided to move his research focus away from Western scholarship. Here was another example. In 1934 he elected to publish a chapter from his book *General History*, entitled "The Development of Chinese historiography." Consider the fact that the book was originally written as a comparative study, He's decision to publish this particular chapter was indicative of his mind at the time.[8]

He's renewed interest in Chinese scholarship reflected a cultural nativism. This cultural nativism also affected his political preference: like many Western trained intellectuals, He chose to support the GMD government, the official leadership of China, rather than other political parties including the CCP. He became actively involved in the social activities sponsored, directly or indirectly, by the GMD and served as the director of the The Association of Chinese Art and Scholarship *(Zhongguo xueyishe)*, an association that gathered intellectuals with similar political inclinations. His activism and leadership caught the attention of some GMD leaders including Chen Lifu (b. 1900).

He's participation in these activities culminated in cosigning a manifesto with nine other professors in 1935, called "Declaration of the Construction of a China-based Culture" (*Zhongguo benwei wenhua jianshe xuanyan*, hereafter "Declaration"), which appeared originally on January 10, 1935, in the *Cultural Construction (Wenhua jianshe)*, a journal endorsed by Chen Lifu's CC clique through the Association for Cultural Construction in China *(Zhongguo wenhua jianshe xiehui)*, and was reprinted in other journals and magazines afterward.[9] Though it was not clear whether He Bingsong himself drafted the Declaration, as a renowned advocate of Western historiography, his signature did contribute to the wide attention the Declaration received after publication.[10] In the ensuing discussions, He played a leading role among the cosigners in defending their position. He presided, for example, over a round table discussion held on January 19 in Shanghai. On January 30, he also delivered a speech about their stance in Nanjing at a similar meeting. In these two meetings, many leading scholars and GMD officials joined the discussion, including Luo Jialun, and showed their support.[11] As many intellectuals, sympathetic with its nationalist tone, endorsed the Declaration, He's friends and former Beida colleagues Hu Shi and Cai Yuanpei were on the other side. Hu Shi sharply criticized the Declaration, regarding it as an unhealthy trend in the academic community. On behalf of all the signers, He responded to Hu's criticism and made more clarifications. It is obvious that though the Declaration was signed by ten scholars, He was the key figure among them.

The Declaration began with an assessment of the status quo of Chinese culture, which was rather gloomy and disappointing: Chinese culture lost not only its position in the world, but also its appeal to the Chinese people. In order to change this situation and enhance the position of Chinese culture vis-à-vis foreign cultures, the authors proposed a China-based approach to "cultural construction" *(wenhua jianshe)*. He and his cosigners admitted that it was not until the twentieth century that Chinese culture encountered a challenge that resulted in fundamental changes; they also acknowledged that it was the May Fourth/New Culture Movement that ushered in a new era of Chinese cultural history as scholars began to embark on cultural reform. However, they asserted, while many scholars took an interest in the reform, they had not yet reached a consensus in regard to its execution. As Chinese scholars were debating back and forth in order to find a workable plan, foreign culture entered China in different forms. As a result, China became a battlefield in which foreign cultures were fully present and vying for superiority, whereas Chinese culture was losing consistently its validity and relevancy. Concerned with this unhealthy situation, these professors declared that only a China-based approach could lead to a constructive cultural reform.

This approach, He and others argued, was constructive for the following reasons. First, it addressed the present needs; "cultural reform must meet the needs of the present society." Second, it advocated the importance of holding a "critical attitude" and using scientific method in dealing with traditional culture. Third, it upheld a "high criterion for judging Western culture" and avoided wholesale Westernization. In a word, the Declaration aimed to create a *Chinese* modern culture, rather than a modern culture *in* China.[12]

The argument was of course nothing new. For one thing, from the mid-nineteenth century when the Chinese began to face the expanded world, the question of how to maintain the substance of Chinese culture while absorbing useful elements from others was a recurrent theme in the writings of Chinese intellectuals. To a large degree, the point made by these ten professors was reminiscent of the *ti* and *yong* dichotomous thinking that prevailed in the late Qing Dynasty. Further, after the May Fourth/New Culture Movement, it became almost a cliché to argue the need for scrutinizing the Chinese tradition. He Bingsong, along with a couple of others who also signed the Declaration, used to be an active participant in such an endeavor in the 1920s.

Though the approach was not original, the Declaration did strike a sensitive chord. By reiterating the need to maintain the Chinese substance, it addressed the identity issue that became extremely sensitive among Chinese people at the time. Due to the Japanese invasion, most Chinese were facing the immediate danger of losing their national identity. Considering He Bingsong's earlier experience in the Commercial Press, his involvement with the Declaration was not surprising. According to some witnesses, He Bingsong was quite emotional in signing the Declaration. And his emotion was shared by many. Tao Xisheng (1899–1986), another signer, admitted to Hu Shi that it was the "nationalist feeling" *(minzu ganqing)* that propelled him to sign his name on the Declaration.[13]

The Declaration also showed an affinity between the scholars and the GMD government. A year earlier, the GMD had launched a New Life campaign, aiming to revive traditional Chinese culture, especially Confucian values. Explaining why such "New Life" was necessary, Chiang Kai-shek proclaimed that he wanted to reach a "social regeneration of China" by reviving the traditional virtues such as "etiquette, justice, integrity and conscientiousness," and creating a "national consciousness and mass psychology." To achieve this goal, Chiang urged people to make sacrifices for the nation and asked them to help the government overcome current difficulties and live their lives by that standard.[14] Thus viewed, the GMD endorsement of the Declaration was only natural. Not only did GMD officials participate in the discussions following its publication, they also invited these professors to many occasions in which they could exchange ideas with them. For example, He Bingsong attended a meeting organized by the GMD party branch and the provincial government in the Jiangxi Province and was asked to deliver a speech about their cultural construction proposal. Zhang Qun (1899–?), the chairman of the GMD party branch, met He afterward and told him that a year earlier, Zhang had given a speech that made a similar argument.[15]

Hu Shi, the Declaration's main critic, understood clearly what this "China-based cultural construction" meant politically and culturally at the time. While he was by no means anti-GMD, he was uncomfortable with the GMD's involvement in what he considered an academic issue. Moreover, he truly believed that what was proposed by these professors was reactionary and detrimental to the ongoing cultural reform. In his response, published in the midst of the discussion in 1935, he pointed out bluntly that what the ten scholars championed was nothing but Zhang Zhidong's well-known *ti-yong* dichotomy; Zhang's proposal had long proven wrong, as shown in history. This China-based approach was also conservative in character, because it reflected a narrow-minded cultural protectionism and celebrated indiscriminately traditional values. Although Hu chose not to comment directly on the New Life movement, he related some activities associated with the movement, especially the warlords' worship of Confucius, to underscore the connection between the movement and the Declaration.[16]

According to Hu, no cultural tradition need be preserved if still viable. Any effort, regardless of its intention, to preserve a culture could only do harm rather than good to it, for culture should be able to preserve itself under all kinds of conditions. There was no need to fend off competitions from different cultures, domestic or foreign, for only through competition could the real value of a culture be shown. If a culture could not survive the competition, from Hu's pragmatist point of view, why should we preserve it? For the same reason, no one should set up a criterion and pass judgment on whether a culture was advanced or backward, useful or useless, and worthwhile or worthless. For Hu Shi cultural construction was an experimentation.

From this pragmatist perspective, Hu declared, scientific method was actually not helpful in settling cultural conflicts, because it could not decide which culture could and would survive in the conflict. He criticized these professors for misunderstanding scientific method, which to him was a method of practice and experiment, not a method of speculation. One could not use scientific method to screen "good" and "bad" cultures; one had to use it in order to know the value of a culture. That is to say, no one knew beforehand how to construct a modern culture, or what kind of culture would be needed by the world. To him, the construction of modern Chinese culture just barely started; China still had a great deal to learn from other cultures.[17]

To answer Hu Shi's harsh criticism as well as other people's questions, He Bingsong and others published another article in May 1935, entitled "Our General Response" *(Women de zongdafu)*, in which they attempted to clarify their position. Their language remained abstract and vague. But the authors did spell out the so-called present needs mentioned earlier, to which this China-based modern culture should respond. These needs were "to enrich people's cultural life, develop the country's economy, and strive for the survival of the nation." The first two of course appeared general, but the last one disclosed that what prompted them to campaign for the China-based approach was the ongoing Sino-Japanese conflict.[18] This avowed nationalist agenda made Hu Shi's criticism sound almost anachronistic.

In addition to the "General Response," He Bingsong in April 1935, gave a speech at Daxia University in Shanghai, responding directly to Hu's criticism. He stated that Hu misread their message in their proposal for the China-based approach. First of all, although they emphasized the importance of building a China-based modern culture, they were not suggesting returning to the past. In fact, they remained quite committed to the enlightenment project of criticizing traditional culture and introducing Western culture. What they recommended was a critical attitude toward both Chinese and Western culture. This critical attitude, He believed, allowed the participants in the cultural construction to become more responsive to the present needs.

In regard to Hu Shi's pragmatic interpretation of cultural development, He Bingsong retorted that culture did need preservation and encouragement, as shown in both Chinese and world history. In the process of preservation, scientific method was needed for designing the future development of the culture. Moreover, in his opinion, whether a culture was valuable and whether this culture could survive were two different questions. Citing examples from world history, He pointed out that many extinct cultures and civilizations achieved great accomplishments in the past, but they still vanished for various reasons.[19] Behind this rhetoric, we find He's strong nationalist concern for the survival of Chinese culture. The Declaration was de facto a political statement.

To better understand its political message, we can use J. G. A. Pocock's wisdom from his study of the political thought of early modern Europe. Pocock discovered that social thinkers often used terms and languages that denoted meanings requiring a contemporary understanding. Accordingly, we must understand a language in its specific context where novel ideas are conveyed through conventional terms—new wine poured into the old bottles. Pocock also states that there were some other cases in which a new language was invented to defend a traditional order.[20]

Pocock's contextual analysis helps us understand why the Declaration precipitated heated debates. Obviously, both sides, its sponsors and critics, were not simply engaged in an academic discussion on the China-based approach. Rather, they were quite clear about its political connotation. For example, much as he liked to make it an academic discussion, Hu Shi himself went beyond the academic arena when he criticized He Bingsong's new approach. He was angry about it not because it emphasized the study of Chinese culture but because it followed a dichotomous (Chinese versus foreign) way of thinking. Indeed, Hu would never oppose the focus on traditional culture—he himself spent most of his life constructing China's scientific tradition—he was concerned about the upsurge of cultural conservatism, which would put China against the other, namely foreign cultures in the world. For him, as always, the success of China's cultural modernization relied on a "complete globalization" *(chongfen shijiehua)*.

What He Bingsong did from 1935 onward seemed to have confirmed Hu Shi's worry. In contrast to his earlier comparative approach, in which China and the West were regarded more or less as equals, He in the late 1930s and the 1940s intended to demonstrate that China was better than the West. In June 1935, amid the boiling discussion of the China-based cultural construction, He published a long essay on China's cultural influence on the West. Like most of his earlier works, this essay was based on a Western scholar's work—German historian Adolf Reichevein's *China und Europa*. But He attempted this time to reach an entirely different conclusion: It was not that China should learn from the West, but vice versa. He pointed out that eighteenth-century European scholars like Voltaire and Leibniz were admirers of Chinese culture. He then continued to describe Goethe's interest in Chinese culture and how Chinese architecture and gardens inspired European designers and architects in the Romantic Movement. However, he ended his discussion abruptly before the twentieth century when Chinese culture was no longer a model but a target of criticism and ridicule. Rather, he chose to close his study with a suggestion: Since Westerners were fascinated with Chinese culture in the past, why should the Chinese people belittle, rather foolhardily, their own culture? What they should do is observe and research their own cultural tradition.[21]

He's involvement in the "cultural construction" also led him to a new career. Apparently, GMD leaders like Chen Lifu and others noticed his role in the discussion. When they proposed to allow more intellectuals to join the government, or the "open door" policy as it was called, they selected He Bingsong. A few months after the publication of the Declaration, due to Chen's recommendation, the GMD government appointed He Bingsong president of the Jinan University in Shanghai, a private university originally established for educating Chinese students living overseas.[22] While private, the university administration was supervised by the government; the latter also decided the appointments of its top administrators. Because of this appointment, He Bingsong embarked on a new life. His historical career was virtually ended. Despite some initial reluctance, He, like many of his cohorts, chose to accept the offer. Their choice reminds us of the mandarin tradition, which found its way back amid the renewed interests in traditional cultural values.

Unlike his student Luo Jialun's administration at Qinghua University, however, He Bingsong remained committed to liberal education in his presidency. He kept some distance from the GMD party and promoted academic freedom on campus. For example, in order to improve the academic level of the university and expose students to various schools of thinking, He tried hard to recruit scholars of different political backgrounds to the university, including a few leftists. He also helped radical students to avoid the harassment of the secret police on campus.[23] To some extent, his administration at Jinan was inspired by Cai Yuanpei's model at Beida in the 1910s, which he eye-witnessed while teaching at Beida during that period.

Yet He Bingsong faced a more difficult situation. During his ten-year tenure as the university president, the Jinan campus, like all other campuses in the country, was extremely tumultuous and turbulent.[24] Not only were the students more active and agitated due to the national crisis, but both the CCP and the GMD were more involved in student activities, turning the campus into a political battleground. Worst of all, only two years after He took over the university, the Japanese army entered the city of Shanghai. Although the campus was located in the English Concession, it was still not safe for both the faculty and students. In 1938, He made a decision to move the university out of the city, refusing to collaborate with the Japanese rule.[25] During the move, He's tremendous courage and endeavor kept the university together as a whole. Whenever He had an opportunity, he appealed to the GMD government for any possible assistance. But most of the time, He and his faculty and students were left unaided. Despite all the plight, in the early 1940s when the university was situated temporarily in Fujian Province for a few years, he even managed to resume classes and admit new students. During the entire period of World War II in China, the university was kept alive.[26]

But the war also took its toll on He's health. In 1945 when the war was finally over, He returned to Shanghai with his students, in an exhausted state and without a place to stay. His family had to live with a friend-cum-student in an old dormitory, belonging to the Chinese Association of Art and Scholarship. Despite these personal setbacks, He continued his efforts to reopen the university. In the following year, when he felt ready to start the new semester, he received an appointment from the government to be the president of the Yingshi University, a newly established provincial school in his hometown, Jinhua, Zhejiang Province. This was quite devastating. But despite his great reluctance, he accepted the appointment, due to the pressure mounted on him from his friends, students, and most of all, the government. After all, He explained, this new university was established for the people of his hometown and home-province.[27] However, before he was able to move physically to Jinhua, He died of pneumonia and fatigue on May 25, 1946. At his death, He and his family were still living in the same dormitory found in their return to Shanghai after the war.

World War II not only tragically claimed He's life at the age of only fifty-six, it also affected his scholarly accomplishment. The last decade of his life was spent at Jinan University in which he could not make substantial contributions to historical study. For many of his students and friends, He's love for his country and his dedication to education were their lasting memory. But there were still some who pointed out that had He not been assigned the administrative duty, he could have achieved much more as a historian. To account for the changes that occurred to He Bingsong, the Sino-Japanese War was definitely an important factor.

But we should also consider his personality. It seems that He often succumbed to pressure, rather than following his own interests.[28] Yet He Bingsong's experience was not unusual at the time; it was rather emblematic of his generation. Others with stronger personalities might have chosen to act differently. But whatever they did, their actions undoubtedly bore the imprint of the war.

History and Public Sphere

During most of the 1930s, Hu Shi remained committed to his ideals of liberalism and kept himself outside the government until 1938 when he became the ambassador to the United States. While an outsider, he was equally concerned about China's political and military situation. In the wake of the loss of Manchuria, he and his close friends founded a journal, entitled *Independent Critique (Duli pinglun)*, in 1932. Stating their goal, Hu Shi wrote, "Fire is already burning and national disaster has befallen everybody. . . . *Independent Critique* is a single thing that my friends and I thought we could do for this country under such a situation."[29] The title and the statement manifested Hu Shi's ideas of liberalism, he would rather be an independent critic of the government than be a participant in the government.

The journal did not receive financial assistance from any party or agency. Hu Shi and his friends supported the journal with their own money and even declined advertisement.[30] In defining this independence, Hu said, "We do not expect that everyone agrees with each other completely, we only hope that everyone can use his/her own knowledge and adopt a balanced attitude to studying problems in today's China. . . . We call this journal *Independent Critique* because we all hope to always keep an independent spirit, which means not to depend upon any political party, not to be capitulated by any bias, but to use responsible words to express the results of everyone's thinking; this is the independent spirit."[31]

Hu Shi's receptiveness to liberalism could be traced back to his college years in the United States. In addition to his study and reading of American democracy, he observed with great enthusiasm the presidential election of 1912 and was excited about the process of democratic operation, in spite of his disappointment with Theodore Roosevelt's defeat. Hu Shi was very proud that he had such an experience.[32] In one of his *Independent Critique* articles that argued for the possibility of establishing democracy in China, he proudly stated that his "long belief in democracy and constitutional government" was through his careful observation of American democracy and his taking courses in political theory and government during his seven-year sojourn in the United States.[33]

Thus viewed, Hu Shi was never a mere academic. In the early years of his career after returning from the United States, he struggled to keep a balance between his political aspiration and his dedication to scholarly pursuit. In the New Culture Movement, he swore that he would "avoid talking politics" *(bu tan zhengzhi)* for twenty years, in order to concentrate on creating a "cultural foundation for Chinese political construction," which influenced Fu Sinian and his friends in the New Tide Society. But the political reality soon forced him to break his promise. In 1919 when Hu's Beida colleague Chen Duxiu was arrested for his political radicalism, Hu Shi took over the editorship of the journal *Weekly Critique (Meizhou pinglun)* and published a controversial article that aroused a heated discussion on "isms and problems."[34] To be sure, at that time Hu Shi had not yet been ready to "talk politics" *(tan zhengzhi)*; consider his argument that what China needed was not discussions on "isms," but solutions to "problems." He urged his fellow scholars to study concrete social problems rather than to indulge in theoretical discussions on what pathway China should take to construct modernization.[35]

Having befriended Ding Wenjiang, Hu Shi became more active in political discussions. In the 1920s, he and Ding edited the *Endeavor Weekly (Nuli zhoubao)* and advocated "good government" *(hao zhengfu)*. He became convinced that political reform was a premise to the cultural and educational reform he had championed in the New Culture Movement.[36] In order to launch such a political reform, Hu Shi urged everyone to "do something" and wrote it into the "Song of Endeavor," the song for the Endeavor Society *(nuli she)*. Noticeably, Hu Shi admitted that what made him to take action then was that he became disappointed with the discussions conducted in the "new public opinion" *(xin yulunjie)*. Apparently, Hu and his friends intended to influence such a "new public opinion" by adding their voices, hoping to find a practical solution to the thrust of all social problems. To Hu Shi and his friends, the origin of China's political problems was the lack of "good people" in government. By asking "good people"—the elites who were well educated and liberals—to participate in government, they believed that China could achieve its goal in political reform. In their definition, "good government" should be constitutional, open to public, and protective of individual freedom, yet all these goals will not be achieved without the active participation of the "good people."[37]

Naive as their proposal appeared, it was "the first systematic summary of opinions that can be identified as 'liberal,'" as put by Hu Shi's biographer Jerome Grieder.[38] Their concern for individualism, their advocacy of political participation, and their opposition to strong government reflected elements of modern liberalism. Yet what is more significant was the liberal approach this "good government group" then adopted in dealing with China's political problems, which merits our attention. Although these liberals advocated a "good government," they did not think that this government could be established overnight. Rather, they believed that it would be the ultimate solution to China's illnesses. Given the unstable political circumstances, however, it could not be an immediate solution. They were not as naive to believe that the warlords would listen to them and give up their power in favor of the "good people." What they really promoted was an activism in the political process, which was regarded as the "only way to initiate the work of political reform." "It is not," Hu Shi wrote, "enough to be a good man—it is necessary to be a good man who can fight. Negative public opinion is not enough—it is necessary to have a militant and decisive public opinion."[39] Thus their real and immediate goal was to create an active public opinion that could influence politics and monitor the operation of a government. In other words, Hu Shi and his liberal friends intended to create a "public sphere" in China.

In his important work *The Structural Transformation of the Public Sphere*, Jürgen Habermas points out that along with the establishment of bourgeois society in modern Europe, a liberal public sphere was formed in which critical discourses on political and social interest were exchanged among a reading public, consisting mainly of scholars and journalists. In Europe such a public sphere began to take shape in the decline of feudalism and experienced subsequently a few fundamental changes that accompanied the rise of state power and the growth of capitalism.[40] Needless to say, China did not witness such a clear process as seen in Europe. Hence whether or not this "public sphere" theory is applicable here or in China, studies as a whole may still be debatable; some China scholars, such as Frederic Wakeman, Jr. and Philip Huang, have raised questions regarding the application of this theory.[41] However, if we exercise caution and notice the contextual differences, this theory is useful for our discussion of the *Independent Critique* journal here.

There are a few reasons for using the theory. First of all, the journal contributors repeatedly used the term "public" *(gong)* in their discussions on the need of the country. They consciously drew the distinction between what was the "public sphere," meaning the will of the people, and what was the official sphere. As said earlier, they published this journal so that it could become a strong voice on behalf of the public. Whatever they accomplished, they were pursuing this independent position, hence the journal title.

If we also consider, drawing on Prasenjit Duara's definition, the *public sphere* as an associated commitment to the "discourse of public issues and to the defense of its autonomy,"[42] the term becomes very relevant and useful here. Not only were the discussions sponsored by the journal focused on public issues that reflect the compelling needs of the country, these discussions were also conducted in the associated manner and drew the attention from the entire Chinese intellectual community.

Lastly, the use of the "public sphere" helps us understand the relation between state and society in 1930s China, a pivotal issue that can be highlighted by the theory. In 1930s China, the tension between state and society was no less acute than eighteenth-century Europe, which provided the basic foundation and necessity for establishing a similar public sphere. This public sphere was needed not only for restoring the political authority that had collapsed with the Qing Dynasty in 1911, but also for founding a unified modern state; the success of the GMD's Northern Expedition had only unified the country by forming a tentative coalition between Chiang Kai-shek and other warlords. In founding their journal, Hu Shi and his friends hoped to make a conscious endeavor to participate in the process of nation building by riding the wave of public opinion.

This wave was pushed by the high tide of nationalism. The *Independent Critique* was a huge success, attracting thousands of subscribers. According to Hu Shi, the journal initially sold 2,000 copies of its first issue. It successfully reached 7,000 copies in its third year and 13,000 copies in its fourth year.[43] Such a success made the journal one of the most important vehicles in venting public opinions on the role of government in the war and the governmental policies toward Japan. Although the *Independent Critique* contributors tended to keep a moderate tone in their criticism of the GMD's nonresistance policy toward Japan, compared to left-wing criticisms found in the *Spring and Autumn* and the much more popular journal *Life Weekly (Shenghuo zhoukan)*, they were very active in launching controversial debates such as the one on democracy versus dictatorship, while the other journals were ambiguous about these issues.[44]

To Hu Shi, democracy was not only suitable to China in peacetime, it was also needed more in wartime such as then. He argues that if China were to survive, it needed to develop a modern society after the Western model with an articulate intelligentsia and an established middle class.[45] To support his argument, Hu referred not only to his own experience in the United States, but also to Western history. When the historian Jiang Tingfu, then chair of the History Department at Qinghua, rebutted that a period of absolute monarchy, as shown in European history, seemed necessary in building a modern nation, Hu expressed his strong objection: "The precondition to the establishment of a modern country was a unified government rather than an absolute monarchy. Such an unified government was not necessarily an absolute monarchy." He pointed out that the English national state was based on several factors besides the absolute rule of the Tudor monarchy, such as the birth of vernacular literature, the English translation of the Bible, the use of the Book of the English Prayer, the development of textile industries, and so forth.[46]

Although Hu Shi and Jiang Tingfu both agreed that China at the time had to put an end to warlordism and unify, they disagreed with each other on how to reach such a goal. To Jiang, only through a military campaign under a strong leadership, or a strong dictator, could the goal be realized. The current problem in China, said Jiang, was the existence of several minor dictators, or warlords; a strong dictator could and had to eliminate them because otherwise there would be no dictatorship. In the process, national unification was established.[47]

But such a unification was the last thing Hu Shi wanted. He advocated a "political unification" instead of "military unification," which meant establishing a national congress and provincial assemblies. He believed that these "democratic apparatus" *(minyi jigou)* would show the will of the people and generate a legitimate political potency that could check and even control warlordism.[48] When his opponents laughed at his democratic approach to political unification as naive, premature, and even utopian, Hu insisted that democracy was not a sophisticated system that required much preparation. "I have a bold opinion," he wrote, "based on my observation of the world politics in the past few decades. I feel that constitutional democracy is a sort of kindergarten political system. It is most suitable to train a nation that lacks political experience. Democracy is government by common sense, whereas enlightened monarchy is government by elites. Elites are hard to find whereas common sense is easy to develop. Our country lacks elites, therefore the best political training is constitutional democracy that can politically empower people in a gradual manner."[49]

But Hu's "bold opinion" aroused even more criticisms, one of which was from his friend and cofounder of the journal Ding Wenjiang. Ding also referred to Western history to make his argument that China then needed a strong dictatorship in order to reach national unification and bring about an effective national defense. "In fact," Ding wrote, "countries that succeeded in practicing constitutional democracy are those nations with rich political experience. By contrast, such countries as Russia, Italy, and Germany that relatively lacked political experience all have given up democracy and have established dictatorship. This shows that constitutional democracy is not a kindergarten system as Mr. Hu Shi believed."[50]

Ding's criticism put Hu in a defensive position. But he never entirely gave up his belief in democracy. He insisted that democracy was the best system for empowering people and giving them political rights. This was best shown in English history. Although the English enjoyed some political rights in the past, universal suffrage was quite recent. It suggested that democratic constitutionalism could gradually broaden its power base in the people.[51]

To be sure, with regard to the use of historical facts, Hu's opponents seem to do a better job. Early modern European history indeed showed that monarchy, absolute and enlightened alike, preceded the establishment of democracy. But Hu's argument seems constructive at the time, when he suggested that democracy can politically empower people and temper their political experience. This is indeed what he attempted to achieve in publishing the journal. Although the *Independent Critique* writers expressed different opinions, their debates amounted to an attempt to promote an activism in political participation in public, hence leading to the establishment of the public sphere. Hu's insistence on political unity through democratic apparatus reflected his unfailing belief in the political effect of public opinion. To him, public opinion *(minyi)* represented in the political arena a "public loyalty" *(gongzhong)* and it should replace the "private loyalty" *(sizhong)* that prevailed at the time in warlord separatism.[52] It was through this "public loyalty" that national unification could be realized.

Although different from Hu in regard to China's unification and political future, Hu's opponents, too, were committed to such an effort to foster an independent public opinion, despite their advocacy of a strong leadership in the central government. They placed their hope on the GMD government in order to make an effective defense against the Japanese invasion. Yet they never believed, it seems to me, that a dictatorial government was the ultimate solution to China's political problems. On the contrary, they only thought that they were living in a transitional period of history in which a strong leadership was necessary to end warlordism, promote economic development, and prepare for the future development of democracy. Their support of strong leadership notwithstanding, they were not hesitant to criticize the government. Both Ding Wenjiang and Jiang Tingfu, for instance, were critical of the GMD policies such as the "first internal pacification, then external resistance" *(Rangwai bixian an'nei)* and Chiang Kai-shek's military operation against the Communist force. Ding wrote a series of articles in 1932 and 1933 opposing Chiang's campaign. He argued that since Japan escalated its military action against China, the GMD government should concentrate on national defense and maintain regional independence. His suggestion to Chiang Kai-shek was that Chiang should "make a truce immediately with the Communists. The only condition to such a truce is not to attack each other during the anti-Japanese war." To Ding, Communism was not agreeable to China's social and economic condition; China was too backward to wage a socialist revolution. But he did not want the Communists to give up their belief either. "I only hope," Ding wrote, "that they take a practical political approach, sever the tie with the Comintern, give up revolution, change from a secret party to a public party, and request the freedom to discuss openly their belief."[53]

Likewise, Jiang Tingfu criticized the GMD government for the lack of open discussions on national defense. He suggested that the GMD lessen its control and separate military and civilian government in order to rally the people to its cause. Jiang attributed the problem to the want of a responsible parliamentary system in China.[54] Such "democratic" means, he strongly believed, were of importance for the GMD leadership in dealing with China's current situation.

As Jiang Tingfu and Ding Wenjiang urged the GMD to take a more liberal approach to its opposition party or opinion, Hu Shi went further. He suggested that the GMD allow opposition parties to participate in the government and believed that the competition could only improve the GMD leadership and rally people behind the constitution.[55] Yet they all showed interest in democratizing the GMD government. As Hu pointed out, the difference between the two sides in the debate on "democracy versus dictatorship" was not that they disagreed on *whether* China should establish democracy, but *when* it should. That his opponents objected to his proposal was simply because they idealized democracy too much to believe that it could be adopted immediately by China. This debate, he hoped, could establish a common political belief that democracy was not only good but also feasible.[56] To Hu Shi, democracy was feasible because it related to individual freedom, which was longed for by everyone. Individualism, he stated, was a major theme in the May Fourth Movement of 1919; the movement promoted free and independent individuality, which provided the genuine foundation of political democracy.[57]

Fu Sinian, another founder of the *Independent Critique*, echoed Hu's opinion about the May Fourth Movement. He urged the GMD government to sanction individual freedom. Among Fu's many publications in the journal, one deserved special attention, which was about Chen Duxiu's arrest. After being arrested in the English Concession in Shanghai, Chen was later turned over to the GMD government in Nanjing. Fu wrote an article requesting a fair trial for Chen, his former Beida teacher, despite the facts that Chen had become a Communist leader and Fu had decided to support the GMD. To give a just assessment of Chen's position, Fu divided Chen's career in three periods and stated that Chen made a great contribution to the "literary revolution" in the New Culture Movement that fostered reform on social morality. Chen's activity during the New Culture Movement was inspired, Fu emphasizes, by his "radical and thorough liberalism," exemplified in the French Revolution. Although Chen became a Communist leader in the third period, his liberalism did not allow him to follow subserviently the Comintern orders. Fu noticed that Chen had been expelled from the Chinese Communist Party at the time when he was apprehended. Hence Fu asked the GMD government to give Chen an open trial in order to "best accord to the law, best reveal the opinion of the people, consider the history of the Chinese revolution in the last twenty years, and show the revolutionary standpoint of the GMD government."[58]

Although Fu praised Chen's liberalism and his leadership role in the social reform—he called it "ethical reform"—during the 1920s, he was conspicuously silent in the "democracy versus dictatorship" discussion, lending no support to his mentor Hu Shi. Wang Fansen explains that "this [Fu's] unusual apathy indicates that Fu did not feel at ease with either of the two positions. He did not support absolutism, but he also perceived that, at that time, calls for democracy were naive."[59] But elsewhere, Fu did indicate his preference. He called for strong leadership from Chiang Kai-shek and believed that without a unified leadership, China would certainly be subjugated by Japan. Because of this, he urged other GMD party leaders not to compete with Chiang for power.[60] Thus viewed, his silence was not without a reason. He was sympathetic with Hu Shi's opponents. But because of his relationship with Hu, he chose not to say anything.

However, like Jiang Tingfu and Ding Wenjiang as well as Hu Shi, Fu Sinian rarely held back his criticisms of the GMD. In 1932, Fu wrote a short article, criticizing the GMD government for its unrealistic economic plans and unattainable promises. He openly expressed his disappointment that "The biggest problem [in the government] seems to be too much talk, too many plans, too many meetings, too much propaganda, yet short on practical planning, short on appropriate procedures. Up to date, the country has drawn to the bottom of the deep loophole, is there any face to brag about any more? It is better to complete some basic things before talking highly of any major constructive plans!"[61] Fu also criticized the GMD government in his article on Manchuria. Having analyzed the domestic and international situation a year after the Manchurian Incident, Fu openly expressed his great disappointment, lamenting that "under such a serious national disaster, it is odd to see that the rulers in China were even unable to find a way out." The GMD government, in Fu's opinion, was too tied down to its internecine political struggle to concentrate on national defense. "Till today, not only was the resistance not organized, but the government itself was neither one thing nor another, neither there nor not-there."[62] Despite his high hopes for Chiang Kai-shek, Fu also maintained an independent position.

The *Independent Critique*'s independence was shown nowhere more clearly in its discussion on China's foreign policy, especially in dealing with Japan's aggression. Hu Shi contributed a series of articles to the journal warning the people that this was not the time to openly engage in a war with Japan, given China's military weakness. Rather, China should seek peaceful negotiations with Japan to solve the crisis. This peaceful solution required both Japan and China to restrain their actions; the Chinese people should not act on emotions and the Japanese government should not escalate its military aggression. According to Hu Shi, Japan now faced choices between "nine generations of enmity or a century of friendship" with China, because "Japan can never conquer China by force. There would be a way for Japan to conquer China, that was to stop immediately the invasion and conquer *(zhengfu)* the mind of the Chinese people,"[63] which meant to develop friendship. Although Hu was not a defeatist but more a pacifist, his statement was tantamount to an endorsement of Chiang Kai-shek's unpopular nonresistance *(bu dikang)* policy, which made him very unpopular among his friends. Fu Sinian and Ding Wenjiang both disagreed with him. Fu even told Ding that he wanted to leave the journal, which made Hu Shi very sad—Fu was later persuaded by Ding not to do so.[64]

Some left-wing writers even accused Hu Shi of betraying the nation.[65]

But Hu Shi had his reasons. As Jerome Grieder has noticed, Hu Shi believed that international politics was no different from domestic politics. An active public opinion would promote China's democracy; in world politics, international organizations such as the League of Nations could, through the pressure of "world public opinion" *(shijie gonglun)*, restrain Japan's aggression. Having heard about the Lytton report, conducted by the League of Nations that condemned Japan's invasion in Manchuria, Hu wrote optimistically that the pressure of world opinion could "sober up the drunken Japanese."[66] Examples in European history were used to justify his optimism. On the one hand, he analyzed, if Japan chose to conquer China by force, it would become Weimar Germany, which ended with a dictatorship; to do otherwise could turn Japan into a strong and wealthy nation like Britain. On the other hand, he wrote, France lost Alsace-Lorraine to Prussia in 1871 but regained it forty-eight years later in World War I. He shared his historical wisdom with his readers: In the long life of a nation, fifty years of loss or suffering did not have a huge impact on the entire course of its history.[67] He called for endurance and restraint, especially by young college students. When many of them were agitated by Japan's aggression, Hu Shi and Ding Wenjiang urged them to focus on their studies, for China would need their talents and education.[68]

But Hu Shi's admonition had no appeal to his students at the time, including the most loyal one—Fu Sinian, nor did his warning have any effect on Japan. Two years after occupying Manchuria, Japan in 1933, concluded the notorious Tanggu Truce with the warlords in northern China, resulting in a pro-Japanese government. But this still did not change Hu's intention to seek a peaceful solution. It was not until 1935 when Japan plotted to establish the "North China Autonomous Zone" that he and Fu Sinian stood together and openly protested against it.

Compared to Hu Shi, Fu Sinian long realized that resisting Japan was the only option for the Chinese people. When Hu praised the Lytton report on the Manchurian Incident for representing world public opinion, Fu, disagreeing with Hu, expressed his suspicion and urged the Chinese people to seek other alternatives. After the Tanggu Truce, he questioned the gesture of the Sino-Japanese reconciliation pursued by both the Japanese and Chinese governments. For him, there would be no peace between two unequal partners. "There is no country that can survive without cost," Fu warned, "there is no nation that can earn freedom without sacrifice and struggle." He advised the government to prepare for the worst, rather than wait under the illusion of peace.[69]

By exchanging different assessments about the domestic and international situations, the *Independent Critique* writers worked toward a common goal in forming an active public opinion. During 1932 and 1937, the journal was an indispensable forum in China's politics, representing a distinct voice from the prominent Chinese intelligentsia. According to some studies, the majority of the contributions to the journal came from university professors and students, especially from Beijing University and Qinghua University.[70] Their opinions received not only public attention, but also the attention of the government.

Although the journal published criticisms of the GMD government, the government leaders, especially Chiang Kai-shek, seemed to be interested in these intellectuals, as were the intellectuals in the government. Jiang Tingfu, for instance, met Chiang a few times, discussing the need for a centralized government, which resulted in Jiang's appointment in the government. Hu Shi also received extensive attention from the GMD leaders, as shown in his receiving of a few appointments from the GMD, although Hu turned them down. He believed that he should maintain his position as a liberal and stay away from governmental posts. On April 8, 1933, Hu wrote to Wang Jingwei (1883–1947), then the head of the executive *Yuan*: "I have thought it over, that I believe I can help the nation more if I stay outside of the government than inside the government. I want to keep myself in an independent position, but the reason is not to pursue fame in vanity, nor to protect myself. I only want to maintain a detached status and say some unbiased words should the nation need them in critical moments. It is not right for a nation not to have that kind of people; the more there are of them, the more stable its social foundation. . . . I hope you can allow me to stay outside the government in order for me to become a critic-minister *(zhengchen)* to the country and a critic-friend *(zhengyou)* to the government."[71]

Obviously, what Hu intended to become was also what he hoped for the journal. But to remain as a "critic-friend" was never easy. At several times the warlords were irritated by the journal's criticisms and ordered its confiscation. Once the journal had to suspend its publication for more than four months as ordered by Song Zheyuan (1885–1940), the warlord in north China.[72] In addition, there were problems within. Although Hu Shi declined a few offers from the government, some of his colleagues, such as Ding Wenjiang, did not. Following Jiang Tingfu and Ding Wenjiang, Weng Wenhao

(1889–1971), the British-educated geologist, also joined the government. After the Sino-Japanese conflict turned into a full-scale war, Hu Shi himself accepted an appointment to become China's ambassador to the United States, although he vowed to make it a temporary assignment. Hu's becoming the ambassador officially ended the publication of the journal. This also ended the attempt by these intellectuals to form an independent political voice based on their understandings of history.

History and Politics

Having analyzed the achievement of Hu Shi and his group in shaping China's politics, Eugene Lubot remarks that Hu Shi was a true liberal in an illiberal age.[73] Indeed, Hu in many discussions was in a defensive position. Intellectuals, even the ones who were exposed to liberal ideas, appeared eager to make contributions to the cause of national salvation, serving the government or supporting a "strong leader." Thus Chinese liberalism incurred a big setback because of the war. In the following pages we shall analyze the impact of the war on the careers of Fu Sinian, Yao Congwu, and Luo Jialun during the 1940s and the 1950s.

If Ding Wenjiang, Jiang Tingfu, and others chose to join the government, Fu Sinian took on a different project. After the loss of Manchuria, Fu gathered a group of historians and decided to write a general history of China. Their goal was to present a Chinese view of Asian history, refuting the Japanese interpretation. As noticed by Tao Xisheng, an *Independent Critique* contributor who also cosigned with He Bingsong the Declaration, by introducing the term *(Toyo no bunmei)* "Eastern civilization", or simply "Eastern history" *(toyoshi)*, Japanese historians reinterpreted Asian history and vindicated Japan's occupation of Manchuria and other Asian regions.[74] Fu Sinian's project thus was an attempt to thwart the Japanese effort and defy their false claim on Manchuria. As a collective project, it initially involved a few scholars. As Fu was to write its first volume about ancient Manchuria, Yao Congwu, Jiang Tingfu, Xu Zhongshu (1898–1991), Fang Zhuangyou (1902–1970), and Xiao Yishan (1902–1978) were to write subsequent volumes about Manchuria's late history, its relations with other regions and the makeup of its people. In 1932 after Fu completed a short history of ancient Manchuria, however, none of the others completed theirs.[75]

Fu called his book *An Outline History of Northeast China (Dongbei shigang)*, avoiding the word *Manchuria*. After he completed it, Li Ji, his colleague in the Institute of History and Philology, translated it into English under the title *Manchuria in Chinese History*. The GMD government presented it, with other documents, to the Lytton Commission to evidence its sovereignty over Manchuria.[76] In its belated report, the Lytton Commission indeed supported China and denounced Japan's invasion. Of course, the Lytton report did not stop Japan from invading China, but Fu must have felt that he did his job by contributing his knowledge to the country. To answer his own question, Fu did what a scholar can for his country.

Fu's argument in the book was quite clear. What remains interesting, however, was his methodological approach. In writing the book he implemented the methods he advocated in leading the Institute of History and Philology. Using the method of history and philology, for instance, he studied the myths in ancient Manchuria and compared them with those known to other Chinese regions. Employing the method of anthropology, he examined ethnic behaviors of the Manchurian inhabitants and compared them with those of the rest of Chinese. He also based his research on a variety of sources, ranging from written and material to linguistic and archaeological. Thus viewed, his book not only provided an exclusive account of Manchurian history, but practiced modern historical methodology. As a conclusion, Fu stated that according to the evidence, Manchuria was always an important part of ancient China and was long ruled by a Chinese government. In fact, he stressed, Manchuria could be considered one of the earliest origins of Chinese civilization. By comparison, its tie with either Korea or Japan was tenuous.[77]

A successful political project notwithstanding, Fu's book was the result of hastiness, containing mistakes and even flaws that were detrimental to his scholarly reputation. No sooner had his book come out than it incurred relentless criticisms from his fellow historians. Interestingly, the criticisms centered on Fu's use and interpretation of the sources, an area in which he had made himself an expert. Miao Fenglin, for example, enumerated a number of factual mistakes Fu committed in the book. At the end, Miao ridiculed that Fu had broken the record for mistake-making in historical writing. Besides Fu's mistakes in treating his sources, Miao and Chen Hesheng (1901–?), another critic, also found that Fu overlooked and discarded, intentionally or unintentionally, many available sources, probably because they would contradict his thesis.[78]

Having made so many avoidable mistakes, Fu's history of Manchuria became almost a mockery to his campaign for scientific history, to which source criticism was considered crucial. How could one believe that it was the same Fu Sinian who had claimed "no historical sources, no history" who had produced such shabby scholarship? Many expected Fu to give an explanation. Fu did nothing. He only kept those critical reviews in his possession and thought about writing a rebuttal, but never did.[79] This could be interpreted to mean that he felt it was difficult to defend his work, hence admitting to the accuracy of the criticisms. But his lack of action could also indicate a different motive. Given Fu's keen nationalist concern, it is possible that he might not have committed these errors by simple mistake. "It is unbelievable," writes Wang Fansen, "that Fu could had been ignorant of the fact that in past dynasties China had exercised no complete control over Manchuria."[80] Obviously, Fu should have known better of the history. But he was compelled to say the opposite in order to defy Japan's claim. He probably thought that his critics made an even bigger mistake, a political mistake, by disclosing his mistakes. In Fu's mind, nationalism outweighed scholarship, at least at that time.

It is thus no coincidence that during the mid- and/or late 1930s, Fu Sinian began writing a national history of China, entitled "*A Revolutionary History of the Chinese Nation*" *(Zhongguo minzu gemingshi)*. While an incomplete and thus never published manuscript, it provides an important source of evidence for us to see the change of Fu's idea of and approach to history, in response to the national crisis. Unlike his previous emphasis on source examination, Fu in the beginning of the book declared that "although the book can be considered a monograph, it is in fact written for a practical purpose, which is didactic, not evidential."[81] In other words, he did not intend to produce a text based on evidential research, or source criticism, but simply to help his readers learn about the past experience for better understanding the present situation. This intention is also shown in his definitions of both "nation" *(minzu)* and "national revolution" *(minzu geming)*, especially the latter. According to Fu Sinian, the term *nation*, by quoting Sun Yat-sen, referred to a group of people who shared the same ethnic origin, lifestyle, language, religion, and culture. While this definition is not so particular, Fu's understanding of "national revolution" seems very specific. He emphasized that "national revolution" referred only to the uprising mounted by an oppressed majority of a nation against the oppressive minority of another nation. That is, "national revolution" is the same as national defense, in which one nation fights to survive the invasion of another.

This definition of "national revolution" shaped the structure of the work. Given his interest in describing the conflict between nations in China, Fu began his work in the third century, after the fall of the Han Dynasty, which was generally considered an end of the classical period of Chinese culture and the beginning of a new age when Han Chinese faced challenges from non-Han ethnic groups in the north and the infiltration of foreign cultures and religion, such as Buddhism. With this focus, Fu left out of his work the political struggles that occurred within the Han Chinese nation, as well as the examples of peaceful assimilation and accommodation of non-Han Chinese groups in Chinese history. The bulk of his writing was centered on the events that depicted Han Chinese heroism in defending their land and culture, such as the unsuccessful yet worthwhile attempts made by both the Northern and Southern Song Dynasties to fend off the invasions of the Jin (Jurchen) and the Mongol during the twelfth and the thirteenth centuries. While this example is the only one given by Fu in his incomplete manuscript, it is sufficient for us to see the scope and focus of his entire project. In a few places, Fu did mention that he also planed to discuss similar events in Chinese history through the founding of the Republic in 1912, which, in his opinion, was a prime example for the success of national revolution in modern China, for Sun Yat-sen and his party successfully overthrew the Manchu rule of the Qing Dynasty.

Although Fu failed to complete his manuscript, he highlighted the main points, or the "general ideas" *(gaiyi)*, he hoped he could accomplish with his writing. These were considered main traits of the Chinese nation:

1. The Chinese nation was peace-loving, cherishing a peaceful relation with her neighbors. When faced with an invasion, however, she would fight back with all her strength.
2. Even if the Chinese nation was overrun by foreign nations from time to time, it would never obliterate the national awareness, which would reemerge whenever there was an opportunity.
3. The Chinese nation would never forget her territorial losses to the enemy.
4. Although there were at times problems and weaknesses, the Chinese nation would always come back and cure her ills once a new and effective leadership was established.

These traits, Fu Sinian concluded, as they were realized and amplified by the modern Chinese, would lead the Chinese nation to a glorious age, rivaling the glory and power of the Tang Dynasty in the past. By stressing these national traits, Fu demonstrated his didactic approach to historiography, which was, quite obviously, different from his earlier scientific and positivist approach. Indeed, during and after the war, it seems that Fu no longer had the same confidence in holding the positivist stance in regard to the universal value of science.[82] His study of history became more and more politicized, as did his career. But due to his untimely death in 1950, we are unable to find more concrete evidence about how the change affected his understanding of history, as well as his leadership at the Institute of History and Philology.

There were still other examples that demonstrate Fu's strong nationalist commitment. As much as he would like to use his book to defy Japan's claim on Manchuria, he was eager to see the Chinese army recover Manchuria. When his son was born, he named him Rengui, after Tang general Liu Rengui (601/2–685) who defeated the Japanese in Korea several centuries previously.[83] As shown in his *A Revolutionary History of the Chinese Nation*, Fu's deep love for the Chinese nation followed the demarcation between the Hans and non-Hans. His friend recalled that Fu at that time would be particularly embarrassed if anyone mentioned his ancestor, Fu Yiqian, an otherwise very honorable figure due to his successes in the civil service examination. Fu despised him because Fu Yiqian took the examinations under the early Qing. His ensuing service to the Manchu ruler disgraced the Han Chinese.[84]

Fu Sinian's nationalist feeling for his country, especially Han China, was far from extraordinary for his generation. Yao Congwu's conduct during the period, also reflected nationalism. First, Yao's return from Germany was related to Japan's occupation of Manchuria, according to Wang Deyi, Yao's assistant during the 1950s and the 1960s at Taiwan University;[85] Yao probably thought he could do something, for China's northern borders were a focus of his study. After his return, in addition to teaching the historical methods course, Yao taught two other courses: the history of the Huns and the histories of the Liao, Jin, and Yuan Dynasties.[86] Both of them had something to do with Manchuria. The Jin Dynasty, for example, was established by the Manchu, then known as the Jurchen, in the twelfth century.

Besides teaching, as mentioned earlier, Yao also participated in Fu Sinian's project on writing the history of Manchuria. Although he failed to complete his writing, his participation indicated that he was no longer a bookish student who cared little about anything around him, as his behavior in the May Fourth Movement suggested. Indeed, Japan's invasion had even changed Yao Congwu. From his return to China in 1934 to 1949 when he followed the GMD to Taiwan, Yao published only about one article every three and a half years. His major publications during that period included an introduction to Franke's Chinese historical study and an article on the religious activities among the Jurchens and Mongols.[87] Some have explained that Yao's meager record of scholarly productivity during the period was a result of his high devotion to teaching.[88] But a more convincing reason, it seems to me, is that Yao probably was involved in many nonacademic projects.

The Sino-Japanese conflict exerted a formidable impact on the lives of the academics and students. In response to Japan's military offensive, for example, Beijing students organized several demonstrations, demanding that the GMD government take prompt military action. The largest student rally was held on December 9, 1935 in Beijing, in which Beida students again played the vanguard role. There was a widely circulated saying in society describing student patriotism at the time: "Despite the largeness of all north China, there was no place to set down a peaceful study table."[89] Political instability and national crisis fundamentally changed the campus climate. Few scholars could remain indifferent to the ebullient tide of nationalism.

When the Japanese army launched a large-scale invasion in 1937, academic life became even more difficult. Refusing to collaborate with the Japanese invaders, Beida faculty and students began a year-long migration and finally reached Kunming, the southwest city on the Yunnan Plateau in 1938. In Kunming the university was incorporated into the National Southwest Associated University *(Xinan Lianda)* with other universities from northern China.[90] Despite all the hardships and changes, Yao proposed to form an ad hoc committee for collecting and preserving sources about the ongoing war. It was called "The Committee for Soliciting Historical Sources of the Sino-Japanese War" *(Zhongri zhanzhengshi shiliao zhengji weiyuanhui)*, and it involved many of his fellow members on the university faculty.[91]

In his proposal, Yao thought it worthwhile to collect the materials as follows:

1. government documents, including statements, reports, telegrams, meeting minutes, and memoirs of firsthand witnesses or participants;

2. foreign reports about the war, especially in the major newspapers such as the American *New York Times* and the English *Times*;
3. published reports and records;
4. war ruins and relics.

The reason for doing so was that, Yao believed, these materials were historical sources. He made it clear that by collecting them, the project would help the work of the historian in the future. In order to do a good job, the committee should provide adequate supervision and hire only qualified people to first categorize the sources and then publish them as source books.[92]

For Yao this kind of source collection was important because it was the foundation of historical writing, both in China and the West. In the Song Dynasty, he noted, historical writing proliferated and overshadowed that of other dynasties because the people paid great attention to the preservation of sources. Sima Guang was able to complete his magnum opus, *Comprehensions Mirror,* because he had access to a great number of sources at the time. However, after completing the writing, Sima decided to eliminate the traces of sources from the text in order to improve the readability of the book (obviously Song historians had not yet learned to use footnotes). The success of Song historiography, Yao explained, lay not in the work of Sima Guang but in the work of many lesser known historians who collected and prepared sources. How much a historian could accomplish in his study depended on the availability of sources.

Yao also referred to his own experience in Germany to emphasize the importance of source preservation. Having worked as an intern in the archives of Berlin and the Rhineland, Yao said, he learned that it was very easy for valuable sources to be lost. If one did not do the collecting early, it would make the job much more difficult when people wanted to collect them later on, for they would find it difficult to place them in the right context.[93] Due to his historian's training and insight, Yao realized that the struggle of modern Chinese against the Japanese at the time was going to be an extremely important event in Chinese history. Having explained the importance of the project and prepared its implementation with his experience, however, Yao wrote to Chen Yinke and Fu Sinian, modestly asking them to be in charge of the project.[94]

Yao was also drawn to other extracurricular activities in Kunming. Like his friends, he chose to support the GMD government.

In 1936, as the chairman of the history department, Yao and 104 other university professors cosigned a petition to the GMD government, expressing their deep concern for the hazardous situation in northern China. In the face of a large-scale Japanese invasion in 1937, Yao and other leading Beida professors telegraphed Chiang Kai-shek, stating their full support of Chiang's belated decision of resisting further Japanese military action.

At the Associated University, he was at one time the coordinator of the Youth League of the Three Principles of People *(Sanminzhuyi qingniantuan)*, an affiliated youth organization of the GMD. His leadership role, although ineffective, made him a target of attack from the pro-CCP students on campus.[95]

After World War II, Yao was appointed president of Henan University by the GMD government. In 1948 he became a member of the National Assembly in which Chiang Kai-shek was elected president of the Republic of China. But all this came at the time when the GMD was losing to the CCP on all grounds. On receiving the appointment Yao returned to his home province. However, he was not able to hold the position. In fact, his days in the mainland were numbered. As a result of the GMD's military fiasco, Henan Province was soon lost to the CCP. To follow the defeated GMD army, Yao disguised himself as a peasant, walking continuously for three days, often on the verge of starvation, until he finally reached the GMD occupied region in the Jiangsu Province. Having retreated to Suzhou, he made a great effort to shelter the students of Henan University, but with little success. As the university by that time was virtually disintegrated, Yao resigned from his presidency and became director of the Palace Museum *(Gugong bowuyuan)*. In 1949, escorting court documents and archives, he went to Taiwan and later was appointed by Fu Sinian as history professor at the National Taiwan University, wherein Fu was a newly appointed president.

Compared to Yao Congwu, Fu Sinian also went through a great deal of agony and frustration during the 1940s. In World War II he was drawn deeper and deeper into politics, taking various positions to help the GMD, aiming to prevent it from a total collapse in World War II and from its defeat by Communists in the ensuing Civil War (1945–1949). For example, he was sent by the GMD on a mission to Yan'an to meet with Mao Zedong, whom he first met at Beida when Mao was a petty clerk in the Beida library, to seek a possibility of fostering a new alliance between the CCP and the GMD. At this reunion, although Fu was not impressed with Mao, he was somewhat struck by Mao's ambition; at the same time, he began to realize

Mao's ability to change China. But he did not give up hope for the GMD. Rather he became more and more critical of the GMD government, hoping to make it better. His courage and outspokenness turned him into a well-known figure for political uprightness and integrity, in contrast to the widespread corruption in the GMD government and society.

Despite his earnest expectation, however, Fu did not see much improvement in the GMD government. In fact, many of his remonstrations fell on deaf ears. He once demanded that the head of the Executive *Yuan* Song Ziwen resign. He did not succeed. Another time, he was insulted by a politician in a debate. Fu was so angry that he challenged the opponent to a duel.[96] Much as he disliked the government, he never lost his loyalty, nor did he become uninterested in politics. His bold criticism of the GMD and the government won over many supporters. In 1948 when Fu was in the United States, treating his hypertension, his friends and supporters at home nominated him to be the candidate for the deputy chair of the Legislative *Yuan*, challenging the GMD candidate Chen Lifu. Fu lost the race, due mainly to the dominance of Chen's C. C. Clique in the Legislative *Yuan*.[97] However, Fu did not seem to mind these "losses"; his commitment to helping the country was above anything else. As his friend Cheng Cangbo (1903–?) put it, Fu Sinian in that period acted like a loyal mandarin *(jingsheng)*—reminding us of his family tradition—who believed that his loyalty should never change when the country was in a profound crisis and when his "prince" was in deep trouble, regardless of his personal gain and interest.[98]

But as a historian, Fu was a disappointment. On various occasions, Fu expressed his frustration because he was not able to pursue his scholarly interest. In a letter to Hu Shi, he wrote that he had planned to write four books in the 1940s: a book of "*Kultur Kampf*" [his own words], another on the origin of human beings, another on "Causality and Chances in history" [his own words], and last, a biography of the Ming Emperor Zhu Yuanzhang, but he did not even start any of them before his death. In the letter, Fu told Hu that he was uneasy about his political involvements which took too much of his time. He was unable even to finish his book on ancient China and its peoples that had been started in the 1930s.[99]

In December 1951, barely two years after the GMD government retreated to Taiwan, Fu, as president of Taiwan University, drew the final and dramatic chapter of his life; he died of a cerebral hemorrhage when he gave an emotional speech defending the need of

Taiwan's higher education at the Senate House of Taipei city. His tragic death ended his hectic and rich life. Fu devoted himself to the nationalist cause for building a modern China. To this end, he helped develop a new understanding of Chinese history, drawing on his knowledge of modern science. But Fu could never fully settle down as a professional historian. If in his study of history he was indebted to traditional learning, in his political involvement he was influenced by the mandarin tradition as well as nationalism, which dictated his attitude toward the government in wartime. To some extent, Fu's life and career were an epitome of the tradition-modernity binary of the May Fourth generation.

Fu Sinian indeed was not alone. Luo Jialun, his long-time friend, showed more willingness to put aside scholarship for political participation. During the 1930s and 1940s, Luo was president of a few universities and these universities were often tied closely to the GMD party. In World War II, he first led the GMD party delegation to Xinjiang, a northwestern province, for cultural and economic investigation, and later was appointed China's ambassador to India.[100]

Moreover, as a government official, unlike Fu Sinian and Hu Shi who remained sometimes critical of the GMD, Luo represented the official position in regard to its foreign and domestic policies. For example, when college students demonstrated in the streets protesting the Japanese invasion in the 1930s, he considered these actions as charged by blind enthusiasm, often incited by "ambitious plotters," namely the Communists.[101] His remark indicated that by that time, Luo, a former student leader, had switched to the other side—the side of the government. He became increasingly suspicious about the same student activism he himself sparked earlier during and after the May Fourth Movement. By comparison, Hu Shi and Fu Sinian took a less partisan (anti-Communist) approach; they tried to persuade the students to focus on their studies.

Luo, too, appeared less enthusiastic about learning from the West but more interested in enhancing national pride in scholarship. In 1928 Luo, as the president of Qinghua University, gave a short farewell speech to a group of students who were departing for the United States for study, in which he emphasized that the students needed to seek an equal scholarly place for Chinese culture in the world.[102] On another occasion, he cautioned his audience that not all American scholars were good enough to teach Chinese students. He attacked H. E. Barnes's work, *A History of Historical Writing*, for its sketchy narration, unsound judgment, and hasty research, especially when it was compared with G. P. Gooch's

History and Historians in the Nineteenth Century in the field of historiographcial study. He also, noticeably, criticized James H. Robinson, one of his Columbia professors, for publishing many books hammering on virtually the same thesis.

To be sure, Luo's criticisms were not completely illegitimate. But like He Bingsong's recommendation of the China-based approach to cultural construction, Luo's remarks suggested a retreat from the May Fourth position in regard to cultural exchange. In order to link scholarship more closely to the cause of national salvation, they became more and more inclined to perceive China's relation with the world in a China-West dichotomous manner. Luo, for instance, pointed out that Western scholars rarely understood the importance of *shu er bu zuo* (lit. to teach rather than write), a Confucian teaching. Instead, they were pressed to publish, which only led to mediocre scholarship. In Luo's opinion, while some Western scholars appeared very productive, they were not as good as their Chinese students might have expected.[103]

As Luo became more critical of Western scholarship, he also changed his view in regard to the significance of the May Fourth/New Culture Movement in Chinese history. As a luminary of the May Fourth era, Luo was asked to write a number of recollections for various occasions. But these commemorative essays hardly followed a consistent line of thinking; most of them were written in response to the political need at a particular time. What remained consistent was his acknowledgment of its historical significance. In an article written in 1950, for example, he praised the movement for creating a new culture. He used both the English word *enlightenment* and German word *Aufklärung* to describe its nature. But he considered the German word more appropriate, because it connoted the meaning: "to clear up." Luo proclaimed that the goal of the May Fourth Movement was to clear up the minds of the people in order to embrace a new culture, which was science and the spirit of freedom.[104] For him, the May Fourth Movement was crucial to the construction of modern Chinese culture.

But in regard to what was cleared up and what was created by the movement, Luo's answer became evasive and vague. Or, he might not want to spell them out due to various political reasons. In the early days, Luo stated that the aim of the May Fourth Movement was to construct modern Chinese culture, which included criticisms of the cultural tradition, replacing literary Chinese with the vernacular, pursuing modern scholarship, the importation of Western culture, and social liberation such as the emancipation of Chinese women.[105] To reach these goals, students alone, Luo believed, were inadequate for the job. In 1920, for example, he stressed that though the movement promoted a new culture in which scientific research was regarded as important, not many students at that time were ready to engage in serious, scientific research. While people looked forward to a new cultural era, students enjoyed their popularity that resulted from political action. Driven by their ambitions for achieving more social fame, some student leaders even became involved in internecine power struggles. According to Luo, this kind of behavior betrayed the spirit of the May Fourth. He suggested that from then on, students should pursue two causes: social revolution and cultural reform. To wage a social revolution, students should go to the people and share their grievances. For a cultural renovation, Luo especially emphasized two things: translating Western works; and fostering modern scholarship. He regretted that he had become too involved in various social activities that he was not suited for temperamentally.[106]

Luo's life turned out quite ironically to be the opposite of what he was looking for in the early 1920s. In the 1930s after taking government positions, he became less and less exhilarated by the student activism embodied by the May Fourth Movement, especially when college students at the time appeared easily swayed by radical and Communist ideas. Some political conservatives charged that radical students were influenced by the May Fourth Movement and that the movement gave birth to Chinese Communism. In order to defend the movement and himself, he in his later writings emphasized that the movement had little to do with Communism. He deliberately downplayed Chen Duxiu's and Li Dazhao's leadership role and promoted Hu Shi as the sole leader of the movement, placing Hu's "literary reform" in the foreground. Moreover, Luo tried to bring Sun Yat-sen into the picture. He tried hard to establish a relationship between the GMD and the May Fourth Movement through Sun Yat-sen, although Sun's influence on the movement was indirect and unnoticeable.[107]

Accordingly, Luo Jialun's reinterpretations of the May Fourth era was a reflection of politics in history. The political influence was also shown in the late years of Yao Congwu, albeit with different manifestations. After settling down in Taiwan in the 1950s, Yao entered a period of efflorescence in publication. He wrote about fifty research articles and some translations and became an authority on the history of mid-imperial China, specializing in the histories of the Song, Jin, Liao, Xixia, and Yuan Dynasties. However, many of his publications carried a perceptible political undertone. For example, from his observation of the interactions between the Han and ethnic Chinese in the past, Yao concluded that while Han Chinese culture suffered many setbacks, it always came out to be the ultimate winner. By stating this, he implied that since China had warded off many challenges in the past, it, represented now by the GMD government, could also overcome the problems caused by the Japanese as well as the Communists.

Noticeably, Yao's understanding of Chinese culture followed both political and ethnic lines. In history, he adopted a Han-centric approach to describe the ebb and flow of Chinese culture and in politics, he supported the GMD. In other words, he used the self-other dichotomy to guide his research and his attitude toward the political change in China, in which the "self" was the Han Chinese nation as represented by the GMD government and the "other" was the non-Hans in the past and Communism at his time. Thus Yao's research was driven by this perceived analogy between history and reality, past and present. In his opinion, while the GMD suffered a great loss by retreating to Taiwan, it would eventually find its victorious destiny, just like the Han Chinese during the Song and Yuan Dynasties.

During the 1950s, Yao wrote two articles that deserved our attention here. One was his "My Opinion of the Evolution of National History" *(Guoshi kuoda mianyan de yidian kanfa)* and the other "The Backbone of the Harmonious East Asian Confucian Culture: A Historical Perspective" *(Cong lishi shang kan dongya rujia datong wenhua de liguo jingshen)*. His first article surveyed the course of Chinese history. He asserted that Chinese history had lasted four thousand years without interruption and that this longevity and continuity resulted from the vitality in Confucianism. Besides Confucianism, Yao pointed out, there were three contributing factors: First, China had a wide geographical terrain and rich resources that helped her people to overcome challenges and accommodate foreign influence. In his opinion, the Great Wall, Yellow River, and Yangzi River were three natural defense lines that helped the Han Chinese fight the nomads and preserve their culture. Second, Confucian philosophy provided the foundation for the development of Chinese culture. According to Yao, Confucianism was humanistic, harmonious, introspective, and knowledge-oriented. Because of this foundation, Chinese culture became unique in comparison with others. Third, the long course of Chinese history provided a variety of experiences to the people and enabled them to cope with different situations. In the past, the Chinese people established powerful empires and developed sophisticated political systems and social institutions that were an important and useful legacy.[108]

As Yao admitted, his emphasis on the importance of Confucianism was drawn on the work of his German mentor Otto Franke. He reiterated Franke's argument, posited originally in the *Geschichte des Chinesischen Reiches*, that the longevity of Chinese history benefited from the development of a harmonious Confucian culture. This harmoniousness was shown in the ability of the Han Chinese to assimilate nomadic peoples and even turned them into successors of Han culture. In the meantime, he also became indebted to some of his fellow Chinese historians, such as Fu Sinian, Lei Haizong (1902–1962), and Liang Qichao, in developing his thesis. Like them, Yao believed that while the growth of Chinese culture was dependent on interactions of border peoples and the Han Chinese, it was the ability of the Han Chinese to assimilate and sinicize the others that accounted for the longevity of Chinese history.[109] He stated:

> When the Tang Dynasty fell in 907, Han culture lost its originality, and the military lost its strength. Border peoples such as the Khitan, Jurchen, Mongol, and Manchu respectively in northeast China came to the mainland and founded their dynasties. But because Confucian culture was appealing and the Song and Ming Dynasties established by the Han Chinese retained some military strength, these nomadic peoples were sinicized as soon as they crossed the Great Wall. As a result, the old culture was supplemented by new elements while the new culture was inspired by the old culture. This [cultural interaction] generated the revival of Confucian culture.[110]

Why did Confucian culture appeal to the nomadic peoples? Yao explained it in his second article. He considered four aspects of Confucian culture, which he thought were advantageous and superior:

1. emphasis on the industriousness of people;
2. humanistic approach to politics;
3. advocacy of meritocracy;
4. sophisticated philosophy of history.[111]

Of course, whether these four actually represented the value of Confucianism is an open question. For example, whether Confucianism, with an emphasis on *li* (rites) rather than *fa* (law), was more humanistic than others is quite debatable, for as a political ideology it supported autocratic monarchies in China for about two millennia. But Yao's intention to commend Confucianism was not only for stating an academic opinion, but also a political one. During the Cold War of the 1950s, especially in the wake of the Korean War, there was a great amount of tension on both sides of the Taiwan Strait: as the GMD leaders were preparing to return to the mainland, providing the U.S. support, the CCP launched political campaigns aiming at re-educating Chinese intellectuals through Marxist and Stalinist doctrines. To Yao Congwu, the Communist victory in China was a foreign cultural invasion, similar to what China had experienced in the past. He hoped that Confucianism could help the GMD, which carried on its legacy, to regain its control of China.

Yao's belief in the efficacy of Confucianism derived from his study of history, especially histories of the Khitan, Jurchen, and Mongol. For example, while the Khitan, who founded the Liao Dynasty in the tenth century in north China, defeated the Song army and established the dynasty on the conquered land, they gradually accepted Han Chinese culture and lifestyle from the Song. After conquering some farmlands, the Khitan chose not to turn it into grassland to raise livestock, which had been the original purpose for invading Han China, but established "Han towns" *(Hancheng)* and allowed the Han Chinese to live on the land and continue their farming. The Han Chinese who lived under the Liao Dynasty were entitled to their social customs, language, and lifestyle. Later on, the Khitan rulers even allowed the Han Chinese to take part in civil service examinations, although the Khitan were recruited from other channels. But despite this "dual" treatment, which was aimed to prevent Khitan culture from being sinicized, the Khitan were not immune to the influence of Han Chinese culture. After about two hundred years, Yao found, the social and political structure of the Liao Dynasty became almost the same as that of the Song Dynasty. In fact, to the peoples in central and northern Asia, Khitan culture represented Chinese culture. In ancient Russian and Persian, he noted, China was known as "Ki-tan" or "Ki-tai." And in ancient English and German, China was sometimes referred to as "Cathay" or "Kathay," indicating the cultural sameness and integration between the Khitan and the Chinese.[112]

The same thing also happened to the Jurchen, Yao claimed. Although the Jurchens did not found their dynasty, the Jin, until the twelfth century, they had challenged the Song Dynasty almost at the same time as the Khitan did. After the establishment of the Jin, the Jurchen became Song's arch-enemy for two hundred years, until they were both subdued by the Mongol in the thirteenth century. Compared to the Khitan, however, the Jurchen appeared much more cautious about the influence of Han Chinese culture. To Yao, the Jin Emperor Shizong's (1123–1189) attitude toward Han culture was representative of the Manchu attitude toward the Han. On the one hand, Jin Shizong acknowledged the necessity of accepting Chinese culture and using Chinese officials in his government. On the other hand, he still hoped to hold on to the values of Jurchen culture, such as straightforwardness, frankness, and martial spirit. What appealed to Jin Shizong was a combination of Jurchen culture with Confucian education. To implement his plan, Jin Shizong required all the Jurchen to learn how to write and read in Chinese as they learned to become riders and hunters. As a result, the Jurchen too were gradually sinicized.

Although reluctant at the beginning, the Manchus' adoption of Han culture, Yao argued, was beneficial to them as well as to the growth of Chinese culture as a whole. The Jin rulers' effort to combine good traits from both cultures paved the way for the Jurchen to rise again in the seventeenth century. The founding of the Qing Dynasty, he believed, represented a success not only of Jurchen culture, but also of Han culture, because it attested to the fact that Han Chinese culture could absorb valuable elements from other cultures. To Yao, the Qing Dynasty embodied the second high tide of Confucian culture—the first occurred prior to the Tang Dynasty.[113]

The success of the Qing Dynasty suggested, Yao contended, that Chinese culture was endowed with "cosmopolitanism" *(shijie zhuyi)* and "objectivity" *(keguanxing)*. By "cosmopolitanism" he meant the openness of the Han Chinese to foreign influences; by "objectivity" he referred to his argument that Han Chinese did not have any prejudice against foreign rulers, as long as the rulers contributed to the growth of their culture.[114] Apparently Yao's argument is very subjective and hence problematic. He not only begged the question that the Qing's reign was indebted to Han cultural influence, he also overlooked, intentionally, the historical fact that the Han Chinese resisted strongly any non-Han invasion, including the Manchu's.[115] If Chinese culture appeared "cosmopolitan" and "objective" in the seventeenth century, or for that matter in any other period, these qualities were not a matter of choice, but of military coercion and political oppression.

Yao's study of Yuan history, which was probably what he plowed most thoroughly during the period, amounted to another attempt to celebrate the success of the sinicization of the non-Han Chinese. In

1966, Yao published a long and detailed treatise on Chinggis Khan (1167–1227), one of the founding fathers of the Mongol Empire and a famous ruler in China. In his biographic study, Yao elected to describe Chinggis Khan's friendship with Qiu Chuji (1148–1227), a priest of the Quanzhen religion that was a sect of Daoism. From this perspective, Yao managed to present a lesser known side of Khan's life: his interest in, or respect for, Daoism, a native Chinese religion. Yao depicted in minute detail how Qiu Chuji won Chinggis Khan's trust and how this trust helped Qiu to spread his religion. In describing the popularity of the Quanzhen religion in northern China, Yao did not forget to add that because of his privilege in Khan's court, Qiu and his other Quanzhen priests helped shield many Han intellectuals from attacks of the brutal Mongol army in its continual conquest of China.[116]

If Chinggis Khan's interest in Han culture was limited to Daoism, his grandson Khubilai Khan (1215–1294), Yao argued, made a systematic attempt to reconcile with the Han Chinese, hence initiating the sinicization process for the Mongol. As a founder of the Yuan Dynasty, a Mongol power in China proper, Khubilai treated the Han Chinese softly, in contrast to the harsh policy in the earlier reigns of his brothers and uncles. In fact, Yao argued, Khubilai respected Confucian culture and used Han intellectuals to be his close advisers. More important, Khubilai's reconciliating policy toward the Han people helped him consolidate the Yuan Dynasty in China. Thus Yao reiterated his thesis that the success of non-Han government depended on whether or not the ruler was willing to embrace Han Confucian culture.[117]

In addition to his study of the sinicization of the non-Hans, Yao tried to present the vitality of Han culture through inspiring examples found in the Han people. Most of them were generals and statesmen, who either defended the territory of the Han Chinese dynasty or extended Confucian culture. Yao's article on Yang Jiye, published in 1955, was such an example. As a general of the Northern Song Dynasty, Yang Jiye was a legendary figure in Chinese history for his courage on the battlefield and his victory over the Khitan. While a solid research paper in which Yao used sources of both sides, Song and Liao, to compose his account, this treatise was written specifically for a political reason. Yao hoped to use it to help boost the morale of the GMD army, which had reached its nadir after its defeat on the mainland.[118]

Yao had hopes not only for army generals but also civilian officials. For that reason, he studied Fu Bi, a loyal and skillful diplomat of the Northern Song Dynasty. Fu's successes in negotiating with the Khitan king, according to Yao, helped prevent several years of military conflict between the Song and the Liao. In discussing the triangular relation of the Song, the Liao, and the Xixia (1032–1227), another non-Han dynasty established around the same time, Yao did not even bother to conceal his bias toward the Han people, namely the Song Dynasty. He simply called the Song generals "national" *(minzu)* heroes for their feats in defending the "country" *(guojia)*,[119] manifesting his avowed belief that the non-Hans could become part of China only if they underwent sinicization.

Biased as it appeared, Yao's research received recognition from the GMD government and praise from his colleagues at Taiwan University and the Academia Sinica. For example, his study of Yu Jie (?–1253), a talented yet lesser known general of the Southern Song Dynasty, turned out to be an award-winning biography. Yao argued that Yu Jie was a great and loyal general who should have the same reputation as Yang Jiye did in history, for Yu was probably the only Han general who was able to stop the Mongol cavalry force. Relying on a mountainous landscape, Yu's infantry succeeded in preventing the Mongolian knights from entering Sichuan for several years. By bringing this to the fore, Yao was awarded the Sun Yat-sen Academic Award by the GMD government, which was also for his treatise on Chinggis Khan and Qiu Chuji.[120] Apparently Yao received this award not only because of his superb research ability but because of his attempt to make history in the service of politics.

It is quite ironic to see that as a scholar noted for his specialty in non-Han Chinese history, Yao was only interested in presenting his study from the Han perspective. Although he acknowledged the contribution different ethnic groups made to the development of Chinese culture, he tried hard to exalt the ability of Chinese culture to assimilate Manchu/Jurchen culture, or for that matter, any non-Han cultures. Of course, what he said often bore evidence to the historical fact that the longer non-Han ethnic rulers ruled China proper, the more likely they were assimilated by Han Chinese culture. But the extent to which he emphasized the success of sinicization and the vitality of Confucianism in Chinese history suggested his Han ethnocentrism.[121] This ethnocentrism, in an extreme form, reflected as much the immediate impact of the war (including the Cold War) politics, which prompted Yao to draw an analogy between history and politics in order to support the GMD, as the endeavor made by scholars, amid the fierce struggle for national survival, to reorient the course of cultural construction.

Yao Congwu's historical practice, no matter his personal bias, underscored the war's impact on the lives of these Chinese intellectuals from the 1930s onward. To some extent, it also epitomized the pursuit of a modern understanding of Chinese history considered in this book. Of course, not everything he put forth would be agreed to by his fellow historians. Yao's Han ethnocentrism, for example, clashed with Gu Jiegang's and early Fu Sinian's belief in a multi-ethnic origin of Chinese civilization.[122] However, his study of the sinicization question in Chinese history was indeed interesting. While it was clearly shaped by China's (including Taiwan's) political situation in the 1950s and the 1960s, it helped characterize the pursuit of these historians in experimenting with scientific history: to construct a past by sinicizing outside influences in order to make it more agreeable and responsive to the task of nation-building and, during World War II, nation-defending in China.

Ti and Yong: A Reconsideration

The issue of sinicization required us, it seems to me, to reconsider the *ti-yong* (substance-function) question. As a dichotomous way of thinking, it proposed to combine parts of each, namely the Chinese substance plus the Western technology, for coping with the problems caused by the Western intrusion. When it failed to work, as evidenced by the failure of the so-called Westernization Movement *(Yangwu yundong)* in 1895, radical intellectuals, especially those in the May Fourth/New Culture Movement, began to ridicule the idea and ponder a new approach. However, the new approach, represented by the May Fourth historians in this work, was not an antithesis of the *ti-yong*. Rather, it attempted a different implementation. If the original *ti-yong* idea was intended for a combination of two cultures, its new practice was for integration, or sinicization—absorbing foreign elements, the *yong* into the *ti*, and making the *yong* part of the *ti*. From combination to integration, the *ti-yong* idea helped highlight a change in modern Chinese intellectual history. Nevertheless, this change was by no means permanent. As we have seen earlier, during the wartime, many scholars became quite uncertain about the effect of and the need for cross-cultural integration.

In order to better analyze the influence of the *ti-yong* philosophy on modern Chinese intellectuals, it seems necessary for us to spend more time on Chen Yinke, whom we mentioned earlier, for he was an ardent believer in the *ti-yong* and his whole career was centered around the idea. Born into a Qing reformer's family in 1890, Chen was instilled with the idea, which his father and others advocated, during his early childhood.[123] After growing up he pursued, relentlessly, both Chinese and Western learning until his mid-thirties. Chen was indebted to his family for building up a solid foundation of traditional Chinese learning; in addition to mastering the writing of traditional poetry, he was well versed in Chinese classical learning. Beginning at the age of fifteen, he too was exposed extensively to Western learning, studying in both Europe and north America.

Having immersed himself in the study of both Chinese and Western learning, Chen was convinced that the *ti-yong* idea represented the best approach to the construction of modern Chinese culture. He stated: "I am interested in neither modern nor ancient history [since he only studied the history of China from the third to tenth centuries], my thoughts are confined to that of the late Qing Dynasty, and my opinions are similar to those of Zeng Guofan and Zhang Zhidong."[124] As known to many, it was Zhang Zhidong who championed the *ti-yong* in the late Qing. Through his life, despite many changes, Chen never gave up his belief.[125]

However, Chen did not perceive the *ti-yong* relation in a dichotomous manner. Rather, he believed that there should be a reciprocal relationship between the foreign and the indigenous so that the former could help strengthen the latter and, at the same time, it also became integrated into the latter. In other words, Chen Yinke did not regard Chinese and Western learning as antagonistic: neither was the Chinese tradition an obstacle to modernity nor was Western knowledge readily applicable to the Chinese situation. Instead, he advocated their integration. Like Yao Congwu, Chen Yinke attempted to draw a historical analogy. He believed that the history of Buddhism in China, or the development of Chinese Buddhism, illustrated the necessity of sinicization, or cultural integration.[126]

Chen began his career first as a philologist. Like the historians discussed earlier, he considered philological study a foundation for the study of history. In this sense, he shared the belief that philological study of historical sources was a meeting place of Eastern and Western historical cultures. However, unlike Hu Shi and others who scientized the Chinese philological tradition, Chen's interest in philology enabled him to perceive the West from a different perspective. As Hu Shi was attracted to the work of Western scientists, Chen Yinke was interested in that of the humanists. As a result, he helped the Chinese to discover a different Western tradition than the scientific one.[127] By emphasizing this humanist approach, he also made Western culture more compatible with Chinese culture. His interest in humanism helped him to nurture his friendship with Wu Mi (1894–1978), whom he met at Harvard. Following the teaching of new humanism of Irving Babbitt, their literature professor at Harvard, Wu Mi and his friends Mei Guangdi and Tang Yongtong (1893–1964) advocated the integration and revival of Chinese and Western humanist traditions and opposed Hu Shi and his followers for their simplistic interpretation of modern Western culture. Their opinions were mostly published in the *Critical Review (Xueheng)*, of which Wu Mi was the editor.[128]

Compared to the historians considered in this study, Chen spent the longest time in the West. Although his education record in the West is far from complete, we can, using World War I as a breakpoint, divide it into two periods. In the first period, he was enrolled in the universities in Berlin, Zurich, and Paris, aiming to acquaint himself with Western classics. He learned most major European languages including Latin and Greek.[129] After World War I, beginning with his study at Harvard with Charles R. Lanman, he started to take an interest in Asia, especially China's relationship with its neighbors. He learned more languages, mostly those of Asia such as Sanskrit and Pali and established some contacts with Western sinologists, such as Paul Pelliot.[130] For his new interest in Asian languages, he went to Berlin to work with Henrich Lueders. Meanwhile, he took courses in comparative philology as well as in other Asian languages, one of them was F. W. K. Mueller's philology course.[131] Even after his return to China, he continued to work with Baron A. von Stael-Holstein to improve his knowledge of Sanskrit.[132]

Thus among Western-educated Chinese scholars, Chen was an outstanding figure. As most Chinese students struggled with one or two foreign languages, Chen had learned more than a dozen. Besides English, French, German, Italian, Russian, Greek, and Latin (which he wrote well according to one source), he also studied Hindi, Pali, Persian, Mongolian, Tibetan, Turkish, Manchu, and other Asian languages.[133] While a definite polyglot, Chen took a pragmatic approach to his language study. He once told a friend that he only learned these languages to facilitate his study of history.[134]

Chen's language aptitude, his photographic memory, and his academic devotion were more than enough to impress his peers. Wu Mi, Chen's fellow student at Harvard, exclaimed that "Chen Yinke is the most learned man I have ever met of our generation. He is erudite in both Chinese and Western learning."[135] Mao Zishui also recalled that in 1923 when he had just arrived in Berlin, Fu Sinian told him that among Chinese students studying in Berlin at the time, Chen was one of the two "real students."[136] Most of all, Chen was remembered for his industriousness and perseverance in pursuing knowledge. Yang Buwei, the wife of Zhao Yuanren who taught linguistics at Harvard, wrote in her memoir that when she and her husband met Chen in Boston, Chen led a very simple life and seemed only to care about his study.[137]

Chen's interest in Chinese Buddhism as well as Chinese history derived from his language study. In 1923 he wrote a letter to his sister from Germany,

> I am now interested in learning Tibetan, because Tibetan and Chinese have the same root. It is just as Sanskrit, Greek, Latin, English, Russian, German, and French are from the same origin. These similarities provide good cases for studying phonetics and philology. For example, Tibetan began to use Sanskrit alphabets thousands of years ago. It thus shows a clearer evolutionary process than Chinese. If I use the methods of modern Western linguistics to compare Chinese and Tibetan, I can achieve a greater success than Qing scholars. However, this is not what I plan to do. I shall only pay attention to two things: one is Tang history, in which Tibetan is essential; the other is Buddhism, especially the Mahayana Sutras written in Sanskrit.[138]

This letter revealed that though Chen was now better known as a Tang historian, he probably developed his interest from his study of Chinese Buddhism, for it was during the Tang that Buddhism consolidated its basis in China.

Chen's interest was shown in his early teaching career. In 1925 he was offered a teaching position at the National Studies Institute at Qinghua University. He taught two courses: Sanskrit, which focused on the translations of Buddhist classics, and a bibliographical study of Western sinology.[139] While the Institute was staffed with senior scholars like Liang Qichao and Wang Guowei, Chen's erudition and language ability made a great impression on his students. To them, Chen mastered both Chinese and Western learning and was a singularly learned man of his generation, echoing Wu Mi's assessment.[140]

Besides his teaching responsibility, Chen in the 1930s was engrossed with his research on Chinese translations of Buddhist sutras. For example, by comparing and collating various translations of a Buddhist sutra, he explained how and why an original text was misunderstood, interpolated, and transfigured in the process of traveling from India to China. While his research seemed to focus on correcting mistranslations of Buddhist doctrines, he was also concerned about a larger question. He was interested in depicting the process of how the Buddhist belief entered and was accepted by the Chinese. To him these mistranslations were not simple mistakes. Rather, they helped reveal the way in which the Chinese appropriated Buddhist ideas and incorporated them in their lives. In other words, in his study of Buddhism, Chen was more interested in ethnological issues than Buddhism per se.

Here is an example. In 1930, Chen published an article analyzing the Chinese version of a Mahayana sutra, in which he argued that Chinese Buddhism represented a multifaceted tradition. In the early days when Buddhism just entered China, Chinese Buddhists used Daoist terms to render Buddhist concepts into Chinese. While their translations were understandable to Chinese readers, hence paving the way for the spread of Buddhism, the practice faced criticisms later on, especially in the Tang time when a few Buddhists, such as Xuanzhuang (Tripitaka, 602–664), managed to travel to India and brought back original texts. The Tang Buddhists changed the way of translation: instead of using existent Chinese words to match Buddhist terms, they retained the Buddhist/Indian terms through transliteration, suggesting an effort to understand Buddhism in its own terms. However, the new translation did not replace the old but often became an addition to the Chinese Buddhist tradition. As a result, a Buddhist concept often appeared in Chinese in two very different ways. Moreover, each translation attained its own meaning through the years, different from one another.[141]

While the difference in translation caused confusion among Chinese Buddhists, it also helped to form different sects. The Tiantai sect, Chen found in his another study, was noted for its emphasis on the concept of *wushi* (five time divisions). Although the concept had been used before by other sects, it was the Tiantai monks who raised its level of importance and made it a key concept in Buddhism that distinguished their sect from the others. Moreover, Chen argued, the *wushi* enabled the Tiantai sect to gain prominence among Chinese Buddhists for it corresponded with the ancient Chinese concept of *wuxing* (five elements), a key term in Daoism and other ancient Chinese philosophies.[142] Through his study of Tiantai Buddhism, Chen demonstrated that appropriation of foreign ideas to mesh them with the indigenous, or sinicization, was essential to the success of cultural exchange.

Indeed, due to the spread of Buddhism, many elements of Indian culture were sinicized and became integrated into Chinese culture. For example, Chen found, many stories and characters in the famous Chinese fiction *The Journey to the West (Xiyouji)* had Indian prototypes. Thus the novel was not a total fiction, but was a romanticization of Indian culture. This kind of sinicization also entered history texts. Chen Shou's (233–297) *A History of the Three Kingdoms (Sanguozhi)*, for instance, recorded a bright Chinese boy who succeeded in determining the weight of an elephant by letting the elephant stand in a boat and measuring the boat draft in water. But this story, Chen revealed, was nothing but a replica of a well-known Indian allegory. Chen also suspected that the legendary doctor, Hua Tuo, in the period of the Three Kingdoms, mentioned by many historians, was simply a transliteration of the Sanskrit word for "medicine god." So Hua Tuo was an anthropomorphic figure that embodied medicine in ancient China. To Chen, however, though it was a mistake for historians to regard Hua Tuo as a real person, the fact that the Indian god of medicine was personified in China showed the sinicization of Buddhism and Indian culture.[143]

Due to his interest in cultural integration, Chen adopted a different approach to understanding the value of historical sources. For him, while source criticism was important, it was not aimed at discarding forged or tempered sources. Rather, the historian should know how to use different sources, including the forged ones, for his study. In other words, all literary works were of value, depending on their use, no matter whether they provided correct information or not. A false record, he argued, could be a valuable piece of information revealing the intercourse among different cultures because forgeries were often produced for a specific reason, either to accommodate a foreign culture or to extend a once celebrated legacy.

From the study of Buddhism, Chen Yinke moved on to Tang history. His main publications were two books, appearing respectively in 1939 and 1941, one focused on Tang institutions and social infrastructure, the other on court politics.[144] His research won him fame as a leading Tang historian. In 1939, Oxford University invited Chen to its campus as a visiting professor. He was also elected to the English Royal Society. Due to the outbreak of World War II, however, Chen failed to reach England. He waited in Hong Kong for a few anxious months, enduring economic hardship resulting from Japan's occupation of the city. Eventually, helped by his friend Fu

Sinian and his student Wu Han (1909–1966), he and his family escaped the city and returned to China.[145] During most of the war, Chen was a professor in both the history and literature departments at Associated University, where he taught Sui and Tang histories as well as Tang poetry.

In his study of Tang history, Chen adopted the same philological approach, which enabled him to examine the validity of historical texts through comparison and contrast. As remembered by his students, Chen often began his class by listing a number of sources on a subject. He then analyzed each of them by comparing their relevance to the subject. In so doing, he allowed credible sources to distinguish themselves from the rest. Through this kind of source criticism, his students learned not only about the subject per se but its historiography. But what impressed the students the most was Chen's erudition. He was able to recite a number of texts without checking their sources. Because of his superb memory, he could also discover a new, different meaning from an otherwise well-known source.[146]

By presenting the sources, ranging from official historical writings to miscellaneous histories, Chen pieced together Tang political history from a geopolitical perspective. He contended that in the early Tang, there was a power shift in central government. The founders, the Li clan, or the Guanlong bloc, of the dynasty came originally from the modern Shandong Province, although they had been mixed with non-Hans. In the process of founding the Tang Dynasty, the clan were sinicized.[147] This Guanlong bloc, however, was not able to maintain its dominance in Tang politics during the reign of the Empress Wu, who, from a different and modest family background, decided to promote Buddhism as well as officials from other regions. Wu's policy was attributed to the decline of the Guanlong bloc and the continued power struggle in the mid-Tang Dynasty.[148] By analyzing the Tang politics, Chen explored the political background of Chinese Buddhism; Buddhism was brought to China for a political purpose.

Due to his obsessive reading and the poor living conditions during the war, Chen began to lose his eye sight in the 1940s. Among his friends whose lives were affected by the war, Chen paid the heaviest toll. From the late 1940s onward, he had to depend on the assistance of others to continue his writing. In the meantime, he relied on his extraordinary memory to plow continuously the field of Tang history and culture. During the 1950s, Chen published a few articles on Tang political history, in addition to a book on Yuan Zhen (779–831) and Bai Juyi (722–846), two famous Tang poets.[149] All his assistants were equally amazed by his knowledge and memory while following his instructions in searching for useful sources.[150]

Chen did not change his research interest while losing his eye sight, nor did he change his belief in the *ti-yong* while witnessing the political change in 1940s China. At the end of the Civil War when the GMD was losing northern China, Chen and his family, accompanying Hu Shi, retreated from Beijing to Nanjing. However, he refused to leave the mainland when he arrived in Guangzhou. Before Guangzhou fell into the CCP hands, Fu Sinian had written and telegraphed Chen several times, hoping to persuade him to leave the city for Taiwan, but to no avail. His decision reflected his political consideration. While he disapproved of Communism, he did not place any hope on Chiang Kai-shek and the GMD government. After witnessing the collapse of the GMD army, he decided to await his destiny while teaching at Lingnan University.[151] In addition, he probably would like to stay close to the *ti* (stem) of the tree of Chinese culture, if we consider the *ti-yong* idea in a center-periphery relation.

Fortunately, from 1949 to 1966, Chen led a relatively peaceful life in Communist China. He was even provided with assistants and other facilities for his teaching and research.[152] His expertise was also appreciated by the CCP in the beginning; he was once invited to head the No. 2 Historical Institute at China's Academy of Social Science in Beijing. He declined the offer with the excuse that he thought the weather in the south better for his health.[153] During the period, he was able to finish a few major works as well, including the well acclaimed *An Informal Biography of Liu Rushi (Liu Rushi biezhuan)*. While a biography of a Qing courtesan, it depicted the cultural transition during the late Ming and early Qing Dynasties and its impact on the intellectuals. In his writing, despite his blindness, Chen presented a wide array of sources, ranging from poems to miscellaneous histories and county gazetteers, best demonstrating his scholarship.[154]

However, this "privileged" treatment did not last long. During the Cultural Revolution beginning in 1966, Chen was deprived of assistants and any other aid. His house was searched by Red Guards. Red Guards hanged Big Character Posters *(Dazibao)* in his room and forced him to confess and be self-criticical. Trying to protect him, his wife was even beaten once by the Red Guards. Chen's life was, as he described it, just like living in hell.[155] The revolutionaries not only took away all his belongings, they also evicted him and his wife from their home. Failed to endure all these torments, Chen died on October 7, 1969. Three months later his wife died as well. Before his death, Chen had made a cynical remark about his life: "I was born as a subject of an empire, but died as a ghost of Communism."[156] This sad statement hardly concluded his entire life, but showed his outrage and despair as he was ending his life. Chen followed the *ti-yong* belief throughout his career. But the Cultural Revolution threw both away. Chen's death marked the end of not only a valuable life but an entire period in modern Chinese intellectual history.

Chapter Six

Epilogue

> Thus, the world and man reveal themselves by *understandings*. And all the undertakings we might speak of reduce themselves to a single one, that of *making history*.
>
> —Jean-Paul Sartre, *What Is Literature?*

During 1948 and 1949 as the GMD retreated to Taiwan, those historians who chose to remain in the mainland, such as Chen Yinke, Gu Jiegang, and many others, did not know what it would be like to live under the rule of a Communist regime; further, they could not foresee the outbreak of the Cultural Revolution in which they would not only be deprived of the rights of academic research, but also suffer from physical and mental abuses that would endanger, if not take, their lives.[1] But those who opted to follow the GMD's retreat to Taiwan were also confronted with a serious challenge: how to explain and cope with the loss of the mainland. The ensuing outbreak of the Korean War in 1950 and the emergence of the Cold War arrangement, wherein the world was basically divided ideologically between the Communist bloc and the so-called Free World, created a tense atmosphere that urged Chinese intellectuals to reflect critically on their cultural pursuit over the previous few decades, especially the possible connection between the rise and triumph of Communism and their endeavor and interest. It did not take them long to find that the Chinese Communist movement originated in the May Fourth era, when scholars and students yearned for Western ideas and culture and extolled them as viable alternatives to the Chinese cultural heritage. During the 1950s and the 1960s, therefore, several intellectuals questioned the attempt to learn from the West as a whole in modern China, especially during the early days of the twentieth century when it appeared particularly prevalent. Zhang Junmai (Carsun Chang), Tang Junyi (1909–1978), Xu Fuguan (1903–1982), and Mou Zongsan (1909–1993), along with Qian Mu, advocated the revival of Confucianism in both Hong Kong and Taiwan—hence the rise of New Confucianism—and criticized the May Fourth/New Culture Movement for its enthusiasm for cultural exchange.[2] Their criticisms forced May Fourth luminaries like Hu Shi and Luo Jialun into a defensive position. As one of the May Fourth's spiritual leaders, Hu Shi was subjected to severe attacks at the time, which contributed partially to his death. On November 6, 1961, three months before his death, Hu gave a speech at a meeting, entitled "Social Reform for the Development of Science" *(Kexue fazhan suo xuyao de shehui gaige)*, in which he stressed that the attempt to contrast Western civilization as "material" vis-à-vis Chinese civilization as "spiritual" was in vain, for a "spiritual civilization" still depended on the development of science and technology, advanced first in the West. His speech provoked many hostile criticisms; some used vulgar language to attack him personally, including such scholars as Xu Fuguan. Hu emotionally mentioned this incident when he, as the president of the Academia Sinica, chaired the election of academicians on February 24, 1962. However, he was unable to finish his remarks, suffered a heart attack, and died subsequently in the early evening of the same day.[3]

If Hu Shi's death had something to do with the seemingly resumed interest in cultural conservatism, this conservatism was somewhat related to the GMD's autocratic rule in the island. Chinese liberalism, which never fully gained its ground in the mainland, suffered more setbacks in Taiwan. Two years before Hu Shi's death, he had already realized, rather painfully, that his advocacy of "tolerance" and "free speech" did not go anywhere in Taiwan; in 1961, the GMD government confiscated the *Free China (Ziyou zhongguo)* journal and arrested its editor Lei Zhen. Hu had been a strong supporter of the journal and had served as its sponsor.[4] As a matter of fact, not only were these political journals not allowed to be published, scholarly publications were also forbidden, as long as the authors remained in the mainland. Gu Jiegang's *Critiques of*

Ancient Histories, for example, was not permitted to circulate. Marxist historians' works, needless to say, faced a harsher restriction. Consequently, most Taiwan history students were quite ignorant of the major discussions in the history of modern Chinese historiography, such as the Social History Discussion, nor were they aware of the influence of Marxism in Western historical writing.[5] This situation remained until 1988 when martial law was finally lifted.

Besides the restrictions on academic freedom, the deaths of Fu Sinian and Hu Shi also resulted in an absence of leadership in the intellectual community. Although prominent figures succeeded to their positions, they lacked equivalent personal charm and social influence to have a visible bearing on the government's policy toward higher education and scholarly research. Facing the Cold War the GMD government also prioritized its limited resources to support its goal of "recovering the mainland" *(fangong dalu)* rather than assisting in academic research. As a result, financial assistance to universities and research institutions dwindled significantly. Lacking adequate research support, historians sought academic positions abroad, including Luo Jialun's protégé Guo Tingyi who, after founding the Institute of Modern History and securing a grant from the Ford Foundation, chose to spend his last years in the United States. Some of Fu Sinian's close assistants in the Institute of History and Philology also left Taiwan for the United States. Indeed, having retreated to Taiwan and been cut off from the connection to the mainland, many historians felt it was virtually impossible to continue practicing Fu's idea of seeking scientific material evidence for ancient history.[6]

Although their attempt to carry on the May Fourth tradition encountered challenges in the political and economic arenas, Taiwan historians by and large remained attracted to the idea that source criticism was the key to modern historiography, an idea advocated by Hu Shi, Fu Sinian, Yao Congwu, and others. As the hostility along the Taiwan Strait prevented them from conducting archaeological research, they concentrated more closely on examining written texts in their research. Monographic studies of a specific subject, often in the form of articles rather than books, became the norm of historical research, at least as seen in the publications of the research fellows at the Institute of History and Philology and history professors at Taiwan University, during most of the second half of the twentieth century. This practice, needless to say, is reminiscent, in part, of Fu Sinian's positivist idea that a modern historian should conduct research, rather than tell a didactic story.[7]

Despite his early death in 1950, Fu's influence was still present in the historical community in Taiwan, probably due to the fact that after moving to the island, he was put in charge of both Taiwan University and the Institute of History and Philology, one produced promising young scholars and the other, namely Academia Sinica, received them and turned them into full-fledged researchers. In today's Taiwan, these two institutions remain the greatest attraction for anyone serious about pursuing an academic career.[8]

There have been, of course, significant changes that occurred in Taiwan's historical circle. From the mid-1960s onward when the first generation of Taiwan-trained scholars returned to the island, either for a long-term appointment or a short-term visit from the United States, where they received more advanced degrees, they brought with them new social theories and methods. Studies of social history that emphasized quantitative research and structural analysis gained in popularity, especially among young students. But more traditional pursuits that demanded a masterful grasp of the rich tradition of Chinese literary culture, such as the study of intellectual history, remained very attractive, especially if historians in their analyses could also demonstrate knowledge of up-to-date theories from the West.[9] Accordingly, while historians in Taiwan closely followed recent trends in modern historical studies, most of them maintained a strong interest in the study of Chinese history and culture, which, in the most recent decade, has included the study of Taiwan. Of course, to some historians, the study of Taiwan should obtain a status of its own in order to demonstrate the distinct characteristics of Taiwan's history and culture.[10]

On the mainland, while the Communist government promised a "New China" *(xin zhongguo)*, it did not present a successful alternative to the pursuit of Chinese modernity. Believing destruction would lead naturally to construction, Mao Zedong orchestrated many political campaigns, including the disastrous Cultural Revolution, for finding a solution to China's problems in "perpetual revolution." His approach however did not succeed; China instead was plunged into cultural chaos and political disorder. As tradition, chastised as the "four olds" *(sijiu)*, was swept away and foreign influences were kept outside China, the country found itself in a cultural desert. This shows that like their predecessors (liberals and traditionalists) of earlier periods, the Communists could not successfully attempt the nation-building project without any backing from the past. In fact, before and after its victory, at least until the early 1960s, the Communist movement in China had been an application of Marxist ideas and the Soviet experience to the Chinese situation. The application involved efforts to appropriate and sinicize Marxist ideas to fit into the circumstances in China.

After taking over the power, for example, Chinese Communist historians zealously followed the work of Soviet historians to search for examples in Marxist historiography. They showed overt enthusiasm for translating Soviet historical works both in Chinese history and world history, along with a few Soviet party doctrines pertinent to the Marxist view of history. These translations served as a point of departure for their own construction of Marxist historiography in China. For Chinese Marxists, Russian historians not only brought Marxism, especially theories on social development and class struggle, into the field of Chinese history, they also provided general interpretations of world history through their studies of the histories of other countries. The latter was equally important for their work on Chinese history; their belief in the validity of Marxism prompted them to search for general rules of historical development worldwide. "As the subject of scientific research," one prominent PRC historian declared, "history has its objective course as well as its objective laws of development."[11]

But to find out these "objective laws" in Chinese history was no light task for Marxists. Chinese Marxists soon found not only the Soviet model, often dogmatic and arbitrary, inadequate for their research, but also the comparative perspective on the developments of Chinese and other Oriental societies awkward and inconclusive.[12] As a result, they were bogged down on almost every major issue when they attempted to follow the Marxian approach to interpreting Chinese history. These issues became major topics for their heated debates, ranging from general questions like the formation of the Chinese nation and the periodization of Chinese history, to specific ones like the "sprouts of capitalism" in the late imperial period, land ownership, and the role of peasant rebellions.[13]

All of these questions were deemed essential to establishing Marxist historiography and some, such as the periodization question, had already caused vigorous discussions in the Social History Discussion in the 1930s.[14] The importance of the question on periodizing Chinese history became more imminent after the Communist triumph. Albert Feuerwerker analyzes,

> The pressure to settle this question finally (and the other periodization problems as well) therefore probably stems as much from the Communist party leadership, who are anxious lest

> any looseness at the beginning of the developmental paradigm raise doubts about its completion, as it does from the historians themselves.[15]

For most Chinese Marxist historians, a correct understanding of the nature of Chinese society was crucial and imperative to their revolution, for a sequential progress of social development was a key component in the Marxist interpretation of history. Some of them argued passionately that like all other societies, especially the European society, China in the past went through a similar process of social development and experienced the same social phases in history. The phases were, as suggested by Karl Marx in his *A Contribution to the Critique of Political Economy:*

> In broad outlines, Asiatic, ancient, feudal, and modern bourgeois modes of production can be designated as progressive epochs in the economic formation of society.[16]

But to acknowledge the need for applying the Marxist viewpoint to interpreting Chinese history was one thing, to actually execute the application, namely, to conform the evolution of Chinese history with the theory, was quite another. In order to place Chinese history in the Marxist scheme of world history, Chinese Marxists had to ignore some distinct, unique (?), features of Chinese history long regarded as part of China's national identity, which resulted in some misgivings even among the most prominent Marxist historians. Fan Wenlan (1893–1969), for instance, who joined the Communists in Yanan as early as the 1930s, refuted Russian historian G. V. Efimov's analysis on the formation of Chinese nation. In contrast to Efimov's opinion that China did not become a nation until the early twentieth century, Fan argued that the unification of China under the Qin Dynasty (221–206 B.C.) had already marked the beginning of the Chinese nation.[17] Thus he opposed a dogmatic application of Marxist theory to interpreting Chinese history, as shown by his position here as well as in the debate on the periodization in Chinese history. Proud of China's past, he stressed the uniqueness of Chinese history. "There were rich characteristics," Fan stated, "in the development of Chinese history. We can see these characteristics if we shake off the yoke of dogmatism."[18]

This nationalist sentiment, of course, was not unique in Fan Wenlan; it was rather ingrained in the cause of the Chinese Communist movement and Chinese Marxist historiography. As Russian historians qualmishly observed in the early 1960s:

> At present, Chinese scholars are carefully summing up all the distinctive aspects, the special features, of the history of China in order to emphasize again and again, not the general, but the particular; it is as though they were striving to secede from, rather than to unite with, the general current of human history.[19]

In fact, the Chinese were much more ambitious. By emphasizing the uniqueness of Chinese history, they were seeking *the* Chinese interpretation of Marxism in order to "shoulder the responsibility of, with independent spirit, making great contributions to human history."[20] This sense of responsibility, or national consciousness, not only prompted them to challenge the Eurocentrism embodied by the work of Russian historians, but also accounted for their ultimate departure from the Soviet practice of Marxist history in the 1960s.

When the Cultural Revolution approached its end in 1976, mainland China began to re-open its door to the West. Chinese intellectuals, therefore, again embarked on the search for cultural construction. Their search resulted in the so-called "culture fever" *(wenhua re)* in the mid-1980s, which dwelled on many issues that had concerned their predecessors in the Republican era. Many young scholars, like a group of unbound Prometheuses, showed an overwhelming zest for knowledge about the West, as in the May Fourth Movement.[21] Among historians, the *ti-yong* relation again attracted considerable attention.[22] This déjà vu suggests that the question of how to deal with the relation between Chinese tradition and foreign cultural influence in search of modernity remains a key and lingering issue to the Chinese people.

The May Fourth project on modern historiography, as considered in this book, had an exemplary value for scholars of the new generation in realizing the intrinsic link between tradition and modernity. In Liang Qichao and He Bingsong's methodological study of Chinese historiography, Hu Shi and Gu Jiegang's critical examination of ancient Chinese history, and Chen Yinke's philological research on China's cultural transformation under the Buddhist influence, there was an apparent concern for the expectation of Chinese civilization. This concern was deeply shared by the young generation who, unlike their predecessors, did not go through the Confucian indoctrination but experienced the fierce years of the Cultural Revolution and the political upheaval. When they finally came out of the "dark house," they were suddenly exposed to the new, colorful world and were quite excited by their "discovery" of the West.

The popular TV series "River elegy" *(He Shang)* epitomized this excitement when the producers urged the viewers to embrace the "blue sea," meaning the Western industrial world. In the wake of this "culture fever," Western translations attracted a large readership. Not only were translations of Western novels reappearing in the market (many of them had been translated before yet were banned in the Cultural Revolution), appealing to readers of different social strata, translations of Western scholarly books, ranging from politics, economics, and psychology, to history, literary criticism, and hermeneutics, were also very popular.[23] Some scholars obtained instant fame simply because they rendered a Western work into Chinese, similar to the experience of He Bingsong in the 1920s. Gan Yang, for example, was first noticed by others for his translation of Ernst Cassirer's (1874–1945) *An Essay on Man: An Introduction to Philosophy of Human Culture*, which took a Chinese title as the *Renlun* (On Human Beings) and became a best-seller in the mid–1980s.

Yet this "culture fever" was not only concerned with the West, but also with the Chinese cultural tradition. While the enthusiasm for Western culture and economic advancement was obvious, this enthusiasm stemmed from an evident apprehension for the outlook of Chinese culture. This anxiousness reflected an inherited May Fourth legacy.[24] Like the May Fourth historians, the participants in the "culture fever" movement sought ways in which they could transform Chinese tradition and reconcile China and the West. The "Chinese Culturalist School," for example, was noted for its attempt to negotiate between modernization and tradition, observed Xudong Zhang. Led by Tang Yijie, son of Tang Yongtong, a Tang Buddhism expert who did his graduate work at Harvard with Irving Babbitt, this school was based in the Academy of Chinese Culture in Beijing. For Tang, what stands at the center of China's modernization is the project on reforming Chinese culture; all discussions on science and technology must revolve around it whereby they can acquire a social meaning. In other words, any attempt to modernize China, either in terms of importing modern technology or developing the country's economy, cannot succeed unless there is equal attention paid to modernizing Chinese culture. Pang Pu, a respected historian in the Academy of Social Sciences, supported Tang's position. Pang states explicitly that what they intend to achieve is simply to carry on the unfinished May Fourth project on reforming the Chinese cultural tradition.[25] Thus in the works of Tang and Pong we discern a recurrent, familiar theme that we have seen in our discussions on modern Chinese historiography. Like their predecessors in the May Fourth era, these scholars have realized that any sensible attempt at coming to grips with China's future must start with a serious consideration of its past. China's cultural tradition, or the "tyranny of history," as analyzed by W. J. F. Jenner, has become a historical problem that circumscribes the pursuit of modernity in China.[26]

For the radicals like Bao Zunxin, to cope with this "tyranny," or the tradition, means to rebel against it, which he defines as certain ideological, moral, and cultural precepts that have shaped and regulated the way of thinking, knowledge structure, social behavior, and aesthetic judgment of modern-day Chinese. In China, Confucianism embodies such a tradition that plays the above roles in society. But he hastens to add, tradition itself is also a powerful spiritual force *(jingshen liliang)*; while it controls people, it also can help to create new culture if people can transcend it and free themselves from its constraint. To Bao, whether or not one can create a new culture and how valuable this new culture can be depends on whether one can make this transcendence.

> Anti-tradition therefore becomes the primary impetus for defending traditional culture and developing national culture. For while every great ancient culture has its perpetual value, this value is [valuable] not because it becomes a tradition, but because people can reflect, rediscover, and recreate it.[27]

While Bao takes an opposite position to that of the New Confucians (the latter believes that Confucian values can prepare the foundation for China's modernization), he does not think that this anti-traditional stance necessarily negates traditional culture per se and amounts to a kind of "cultural nihilism" *(wenhua xuwu zhuyi)*. What he champions is rather an attitude change; through this change, he hopes that one can search for new values in Chinese culture beyond Confucianism.

Thus this antitraditionalism, portrayed by Bao Zunxin, connotes an attempt to transcend Confucianism and discover a new past in Chinese tradition. This search for multiple pasts characterizes the work of the historians in the Peoples' Republic as well as of those in the Republican era. In both periods, intellectuals have attempted and managed to (re)discover history. This discovery is premised on a historical relativism that aims to reconfigure in constancy the course and manifestation of history. Their discoveries show that, to use Foucault's words, "the world we know is not this ultimately simple configuration where events are reduced to accentuate their essential traits, their final meaning, or their initial and final value. On the contrary, it is a profusion of entangled events."[28] To acknowledge this "profusion" of multiple pasts in Chinese history allows these intellectuals to defy the absolute value of Confucian tradition and construct a new history.

If the "culture fever" movement has as its underlying concern the reform of tradition, this concern also unites the moderates like Tang Yijie, Pang Pu, and the radicals like Bao Zunxin and Gan Yang. While they hold different views in regard to the importance and relevance of Western culture to their project, they all believe that the purpose of learning from the West is for (re)forming what China had in the past to meet the needs of the present. This backward-looking approach to seeking a future in modern China determines that their project must focus on history. Zhu Weizheng, a history professor of Fudan University and a noted figure in the "culture fever" movement in Shanghai, stresses that since "traditional culture is a historical existence," any attempt to understand this culture must be based on a knowledge of "historical facts" *(lishi shishi)*. To acquire this knowledge, one needs to employ the method of history. Gaining this knowledge enables one to discern that traditional culture is a historical continuum, composed of two parts; one is known as the "dead culture" *(si wenhua)* whereas the other as the "living culture" *(huo wenhua)*. Nevertheless, a "dead culture" is not necessarily undesirable and a "living culture" is not always desirable. Rather, provided with historical knowledge, people can reverse the nature of these two to meet their needs and develop a more viable, useful tradition.[29]

Thus, seeking a new tradition is always in juxtaposition with the attempt at writing a new history. In so doing, historians and intellectuals challenge their given past embodied in the form of tradition, and change it in order to make it more harmonious with the changing social milieu. The way in which modern historians summon the past for the present leads to the creation of not only a new form of historiography, but history in its philosophical sense, as argued by Benedetto Croce. "What constitutes history," claimed Croce, "may be thus described: it is the act of comprehending and understanding induced by the requirements of practical life." In other words, every true history is contemporary history; it is produced to correspond to the present need.[30] In its production, historians dismantle the image of an accepted past and construct a new one with a new perspective and a new method. "History thus transformed," says David Lowenthal, "becomes larger than life, merging intention with performance, ideal with actuality."[31] I hope this book is a contribution to our knowledge of the significant transformation in both Chinese history and historical writing of the twentieth century.

Glossary

Ban Gu 班固
Bao Zunxin 包遵信
Beida 北大
Beiwen 碑文
Bianshiguan 編史館
Budikang 不抵抗
Butan zhengzhi 不談政治
Cai, xue, shi, de 才、學、識、德
Cai Yuanpei (Tsai Yuen-pei) 蔡元培
Chen Duxiu 陳獨秀
Chengzhu bianyi 程朱辨異
Chen Lifu 陳立夫
Chen Yinke 陳寅恪
Chongfen shijiehua 充分世界化
Chouxiang 抽象
Chunqiu/Chunqiu bifa 春秋╲春秋筆法
Cui Shu 崔述
Dadan de jiashe, xiaoxin de qiuzheng 大膽的假設、小心的求證
Dadong xiaodong shuo 大東小東說
Danghua 黨化
Daoguang yangsou zhengfu ji 道光洋艘征撫紀
Datong 大同
Dazibao 大字報
Ding Wenjiang (Ting Wen-ch'iang) 丁文江
Dixue zazhi 地學雜誌
Dongbei shigang 東北史綱
Duli pinglun 獨立評論
Faguo zhilue 法國志略
Fangong dalu 反攻大陸
Fan Wenlan 范文瀾

Feng Youlan (Feng Yu-lan) 馮友蘭
Fuqiang 富強
Furen xuezhi 輔仁學誌
Fu Sinian (Fu Ssu-nien) 傅斯年
Gaiyi 概義
Gangchang 綱常
Gan Yang 甘陽
Gongzhong 公忠
Gong Zizhen 龔自珍
Guancha dian 觀察點
Guangshu 廣書
Gu Jiegang (Ku Ch'ieh-kang) 顧頡剛
Guocui xuebao 國粹學報
Guo Tingyi 郭廷以
Guoxue, guoxue yanjiusuo 國學，國學研究所
Gushibian 古史辯
Guwei jinyong 古為今用
Gu Yanwu 顧炎武
Haiguo sishuo 海國四説
Haiguo tuzhi 海國圖志
Hancheng 漢城
Hanhua 漢化
Hao zhengfu 好政府
He Bingsong (Ho Ping-sung) 何炳松
He Shang 河殤
Huang Kan 黃侃
Hu Shi (Hu Shih) 胡適
Jiang Tingfu 蔣廷黻
Jianwang zhilai 鑑往知來
Jiaohu xing 交互性
Jiji de 積極的
Jindaishi 近代史
Jing, shi, zi, ji 經、史、子、集
Jingshen liliang 精神力量
Jingshi zhiyong 經世致用
Jinhua 進化
Jinsheng 縉生
Jinwen 金文
Jishi benmo 記事本末
Jiuwo 舊我
Juti 具體
Kaishanzu 開山祖
Kangri zhanzheng 抗日戰爭
Kang Youwei (Yu-wei) 康有為
Kaoju jia 考據家
Kaozheng (Kao-ch'eng) 考證
Keguan/Keguan xing 客觀＼客觀性

Liangjiu 良久
Liang Qichao (Ch'i-ch'ao) 梁啟超
Liang Tingnan 梁廷枏
Lianxu xing 連續性
Li Dazhao 李大釗
Liezhuan 列傳
Li Ji 李濟
Lishi de cailiao 歷史的材料
Lishi yanjiufa 歷史研究法
Lishi yuyan yanjiusuo 歷史語言研究所
Liujing jieshi 六經皆史
Liu Rushi biezhuan 柳如是別傳
Liu Shipei 劉師培
Liu Xin 劉歆
Liu Yizheng 柳怡徵
Liu Zhiji 劉知幾
Luo Jialun (Lo Chia-lun) 羅家倫
Luo Zhenyu 羅振玉
Mao Zishui 毛子水
Mei Guangdi 梅光迪
Meizhou pinglun 每週評論
Miao Fenglin 繆鳳林
Minyi/minyi jigou 民意＼民意機構
Minzu fuxing congshu 民族復興叢書
Minzu ganqing 民族感情
Minzu/minzu geming 民族＼民族革命
Mou Zongsan 牟宗三
Nuli she/nuli zhoubao 努力社＼努力周報
Pang Pu 龐樸
Pufa zhanji 普法戰紀
Puxue 樸學
Qian Mu 錢穆
Qian Xuantong 錢玄同
Qilue 七略
Qinghua liumei yubei xuexiao 清華留美預備學校
Qingyi bao 清議報
Quanpan xihua 全盤西化
Rangwai bixian annei 攘外必先安內
Ru 儒
Sanguozhi 三國志
Sanshishuo 三世說
Shengping 昇平
Shengwuji 聖武記
Shidi congkan 史地叢刊
Shifa 史法
Shiji 史記
Shijie geming 史界革命

Shijie gonglun 世界公論
Shijie zhuyi 世界主義
Shiming 使命
Shiping 史評
Shitong 史通
Shiyan zhuyi 實驗主義
Shiyi 史意
Shiyi zhi changji yi zhiyi/Shiyi zhiyi 師夷之長技以制夷＼師夷制夷
Shu 書
Shuailuan 衰亂
Shuer buzuo 述而不作
Sijiu 四舊
Sima Guang 司馬光
Sima Qian 司馬遷
Sizhong 私忠
Sizhouzhi 四洲志
Taiping 太平
Tang Junyi 唐君毅
Tang Yijie 湯一介
Tang Yongtong 湯用彤
Tao Xisheng 陶希聖
Tongshi xinyi 通史新義
Wang Guowei 王國維
Wang Tao 王韜
Wang Yangming 王陽明
Wei 僞
Wei Yuan 魏源
Weng Wenhao 翁文灝
Wenhua jianshe 文化建設
Wenhua re 文化熱
Wenhua xuwu zhuyi 文化虛無主義
Wenshi tongyi 文史通義
Wenxue geming 文學革命
Wenyi fuxing 文藝復興
Wu 誤
Wu Mi 吳宓
Wushi 五時
Wushiliao jiwu shixue 無史料即無史學
Xiandaishi 現代史
Xiaoji de 消極的
Xinan lianda 西南聯大
Xinchao 新潮
Xinmin congbao 新民叢報
Xinqingnian 新青年
Xinshi 信史
Xinshixue 新史學
Xinwo 新我

Xin yulunjie 新輿論界
Xin zhongguo 新中國
Xixue yuanshikao 西學源始考
Xiyouji 西遊記
Xueheng 學衡
Xu Fuguan 徐復觀
Xu Jiyu 徐繼畬
Xungu 訓詁
Xu Zhongshu 徐中舒
Yangwu yundong 洋務運動
Yao Congwu (Tsung-wu) 姚從吾
Yao Jiheng 姚際恒
Yigupai 疑古派
Yinghuan zhilue 瀛環志略
Yinguo guanxi 因果關係
Yixia dongxi shuo 夷夏東西說
You tiaoli de zhishi 有條理的知識
Yu Dawei 俞大維
Zhang Junmai 張君邁
Zhang Taiyan 章太炎
Zhang Xuecheng 章學誠
Zhao Yi 趙翼
Zhao Yuanren 趙元任
Zhedong xuepai/suyuan 浙東學派＼溯源
Zhengchen/Zhengyou 諍臣＼諍友
Zhengju 證據
Zhengli guogu, Zaizao wenming 整理國故，再造文明
Zhengshi 正史
Zhengtong lun 正統論
Zhenxiang 真相
Zhongguo benwei wenhua 中國本位文化
Zhongguo lishi yanjiufa/bubian 中國歷史研究法＼補編
Zhongguo minzu gemingshi 中國民族革命史
Zhongguoshi xulun 中國史序論
Zhongguo zhexueshi dagang 中國哲學史大綱
Zhongri 終日
Zhongxue weiti, xixue weiyong 中學為體，西學為用
Zhongyang yanjiuyuan 中央研究院
Zhuguan 主觀
Zhu Jiahua 朱家驊
Zhu Weizheng 朱維錚
Zhu Xi 朱熹
Zhu Xizu 朱希祖
Ziyou zhongguo 自由中國
Zizhi tongjian 資治通鑒

Notes

Chapter One

1. Cf. Robert E. Frykenberg, *History and Belief: The Foundation of Historical Understanding* (Grand Rapids, MI: Wm B. Eerdmans Publishing Co., 1996).

2. Gordon Graham, *The Shape of the Past: A Philosophical Approach to History* (Oxford: Oxford University Press, 1997), 2.

3. Ibid.

4. Although most Chinese scholars pronounce his name Chen Yinque, it seems Chen himself used "Yinke," or its Wade-Giles version "Yin-ko," overseas, both in the 1920s and in the 1940s. In a letter to Fu Sinian while he was in Oxford after World War II, Chen asked Fu to write him back, using the name "Chen Yin-ke." See "Fu Sinian dangan" (Fu Sinian's archive), I–709, Fu Sinian Library, Institute of History and Philology, Academia Sinica, Taiwan. Zhao Yuanren, an acclaimed Chinese linguist and Chen's friend and colleague, also said that one should pronounce "Yinke" rather than "Yinque." See Zhao and Yang Buwei's "Yi Yinke" (Chen Yinke remembered), in Yu Dawei et al. *Tan Chen Yinke* (About Chen Yinke) (Taipei: Zhuanji wenxue chubanshe, 1970), 26.

5. Prasenjit Duara, *Rescuing History from the Nation: Questioning Narratives of Modern China* (Chicago: Chicago University Press, 1993), 4.

6. See Eric Hobsbawm and Terence Ranger, eds. *The Invention of Tradition* (Cambridge: Cambridge University Press, 1983) and Jocelyn Linnekin, "Defining Tradition: Variations on the Hawaiian Identity," *American Ethnologist*, 10 (1983), 241–252.

7. Partha Chatterjee, *The Nation and Its Fragments: Colonial and Postcolonial Histories* (Princeton: Princeton University Press, 1993), 4–5.

8. Cf. Tu Wei-ming, ed., *The Living Tree: The Changing Meaning of Being Chinese Today* (Stanford: Stanford University Press, 1994).

9. *Confucian China and Its Modern Fate: A Trilogy* (Berkeley: University of California Press, 1968), III, 85–109, the quotation is on 94.

10. A concise version of Levenson's argument is found in his "'History' and 'Value': the Tension of Intellectual Choice in Modern China," *Studies in Chinese Thought*, ed. Arthur Wright (Chicago: University of Chicago Press, 1953), 146–194. See also, Eugene Lubot, *Liberalism in An Illiberal Age: New Culture Liberals in Republican China, 1919–1937* (Westport: Greenwood Press, 1982).

11. Cf. Duara, *Rescuing History from the Nation*, 3–16, especially 5.

12. Laurence Schneider, *Ku Chieh-kang and China's New History: Nationalism and the Quest for Alternative Traditions* (Berkeley: University of California Press, 1971), Introduction, 1–17.

13. Arif Dirlik, *Revolution and History: The Origins of Marxist Historiography in China, 1919–1937* (Berkeley: University of California Press, 1978), 1–18, the quote is on 10.

14. Zheng Shiqu, *Wanqing Guocui pai* (The National Essence group in the late Qing) (Beijing: Beijing shifan daxue chubanshe, 1997). See essays by Laurence Schneider, Martin Bernal, and Charlotte Furth in The *Limits of Change: Essays on Conservative Alternatives in Republican China* (Cambridge, MA: Harvard University Press, 1976), ed. Charlotte Furth, Also, Yu Ying-shih, "Changing Conceptions of National History in Twentieth-Century China," *Conceptions of National History: Proceedings of Nobel Symposium 78*, eds. Erik Lönnroth, Karl Molin, and Ragnar Björk (Berlin: Walter de Gruyter, 1994), 155–174; and "Rethinking Culture and National Essence" written by Lydia H. Liu in her *Translingual Practice: Literature, National Culture, and Translated Modernity—China, 1900–1937* (Stanford: Stanford University Press, 1995), 239–264.

15. Duara, *Rescuing History from the Nation*, 5, and Lydia Liu, *Translingual Practice,* 29.

16. Duara, *Rescuing History from the Nation*, 5. The italics are his.

17. Xiaobing Tang, *Global Space and the Nationalist Discourse of Modernity: The Historical Thinking of Liang Qichao* (Stanford: Stanford University Press, 1996).

18. See Liang Qichao's *Xinshixue* and *Zhongguo lishi yanjiufa* (Methods for the study of Chinese history), in *Liang Qichao shixue lunzhu sanzhong* (Liang Qichao's three works on history) (Hong Kong: Sanlian shudian, 1980; hereafter *sanzhong*), 10–15, 45–51.

19. Tang, *Global Space*, 9.

20. Lionel M. Jensen, *Manufacturing Confucianism: Chinese Tradition and Universal Civilization* (Durham, NC: Duke University Press, 1997), 158.

21. Hobsbawm and Ranger, *Invention of Tradition*, 1.

22. Prasenjit Duara offers his analysis of the influence and manifestations of transnationalism in modern China in "Transnationalism and the Predicament of Sovereignty: China, 1900–1945," *American Historical Review*, 102:4 (Oct. 1997), 1030–1051. A discussion on transnationality of a more recent period is found in Ong Aihwa's *Flexible Citizenship: The Cultural Logics of Transnationality* (Durham, NC: Duke University Press, 1999).

23. Toby Huff, *The Rise of Early Modern Science: Islam, China, and the West* (New York: Cambridge University Press, 1995), 12.

24. See Peter Burke, *The Renaissance Sense of the Past* (London, 1969); Nancy Struever, *The Language of History in the Renaissance: Rhetoric and Historical Consciousness in Florentine Humanism* (Princeton: Princeton University Press, 1970); Eric Cochrane, *Historians and Historiography in the Italian Renaissance* (Chicago: University of Chicago Press, 1981); Donald Kelley, *Foundations of Modern Historical Scholarship: Language, Law, and History in the French Renaissance* (New York: Columbia University Press, 1970); Joseph M. Levine, *Humanism and History: Origins of Modern English Historiography* (Ithaca: Cornell University Press, 1987); M. S. Anderson, *Historians and Eighteenth century Europe, 1715–1789* (Oxford: Clarendon Press, 1979); Peter Reill, *The German Enlightenment and the Rise of Historicism* (Berkeley: University of California Press, 1975); and of course Friedrich Meinecke, *Historism: The Rise of a New Historical Outlook*, trans. J. E. Anderson (London: Routledge & Kegan Paul, 1972).

25. Arnold Momigliano, "Ancient History and the Antiquarian," *Studies in Historiography* (New York: Harper & Row Publishers, 1966), 1–39.

26. See G. P. Gooch, *History and Historians in the Nineteenth Century* (Boston: Beacon Press, 1959), Georg G. Iggers, *The German Conception of History: The National Tradition of Historical Thought from Herder to the Present* (Middletown, CT: Wesleyan University Press, 1968) and his "The Image of Ranke in American and German Historical Thought," *History and Theory*, 2 (1962), 17–40.

27. For the New Historians' challenge to Rankean historiography, see Harry E. Barnes, *The New History and the Social Studies* (New York: Century Co., 1925); John Higham, *History: Professional Scholarship in America* (Baltimore: Johns Hopkins University Press, 1983); Cushing Strout, *The Pragmatic Revolt in American History: Carl Becker and Charles Beard* (New Haven: Yale University Press, 1958); Peter Novick, *That Noble Dream: The "Objectivity Question" and the American Historical Profession*

(Cambridge: Cambridge University Press, 1988); and Ernst Breisach, *American Progressive History: An Experiment in Modernization* (Chicago: University of Chicago Press, 1993). For the recent trends in Western historiography and the rise of social, quantitative, and psycho-history, see Michael Kammen, ed. *The Past before Us: Contemporary Historical Writing in the U.S.* (Ithaca: Cornell University Press, 1980); Lawrence Stone, *The Past and the Present Revisited* (New York: Routledge & Kegan Paul, 1987); Geoffrey Barraclough, *Main Trends in History* (New York: Holmes & Meier, 1979); Georg Iggers and Harold Parker, eds. *International Handbook of Historical Studies: Contemporary Research and Theory* (Westport, CT: Greenwood Press, 1979); and Henry Kozicki, ed. *Developments in Modern Historiography* (New York: St. Martin's Press, 1993).

28. See Chang Hsin-pao, *Commissioner Lin and the Opium War* (Cambridge, MA: Harvard University Press, 1964); Jane K. Leonard, *Wei Yuan and China's Rediscovery of the Maritime World* (Cambridge, MA: Harvard University Press, 1984); and Paul A. Cohen, *Between Tradition and Modernity: Wang T'ao and Reform in Late Imperial China* (Cambridge, MA: Harvard University Press, 1987).

29. See Paul A. Cohen, *Wang T'ao,* Jane K. Leonard, *Wei Yuan,* and Noriko Kamachi, *Reform in China: Huang Tsun-hsien and the Japanese Model* (Cambridge, MA: Harvard University Press, 1981). Most PRC historian believe that the Opium War (1838–1842) signaled the beginning of modern Chinese historiography: see *Zhongguo jindai shixueshi* (History of modern Chinese historiography) 2 vols. ed. Wu Ze (Nanjing: Jiangsu guji chubanshe, 1989).

30. See Hao Chang, *Chinese Intellectuals in Crisis: Search for Order and Meaning (1890–1911)* (Berkeley: University of California Press, 1987) and Michael Gasster, *Chinese Intellectuals and the Revolution of 1911: The Birth of Modern Chinese Radicalism* (Seattle: University of Washington Press, 1969).

31. See Fukuzawa Yukichi, *An Outline of a Theory of Civilization*, trans. David A. Dilworth and G. Cameron Hurst (Tokyo: Sophia University Press, 1973), chs. III and IV; also Carmen Blacker, *The Japanese Enlightenment, A Study of the Writings of Fukuzawa Yukichi* (Cambridge: Cambridge University Press, 1964), 93–94 and Masayuki Sato, "Historiographical Encounters: the Chinese and Western Traditions in Turn-of-the-century Japan," *Storia della Storiografia*, 19 (1991), 13–21.

32. *Xin shixue*, in *sanzhong*, 3. There have been a few English monographs on Liang Qichao, see Joseph R. Levenson, *Liang Ch'i-ch'ao and the Mind of Modern China* (Cambridge, MA: Harvard University Press, 1959); Hao Chang, *Liang Ch'i-ch'ao and Intellectual Transition in China, 1890–1907* (Cambridge, MA: Harvard University Press, 1971); and Philip C. Huang, *Liang Ch'i-ch'ao and Modern Chinese Liberalism* (Seattle: University of Washington Press, 1972).

33. Tang, *Global Space,* 6–8.

34. For the works written in English on the Chinese historiographical tradition, see Charles Gardner, *Chinese Traditional Historiography* (Cambridge, MA: Harvard University Press, 1961); Han Yu-shan, *Elements of Chinese Historiography* (Hollywood: W. M. Hawley, 1955); E. G. Pulleyblank, "The Historiographical Tradition," *The Legacy of China*, ed. Raymond Dawson (Oxford: Clarendon Press, 1964), 143–164; W. G. Beasley and E. G. Pulleyblank, *Historians of China and Japan* (London: Oxford University Press, 1961); Donald D. Leslie, Colin Mackerras, and Wang Gungwu, eds. *Essays on the Sources for Chinese History* (Columbia: University of South Carolina Press, 1975); and, with a focus, Denis Twitchett, *The Writing of Official History under the T'ang* (New York: Cambridge University Press, 1992).

35. It was long believed in the West that there was not much historical criticism in ancient China. But E. G. Pulleyblank challenged this notion in his "Chinese Historical Criticism: Liu Chih-chi and Ssu-ma Kuang," *Historians of China and Japan*, 135–166, so did Xu Guansan (Hsu Kwan-san), "The Chinese Critical Tradition," *The Historical Journal*, 26:2 (1983), 431–446. For the historical practice in the Ming and Qing period, see Benjamin Elman, *From Philosophy to Philology: Intellectual and Social Aspects of Change in Late Imperial China* (Cambridge, MA: Harvard University Press, 1984); Du Weiyun, *Qingdai shixue yu shijia* (History and historians in the Qing) (Beijing: Zhonghua shuju, 1984); and Yu Ying-shih, *Lun Dai Zheng yu Zhang Xuecheng* (On Dai Zheng and Zhang Xuecheng) (Taipei, 1975).

36. Hu, "Introduction," *Development of Logical Method in Ancient China*, 1. In his later years, Hu again emphasized that all his works were centered around methodology and that methodology had underscored his forty-year scholarly career. See *Hu Shi koushu zichuan* (Hu Shi's oral autobiography), ed. Tang Degang (Taipei, 1981), 94.

37. A definitive study of Gu Jiegang's historical career is in Laurence Schneider's *Ku Chieh-kang and China's New History: Nationalism and the Quest for Alternative Traditions*. There are also quite a few works in Chinese such as: Wang Fansen, *Gushibian yundong de xingqi* (The rise of the National studies movement) (Taipei: Yuncheng wenhua shiye gongsi, 1987); Liu Qiyu, *Gu Jiegang xiansheng xueshu* (Gu Jiegang's works) (Beijing: Zhonghua shuju, 1988); Chen Zhiming, *Gu Jiegang de yigu shixue* (Gu Jiegang and his critical historiography) (Taipei: Shangding wenhua chubanshe, 1993). Ursula Richter's *Zweifel am Altertum: Gu Jiegang und die Diskussion ueber Chinas alte Geschichte als Konsequenz der "Neuen Kulturbewegung" ca. 1915–1923* (Doubting antiquity: Gu Jiegang and the discussion on China's ancient history as the consequence of the New Culture Movement) (Stuttgart: Franz Steiner Verlag, 1992) is another recent study, as well as Tze-ki Hon's "Ethnic and Cultural Pluralism: Gu

Jiegang's Vision of a New China in His Studies of Ancient History," *Modern China*, 22:3 (July 1996), 315–340.

38. Vera Schwarcz, *The Chinese Enlightenment: Intellectuals and the Legacy of the May Fourth Movement of 1919* (Berkeley: University of California Press, 1986).

39. Hans-Georg Gadamer, *Truth and Method* (New York: Crossroad Publishing Company, 1984), 250. See also, Carl Becker's *Heavenly City of the Eighteenth-Century Philosophers* (New Haven: Yale University Press, 1932).

40. Anthony Kemp, *The Estrangement of the Past: A Study in the Origins of Modern Historical Consciousness* (New York: Oxford University Press, 1992), 106.

41. Hu Shi himself used it to call the New Culture Movement, see his *The Chinese Renaissance: the Haskell Lectures, 1933* (New York: Paragon Book Reprint Corp. 1963), and Jerome Grieder, *Hu Shih and the Chinese Renaissance: Liberalism in the Chinese Revolution, 1917–1937* (Cambridge, MA: Harvard University Press, 1970).

42. See Partha Chatterjee, *Nationalist Thought and the Colonial World: A Derivative Discourse* (London: Zed Books Ltd., 1986), chapter 1, 1–35.

43. Schwarcz, *Chinese Enlightenment*, 4.

44. See Yu Ying-shih, "Wenyi fuxing hu? Qimeng yundong hu?—yige shixuejia dui wusi yundong de fanxi" (Renaissance or Enlightenment? A historian's reflection on the May Fourth Movement), in Yu Ying-shih et al., *Wusi xinlun: jifei wenyi fuxing, yifei qimeng yundong* (May Fourth reconsidered: neither Renaissance nor Enlightenment) (Taipei: Lianjing chuban shiye gongsi, 1999), 1–32. While focusing on a more recent period, Zhang Longxi's *Mighty Opposites: From Dichotomies to Differences in the Comparative Study of China* (Stanford: Stanford University Press, 1998) also offers thoughtful discussions on the intricate interplay of the native and the foreign in modern Chinese culture.

45. For the *Xueheng* group, see Shen Songqiao, *Xueheng pai yu wusi shiqi de fan xinwenhua yundong* (The Xueheng group and the anti-New Culture Movement in the May Fourth era) (Taipei: National Taiwan University Press, 1984) and Richard Rosen, "The National Heritage Opposition to the New Culture and Literary Movements of China in the 1920s" (Ph.D. Dissertation, University of California/Berkeley, 1969). For the debates on Chinese culture vis-à-vis Western culture, see Guy Alitto, *The Last Confucian: Liang Shu-ming and the Chinese Dilemma of Modernity* (Berkeley: University of California Press, 1979); Ma Yong, *Liang Shuming wenhua lilun yanjiu* (A study of Liang Shuming's cultural theory) (Shanghai: Shanghai renmin chubanshe, 1991). See also Furth, *The Limits of Change* and Y. C. Wang, *Chinese Intellectuals and the West, 1872–1949* (Chapel Hill: University of North Carolina Press, 1966), as well as Charlotte Furth, *Ting*

Wen-chiang: Science and China's New Culture (Cambridge, MA: Harvard University Press, 1979).

46. Tang, *Global Space,* 9–10.

47. See a concise English version of Hu's opinion in "The Scientific Spirit and Method in Chinese Philosophy," *The Chinese Mind: Essentials of Chinese Philosophy and Culture*, ed. Charles Moore (Honolulu: University of Hawaii Press, 1967), 104–131.

48. See Richard Handler and Jocelyn Linnekin, "Tradition, Genuine or Spurious," *Journal of American Folklore*, 97:385 (1984), 273. See also, Nicholas Thomas, "The Inversion of Tradition," *American Ethnologist*, 19:213–232.

49. Cf. Jonathan Friedman, "The Past in the Future: History and the Politics of Identity," *American Anthropologist*, 94:4 (1992), 837–859.

50. Chatterjee, *Nationalist Thought*, 36–43.

51. See John Israel, *Lianda: A Chinese University in War and Revolution* (Stanford: Stanford University Press, 1998).

52. Jürgen Habermas, *The Structural Transformation of the Public Sphere: An Inquiry into a Category of Bourgeois Society*, trans. Thomas Burger (Cambridge, MA: MIT Press, 1989), 25–26.

Chapter Two

1. See "Yiwenzhi" (History of Literature), in Ban Gu, *Hanshu (Han History)* (Beijing: Zhonghua Shuju).

2. Cf. Li Zongye, *Zhongguo lishi yaoji jieshao* (An introduction to essential works in Chinese history) (Shanghai: Shanghai Guji Chubanshe, 1982), 12–13; Cang Xiuliang, et al., *Zhongguo gudai shixueshi jianbian* (A concise history of ancient Chinese historiography) (Harbin: Heilongjiang Renmin Chubanshe, 1983), 114–115; and Zeng Yifen, "Suitang shiqi sibu fenfa de queli" (The application of four divisions in bibliography in the Sui and Tang Dynasty), *Shixueshi yanjiu (Journal of Historiography)*, 3 (1990), 46–52. See also E. G. Pulleyblank, "The Historiographical Tradition," *The Legacy of China*, ed. Raymond Dawson (Oxford: Clarendon Press, 1964), 153; and *Historians of China and Japan,* 3.

3. Zhang Xuecheng, "Yijiao" (The teaching of the *Changes*), part 1, *Wenshi tongyi* (Taiwan: Zhonghua Shuju). See also Jin Yufu, *Zhongguo shixueshi* (A history of Chinese historiography) (Beijing: Zhonghua Shuju), chapter 2.

4. *Zhangshi yishu* (Literary remains of Zhang Xuecheng), ed. Liu Chengkan (Shanghai: Wuxin, 1922), vol. 4. Cf. David S. Nivison, *The Life*

and Thought of Chang Hsüeh-ch'eng (Stanford: Stanford University Press, 1966), 99–100.

5. Sima Qian, "Taishigong zixu" (Self-Preface of the Grand Historian), *Shiji*. Translated by Burton Watson in his *Ssu-ma Ch'ien: Grand Historian of China* (New York: Columbia University Press, 1958), 87.

6. See his "zun shi" (respect history), *Gong Zizhen quanji* (The complete works of Gong Zizhen) (Shanghai: Shanghai renmin chubanshe, 1975), 80–81. See also Chang Hao, "On the *ching-shih* Ideal in Neo-Confucianism," *Ch'ing-shih wen-t'i*, 3:1 (1974), 36–61. A detailed study on Gong's pragmatic approach to classical learning is found in On-cho Ng's "Revisiting Kung Tzu-chen's (1792–1841) *Chin-wen* (new text) Precepts: An Excursion in the History of Ideas," *Journal of Oriental Studies*, 31:2 (1993), 237–263.

7. Gong, *Gong Zizhen quanji*, 21.

8. "Shang daxueshi shu" (A memorial to the cabinet member), ibid., 319. Translations is based on Shirleen S. Wong's *Kung Tzu-chen* (Boston: Tawayne Publishers, 1975), 30.

9. Gong's examination of the three-age theory is mainly seen in his "Wujing dayi zhongshi daiwen" (The complete meaning of the Five Classics: An answer), *Gong Zizhen quanji*, 46–48.

10. See Kang's *Kongzi gaizhi kao* (Confucius: the reformer) (Beijing: Zhonghua shuju, 1958) and Hao Chang, *Chinese Intellectuals in Crisis*.

11. "Ruan Shangshu nianpu diyi xu" (The first preface to Ruan Yuan's chronological biography), *Gong Zizhen quanji*, 229.

12. Cf. On-cho Ng's "World Making, *Habitus* and Hermeneutics: A Re-reading of Wei Yuan's (1794–1856) New Script (*chin-wen*) Classicism," *Worldmaking*, ed. William Peucak (New York: Peter Lang, 1996), 57–97.

13. "Mogu xia, zhipian" (Mogu 2, governance 9), *Wei Yuan ji* (Works of Wei Yuan) (Beijing: Zhonghua shuju, 1983), 60.

14. Ibid., 48. For Wei's ideas of history, see Wu Ze, "Wei Yuan de bianyi sixiang he lishi jinhua guannian (Wei Yuan's thought on change and view-point on historical progress), *Lishi yanjiu* (Historical research), 5 (1962), 33–59; Qi Sihe "Wei Yuan yu wan Qing xuefeng" (Wei Yuan and late Qing scholarship), *Yen-ching xuebao*, 39 (1950), 177–226; and Leonard, *Wei Yuan* 15–16, 103–105.

15. See *Shengwu ji* (Yangzhou: 1846, rep. Taipei: Wenhai chubanshe), chapter 12, 935–944.

16. Peter Gay, *Style in History* (New York: Basic Books, 1974), 3–17.

17. Wei, *Shengwu ji*, 651 and 677.

18. See *Wei Yuan ji*, 206. *Daoguang yangsou zhengfuji* is sometimes included into the 1846 edition of the *Shengwu ji* and is the first Chinese account of the Opium War.

19. About Lin's effort to learn about the West, see Chen Shenglin, *Lin Zexu yu Yapian Zhanzheng lungao* (Essays on Lin Zexu and the Opium War) (Guangzhou: Zhongshan daxue chubanshe, 1990), 421–506. For Lin's role in the War, see Chang Hsin-pao, *Commissioner Lin.*

20. See Wei's preface to the *Haiguo tuzhi*, *Wei Yuan ji*, 207.

21. Ibid.

22. In Wei's *Shengwu ji*, he discusses the ignorance of the Qing scholars about foreign countries. See volume 12, 944–946.

23. Wei's criticism of the geographical writings in Chinese historiography has been discussed in Leonard, *Wei Yuan*, 94–104.

24. See Wei's preface to the *Haiguo tuzhi*, *Wei Yuan ji*, 208–209.

25. Q. Edward Wang, "World History in Traditional China," *Storia della Storiografia*, 35 (1999), 83–96, especially 91–96.

26. See Xin Ping, *Wang Tao pingzhuan* (A critical biography of Wang Tao) (Shanghai: Huadong shifan daxue chubanshe, 1990), 1–102 and Cohen, *Wang T'ao,* 3–86.

27. Wang attributed Wei's deficiency to his insufficient knowledge about the West, given the limited contact between China and the West at the time. See Wang's *Taoyuan chidu* (The letters of Wang Tao), 12 juan (Hong Kong: 1880), juan 8, 8a–b.

28. About Wang and the origin of modern journalism in China, see Cohen, *Wang T'ao*, 73–81.

29. Grant Hardy, "Can an Ancient Chinese Historian Contribute to Modern Western Theory?—The Multiple Narratives of Ssu-ma Ch'ien," *History and Theory*, 33:1 (1994), 20–38.

30. For Wang's style in writing Western history, see Zhang Chengzong, "Wang Tao de Faguo zhilue he Pufa zhanji" (Wang Tao's General history of France and Account of the Prusso-France War), *Zhongguo shixue lunji* (Essays on Chinese historiography) (Nanjing: Jiangsu guji chubanshe, 1987), vol. 1, 220–234.

31. Wang, *Taoyuan chidu*, 3 juan, 121–122.

32. Wang, *Faguo zhilue*, 24 juan (Hong Kong: 1890). Paul Cohen's discussion is in *Wang T'ao*, 114–130. For Wang's historiographical innovation, see Zhang Chengzong, 233.

33. See Wang's first preface *(qianxu)* to the *Pufa zhanji* (Shanghai: 1895), 1. Paul Cohen has discussed Wang Tao's negative image of Russia in his work, 96–98.

34. For Wang's ideas of history, see Cohen, *Wang T'ao*, 91–96, 110–139.

35. Quoted in Cohen, *Wang T'ao*, 118.

36. See Wang, *Taoyuan wenlu waibian* (Additional essays of Wang Tao) (Shanghai: 1897), chapter 10, 11a, 18a, and chapter 7, 16a.

37. According to Chen Xulu, the *ti-yong* idea was indeed well-liked among most Qing scholar-officials in the late nineteenth century. See "Lun zhongti xiyong" (On Chinese substance and Western function), in *Chen Xulu xueshu wencun* (Chen Xulu's scholarly essays) (Shanghai: Shanghai renmin chubanshe, 1990), 274–300. Xue Huayuan's *Wanqing "zhongti xiyong" sixianglun, 1861–1900* (On the idea of "substance vs. function" in the late Qing) (Taipei: Daoxiang chubanshe, 1991) gives a comprehensive discussion on the formation and evolution of the *ti-yong* ideology.

38. Wang Tao's speculation on the future of history is seen in his "Yuan dao" (Explanation of the *Dao*), *Taoyuan wenlu waibian*, vol. 1.

39. Cohen, *Wang T'ao*, 87–88.

40. Kang attempted to change the image of Confucius from a conservative to a reformer by developing a new interpretation of the *Chunqiu*. He emphasized especially the three-epoch historical theory Confucius allegedly connoted in the *Chunqiu*. His effort thus challenged the conventional interpretation of Confucian historiography and helped generate a skeptical attitude toward the past. See Chang, *Chinese Intellectuals in Crisis*, 50–55.

41. For translations of Western books at the time, see Tsuen-hsuin Tsien, "Western Impact on China through Translation," *Far Eastern Quarterly*, 13:3 (1954), 305–327. According to Tsien, Liang Qichao was an attentive reader of Western books. Paula Harrell's *Sowing the Seeds of Change: Chinese Students, Japanese Teachers, 1895–1905* (Stanford: Stanford University Press, 1992) discusses how Chinese students learned Western knowledge through Japanese translations during the period, 89–94.

42. "Sanshi Zisu" (My recollections at thirty), in Liang Qichao, *Yinbingshi quanji* (The complete works from the Ice-drinker's studio) (Taipei: 1986), 490.

43. See Benjamin Schwartz *In Search of Wealth and Power: Yen Fu and the West* (Cambridge, MA: Harvard University Press, 1964). Also, James Pusey, *China and Charles Darwin* (Cambridge, MA: Harvard University Press, 1983), chapter 2. Fung Yu-lan's *A Short History of Chinese Philosophy* (New York: Free Press, 1948) gives a list of the Western works translated by Yan Fu. Fung also explains why these books were popular at the time.

44. For the influence of Darwinism in modern China, see James Pusey, *China and Charles Darwin*, passim.

45. Liang, "Sanshi zisu," *Yinbingshi quanji*, 492.

46. See Fukuzawa Yukichi, *An Outline of a Theory of Civilization*.

47. According to Paula Harrell, Fukuzawa's *A General Outline of Civilization* and *Comments on Current Affairs* were translated into Chinese at

the time, 93. Stefan Tanaka has studied Japanese historiography during the nineteenth and twentieth centuries in his *Japan's Orient: Rendering Pasts into History* (Berkeley, CA: University of California Press, 1993). For Fukuzawa's influence on Liang, see Xiao Lang, "Fukuzawa Yukichi to Chugoku no keimou shisou: Liang Qichao to no shisouteki kanren o chushin ni" (Fukuzawa and the Chinese Enlightenment: A Study on Liang Qichao and the Japanese Enlightenment," *Nagoya Daigaku Kyoikugakubu Kiyou*, 40, 1 (Sept. 1994), 63–81.

48. See Philip Huang in his *Liang Ch'i-ch'ao and Modern Chinese Liberalism*, chapters 3 and 4.

49. In his *Liang Ch'i-ch'ao and the Mind of Modern China*, Joseph Levenson put forth his "history" and "value" thesis. Hao Chang's *Liang Ch'i-ch'ao and Intellectual Transition in China, 1890–1907*, puts forth a different perspective. Paul Cohen discusses the difference in his *Discovering History in China: American Historical Writing on the Recent Chinese Past* (New York: Columbia University Press, 1984). Philip Huang and Xiaobing Tang both noticed that Liang intended to syncretize the two cultures.

50. In 1901 Liang wrote *Zhongguoshi rumen* (Introduction to Chinese history) and later incorporated some (of its) ideas in *Xin shixue*.

51. Liang, *Xin shixue*, 3–5.

52. Ibid., 4–9.

53. For Liang Qichao's attraction to Japanese Enlightenment thinkers such as Fukuzawa Yukichi, see Xiao Lang's article cited in note 47. In his *Zhongguo shixue jindaihua jincheng* (The modernization of Chinese historiography) (Jinan: Qilu Shushe, 1995), Jiang Jun states that Liang Qichao's *Xinshixue* was basically a modified replica of Ukita Kazutami's (1860–1946) *Shi gaku tu ron* (An introduction to history), 33–34.

54. It is quite interesting that Robinson also thought that historians' attention to elite people was the deficiency of old-style historiography. "Our so-called standard works on history deal at length with kings and popes, with courtiers and statesmen, with wars waged for territory or thrones, with laws passed by princes and parliaments. But these matters form only a very small part of history, . . . What assurance have we that, from the boundless wealth of the past, the most important and pertinent of the experiences of mankind have been sifted out and brought into due prominence by those who popularize history and squeeze it into such compendious forms as they believe best adapted to the instruction of youth? I think that we have no such assurance." *The New History* (New York: 1912), 135–136.

55. Xu Guansan, *Xin shixue jiushi nian* (New history in the last ninety years) (Hong Kong: Zhongwen daxue chubanshe, 1986), I, xi.

56. Although Liang and Robinson shared some of the views in historiography, there is no evidence that the two have ever met. Liang visited

the United States in 1903, a year after he wrote his *Xin shixue*, while Robinson probably just started to write his.

57. Cf. Rao Yuyi, *Zhongguo lishi shang zhi zhengtonglun* (The legitimacy issue in Chinese historiography) (Hong Kong: Longmen Shudian, 1977).

58. Liang, *Xin shixue*, 33–34.

59. Ibid., 36.

60. Pusey's analysis of Yan Fu here is applicable in Liang's case. See James Pusey, *China and C. Darwin*, 51.

61. Liang, *Xin shixue*, 10–15.

Chapter Three

1. Tang, *Global Space*, 165–223.

2. See Geng Yunzhi, *Hu Shi nianpu* (Chronological biography of Hu Shi) (Hong Kong: Zhonghua shuju, 1986), 5.

3. See Tang Degang, ed. *Hu Shi de zizhuan* (Hu Shi's autobiography), in Ge Maochun et al., eds. *Hu Shi zhexue sixiang ziliaoxuan*, 2 vols. (Shanghai: Huadong shifan daxue chubanshe, 1979), vol. 1, 18, and Wang Zhiwei's *Hu Shi xiansheng nianpu* (Hu Shi's chronological biography), *Hu Shi* (Taipei: Huaxin Cultural Center, 1979), 269. See also, Jerome Grieder, *Hu Shih*, 351–354.

4. Hu Shi, *Sishi zishu* (Autobiography at forty) (Shanghai, 1933), 49–54.

5. See *Hu Shi xuanji—riji* (Selected works of Hu Shi—diary) (Taipei: Wenxin Shudian, 1966), especially 1–109. While studying agriculture at Cornell between 1910 and 1915, Hu read many literary and philosophical works, including those of Charles Darwin and Thomas Huxley.

6. In Hu Shi's *The Chinese Renaissance*, he recalled his earlier attempt at writing new style poems at Ithaca and how he disputed with his friends. "The original dispute was," Hu says, "one of poetic diction; and a great many letters were exchanged between Ithaca, New York City, Cambridge, Poughkeepsie, and Washington, D.C. From an interest in the minor problem of poetic diction I was led to see that the problem was really one of a suitable medium for all branches of Chinese literature. The question now became: In what language shall the New China produce its future literature? My answer was: The classical language, so long dead, can never be the medium of a living literature of a living nation; the future literature of China must be written in the living language of the people," 50–51.

7. Hu tells us in his preface to the anthology of poems—*Changshi ji* (Experiments)—that he had many supporters, including Fu Sinian, Lu Xun, Chen Hengzhe, and others at Beida. For Hu Shi's position in the May

Fourth Movement, see Chow Tse-tsung, *The May Fourth Movement: Intellectual Revolution in Modern China* (Cambridge MA: Harvard University Press, 1960), 28–31, 44–47; and Schwarcz, *Chinese Enlightenment*, 59, 80–81; and Yu Ying-shih, *Zhongguo jindai sixiangshi shangde Hu Shi* (Hu Shi's position in modern Chinese intellectual history) (Taipei: Lianjing chuban shiye gongsi, 1984) and Chow Tse-tsung ed. *Hu Shi yu jindai Zhongguo* (Hu Shi and modern China) (Taipei: Shibao wenhua chuban qiye youxian gongsi, 1991).

8. In Dewey's own words, "(i) a felt difficulty; (ii) its location and definition; (iii) suggestion of possible solution; (iv) development by reasoning of the bearings of the suggestion; (v) further observation and experiment leading to its acceptance or rejection; that is, the conclusion of belief or disbelief." See John Dewey, *How We Think* (Boston: D. C. Heath & Co., Publishers, 1910), 72.

9. John Dewey et al. *Living Philosophies: A Series of Intimate Credos* (New York: Simon & Schuster, 1931), 255.

10. For Dewey and China, see Barry Keenan, *The Dewey Experiment in China: Educational Reform and Political Power in the Early Republic* (Cambridge MA: Harvard University Press, 1977). Dewey's lectures were translated and published in China by Shanghai Great Harmony Press in 1921 and by Shanghai Commercial Press in 1931. Dewey also wrote extensively about his impression of China that appeared mostly in *Asia* and the *New Republic* during the 1920s.

11. Hu "*Qing dai xuezhe de zhixue fangfa*" (The research method of the Qing scholars), *Hu Shi zhexue sixiang ziliao xuan*, vol. 1, 208.

12. For the relationship between these two books, see Hu Shi's "A Note," in *Development of Logical Method in Ancient China* (New York: Paragon Book Reprint Corp., 1963), which precedes his Introduction.

13. Hu Shi, "Introduction," *Zhongguo zhexueshi dagang* (I), in *Hu Shi zhexue sixiang ziliao xuan*, vol. 2, 28–30.

14. Ibid., 2, 34–37.

15. Windelband *History of Ancient Philosophy*, trans. Herbert E. Cushman (New York: Charles Scribner's Sons, 1898), 6.

16. Hu, "Introduction," *Development of Logical Method in Ancient China*, 1.

17. Hu, "Introduction," *Zhongguo zhexueshi dagang* (I), in *Hu Shi zhexue sixiang ziliao xuan*, vol. 2, 38–44.

18. See Liang's *Zhongguo lishi Yanjiufa*, 107, note 9. For Liang's praise of Hu's new approach, see his "Ping Hu Shizhi *Zhongguo zhexueshi dagang*," in *Yinbingshi wenji*.

19. Gu Jiegang, *The Autobiography of a Chinese Historian*, trans. Arthur W. Hummel (Leyden: Late E. J. Brill Ltd., 1931), 65–66. Hu's Beida and Columbia alumnus and later his colleague Feng Youlan (1895–1990) also provided a similar description of Hu Shi's teaching at Beida and the impact of his book, see Feng's "Sansongtang zixu (Self-preface to the works of Three-Pine-Hall)," *Sansongtang quanji* (The complete works of the Three-Pine-Hall), 3 vols. (Zhengzhou: Henan Renmin Chubanshe, 1985), vol. 1, 199–213.

20. See his "Zhengli guogu yu 'dagui'" (National studies and "to beat the devil"), in *Zhongguo xiandai sixiangshi ziliao*, vol. 2, 126.

21. Hu, "Introduction," *Development of Logical Method in Ancient China*, 9.

22. Ibid., 1–4. Also chapter 1.

23. In his "The Scientific Spirit and Method in Chinese Philosophy" (1939), Hu elaborates on the methods of Zhu Xi and other Confucian scholars in the Song Dynasty. In C. Moore, *Chinese Mind: Essentials of Chinese Philosophy and Culture*, 104–131.

24. Hu Shi, "Qingdai xuezhe de zhixue fangfa" (Qing scholars' methods in their study), *Hu Shi zhexue sixiang ziliaoxuan*, vol. 1, 184–208. Some Western scholars also wrote that Chinese historians applied scientific method to historical study. See Pierre Ryckmans, *The Chinese Attitude toward the Past*, 9.

25. Hu Shi's argument is in ibid., 208–211.

26. Hu Shi, "Intellectual Life, Past and Present," *Chinese Renaissance*, 66–71.

27. In his lecture delivered in 1981 at Hong Kong, Needham said, "When we say that modern science developed only in Western Europe in the time of Galileo during the Renaissance and during the scientific revolution, we mean, I think, that it was there alone, that there developed the fundamental bases of *modern* science, such as the application of mathematical hypotheses to Nature, and the full understanding and use of the experimental method, the distinction between primary and secondary qualities, and the systematic accumulation of openly published scientific data. Indeed, it has been said that it was in the time of Galileo that the most effective method of discovery about Nature was itself, and I think that is still quite true." *Science in Traditional China* (Cambridge, MA: Harvard University Press, 1981), 9.

28. J. Needham, *Science and Civilization in China* (Cambridge, England: 1956), vol. 2, 279–293.

29. C. Furth, *Ting Wen-chiang*, 7–10.

30. D. Kwok, *Scientism in Chinese Thought, 1900–50* (New Haven: Yale University Press, 1965), 26–30, 91–97.

31. See Hu Shi "Lun guogu xue" (On the studies of national heritage), *Zhongguo xiandai sixiang shi ziliao jianbian*, vol. 1, 299–300. Mao's article, entitled "Guogu he kexue de jingshen" (National heritage and scientific spirit), appeared in *Xinchao*, 1, 5 (May 1, 1919).

32. "Xin sichao de yiyi," *Hu Shi zhexue sixiang ziliao xuan*, vol. 1, 125–133.

33. See Gu's letter to Qian Xuantong in *Gushibian* (Beijing: Pushe, 1926), vol. 1, 59–66.

34. For the influence of Cui Shu and other late Qing scholars on Hu Shi and Gu Jiegang, see Joshua Fogel's excellent article, "On the 'Rediscovery' of the Chinese Past: Cui Shu and Related Cases," in his *The Cultural Dimension of Sino-Japanese Relations: Essays on the Nineteenth and Twentieth Centuries* (Armonk, NY: M. E. Sharpe, 1995), 3–21.

35. See *Hu Shi zhexue sixiang ziliao xuan*, vol. 1, especially 1–23, 29–31, 40–47, 50–57.

36. Hu learned this method from John Dewey, which means to look for evidence and describe how the problem arose. See Hu Shi, "Duwei xiansheng yu zhongguo" (Mr. Dewey and China), *Hu Shi zhexue sixiang ziliaoxuan*, vol. 1, 182. Dewey's other student Feng Youlan also remembered that Dewey had asked him a question about the relationship among philosophical schools in his oral defense. Feng deemed the genetic method a main feature of Deweyan pragmatism. See Feng Youlan, "Sansongtang zixu" (Self-preface to the works of Three-Pine-Hall), *Sansongtang quanji*, vol. 1, 193, 201.

37. Gu Jiegang, "Zixu" (Self-preface), *Gushibian*, vol. 1, 1–103, especially 59–60, 77–80. Laurence Schneider and Wang Fansen have analyzed Gu's debts to Hu Shi, Qian Xuantong, and others, see Schneider, *Ku Chieh-Kang*, 53–83, 188–217; and Wang Fansen, *Gushibian yundong de xingqi*.

38. For the affinity between Gu's folklore and historical studies, see Xu Guansan, *Xinshixue jiushinian*, vol. 1, 178–182.

39. See Liu's letter to Gu, *Gushibian*, vol. 1, 217–222, and Gu's response, 223–231.

40. See Gu Jiegang's self-prefaces to *Gushibian*, vol. 4, 4, 19, vol. 3, 6. Although he had an ambitious plan to reconstruct ancient history, he actually achieved less than he had hoped for, due to various interruptions. See Xu Guansan, *Xinshixue jiushinian*, vol. 1, 182–204 and Ursula Richter, "Gu Jiegang: His Last Thirty Years," *The China Quarterly*, 90 (June 1982), 286–295. And the biography written by Gu Chao, Gu Jiegang's daughter, *Lijie zhongjiao zhibuhui: wode fuqin Gu Jiegang* (My father Gu Jiegang) (Shanghai: Huadong shifan daxue chubanshe, 1997).

41. In his diary, Hu Shi compared Gu with Fu Sinian, his most favorite student, and expressed his obvious disappointment at Fu: "Fu has led an

undisciplined life (in the past years in Europe). He has not been as diligent as Gu Jiegang." *Hu Shi de riji*, September 5, 1926. Quoted in Wang Fansen, "*Fu Ssu-nien: An Intellectual Biography*" (Ph.D. Dissertation, Princeton University, 1993), 97, footnote 210.

42. For Hu Shi's social life, see Lu Yaodong's "Hu Shi guang gongyuan" (Hu Shi sauntered in the park), *Qiezuo shenzhou xiushouren* (Let's be spectators in China) (Taipei: Yuncheng wenhua shiye youxian gongsi, 1989), 109–131.

43. Hu Shi, "*Hong Lou Meng* kaozheng" (An evidential study of the *Dream of the Red Chamber*), *Hu Shi*, 99–142.

44. For Hu Shi's scholarly influence, see Feng Aiqun, ed. *Hu Shi Zhi xiansheng jinianji* (A commemorative volume for Hu Shi) (Taipei: Xuesheng shuju, 1962).

45. For the debate, see the works of Kwok, *Scientism in Chinese Thought*, 26–30, 91–97 and Furth, *Ting Wen chiang*, 7–10. For Hu Shi's opinion, see his "*Kexue yu renshengguan* xu" (Preface to *Science and Outlook of Life*), *Kexue yu renshengguan (Science and outlooks of life)* (Shanghai: Dongya shudian, 1923).

46. This was shown in Hu's last speech (1961), delivered in Taipei, called "Kexue fazhan suo xuyao de shehui gaige" (Social reforms for developing science), *Zhuanji wenxue (Biographical Literature)*, 55:1 (1987), 38–40. For a discussion of the attitudes of Liang Qichao and Hu Shi toward Western science in English, see Grieder, *Hu Shih*, 129–169.

47. See *Hu Shi zhexue sixiang ziliaoxuan*, vol. 1, 198.

48. Keenan, *The Dewey Experiment in China*, 18–19.

49. See Luo Jialun's "Pingdiao Jiang Tingfu xiansheng" (In memory of Jiang Tingfu), *Luo Jialun xiansheng wencun* (The works of Luo Jialun), 10 vols. (Taipei, Guoshiguan, 1976), vol. 10, 191–194.

50. See Richard Hofstadter, *The Progressive Historians: Turner, Beard, and Parrington* (New York: Vintage, 1968) and Ernst Breisach, *American Progressive History: An Experiment in Modernization* (Chicago: University of Chicago Press, 1993).

51. Tan, "Benshiji chu de yibu zhuming shixue yizhu—*Xin shixue*" (*The New History*—an influential translated historical book at the beginning of the twentieth century), *He Bingsong jinian wenji* (Commemorative volume for He Bingsong), eds. Liu Yinsheng, et al. (Shanghai: Huadong shifan daxue chubanshe, 1990), 74–75. About Hu Shi's encouragement, see He Bingsong's "Zengbu Zhang Shizhai nianpu xu" (Preface to the expanded chronological biography of Zhang Xuecheng), *He Bingsong lunwenji* (Works of He Bingsong), eds. Liu Yinsheng, et al. (Beijing: Shangwu yinshuguan, 1990), 134.

52. He changed the title to "Cong lishi dao zhexue" (From history to philosophy). The translation appeared in *Shidi congkan*, 2 (1921).

53. He Bingsong "Suiyu er'an" (My adaptable temperament)—it is actually his own description about his personality. *He Bingsong lunwenji*, 507–508.

54. Jin Zhaoxin, He's childhood friend, recalled that because He's knowledge was superior to many of his cohorts; he was a model in school for other children to look after. See Jin's *He Bingsong zhuan* (Biography of He Bingsong), ibid., 526.

55. UC/Berkeley does not have any record of He Bingsong.

56. Their communication began because of the *Liumei xuesheng jibao* (The Chinese Students' Monthly), to which they both contributed. For He's recollection about Hu Shi, see his "Zengbu Zhang Shizhai nianpu xu" (Preface to the expanded chronological biography of Zhang Xuecheng), *Minduo zazhi* (People's Will Miscellaneous), IX:5. Also Fang Xinliang's "He Bingsong pingzhuan" (A critical biography of He Bingsong), *He Bingsong jinian wenji*, 419.

57. He's thesis is untraceable. Princeton only has He's course registration, which shows that he took courses in modern European history and international relations. The information about the title of his MA thesis was given by Ho Ping-ti, his nephew and the history professor emeritus at the University of Chicago. In 1920, He published an article entitled "Zhongguo gudai guojifa" (A study of ancient Chinese international law) in *Fazheng xuebao*, 2:5 (1920). It was probably based on his master thesis.

58. He later published part of his English essay on Chinese parties in Chinese in *Fazheng xuebao* (Journal of Law and Politics), 2:1 (1919). See *He Bingsong lunwenji*, 1–5.

59. He started the project in February 1921; his student Jiang Xinruo at Beijing Normal College helped him. When Jiang left Beijing in May, He's friend Fu Donghua became his assistant. In August, they finished the translation. He's Beida colleagues Zhu Xizu, Zhang Weizi, and Hu Shi read the manuscript. Zhu wrote a forward while Hu pointed out a few mistakes. See He's "*Xinshixue* daoyan" (An introduction to *The New History*), *He Bingsong lunwenji*, 63–64. Zhu's forward is in Si Qi, ed., *He Bingsong xiaozhang wenji* (Works of chancellor He Bingsong) (Taipei: Commercial Press, 1988), Appendix II, 298–301.

60. Many of his students got to know He by reading his translation of Robinson's *The New History*, see Tan Qixiang "Benshiji chu de yibu zhuming shixue yizhu—*Xin shixue*" (*The New History*—an influential translated history book at the beginning of the twentieth century), Xia Yande "He Bingsong xiansheng zai shixue yu wenjiao fangmian de gongxian" (He Bingsong's contribution to China's historiography and education), Hu Daojing "Bocheng xiansheng xueenlu" (What I learned from He Bing-

song), and Zhu Shaotang "He Bingsong xiansheng zai jiaoyu ji shixue fangmian de gongji" (He Bingsong's achievements in history and education), *He Bingsong jinian wenji*, 74–75, 308–317, 344–348, 378–379.

61. "*Xin shixue* daoyan" (An introduction to *The New History*), *He Bingsong lunwenji*, 51–52.

62. Ibid., 52–63.

63. At the same time when He and Guo translated Shotwell's book, they also began to translate George Gooch's *History and Historians in the Nineteenth Century*. However, Gooch's book was only half done and never formally published.

64. "*Shidi congkan* fakanci" (An introduction to *Journal of History and Geography*), *He Bingsong lunwenji*, 6–7.

65. John Higham et al., *History: Professional Scholarship in America*, 111–112.

66. "Xiyangshi yu tazhong kemu de guanxi" (The relationship between the study of Western history and other disciplines), ibid., 65–72. He also published another article based on Johnson's book, "Xiyang zhongxiaoxue zhongde shixue yanjiufa" (Historical methods in Western elementary and secondary schools), ibid., 14–26.

67. "Zenyang yanjiu shidi" (How to study history and geography), ibid., 205–207.

68. *The Varieties of History*, ed. Fritz Stern (New York: Meridian Books, 1956), 209–245.

69. Ibid., 207–208.

70. See Lin Yu-sheng, *The Crisis of Chinese Consciousness: Radical Antitraditionalism in the May Fourth Era* (Madison: University of Wisconsin Press, 1979), passim.

71. Age is always important in the relationship between teachers and students in China. Teacher in Chinese: *"Xiansheng"* literally means "the elder born."

72. Gu Jiegang, *The Autobiography of a Chinese Historian*, 65–66.

73. Luo Jialun recalled that Fu once united his class to humiliate their literature professor for his misinterpretation of literary Classics. Fu made a list of the professor's thirty mistakes and gave them to the president Cai Yuanpei. As a result, the professor left the university. See Luo Jialun, "Yuanqi linli de Fu Mengzhen" (Fu Sinian: an energetic figure), *Shizhe rusi ji* (Recollections) (Taipei: Zhuanji Wenxue Chubanshe, 1967), 167–168.

74. Zhou Zuoren, *Zhitang huiyilu* (Zhou Zuoren's memoir) (Taipei: Longwen Chubanshe, 1989), vol. 2, 475–476.

75. "Hu Shi Xiansheng Yanhan" (Hu Shi's letter of condolence), *Hu Shi xuanji—shuxin* (Selected works of Hu Shi—correspondence), 113–114. At the first anniversary of Fu's death in 1952, Hu again called Fu his "protector." See Hu Shi, "Fu Mengzhen xiansheng de sixiang" (Fu Sinian's thoughts), in *Hu Shi yanlunji* (Hu Shi's words) (Taipei, 1955), vol. 1, 94–95.

76. *Hu Shi laiwang shuxin xuan*, vol. 1, 107.

77. Luo, "Yuanqi linli de Fu Mengzhen" (Fu Sinian: an energetic figure), *Shizhe rusi ji*, 175.

78. See Mao Zishui "Fu Mengzheng xiansheng zhuanlue" (Biography of Fu Sinian), in Mao Zishui, *Shiyou ji* (About my friends) (Taipei: Zhuanji Wenxue Chubanshe, 1967), 89–90.

79. Fu Lecheng, *Fu Mengzhen xiansheng nianpu* (Chronological biography of Fu Sinian) (Taipei: Wenxin Shudian, 1964), 5.

80. Mao Zishui, *Shiyou ji*, 90.

81. Fu Lecheng, *Fu Mengzhen*, 11.

82. Mao Zishui, *Shiyou ji*, 92. Because Fu had studied rather extensively classical learning, he could have become another follower of Zhang Taiyan, as Zhang's three disciples who taught at Beida expected. But Fu later committed himself to the New Culture movement. See Luo Jialun, "Yuanqi linli de Fu Mengzhen" (Fu Sinian: an energetic figure), *Shizhe rusi ji*, 166–167.

83. Cf. Charlotte Furth, "The Sage as Rebel: The Inner World of Chang Ping-lin," *The Limits of Change*, 113–150.

84. For Zhang's scholarship and revolutionary activities, see Charlotte Furth's, ibid., and Liang Chi-chao's *Intellectual Trends in the Ch'ing Period*, 111–112. For his impact on the May Fourth Movement, see Schwarcz, *Chinese Enlightenment*, 35–37.

85. Mao Zishui, *Shiyou ji*, 92–93. Also, Luo Jialun, "Yuanqi linli de Fu Mengzhen" (Fu Sinian: an energetic figure), *Shizhe rusi ji*, 166–167.

86. For the founding of the New Tide and its early members, see Chow Tse-tsung, *The May Fourth Movement*, 51–57; see also Schwarcz, *The Chinese Enlightenment*, 67–76. Lu Xun recorded in his diary that both Fu and Luo wrote to him at the time; Luo visited Lu quite a few times and presented their journal to him. *Lu Xun riji* (Lu Xun's diary) (Beijing: Renmin Wenxue Chubanshe, 1962), vol. 1, 359–403.

87. "*Xinchao* fakan zhiqushu" (An introduction to *New Tide*), *Fu Sinian quanji* (The complete works of Fu Sinian), 7 vols. (Taipei: Lianjing Publishing Co., 1980), vol. 4, 349–353.

88. "Zhongguo xueshu sixiangjie zhi jiben wumiu" (Essential flaws of Chinese scholarship), ibid., vol. 4, 165–171.

89. Ibid., 174–175.

90. Fu Sinian, "Zhongguo lishi fenqi zhi yanjiu" (A study of the division of Chinese history), *Fu Sinian quanji*, vol. 4, 176–182.

91. Ibid., 182–185.

92. Ibid., 185. Fu considered it novel to emphasize the ethnicity question.

93. See Yao Congwu, "Guoshi kuoda mianyan de yidian kanfa," *Yao Congwu* (Taipei: Huaxin Cultural Center, 1979), 235–239.

94. See "Zhongguo wenxueshi fenqi zhi yanjiu" (A study of the division in the history of Chinese literature), *Fu Sinian quanji*, vol. 4, 64–70.

95. "Zenyang zuo baihuawen" (How to use vernacular Chinese), ibid., 71–87.

96. "Hanyu gaiyong pinyin wenzi de chubutan" (A tentative suggestion for romanizing Chinese), ibid., 90–117.

97. Luo Jialun, "Yuanqi linli de Fu Mengzhen" (Fu Sinian: an energetic figure), *Shizhe rusi ji*, 166, 171. In the Fu Sinian Library, which was based on Fu's own possessions, in the Institute of History and Philology, Academia Sinica in Taipei, Taiwan, I found a great number of books owned by Fu that covered a great variety of subjects, ranging from the humanities, social sciences to natural sciences; most of them were purchased by Fu during his European sojourn.

98. Wen-hsin Yeh, *The Alienated Academy: Culture and Politics in Republican China, 1919–1937* (Cambridge, MA: Harvard University Press, 1990), chapters 2, 6, 7. Qian Zhongshu's novel, *Fortress Besieged*, trans. Jeanne Kelly and Nathan K. Mao (Bloomington: Indiana University Press, 1979), also describes these returned, "Westernized" students in 1930s–1940s China.

99. "Hanyu gaiyong pinyin wenzi de chubutan," *Fu Sinian quanji*, vol. 4, 116–117.

100. Edward Shils, "Intellectuals, Traditions, and the Traditions of Intellectuals: Some Preliminary Considerations," *Intellectuals and Tradition*, eds. S. N. Eisenstadt and S. R. Graubard (New York: Humanities Press, 1973), 24.

101. See Luo Jialun, "Yuanqi linli de Fu Mengzhen," *Shizhe rusi ji*, 171–172. For the students' action of May 4, 1919, see Chow Tse-tsung, *The May Fourth Movement*, 99–116. Fu himself also recalled his involvement in the May Fourth Movement. See his "Wusi outan" (About the May Fourth), *Zhongyang ribao* (Central China Daily) (Chongqing), May 4, 1943.

102. "Xinchao zhi huigu yu qianzhan" (New Tide: Recollections of the past and future prospect), *Fu Sinian quanji*, vol. 4, 156. I think what Fu

said here was true and I therefore disagree with Vera Schwarcz's argument that it was coprovincials, roommates, classmates rather than the "shared mind-set" that motivated them to form the "New Tide." For Vera Schwarcz's argument, see 69–71.

103. Fu Sinian, "Liuying jixing" (My studies in Britain), *Chenbao*, August 6–7, 1920. Also Mao Zishui, *Shiyou ji*, 90.

104. Luo Jialun, "Yuanqi linli de Fu Mengzhen," *Shizhe rusi ji*, 172.

105. See Keenan, *The Dewey Experiment in China*, Keenan points out that while the content of Dewey's lectures fell into three categories: modern science, democracy, and education, experimental methodology was certainly his main focus. Through Hu Shi's assistance, Dewey's theory became an authoritative interpretation of Western science and scientific method for the Chinese at the time. 21–42.

106. "Liuying jixing," *Chenbao*, August 6–7, 1920. Fu also said elsewhere at the time that besides Western science, there was no other "true scholarship" *(zhen xuewen)*. See Wang Fansen, *Fu Ssu-nien*, 65–70.

107. "Rensheng wenti faduan" (An introduction to the discussion of human being), *Fu Sinian quanji*, vol. 4, 186–201.

108. The quotation is in Fu's "Duiyu Zhongguo jinri tan zhexuezhe zhi gannian" (A suggestion to those who are discussing philosophy in today's China), ibid., 204. His other essays and book reviews are: "Xinli fenxi daoyin" (An introduction to psychoanalysis), 212–252; "Yingguo yefangsi zhi kexue yuanli" (Jevons's scientific principles in England), 389–390; "Shile xiansheng de xingshi luoji" (Dr. Schiller's formal logic), 397–403. Besides the works of Jevons and Schiller, Fu also read Karl Person's *Grammar of Science* and *Law of Probability*, and T. M. Keynes's *A Treatise of Probability*. See Luo Jialun, "Yuanqi linli de Fu Mengzhen," *Shizhe rusi ji*, 172–173.

109. See *Hu Shi laiwang shuxin xuan*, vol. 1, 103–108.

110. See Fu's collection of books in Fu Sinian Library, Academia Sinica. In some of his notebooks, there is also information about the books he bought during that time and later in 1948 when he was in the United States. See "Fu Sinian dangan" (Fu Sinian's archive), I-817, I-820, I-1683.

111. See Luo Jialun, "Yuanqi linli de Fu Mengzhen," *Shizhe rusi ji*, 172–176.

112. Lin Yu-sheng, *The Crisis of Chinese Consciousness*, Introduction.

113. Mao Zishui, "Guogu he kexue de jingsheng" (National cultural legacy and scientific spirit), *Xinchao*, I:5 (May 1919). As the editor, Fu wrote instead a comment in which he stated that because this paper was so well written, he felt it unnecessary to write one himself.

114. Luo Jialun, "Yuanqi linli de Fu Mengzhen," *Shizhe rusi ji*, 166.

115. According to the Senate House Records of University of London, Fu was a registered student in the Psychology Department from October 1920 to July 1923. In 1922, he obtained his BA degree and was admitted in the MA program of the Department, but Fu did not finish the graduate program.

116. In his letter to Hu Shi from England, Fu mentioned his English professors. He thought Spearman was a bit bookish. He was instead attracted to the fame of George Hicks and L. T. Hobhouse, two prominent philosophers in the school. It seems that he could not totally eliminate his interest in the humanities. *Hu Shi laiwang shuxin xuan*, vol. 1, 107.

117. Luo Jialun, "Yuanqi linli de Fu Mengzhen," *Shizhe rusi ji*, 172–173.

118. "Wo dui shao bona de kanfa" (I see Bernard Shaw), *Fu Sinian quanji*, vol. 7, 32–42.

119. The reason is unknown, but possibly economic. Because of the 1924 inflation, the German mark fell rapidly against the Chinese yuan, and many Chinese students went to Berlin to live on the high exchange rate. Fu's going to Germany gave him an opportunity to meet his Beida friends. Cf. Y. C. Wang, 165. In Fu's letters to Luo Jialun, discovered and published by Luo's daughter Luo Jiufang, he often joked about their poor student lives. See *Dangdai* (Contemporary), 127 (March 1, 1998), 104–119. But it is also possible that he was not so successful in pursuing the degree in psychology. See Wang Fansen, *Fu Ssu-nien*, 84–85.

120. Mao Zishui, *Shiyou ji*, 90.

121. Luo Jialun, "Yuanqi linli de Fu Mengzhen," *Shizhe rusi ji*, 173.

122. Luo Jialun later told a story about Fu's stay in Germany. One day they gathered together in a Chinese restaurant in Berlin, Fu brought a thick three-volume geology book to the party. His friends kidded about his science fetish. Ibid., 175. Although ambitious, Fu's student life in Berlin was not very successful. Lacking a focus, he actually, according to the registration record at Berlin University, failed three courses: Sanskrit, Sanskrit grammar, and astrology.

123. "Yu Gu Jiegang lun gushishu," *Zhongshan daxue zhoukan* (Weekly Journal of Sun Yat-sen University), ed. The Institute of History and Philology, II:13, 14 (Jan. 1928), 359–398. Also, *Fu Sinian quanji*, vol. 4, 454–494. About Fu's impression of Gu's paper, vol. 3, 225.

124. See Wang Fansen, *Fu Ssu-nien*, 96–97, note 209.

125. Fu admitted that because his scientific excitement came after his extensive exposure to classical learning, it was thus not effective. It only served as a kind of mind-training. *Fu Sinian quanji*, vol. 7, 17–27.

126. In his library, there were works of Leopold von Ranke, Georg Hegel, Heinrich Treitschke, and other German scholars. "Fu Sinian dangan" (Fu Sinian's archive), I-817.

127. Fu mentioned Ranke and Mommsen in his forward to the *Shiliao yu shixue* (Historical sources and history). He also praised Sima Guang's historical method. *Fu Sinian quanji*, vol. 4, 354–356.

128. Zhu Jiahua, a GMD veteran and a student returned from Germany, recalled that when he was then the vice-president of the university, he tried to look for a modern scholar to head the School of Humanities. He chose Fu for his new approach to Chinese tradition. "Dao wangyou Fu Mengzhen xiansheng" (In memory of my friend Fu Sinian), in Fu Lecheng, *Fu Mengzhen*, 23.

129. His student recalled that Fu taught five courses at the university: *Shujing* (Book of history), ancient Chinese literature, psychology and others. See Zhong Gongxun "Mengzhen xiansheng zai Zhongshan Daxue shiqi de yidian buchong" (Some supplement materials about Fu Sinian when he was at Sun Yat-sen University), *Zhuanji wenxue*, 28:3 (1976), 51.

130. See *Fu Sinian quanji*, vol. 7, 96–101.

131. See Schwarcz *The Chinese Enlightenment*, passim and Tse-tsung *The May Fourth Movement*.

132. In his assessment of Hu Shi's position in modern Chinese history, Yu Ying-shi has argued that Hu is more relevant today for his commitment to liberalism than his scholarly work. *Zhongguo jindai sixiangshi shang de Hu Shi* (Hu Shi's position in modern Chinese intellectual history) (Taipei: Lianjing chuban shiye gongsi, 1986).

133. Zhang Binsheng, "Yao Congwu xiansheng zhuan" (Biography of Yao Congwu), *Yao Congwu*, 1.

134. Zhao Tiehan, "Daonian yige chunchui de xueren" (In memory of a pure scholar), *Yao Congwu xiansheng aisilu* (Memories for Yao Congwu) (Taipei, 1971), 134–136. Another memoir complains that the media in Taiwan did not pay sufficient attention to Yao's death, because Yao was a scholar, not a popular singer. Peng Ge, "Xueren yu mingxing zhi si" (The death of a scholar and the death of a pop singer), 132–133.

135. Mao Zishui, "Daonian Yao Congwu xiansheng" (In memory of Yao Congwu), *Yao Congwu xiansheng aisilu*, 51.

136. Wang Deyi, *Yao Congwu xiansheng nianbiao* (Chronology of Yao Congwu), *Yaoshi Congwu xiansheng jinian lunwenji* (Commemorative volume for Yao Congwu), ed. History Department, Taiwan University (Taipei, 1971), 5.

137. Ibid., 7–8. Huntington was a geography professor at Yale. This was Yao's first attempt to work with a foreign language. He acknowledged some mistakes in his endnotes.

138. In the 1920s, Yao wrote a series of articles exploring the geographical influence on human history: "Cong lishi guannian guancha dili bianqian yu rensheng zhi guanxi" (The relationship between the changing geography and human life, a historical perspective), *Dixue zazhi* (Journal

of Geography), 11:5, 6 (1920), "Dili yu wenhua" (Geography and culture), ibid., 11:11 (1920), "Wenming yu qihou" (Civilization and climate), ibid., 13:1 (1922), "Hewei dili huanjing, dili huanjing yu renlei shenghuo youruohe zhi guanxi" (What is geographical environment? What is the relationship between geographical environment and human life?), ibid., 13:3 (1922).

139. There are different opinions about how many years Yao studied in Germany. One is in his daughter's memoir which states that his father went to Germany in 1922 and returned to China in 1934. See Yao Ta-liang's "My Father—Tsung-wu Yao," *Yao Congwu xiansheng aisilu*, 14–15. Yao's biographer and his life long friend Zhang Binsheng agrees that Yao returned to China in 1934, but Zhang says that Yao went to Germany in 1923. See Zhang's "Yao Congwu xiansheng zhuan," *Yao Congwu*, 1. A few memoirs written by Yao's friends and colleagues recall that Yao returned to China in 1931. See Tao Xisheng's "Yao Congwu xiansheng lei" (Recollection of Yao Congwu), *Yao Congwu xiansheng aisilu*, 14–15, 98. I accept Zhang's opinion because I also checked these dates with Wang Deyi's *Yao Congwu xiansheng nianbiao*, which matches Zhang's finding. I do not think Yao went to Germany in 1922 for he, according to Mao Zishui's memoir, passed the examination in that fall, and according to Wang Deyi, Yao spent some days at home after passing the examination. Yao actually sailed to Germany on January 5, 1923, and arrived in February. See *Yao Congwu xiansheng nianbiao*, *Yao Congwu xiansheng jinian lunwenji*, 9–10. As for the date of his return, I believe his daughter's memory is more reliable.

140. Yu Dawei, Yao's friend in Germany, recalled that to have a degree from European countries was honorable at the time. There was a saying: "A doctorate from Japan coats you with silver, a doctorate from Europe coats you with gold." Quoted in Hsi-Huey Liang, *The Sino-German Connection: Alexander von Falkenhausen between China and Germany, 1900–41* (Amsterdam: Van Gorcum, Assen, 1978), 26.

141. See Max Linde, "Chinese Students in Germany," *Ostasiatische Rundschau*, 7:11 (1926), 234–235; and Y. C. Wang, *Chinese Intellectuals and the West*, 165. For general information about Chinese students in Berlin in the early twentieth century, see Hsi-Huey Liang, 23–38. About Luo Jialun's sojourn in Germany, see his daughter's memoir, "Zhuinian wode fuqing" (In memory of my father), in *Luo Zhixi xiansheng zhuanji ji zhusu ziliao* (Biography of Luo Jialun and his writings) (Taipei, 1969), 30.

142. In his introduction Hu probably made a mistake. He said that Yao stayed in Germany for seven years; but it was actually eleven years. See Tao Xisheng, "Yao Congwu xiansheng lei," in *Yao Congwu xiansheng aisilu*, 98. Of course, it is also possible that it was Tao, instead of Hu, who made the mistake. Tao explains that at that time, his and other's reverence for Yao is because, on the one hand, not many people have stayed abroad as long as Yao, on the other hand, many students at the time regarded European scholarship as superior to American scholarship.

143. For a brief introduction to their careers, see sections of Mechthild Leutner's "Sinologie in Berlin," *Berlin und China: Dreihundert Jahre wechselvolle Beziehungen*, ed. Kuo Heng-yu (Berlin: Colloquium Verlag, 1987), 44–46, 49–52.

144. My description of Otto Franke's career is largely based on Yao Congwu's own work, "Guoshi kuoda mianyan de yidian kanfa" (My opinion of the evolution of national history), in which he recalls his German professors. *Yao Congwu*, 237–239. The following discussions are based on the same source.

145. Though different from Ranke in understanding history, Johann Droysen was a faithful student of Ranke's concept of historical sources. His *verstehen* approach to history addressed the problem of whether human cognition was able to reach an objective knowledge, but in general, Droysen did not refute the ideal of objectivity. Rather, he wanted to attain it with speculation. Cf. Georg Iggers, *German Conception of History*, 109–115. Wilhelm Wattenbach was known for his work on German historical sources. His achievement in history lay in his editorship of the *Monumenta Germaniae Historica*.

146. See Du Weiyun, "Yao Congwu shi yu lishi fangfalun" (Professor Yao Congwu and historical methodology). Du also recalls that Yao suggested that they teach the course together in the 1960s. *Yao Congwu xiansheng aisilu*, 84–85.

147. Yao Congwu, "Guoshi kuodai mianyan de yidian kanfa," *Yao Congwu*, 231–258.

148. Yao and Haenisch kept contact after Yao returned to China. In a letter written by Yao to Fu Sinian, he mentioned that Haenisch would like him to recommend someone to teach Chinese at Berlin University. Yao thought of Fu Lehuan, Fu Sinian's nephew. See "Fu Sinian dangan" (Fu Sinian's archive), II-345.

149. Wang Deyi, *Yao Congwu xiansheng nianbiao, Yao Congwu xiansheng jinian lunwenji*, 11.

150. *Meng-ta Pei-lu und Hei-ta Shih-lueh, Chinesische Gesandtenberichte uber die fruehen Mongolen 1221 und 1237*, nach Vorarbeiten von Erich Haenisch und Yao Tsung-wu, ubsersetzt und kommentiert von Peter Olbricht und Elisabeth Pinks (Wiesbaden: Otto Harrassowitz, 1980). The translators write that Yao translated a part of the two books in the 1930s, see xvii.

151. "Zhongguo zaozhishu shuru ouzhou kao" (A critical study of the transmission of Chinese paper-making technology to Europe), *Furen xuezhi* (Journal of Furen University), I:1 (1928). It was republished for the last time in the fall of 1966 in *Shumu jikan* (A Quarterly Journal of Bibliography), I:2 (1966).

152. See Yao's own note to the work when it was reprinted in *Shumu jikan*, I:3 (1966).

153. Wang Deyi, *Yao Congwu xiansheng nianbiao, Yao Congwu xiansheng jinian lunwenji*, 25.

154. As Lamprecht's student, Breysig's argument represented an effort to interpret history from a positivist perspective. Corresponding to an international trend in modern European historiography, it was however not the mainstay of German historiography at the beginning of the twentieth century. Cf. Georg Iggers, "The Tragic Course of German Historiography: The Political Function of Historical Scholarship in Germany in the nineteenth and twentieth Centuries," *German Life and Letters*, 34:2 (Jan. 1981), 223–233. With Breysig, Yao studied the works of Vico, Hegel, Comte, Buckle, and Burckhardt. For his recollection of Breysig, see *Yao Congwu xiansheng quanji* (The complete works of Yao Congwu) (Taipei: Zhengzhong Shuju, 1982), vol. 5, 221, note 1.

155. Yao Congwu, "Deguo fulangke jiaoshou dui zhongguo lishi zhi gongxian" (German historian Franke's contribution to the study of Chinese history), *Xin zhonghua* (New China), 4:1 (1936).

156. Yao's "Ouzhou xuezhe dui xiongnu de yanjiu" was first published in *Guoxue jikan* (A Quarterly Journal of National Studies), at Beijing University, 2:3. It was revised and included in *Dongbeishi luncong* (Essays on northeast Chinese history) (Taipei, 1955).

157. This information was given to me by Professor Herbert Franke in his letter of February 19, 1995. Professor Franke is the professor emeritus at the University of Munich who succeeded E. Haenisch.

158. Yang Yixiang, Yao's student at the university and now a renowned specialist in Chinese historiography, recalled recently that it was Yao's influence that he took the study of historiography as his specialty. See Ning Bo, "Shixueshi yaniu de jin yu xi—fang Yang Yixiang xiansheng" (The past and present in the study of historiography: an interview with Mr. Yang Yixiang), *Shixueshi yanjiu*, 4 (1994), 10–15. Due to the Sino-Japanese War, Yao's lecture notes on German historical methodology failed to publish. But he wrote extensively on the subject.

159. See Du's "Yao Congwu shi yu lishi fangfalun" (Professor Yao Congwu and historical methodology), *Yao Congwu xiansheng aisilu*, 81–85.

160. "Lishi fangfa daolun" (Introduction to historical methodology), *Yao Congwu xiansheng quanji*, vol. 1, 1.

161. Ibid., 8–9. Yao gave examples that in order to learn how to swim, one had to jump into the water. Similarly, in order to learn historical method, one had to do history.

162. Ibid., 9–12. Yao suggested that students read Chinese translations of English historian E. H. Carr's *What Is history?* and American writers

Will and Ariel Durant's *The Lessons of History*. As for Hegel, he later wrote that Hegel's statement encouraged historians to look for explanations for historical events. See ibid., vol. 5, 121.

163. Ranke's awareness of the difference between history and philosophy is discussed in *Leopold von Ranke, The Theory and Practice of History*, eds. Georg Iggers and Konrad von Moltke (Indianapolis, 1973), passim.

164. "Ouzhou lishi fangfalun de qiyuan" (The origins of European historical methodology), *Yao Congwu xiansheng quanji*, vol. 1, 16–17. Although published in 1970, it is possible that Yao wrote it for the methodology class in the early years.

165. Ibid., 10–11.

166. "Shuo shiliao de jieshi" (On interpretations of historical sources), ibid., 33.

167. Ibid., 34–37.

168. Ibid., 81–82, 37–45.

Chapter Four

1. For Ranke's influence in the English-speaking world, see Georg Iggers's "The Image of Ranke in American and German Historical Thought." *History and Theory*, 2 (1962), 17–40.

2. Shils, "Intellectuals, Traditions, and the Traditions of Intellectuals," *Intellectuals and Tradition*, eds. Eisenstadt & Graubard, 27.

3. Levenson, "'History' and 'Value': The Tensions of Intellectual Choice in Modern China," 146–194.

4. Xu Guansan made such a comment in his *Xinshixue jiushinian*, vol. 1, xi.

5. Liang published his journey, entitled *Ouyou xinying lu* (Reflections on my trip to Europe), *Liang Rengong jinzhu* (Liang Qichao's recent works) (Taipei: Wenhai chubanshe, 1922), vol. 1.

6. See Li Zongtong's preface to *Ershi shiji zhi kexue* (Sciences in the twentieth century), vol. 9, *Shixue* (history) (Taipei: Zhengzhong shuju), quoted in Du Weiyun, "Xifang shixue shuru zhongguo kao" (A study of the importation of Western history into China), *Bulletin of the Department of History*, National Taiwan University, 3 (1976), 417.

7. Liang's *Zhongguo lishi yanjiufa* (Shanghai: Shanghai Guji Chubanshe, 1987) and its *Bubian* were both his lecture notes. He wrote them in 1922 and 1926–1927 respectively, when he was a history professor at Qinghua University in Beijing.

8. In his *Ouyou xinyinglu*, Liang described how Western intellectuals had developed a sense of despair and pessimism after World War I and what they hoped for China. See also Tang, *Global Space* 165–223.

9. Liang, *Zhongguo lishi yanjiufa*, 1.

10. Ibid., 6.

11. Ibid., 10–11.

12. See chapter 1. For Liu's opinion about the royal historical institute, see *Shitong tongshi* (Perspectives in historiography) (Shanghai: Guji Chubanshe, 1983), "Shiguan jianzhi" (The Establishment of Historical Officer), chapter 11, 303–327; "Bianzhi" Clarification of the Position), chapter 10, 281–288; "Zixu" (Self-preface), chapter 10, 288–299; and "Wushi" (Against the Fashion), chapter 20, 589–599. See also, Denis Twitchett, *The Writing of Official History under the T'ang*.

13. Liang, *Zhongguo lishi yanjiufa*, 36–37.

14. Ibid., 87. In his "Yanjiu wenhuashi de jige zhongyao wenti—duiyu jiuzhu *zhongguo lishi yanjiufa* zhi xiubu ji xiuzheng" (Some important issues in the study of cultural history—revisions of my *Method for the study of Chinese history*), he further confirmed that the scientific method was an inductive method. Ibid., 137. Liang's opinion was possibly influenced by his friend Hu Shi, who published "Qingdai xuezhe de zhixue fangfa" (Qing scholars' methods in their study) in 1919, in which Hu praised Qing scholars for their scientific methods in examining ancient histories. See *Hu Shi zhexue sixiang ziliao xuan*, vol. 1, 184–208.

15. Liang, *Zhongguo lishi yanjiufa*, 39–39.

16. Charles Langlois and Charles Seignobos, *Introduction to the Study of History*, trans. G. G. Berry (New York: Henry Holt & Company, 1926), 19–22. There were two possibilities for Liang to get to know this book. One was through the help of the Chinese students in France whom he met. The other was through the Japanese translation (the Chinese translation of the book, incidentally, was not published until the 1930s). The Japanese translated this book at the end of the nineteenth century. See Masayuki Sato, "Historiographical Encounters: the Chinese and Western Traditions in Turn-of-the-century Japan," *Storia della Storiografia / History of Historiography*, 19 (1991), 17 note 14.

17. *Zhongguo lishi yanjiufa*, 41–42. Liang probably did not know that although H. Bancroft's wide coverage of records made his book valuable to some readers, American historians accused him of lacking a critical examination of his sources. Cf. Barnes, *A History of Historical Writing*, 230, 237.

18. Liang, *Zhongguo lishi yanjiufa*, 67–68.

19. Hu Shi noticed Liang's mistake in his diary *Hu Shi de riji* (Hu Shi's diary) (Hong Kong: Zhonghua shuju, 1985), vol. 3, 255.

20. Liang, *Zhongguo lishi yanjiufa*, 69–73.

21. Ibid., 71–77.

22. Ibid., 77–94.

23. For example, in his *Shitong*, Liu Zhiji discussed historical distortion *(Qubi)*, in two chapters of the book. Instead of pointing out that careful examination of the validity of sources was the way in which historians could avoid distortion in their writings, Liu devoted his discussions to historians' association with the royal court and believed that this kind of affiliation adversely affected historical truth. See *Shitong tongshi*, chapters 24 and 25.

24. Ibid., 71–77. F. Hirth, *The Ancient History of China to the End of the Chou Dynasty* (New York: Columbia University Press, 1908). Having received historical training in Germany, Hirth often intended to meet the German standard in his research. In his preface to the *China and the Roman Orient*, Hirth declared that "I have endeavored to please the German critic rather than the learned of any other country" (New York: Paragon Book Reprint Corp. 1966), iii. This book was first published in Shanghai in 1885 and included in Liang's bibliography here. Liang's acquanitance with Hirth's book was likely through Hu Shi, who was Hirth's student at Columbia.

25. Liang, *Zhongguo lishi yanjiufa*, 108–119.

26. Ibid., 120–136.

27. "Yanjiu wenhuashi de jige zhongyao wenti," ibid, 138. It was however also possible that Liang had read Rickert's work before he wrote the *Zhongguo lishi yanjiufa*. But it seems that his "careful" reading of Rickert occurred afterward.

28. Ibid., 138–140.

29. For a general yet concise discussion on German historicism, including the work of Rickert, see Jörn Rüsen and Friedrich Jaeger, *Geschichte des Historismus* (München, 1992).

30. Liang, *Zhongguo lishi yanjiufa*, 137–138.

31. Ibid., 141–143.

32. Tang, *Global Space*, 165–223.

33. Liang's elaboration on biographical methods constitutes the main part of the *Zhongguo lishi yanjiufa bubian*, 181–323.

34. Ibid., 156–171.

35. Ibid., 299–300.

36. Even after 1949 Liang's two books were reprinted in different versions. Cf. Wu Ze, ed. *Zhongguo Jindai Shixueshi* (Modern Chinese historiography), vol. 1, 495–525; vol. 2, 114–131.

37. P. Demiéville, "Chang Hsueh-cheng and His Historiography," *Historians in China and Japan*, 167–185.

38. For Naito Konan's study of Zhang Xuecheng, see Joshua Fogel's *Politics and Sinology: The Case of Naito Konan (1866–1934)* (Cambridge, MA: Harvard University Press, 1984), 154–156.

39. "Zhang Xuecheng shixue guankui," in *He Bingsong lunwenji*, 89–119. Before this article, He had published a review article of Zhang's work—"Du Zhang Xuecheng *Wenshi tongyi* zhaji" (Reflections on Zhang's *General Meanings of Literature and History*)—in 1922. Ibid., 27–50. In his introduction to Hu's biography, he quoted Hu's diary to describe Hu's "experiment" and related their common interest. See "Zengbu Zhang Shizhai nianpu xu" (An introduction to the Chronological biography of Zhang Xuecheng), ibid., 132–146.

40. "Zhang Xuecheng shixue guankui" (A study of Zhang Xuecheng's ideas of history), ibid., 91–93, 100–103.

41. Ibid., 107–112.

42. Ibid., 93–96.

43. Zhang, *Wenshi tongyi*, chapter 1.

44. "Zengbu Zhang Shizhai nianpu xu" (Preface to the expanded chronological biography of Zhang Xuecheng), *He Bingsong lunwenji*, 146. In his work on the eastern Zhejiang School, he reiterated the importance of introducing Western culture to China for creating a modern culture. See *Zhedong xuepai suyuan* (Shanghai: Commercial Press, 1932), 14, 205.

45. He, "Lun suowei guoxue" (On the so-called national study), *He Bingsong lunwenji*, 481–490.

46. He, "*Tongshi xinyi* zixu" (Self-preface to *A New Perspective on General History*), *He Bingsong jinian wenji*, 1–12.

47. Ibid.

48. Ibid., 97–99, 108.

49. According to Leonard Krieger, the term *scientific history* means two things: critical methods and the search for a lawful generalization. Both these two kinds of the "scientific history" were introduced to the United States from Europe but in the beginning, critical method were dominant. The "New History" school appeared closer to the second kind and it was, Krieger said, a result of the status quo of the study of European history in the United States at the time. "European History in America," *History: The Development of Historical Studies in the US*, eds. John Higham et al. (Englewood Cliffs, NJ: Prentice-Hall, 1968), 255–267.

50. He, "Lishi yanjiufa" (Historical methodology), *He Bingsong lunwenji*, 149.

51. Ibid., 151.

52. Ibid., 152–153.

53. Ibid., 154–155.

54. Ibid., 147–148.

55. Ibid., 152–167. "Nibian zhongguo jiuji suoyin liyi" (A suggestion for indexing historic books in China), ibid., 457–458.

56. See He's preface to the book, *Lishi Yanjiufa* (Shanghai: Commercial Press, 1927), 1–3. He's records at University of Wisconsin/Madison shows that he learned German at the time.

57. See He's letter to Yao Mingda in 1925, entitled "Lun shixue" (On history), *He Bingsong lunwenji*, 123–125.

58. See He's preface to *Lishi Yanjiufa*.

59. Ibid.

60. Wen-hsin Yeh's *Provincial Passages: Culture, Space, and the Origins of Chinese Communism* (Berkeley: University of California Press, 1996) has provided a detailed description of the Zhejiang No. 1 Normal School. See chapter 4, 71–93.

61. It is still a mystery as to who actually did that. He's friends recalled that He might have known something afterward, but he dared not tell, given the political pressure. But it was hardly possible that He had real enemies, for he was indeed a gentle scholar all his life. It might just have been an accident. About the poison case, see He's "Yishi du'an zhi huigu" (My recollection of the poison case at the No. 1 Normal College), Ruan Yicheng, "Ji He Bingsong xiansheng" (About He Bingsong), *He Bingsong jinian wenji*, 33–35, 260–269.

62. In the Commercial Press, He planned to publish a series of translations of Western historical works. His translations of Shotwell's *An Introduction to History and History* and Gooch's *History and Historians in the Nineteenth Century* represented his initial efforts. Although He was unable to continue the plan, the press maintained this tradition of translating Western works in today's China. For He's plan, see his "*Xiyang shixueshi* yizhexu" (Translator's preface to *An Introduction to History and History*) (Shanghai: Commercial Press, 1929).

63. In the 1930s, He was an adjunct history professor at Daxia (Great China) University and Guanghua University.

64. For English scholarship on the Zhedong School, see Lynn Struve, "Chen Que versus Huang Zongxi: Confucian Faces Modern Times in the seventeenth-century," *Journal of Chinese Philosophy*, 18:1 (March 1991), 5–23 and "The Hsu Brothers and Semiofficial Patronage of Scholars in the Kang-hsi Period," *Harvard Journal of Asiatic Studies*, 42:1 (June 1982), 231–266.

65. Ernst Breisach has noticed this lack of interest in epistemology as shown in American Progressive historiography of the early twentieth century. See his article "The American Quest for a New History: Observations on Developments and Trends," *Western and Russian Historiography: Recent Views*, ed. Henry Kozicki (New York: St. Martin's Press, 1993), 25–44, especially 30.

66. Robinson, *The New History*, 25.

67. Fu, "Lishi yuyan yanjiusuo gongzuo zhi zhiqu" (An introduction to the work of the Institute of History and Philology), *Fu Sinian quanji*, vol. 4, 253.

68. Ibid., 254–256.

69. Ibid., 266–267.

70. Fu's student and historian Lao Gan wrote that Fu was then eager to make history analogous to geology and biology. Fu believed that they all belonged to the "empirical sciences." "Fu Mengzhen xiansheng yu jin ershinian lai zhongguo lishixue de fazhan" (Fu Sinian and the development of Chinese historiography in the past twenty years), *Fu guxiaozhang aiwanlu (In memory of former president Fu Sinian)* (Taipei: National Taiwan University Press, 1951), 70.

71. This was actually from Fu's reading of Langlois and Seignobos' *Introduction to the Study of History*, in which Langlois puts forth the slogan "no documents, no history." 17.

72. Fu pronounced in a report that the reason for the founding of the Institute of History and Philology was to put history and philology on a par with astronomy, geology, physics, and chemistry. See Dong Zuobin, "Lishi yuyan yanjiusuo zai xueshu shangde gongxian" (The Institute of History and Philology and its contribution to scholarship), *Fu guxiaozhang aiwanlu*, 64. Fu's report is not found in *Fu Sinian quanji*.

73. Fu, *Fu Sinian quanji*, IV, 256–260.

74. Ibid. Fu's remark here was coined in G. M. Trevelian's phrase: "Collect the facts of the French Revolution! You must go down to Hell and up to Heaven to fetch them." *Clio A Muse* (London, 1913), quoted in Xu Guansan, *Xin shixue jiushinian*, vol. 1, 221, footnote 47.

75. In this article, Fu expressed his full confidence in the effectiveness of archaeological study in solving problems in ancient history. Archaeological study, he declared, is not only a new approach, but also will become the foundation of the study of ancient history. See "Fu Sinian dangan" (Fu Sinian's archive), I-807.

76. Ibid.

77. The Bulletin of the University *Yuan (Daxue yuan gongbao)*, namely the Department of Education in the GMD government headed by Cai

Yuanpei, provides information on how Fu Sinian managed to turn the Institute into a new branch of the Academia Sinica. When the Academia Sinica was first founded in July 1927, there was no plan for establishing the Institute of History and Philology, only an Institute of Social Sciences. Fu Sinian was listed as a member of the committee for founding the Institute of Psychology. But in January 1928 the Institute of History and Philology appeared in the organizational chart of the University *Yuan*. On April 10, 1928 when the Academia Sinica officially announced its establishment, the Institute of History and Philology became one of its eleven research institutes. See *Daxue yuan gongbao* (Taipei: Wenhai chubanshe, n.d.), Year 1, No. 1, 63, 155–166; No. 3, 56; No. 5, 29–30. Also, Pan Guangzhe, "Cai Yuanpei yu shiyusuo" (Cai Yuanpei and the Institute of History and Philology), *Xinxueshu zhilu: Zhongyang yanjiuyuan lishi yuyan yanjiusuo qishi zhounian jinian wenji* (Along new pathways of research: Essays in honor of the seventieth anniversary of the Institute of History and Philology), eds. Du Zhengsheng and Wang Fansen (Taipei: Institute of History and Philology, Academia Sinica, 1998), 1, 189–216.

78. See Li Ji, "Fu Mengzhen xiansheng lingdao de lishi yuyan yanjiusuo" (Fu Sinian and the Institute of History and Philology), *Fu suozhang jinian tekan (Special publication for Director Fu Sinian)* (Taipei: the Institute of History and Philology, Academia Sinica, 1951), 12–13.

79. Fu, "Lishi yuyan yanjiusuo gongzuo zhi zhiqu" (An introduction to the Institute of History and Philology), *Fu Sinian quanji*, vol. 4, 254.

80. In Fu's letter to Cai Yuanpei, the head of the Academia Sinica, for funding he argued that the success of the project would enhance China's scholarly reputation. Ibid. vol. 7, 94–96.

81. Fu, "*Ming Qing shiliao* fakan liyan" (Foreword to *Ming Qing Archives*), ibid., vol. 4, 357–359.

82. "*Ming Qing Shiliao* fukanzhi" (Foreword to the resumed *Ming Qing Archives*), ibid., 360–361.

83. See Li Ji "Fu Mengzhen xiansheng lingdao de lishi yuyan yanjiusuo" (Fu Sinian and the Institute of History and Philology), *Fu suozhang jinian tekan*, 16.

84. On May 25, 1948, Fu Sinian wrote Zhu Jiahua from the United States, describing the "happy conversation" *(kuaitan)* between B. Karlgren and him in Karlgren's visit to New Haven, regarding Karlgren as a sinological authority in Europe and having great influence on Chinese scholars. Karlgren also wrote to Fu from New York on May 31, which read I "offer you our hearty thanks for your great kindness during the happy days we passed in New Haven." See "Fu Sinian dangan" (Fu Sinian's archive), IV-188, I-1189.

85. Li Ji recalled that once he and Fu had lunch together and chatted about the archive project, Fu said to Li that there was no important dis-

covery from these archives. Li kidded about Fu's preference for excavated sources. See "Fu Mengzhen xiansheng lingdao de lishi yuyan yanjiusuo" (Fu Sinian and the Institute of History and Philology), *Fu suozhang jinian tekan* (Special publication for Director Fu Sinian), 16.

86. Paul Pelliot, "The Royal Tombs of An-yang," *Independence, Convergence, and Borrowing in Institutions, Thought, and Art* (New York: 1964), 272.

87. Li Ji, *Anyang: A Chronicle of the Discovery, Excavation, and Reconstruction of the Ancient Capital of the Shang Dynasty* (Seattle: 1977). Also Fu Sinian "Bensuo fajue anyang yinxu zhi jingguo" (A report of the excavation of Shang ruins in Anyang, the Institute of History and Philology). Fu also discussed the new methods used in archeology: "Kaoguxue de xinfangfa" (New methods in archaeology). See *Fu Sinian quanji*, IV, 267–288, 289–299.

88. Hu Shi for example told Gu Jiegang that "now my thinking has changed. I do not doubt antiquity any longer. I believe the authenticity of ancient Chinese history." Quoted in Liu Qiyu, 262. In 1933, the Institute started another archaeological project in Chengziya of Shandong Province. Fu announced that the new project was to probe the scope of the Shang Dynasty and to test the hypothesis as to whether Chinese civilization had been influenced by the sea. See "*Chengziya* xu" (Preface to *Chengziya*), *Fu Sinian quanji*, III, 206–211.

89. For Fu's view of ancient China, see Wang Fansen, *Fu Ssu-nien*, 143–196.

90. About the impression of Fu's leadership of the Institute on others, see Dong Zuobin, "Lishi yuyan yanjiusuo zai xueshu shangde gongxian" (The Institute of History and Philology and its contribution to scholarship), *Fu guxiaozhang aiwanlu*, 64–69.

91. Wang Fansen describes the rivalry between Fu and Gu. *Fu Ssu-nien*, 96–97, footnote 209.

92. All these publications are in *Fu Sinian quanji*, vol. 4. About the influence of Fu's theory, see Wang Fansen, *Fu Ssu-nien*, 143–196.

93. Fu's lecture notes for that course originally contained seven parts, including a part in which Fu compared similarities and differences between European and Chinese scholars in understanding history. However, all these notes later were lost, except their headings and the one on historical sources *(Shiliao lunlue)*. *Fu Sinian quanji*, vol. 2, 3–4.

94. Ibid., 5–40.

95. Ibid., 41–60.

96. See Luo, *Luo Jialun xiansheng wencun*, I, 1.

97. Luo, "Wusi yundong de jingshen" (The spirit of the May Fourth movement). *Meizhou pinglun* (Weekly critique), 23 (May 1919). Also *Luo Jialun xiansheng wencun*, I, 2–3. Cf. Wu Xiangxiang, *Minguo bairenzhuan* (A hundred biographies in the Republic of China) (Taipei, 1976), 199–200.

98. See Chen Chunsheng, *Xinwenhua de qishou—Luo Jialun zhuan* (The forerunner of the new culture—biography of Luo Jialun) (Taipei: Jindai Zhongguo Chubanshe, 1985), 6–13, and Wu Xiangxiang, 198.

99. *Luo Jialun ziliaoji (Sources of Luo Jialun)*, found at Yale University (n.p. and n.d.), 3.

100. See Fu, *Fu Sinian quanji*, IV, 152–153. Chen Chunsheng, *Xinwenhua de qishou* 19–27, and Wu, 198.

101. Luo, *Luo Jialun xiansheng wencun*, I, 2–3. The translation was given in Schwarcz, *The Chinese Enlightenment*, 22.

102. See Luo Jialun's "Pingdiao Jiang Tingfu xiansheng" (In memory of Jiang Tingfu), *Luo Jialun xiansheng wencun*, X, 191–194. Because of John Dewey, particularly because of his series of lectures in China during 1919 and 1921, Columbia University became a symbol of American education. In 1909, there were 24 Chinese students at Columbia. By 1920 when Luo arrived in the United States, the number reached 123. See Keenan, *The Dewey Experiment in China*, 18–19.

103. There was an interesting episode about Luo's assignment. Luo wrote to Hu Shi in 1920 telling him that he lost the notebook of Dewey's four lectures about the philosophy of education. Luo asked whether Dewey or Hu still had the original lecture notes, because Hu was Dewey's interpreter. In *Hu Shi laiwang shuxin xuan*, I, 95–97.

104. In *Hu Shi laiwang shuxin xuan*, I, 226–227. Luo's presentation is entitled "The Present Outlook for Chinese Historical Studies," in which he reviews works written by Hu Shi, Liang Qichao, and other Chinese scholars at the turn of the century. He reports to American historians that the achievement of Chinese historical study in China lay in the fact that besides some conceptual changes, the discovery of many new sources, particularly sources unearthed in the archaeological remains such as inscriptions on tortoise shells and animal bones, greatly enriched the historians' knowledge of ancient Chinese history. He also notices that some of these discoveries were assisted by Western scholars and that some Chinese historians used Western books in their study of Yuan history. In AHA Annual Report, 1922, 293.

105. In 1917, Zhang Xiangwen (1867–1933), a geography professor at Beida, founded the Office of National History *(Guoshi bianzhuan chu)* on Beida campus, which involved Cai Yuanpei and a few Beida students. But

the Office only lasted two years and was abolished in August 1919. We are not sure if Luo Jialun had been involved in some of projects organized by the Office. Judging by its interest in source collection, however, it might have a bearing on Luo Jialun. See Zhang Zhishan, "Zhang Xiangwen he Beijing Daxue fushe Guoshi bianzhuanchu" (Zhang Xiangwen and the Office of National History at Peking University), *Shixueshi yanjiu* (Journal of Historiography), 3 (September 1991), 44–47.

106. Jiang Tingfu later recalled appreciatively that it was Luo who first called his attention to the importance of modern Chinese history. See Luo Jialun, *Shizhe rusi ji*, 201. About Luo's friendship with Jiang, see Luo's "Pingdiao Jiang Tingfu Xiansheng" (In memory of Jiang Tingfu), ibid. Like Luo Jialun, Jiang was later also involved in politics; he was the head of the Executive *Yuan* of the GMD government in the 1940s. John K. Fairbank described Jiang Tingfu's scholarly and political career in his *Chinabound: A Fifty-year Memoir* (New York: Harper & Row, 1982), 86–91.

107. See Luo, *Shizhe rusi ji*, 158.

108. The translation took him a long time because he found what he had translated earlier was far from satisfactory. He had almost to translate it again in order to make it publishable. This book was finally published in 1927 by the Commercial Press in Shanghai.

109. Luo spent the rest of his time in Germany traveling and attending concerts, lived better than ordinary German people, as he recalled to his daughter. In *Luo Zhixi xiansheng zhuanji ji zhusu ziliao* (Biography of Luo Jialun and his writings), 30. Luo's experience in Germany was not unique for Chinese students at the time. The inflation of 1924 Germany gave many Chinese students an advantage in supporting their lives; consequently, many came to Germany from other European countries. The number of Chinese students in Berlin in this particular year reached one thousand. For general information about the Chinese students in Berlin, see Hsi-Huey Liang, 23–38; for their economic condition, see Y. C. Wang, *Chinese Intellectuals and the West* 165.

110. Zhang Youyi recalled Luo's frequent visits to her apartment in Berlin during the period, when she went through an emotional distress after Xu's abandonment. Zhang appreciated Luo's kindness but declined his suggestion for considering a new marriage. See Pang-mei Natasha Chang, *Bound Feet and Western Dress* (New York: Doubleday, 1996), 155–156. Xu Zhimo's and Zhang Youyi's divorce was the first modern kind at that time.

111. These letters were discovered by Luo Jiufang, Luo Jialun's daughter, and published in *Dangdai* (Contemporary), 127 (March 1, 1998), 104–119, in which Fu described, humorously, his and their poor student lives. A couple of letters were sent to Luo in Paris.

112. See Chen, *Xinwenhua de qishou*, 66–67.

113. In his article written in 1931, Luo also mentioned the *Rolls Series* in England and *Collection des Documents inedits sur l'histoire de France*. *Luo Jialun xiansheng wencun*, II, 60.

114. Ibid., 399–400.

115. Luo, *Zhongshan daxue zhoukan*, 2:14 (January 1928), 400–401. Li was an important general of the Taiping rebellion. When he was defeated and captured by Zeng, he wrote his confession.

116. Luo, *Luo Jialun xiansheng wencun*, 400.

117. Chen Jiageng was not only the founder of the University, he was also a well-known patriotic merchant at the time. It was legitimate for Luo to hope to obtain Chen's support. Ibid.

118. "Yanjiu zhongguo jindaishi de jihua" (A proposal for the study of modern Chinese history), Luo's letter to Gu Jiegang was dated September 8, 1926, but it was published in the *Zhongshan daxue zhoukan (Weekly Journal of Sun Yat-sen University)*, ed. the Institute of History and Philology at Sun Yat-sen University, 2:14 (January 1928), 399–401. It was not coincidental that the institute was founded by Luo's friend Fu Sinian and the journal was run by Gu Jiegang.

119. See *Guo Tingyi xiansheng fangwen jilu* (The reminisences of Mr. Guo Tingyi), eds. Zhang Pengyuan et al. (Taipei: Institute of Modern History, Academia Sinica, 1987), 121, and 149. Zhang Pengyuan's new book, *Guo Tingyi, Fei Zhengqing, Wei Muting: Taiwan yu meiguo xueshu jiaoliu gean chutan* (Triangular Partnership: Kuo Ting-yee [Guo Tingyi], John Fairbank, and C. Martin Wilbur and Their Contribution to Taiwan-U.S. Academic Exchange) (Taipei: Institute of Modern History, Academia Sinica, 1997) details the collaboration between the Institute of Modern History and American universities and foundations.

120. About Luo's joining the GMD and his role in composing the source book, see ibid., 163–166, 243. The source book only had two volumes, yet Luo's ideas of the whole project were written into its preface.

121. See Luo's "Zhi Qinghua daxue dongshihui baogao zhengli xiaowu zhi jingguo ji jihua" (Report to the Qinghua Trustee Committee about the plan and procedure of the administrative reform), *Luo Jialun xiansheng wencun*, I, 450–484.

122. See Wen-hsin Yeh, *The Alienated Academy*, chapter 5, 167–182.

123. An example was that Luo required all the students to join morning exercise before class, which was later abandoned because of resistance. See Feng Youlan, *Sansongtang zixu*, 308–320. Feng was Luo's Beida mate whom Luo invited to Qinghua to teach Chinese philosophy. Feng gives a firsthand account of Luo's administration at Qinghua. He also shares his assessments of Luo's four emphases at Qinghua. For general information on Luo's administration at Qinghua, see Su Yunfeng, "Luo

Jialun yu Qinghua daxue" (Luo Jialun and Qinghua University), *Zhongyang yanjiuyuan jindaishi yanjiusuo jikan* (Bulletin of the Institute of Modern History, Academia Sinica, Taiwan), 16 (June 1987), 367–382. See also, Chen Chunsheng, 88–99, and *Luo Zhixi xiansheng zhuanji ji zhusu ziliao*, 47–53.

124. Luo, *Luo Jialun xiansheng wencun*, II, 37–38.

125. For a representative work from the PRC historians, see Fan Wenlan's *Zhongguo jindaishi* (modern Chinese history), which was long regarded as an authoritative text in teaching modern Chinese history in the PRC. Li Yunhan, a modern historian in Taiwan, also adopted Luo's periodization in writing his same-titled textbook.

126. See Charles Beard, "Written History as an Act of Faith," *American Historical Review* 39 (1934), 219–231, also "That Noble Dream," ibid., 41 (1935), 74–87.

127. Luo's letter to Hu Shi, in *Hu Shi laiwang shuxin xuan*, I, 226–227.

128. *Luo Jialun xiansheng wencun*, X, 193. In his article about the educational reform in 1932, Luo praised the reading habit of F. J. E. Woodbridge that he learned from his class. Ibid., I, 496.

129. See C. E. Delaney, *Mind and Nature: A Study of the Naturalistic Philosophers of Cohen, Woodbridge and Sellars* (Notre Dame: University of Notre Dame Press, 1969), 6.

130. F. J. E. Woodbridge, *The Purpose of History* (New York: Columbia University Press, 1916), 17.

131. F. J. E. Woodbridge, *Nature and Mind, Selected Essays of F. J. E. Woodbridge* (New York: Russell and Rusell, 1965), 448, 178. Emphasis is mine.

132. Wilfred Trotter (1872–1939) was an English surgeon and sociologist. He was known for his study of "herd instinct" on which he built his theory of social development. Jean-Gabriel Tarde (1843–1904) was a French sociologist who was famous for his theory of imitation, which stipulates that progress in history was made through imitation.

133. Luo, "Lishi zhexue de paibei he wode yijian" (Various schools of the philosophy of history and my opinion), *Luo Jialun xiansheng wencun*, II, 81–85.

134. Luo's other articles on the philosophy of history are "Lishi zhexue zhi niaokan" (A survey of the philosophy of history), ibid, V, 279–287; "Shiguan" (Historical interpretations), VI, 24–35.

135. Luo, "Shiguan" (Historical interpretations), 24–25.

136. Ibid., 24–26.

137. Luo, "Lishi zhexue niaokan," V, 279.

138. Ibid., V, 286.

139. Woodbridge, "Confessions," *Nature and Mind*, 5.

140. Cf. Delaney, *Mind and Nature*, 144.

141. Luo "Yanjiu zhongguo jindaishi de yiyi he fangfa" (Why we should study modern Chinese history and its method), *Luo Jialun xiansheng wencun*, II, 51–76.

142. Ibid., II, 51. Besides the citation, words with quotation marks are Luo's own hereafter.

143. Ibid., II, 54–55.

144. The "heuristik" (heuristic) refers to the art of discovering documents, which Langlois regarded as the primary step of modern historical scholarship. See *Introduction to the Study of History*, chapter 1, 17–41. Luo used Langlois's analysis to argue for the establishment of a source collection for the study of modern Chinese history.

145. Luo, *Luo Jialun xiansheng wencun*, II, 55–76.

146. Luo recalled that no sooner had he settled down at Wuhan University and started to teach history then he was called up by Chiang Kai-shek for the appointment. He wanted to decline the offer but he failed to do so, even with the help of the president of Wuhan university. See Luo's "Zhengda de dansheng yu chengzhang" (The founding and development of the Central Political Institute), ibid. I, 696.

147. Wu, *Minguo bairenzhuan* III, 214.

148. See Luo, "Guoshiguan sishiliu niandu shizheng gangyao" (Highlights of the programs in the Institute of National History, 1957), *Luo Jialun xiansheng wencun*, I, 345–347. For a complete bibliography of the historical source works published under Luo's patronage in the 1960s, see Jiang Yongjing, "Luo Jialun xiansheng de shengping Jiqi dui zhongguo jindaishi yanjiu de gongxian" (Luo Jialun's life and his contribution to the study of modern Chinese history), in Luo, *Luo Zhixi xiansheng zhuanji ji zhusu ziliao*, 81–82, notes 101 and 106.

149. Luo, "Yige jihu beishiluo de lishi zhengjian" (An almost lost historical document), Luo, *Luo Jialun xiansheng wencun*, I, 481–489.

150. Dai Yi, "Wuxu bianfa zhong Yuan Shikai gaomi zhenxiang" (A new discovery of Yuan Shikai's betrayal in the 1898 Reform), *Beijing ribao* (Beijing daily), June 23, 1999.

Chapter Five

1. Vera Schwarcz, Li Zehou, and Gu Xin, have discussed extensively in their works the antithetic relation between the Chinese enlightenment and

the task of national salvation, see Li Zehou, "qimeng yu jiuwang de shuangchong bianzou" (A dual, intertwined tone of enlightenment and national salvation), *Zhongguo xiandai sixiangshi lun* (On modern Chinese intellectual history) (Beijing: Dongfang chubanshe, 1987), 7–49. See also Schwarcz *The Chinese Enlightenment*; and Gu Xin, *Zhongguo qimeng de lishi tujing* (A history of the Chinese enlightenment) (Hong Kong: Oxford University Press, 1992), and Li Zehou's other book, *Zhongguo jindai sixiang shilun* (Essays on modern Chinese intellectual history) (Beijing: Renmin chubanshe, 1979), 472–488.

2. For student radicalism during the wartime, see John Israel, *Student Nationalism in China, 1927–1937* (Stanford: Stanford University Press, 1966). Israel's new book, *Lianda*, has offered detailed research on how the academics reacted to the war, including Feng Youlan's new works on Confucian philosophy. Qian Mu in 1941 published *Guoshi dagang* (An outline of national history), an instantly best-seller, in which he praised the vitality of Chinese culture shown in its long history. Jerry Dennerline's *Qian Mu and the World of the Seven Mansions* (New Haven: Yale University Press, 1988) has discussions on Qian and his career.

3. Yu Ying-shih used the term *radicalization* to describe the intellectual change in turn-of-the-century China and regarded the May Fourth as a prime example. See his "The Radicalization of China in the Twentieth Century," *Daedalus*, 122:2 (Spring 1993), 125–150. I borrow his term here to emphasize that this "radicalization" was more developed from the late 1930s onward.

4. He wrote about the losses of the Commercial Press. See his "Shangwu yinshuguan beihui jilue" (A record of the devastation of the Commercial Press), *He Bingsong jinian wenji*, 19–29.

5. He wrote a report about the destruction and expressed his angry at the Japanese. "Shangwu yinshuguan beihui jilue" (The destruction of the Commercial Press), ibid., 19–38.

6. He also wrote an article about Chinese social customs in the year: "Zhongguo de fengsu" (On Chinese social customs), *He Bingsong lunwenji*, 259–269.

7. He wrote two textbooks with the same title *Waiguoshi (History of foreign countries)* for high and middle schools in the 1930s, both were published by the Commercial Press.

8. He,"Zhongguo shixue zhi fazhan," *He Bingsong lunwenji*, 202–204.

9. Chen Lifu's official title was the head of the Control *Yuan* of the GMD government. But his real power lay in his leadership of the CC clique, an intelligence agency of the GMD party. For the English translation of the Declaration, see W. T. DeBary, ed., *Sources of Chinese Tradition* (New York, 1960), II, 192–193. About social and political background of the movement, see Zhang Jun, "Sanshi niandai zhongguo benwei wenhua jianshe yundong

fasheng de yuanyin beijing" (Origins and background of the construction of a China-centered culture movement in the 1930s), *Shiyuan* (History of history), 16 (November 1987), 191–216.

10. Liu Baimin, He's friend and colleague in the 1930s, recalled that it was He who drafted the Declaration. However, He's name was actually listed as the second on the Declaration. See Liu's "Ku He Bocheng xiansheng" (Cry for Mr. He Bingsong), *He Bingsong jinian wenji*, 241.

11. Although it was not known whether Luo supported the ten professors, it was quite possible that he and many GMD officials did. For the debate, see *Zhongguo wenhua jianshe taolunji* (Anthology of the discussions on the cultural construction in China) (Shanghai, 1935).

12. He, "Zhongguo benwei de wenhua jianshe," *He Bingsong lunwenji*, 270–273.

13. Liu Baimin described He's emotions. See *He Bingsong jinian wenji*, 240–242. Tao Xisheng mentioned his motive to sign the Declaration to Hu Shi in *Hu Shizhi xiansheng nianpu changbian*, ed. Hu Songping (Taipei: Lianjing chuban shiye gongsi), IV, 1381.

14. Cf. Arif Dirlik, "The Ideological Foundations of the New Life Movement: A Study in Counterrevolution," *Journal of Asian Studies* (August 1975); and Jonathan Spence, *The Search for Modern China* (New York: W. W. Norton, 1989), 414–415.

15. See He, "He Bingsong nianpu" (Chronological biography of He Bingsong), *He Bingsong lunwenji*, 226.

16. Hu Shi's article appeared in *Dagongbao* (Dagong Daily) in 1935 and was reprinted in *Duli pinglun* and *Wenhua jianshe* (Cultural construction) in 1936. See *He Bingsong xiaozhang wenji*, 224–228.

17. Ibid.

18. See He, *He Bingsong lunwenji*, 282–285.

19. "Lun zhongguo benwei wenhua jianshe da Hu Shi xiansheng" (On China-based cultural construction—a response to Mr. Hu Shi), ibid., 274–281.

20. Pocock wrote: "One is that the creation of new language may take place in the attempt to maintain the old language no less than in the attempt to change it; cases can be found in which a deliberate and conscious stress on change, process and modernity is among the strategies of those defending a traditional order, and it is in the logic of the concept of tradition that this should be so." "The concept of a language and the metier d'historien: some considerations on practice," *The Languages of Political Theory in Early-Modern Europe*, ed. Anthony Pagden (Cambridge: Cambridge University Press, 1987), 32. Also see Pocock's *Virtue, Commerce, and History: Essays on Political Thought and History, Chiefly in the Eighteenth*

Century (Cambridge: Cambridge University Press, 1985), particularly his introduction in which he explicates his approach to the study of political discourse.

21. He, "Zhongguo wenhua xichuankao" (A study of China's cultural influence on Europe), *He Bingsong lunwenji*, 286–313.

22. See Wang Xinming, *Xinwenquan li sishi nian* (Forty-year career as a journalist) (Taipei: Longwen chubanshe, 1993), 2:450–455. Wang was the first signer on the Declaration. Xu Jie, a professor at the Jinan University, also believed that He's appointment resulted from his activities in the cultural discussion. See Chen Fukang "He Bingsong and Zheng Zhenduo," *He Bingsong jinian wenji*, 358–359.

23. There is ample evidence of this found in the memoirs of He's students and colleagues. *He Bingsong jinian wenji*, passim.

24. Zhou Yutong, "Aidao He Bocheng xiansheng" (In memory of He Bingsong), ibid., 233–235.

25. He's decision to move the university from Shanghai indicated his determination not to collaborate with the Japanese in the war, while some Chinese scholars did.

26. See students' and colleagues' recollections in *He Bingsong jinian wenji*.

27. Zhou Yutong, He's colleague at Jinan University, wrote that he had discouraged He to accept the appointment. Zhou thought that He could contribute much more to historical study if he worked as an editor or professor. He eventually accepted the position. According to Zhou, it was partially because of his economic hardship and He's family responsibility. "Aidao He Bocheng xiansheng" (In memory of He Bingsong), ibid., 234–235.

28. He's students' and colleagues' recollection of He's achievement as the chancellor were seen in *He Bingsong jinian wenji*, including those, Zhou Yutong and Ruan Yicheng, that pointed out that He sacrificed his scholarship for administrative responsibilities. He's own memoir entitled "Suiyu er'an" that describes his personality is in *He Bingsong wenji*, 507–508.

29. Hu Shi, *Ding Wenjiang de zhuanji* (Biography of Ding Wenjiang) (Taipei: Yuanliu chuban gongsi, 1986), 136. The chief editor of the *Duli pinglun* was Hu Shi, Jiang Tingfu and Ding Wenjiang were associate editors, Fu Sinian, Ren Hongjun, Chen Hengzhe (Ren and Chen were husband and wife and Hu's friends in the United States), and others were main contributors.

30. Everyone had to contribute five percent of their monthly income to the journal. According to Jiang Tingfu's memoir, the journal did not accept any outside financial support, including advertisement. *Jiang Tingfu*

huiyilu (Jiang Tingfu's memoir), trans. Xie Zhonglian (Taipei: Zhuanji wenxue chubanshe, 1972), 140.

31. Hu, "*Yinyan*" (Introductory statement), *Duli pinglun*, 1 (May 22, 1932).

32. Hu, *Hu Shi de riji*, 112–116.

33. Hu, "Zai tan tan xianzheng" (A continued discussion on constitutional government), *Duli pinglun*, 236:5–6 (May 30, 1937).

34. Hu Shi recalled how he became involved in politics in "Wo de qilu" (My crossroads), *Hu Shi zuopingji* (Hu Shi's works)—*Women de zhengzhi zhuzhang* (Our political proposal) (Taipei: Yuanliu chubanshe, 1986), V. 9, 64–65. For Fu Sinian's focused attention on social problems instead on politics, see Wang Fansen, *Fu Ssu-nien*, 65–66.

35. About the whole discussion on "problems and isms," see *Hu Shi zuopingji—Wenti yu zhuyi* (problems and isms), V. 5.

36. About Ding Wenjiang's influence on Hu Shi, see Li Dajia, "Hu Shi zai 'qilu' shang" (Hu Shi at the crossroads), *Hu Shi yu jindai zhongguo*, 226–227.

37. Hu, "Women de zhengzhi zhuzhang," V. 9, 21–26.

38. Jerome Grieder, *Hu Shih*, 190 and Lubot, *Liberalism in an Illiberal Age*.

39. Hu, "Women de zhengzhi zhuzhang," 22–23.

40. Habermas, *The Structural Transformation of the Public Sphere*, 1–26.

41. Frederic Wakeman Jr., "The Civil Society and Public Sphere Debate: Western Reflections on Chinese Political Culture" and Philip Huang, "'Public Sphere'/'Civil Society' in China?: The Third Realm Between State and Society," *Modern China*, 192:2 (1993), 108–138, 216–240. For the public sphere theory in general, see Craig Calhoun, ed. *Habermas and the Public Sphere* (Cambridge, MA: MIT Press, 1993).

42. Duara, *Rescuing History From the Nation*, 148–150.

43. Hu Shi, "*Duli pinglun* de sizhounian" (The fourth year anniversary of the *Independent critique*), *Duli pinglun*, 201:3.

44. See Parks M. Coble, *Facing Japan: Chinese Politics and Japanese Imperialism, 1931–1937* (Cambridge, MA: Harvard University Press, 1991), 76–89. A definitive study on the *Duli pinglun* is done by Chen Yishen's *Duli pinglun de minzhu sixiang* (The democratic ideas of the *Independent Critique*) (Taipei: Lianjing chuban shiye gongsi, 1989).

45. Hu, "Cantong de huiyi yu fansheng" (painful memories and reflections), *Duli pinglun*, 18:8–13 (September 18, 1932).

46. Hu, "Jianguo yu zhuanzhi" (National reconstruction and dictatorship) and "Zailun jianguo yu zhuanzhi" (Continued discussion on national reconstruction and dictatorship), *Duli pinglun*, 81:2–5 (December 17, 1933); 82:2–5 (December 24, 1933). Jiang Tingfu's article, entitled "Geming yu zhuanzhi" (Revolution and dictatorship), appeared in *Duli pinglun*, 80:2–5 (December 10, 1933).

47. Jiang, "Lun zhuanzhi bing da Hu Shizhi xiansheng" (On dictatorship in response to Mr. Hu Shi), *Duli pinglun*, 83:2–6 (December 31, 1933).

48. Hu, "Tongyi de lu" (The road to unification), *Duli pinglun*, 28:2–6 (November 27, 1932).

49. Hu, "Zailun jianguo yu zhuanzhi" (Continued discussion on national reconstruction and dictatorship), *Duli pinglun*, 82:2–5 (December 24, 1933).

50. Ding, "Minzhu zhengzhi yu ducai zhengzhi" (democratic politics and dictatorial politics), *Duli pinglun*, 133:5–6 (December 30, 1934).

51. Hu, "Da Ding Zaijun xiansheng lun minzhu yu ducai" (On democracy and dictatorship in response to Mr. Ding Wenjiang), *Duli pinglun*, 133:7–8 (December 30, 1934).

52. Hu, "Zhengzhi tongyi de tujing" (The road to political unification), *Duli pinglun*, 86:6 (January 21, 1934).

53. Ding, "Feizhji neizhan de yundong" (Stop the civil war); "Jiaru woshi Chiang Kai-shek" (If I were Chiang Kai-shek); and "Pinglun gongchan zhuyi bing zhonggao zhongguo gongchan dangyuan" (On Communism and to advise the Chinese Communists), *Duli pinglun*, 25:3–4 (November 6, 1932), 35:5 (January 15, 1933), 51:5–15 (May 21, 1933).

54. Jiang, "Nanjing de jihui" (Nanjing's opportunity); "Jiuyiba de zeren wenti" (The question of responsibility for the Manchurian Incident), *Duli pinglun*, 31:2–4 (December 18, 1932), 18:14 (September 18, 1932).

55. Hu, "Zhengzhi gaige de dalu" (The road to political reform), *Duli pinglun*, 163:3–4 (August 11, 1935).

56. Hu, "Cong minzhu yu ducai de taolun li qiude yige gongtong zhengzhi xinyang" (To establish a common political belief through the discussion on democracy versus dictatorship), *Duli pinglun*, 141:17 (March 10, 1935).

57. Hu, "Geren ziyou yu shehui jinbu—zaitan wusi yundong" (Individual freedom and social progress—a continued discussion on the May Fourth Movement), *Duli pinglun*, 150:2–5 (May 12, 1935).

58. Fu, "Chen Duxiu an" (The case of Chen Duxiu), *Duli pinglun*, 24 (October 30, 1932).

59. Wang Fansen, *Fu Ssu-nien*, 268.

60. Fu, *Fu Sinian quanji*, 1612–1613.

61. Fu, "Duoyan de zhengfu" (The big mouth government), *Duli pinglun*, 30 (December 11, 1932).

62. Fu, "Jiuyiba yinian le!" (A year after the Manchurian Incident!), *Duli pinglun*, 18 (September 18, 1932).

63. Hu, "Riben ren yinggai xingxing le!" (The Japanese must wake up!), *Duli pinglun*, 42:2–4 (March 19, 1933). His other writings are "Lun duiri waijiao fangzhen" (On the foreign policy toward Japan), 5 (June 26, 1932); "Women keyi denghou wushinian" (We can wait for half a century), 44 (April 2, 1933); and "Wo de yijian ye buguo ruci" (My opinion is nothing more than this), 46 (April 16, 1933).

64. After receiving Fu's letter of resigning from the editorial board, Ding Wenjiang wrote him back, asking him to think twice, especially about his friendship with Hu Shi. See "Fu Sinian dangan" (Fu Sinian's archive), III-197.

65. Qu Qiubai (1899–1935), for example, called Hu the "adviser to the Japanese imperialism." Lu Xun, Hu's Beida colleague in the New Culture Movement, attacked him for "selling his soul." Quoted in Shen Weiwei, *Hu Shi zhuan* (Biography of Hu Shi) (Taipei: Fengyun shidai chuban gongsi, 1990), 214.

66. Hu, "Yige daibiao shijie gonglun de baogao" (A report that represents world public opinion), *Duli pinglun*, 21:2–6 (October 9, 1932).

67. Hu, "Zhongri tixie: da ke wen" (Sino-Japanese reconciliation: an interview); "Women keyi denghou wushinian" (We can wait for half a century), *Duli pinglun*, 143:2–3 (March 25, 1935) and 44:2–5 (April 2, 1933).

68. Hu, "Zengyu jinnian de daxue biyesheng" (Advice to this year's university graduates) and "Chenmo de renshou" (Silent endurance); Ding, "Kangri de xiaoneng yu qingnian de zeren" (The feasibility of resisting Japan, and youth's responsibility), *Duli pinglun*, 7:2–5 (July 3, 1932); 16:2–3 (September 4, 1932); and 37:2–8 (February 12, 1933).

69. Fu, "Guolian diaochantuan baogaoshu yipie" (A glimpse at the investigation report of the delegation of the League of Nations); "Zhongri qinshan?" (Sino-Japanese cooperation?), *Duli pinglun*, 22 (October 16, 1932); 140 (March 3, 1935).

70. Shao Minghuang has done a statistical study of the contributors and found that among 203 writers, university professors were 79, lecturers 7, teaching assistants 5, university students 44, and independent scholars 30. See his "Kangzhan qian beifang xueren yu *Duli pinglun*" (The intellectuals in northern China and the *Independent critic* before the Sino-Japanese War) (MA thesis, National Cheng-chi University, Taipei, 1979), 70. See also Chen *Duli pinglun de minzhu sixiang*, 12–15.

71. *Hu Shi micang shuxin xuan* (Hu Shi's selected secret correspondence), ed. Liang Xihua (Taipei: Fengyun shidai chuban gongsi, 1990), 1:59–60.

72. See Chen, *Duli pinglun de minzhu sixiang*, 10–11.

73. See Lubot, *Liberalism in an Illiberal Age*.

74. About Japan's historiographical advances in the period, see Stefan Tanaka, *Japan's Orient*, especially 31–104. Tao Xisheng's letter was quoted in Wang Fansen, *Fu Ssu-nien*, 243.

75. See Hu Houxuan, "Dongbei shigang de zuozhe shi Fu Sinian" (The author of the Outline history of northeast China is Fu Sinian), *Shixueshi yanjiu* (Journal of historiography), 3 (1991): 48–49.

76. Fu Lecheng, *Fu Mengzhen*, 33–34.

77. Fu, *Dongbei shigang*, 31–32.

78. See Hu Houxuan. See also Wang Fansen, *Fu Ssu-nien*, 245–247. However, we must point out that both Miao and Chen opposed cultural reform. Their criticism of Fu was not just for correcting the mistakes, but to attack Fu and his leadership in promoting modern historiography.

79. Fu seems to have kept all criticisms, some were from Western scholars, of his work along with his papers in the Fu Sinian Library. On a scrap paper (no date), however, he did write down a few works he planed to do, which included the writing a rebuttal to Miao Fenglin's and others' criticism of his *Dongbei shigang*. See Fu, "Fu Sinian dangan" (Fu Sinian's archive), I-779.

80. Wang Fansen, *Fu Ssu-nien*, 248.

81. See Fu Sinian, "Fu Sinian dangan" (Fu Sinian's archive), I-702 and/or I-707. The following discussion is based on reading the manuscript. Schwarcz mentions the manuscript in *The Chinese Enlightenment*, 232–233.

82. In 1948 Fu Sinian went to cure his hypertension in the United States and during that time he wrote a few letters to Zhao Yuanren, his colleague at the Institute and a professor at UC/Berkeley, with whom he discussed some of his readings and new development in modern physics. Fu found that the "infallibility" of physics was no longer held true at that time, and himself more and more interested in Kantian philosophy. See Fu, "Fu Sinian dangan" (Fu Sinian's archive), I-195, I-196.

83. Wang Fansen, *Fu Ssu-nien*, 179.

84. Wang Shijie, "Fu Sinian xiansheng ersan shi" (My recollection of Fu Sinian), *Zhuanji wenxue*, 28:1 (1976), 14.

85. Wang Deyi, *Yao Congwu xiansheng nianbiao* (Chronology of Yao Congwu), *Yao Congwu xiansheng jinian lunwenji* (Commemorative volume

for Yao Congwu), 12. Another reason for Yao's return at the time was probably the political changes in Germany itself. After the Nazis' seizure of power in Germany in 1933, Yao's continuing stay in the country would be obviously very difficult, due to the Nazis' racist policy.

86. Yao's lecture notes of these two courses are in *Yao Congwu xiansheng quanji*, II–IV.

87. "Jin Yuan Quanzhen jiao de minzu sixiang yu jiushi sixiang" (On the nationalist aspects and the worship of a savior in the Quanzhen religion in the Jin and Yuan Dynasties), *Zhishi zazhi (Journal of historical study)*, 2 (1939). Apparently, Yao's study of the subject reflects his wartime concerns.

88. His student Wang Mingxin explains the reasons for Yao's sparse publications at the time: (1) spending too much time on teaching; (2) leading an unstable life because of the Sino-Japanese War and the following civil war; and (3) assuming some administrative work. His analysis is fair. One instance is that Yao often expended a large amount of time in preparing lecture notes; his lecture notes are well-organized and in great detail. For Wang's explanation, see *Yao Congwu xiansheng quanji*, VII, 479. For his lecture notes, ibid., II–IV.

89. About the student activism during this period, see John Israel, *Student Nationalism in China, 1927–1937*; John Israel and Donald W. Klein, *Rebels and Bureaucrats: China's December 9ers* (Berkeley: University of California Press, 1976); and Coble, *Facing Japan.*

90. See Israel, *Lianda*, especially part I & II.

91. Israel's *Lianda* mentioned this project, 72.

92. Yao Congwu, *Lugouqiao shibian yilai zhongri zhanzheng shiliao souji jihuashu* (Proposal for source collection for the Sino-Japanese War after the Marco Polo Bridge incident) (Kunming, 1939), no publisher, seen at Harvard-Yenching Library, 1–26.

93. Ibid., 26–27.

94. See Fu, "Fu Sinian dangan" (Fu Sinian's archive), III-454.

95. Through the Youth League Yao helped recruit many students for the army. *Yao Congwu xiansheng jinian lunwenji*, 15. But in general, according to John Israel, Yao lacked leadership quality; his appointment was due to his friendship with Zhu Jiahua, whom he befriended with while in Germany. A year later, Yao resigned from his position. Israel, *Lianda*, 263–264.

96. Luo Jialun, "Yuanqi linli de Fu Mengzhen," *Shizhe rusi ji*, 181–182.

97. Xia Nai (1910–1985), Fu's colleague and an archaeologist, wrote a letter to Fu right after the election, reporting the result: Chen received 343 votes and Fu 243. A not too bad result given the fact that Fu was absent to the election. See "Fu Sinian dangan" (Fu Sinian's archive), IV-193.

98. Fu Lecheng, "Fu Mengzhen," 64–66.

99. Ibid., 50. Fu's writing plan was also scrapped on a paper. I suspect that the book he mentioned to Hu Shi was the same *A Revolutionary History of the Chinese Nation*. It was just under a new title: "Minzu yu gudai zhongguoshi" (Nation and ancient Chinese history), which Fu said was already completed two third. See "Fu Sinian dangan" (Fu Sinian's archive), I-779.

100. Luo was also a poet. On his trips to India and Xinjiang, he wrote many poems. But he only wrote them in the traditional form, which appeared inconsistent with his overall advocacy of modern culture, particularly because Hu Shi endeavored to write new and prosaic poems in the New Culture movement.

101. Luo, "Qingnian dang queli renge shixue buyingwei yexin fenzi suo liyong" (Advice to young people for the vigilance against ambitious plotters), *Luo Jialun xiansheng wencun*, I, 94. For the student movement at the time, see John Israel, *Student Nationalism*. Also Jeffrey Wasserstrom, *Student Protests in Twentieth century China: the View from Shanghai* (Stanford: Stanford University Press, 1991).

102. Luo, "Mian liumei tongxue" (An exhortation for the students who are going to study in the United States), *Luo Jialun xiansheng wencun*, I, 486.

103. Luo, "Du biaozhun de shuji xie fuze de wenzi" (To read standard books, to write responsible works), ibid., I, 496–497.

104. Luo, "Wusi de zhen jingshen" (The true spirit of the May Fourth Movement), *Luo Jialun xiansheng wenchun*, I, 311–313. About Luo's comparison of the meaning of "Aufklärung" and "enlightenment," also see his "Shuangshi jie zhi ganxiang" (Reflections on the national holiday, October 10), ibid., I, 84.

105. Luo's opinions about these matters were mainly expressed in the 1920s and 1930s. See his "Funu jiefang" (Emancipation of women), *Luo Jialun xiansheng wenchun*, I, 4–25, and "Zhi Hu Xianxiao jun de zhongguo wenxue gailiang Lun" (On Mr. Hu Xianxiao's approach to the reform of Chinese literature), I, 389–414.

106. Luo, "Yinianlai women xuesheng yundong di chenggong shibai he jianglai yingqu de fangzhen" (Successes and failures of the past one year student movement and the plan for its future), ibid., I, 415–436. Luo wrote at the end that he was then engaged in a project of translation, which is very possibly his translation of J. B. Bury's *History of Freedom of Thought*.

107. See Luo's "Beijing daxue de jingsheng" (The spirit of the Beijing University), ibid., I, 610–620; "Dui wusi yundong de yixie ganxiang" (Some reflections on the May Fourth Movement), I, 352–356.

108. Yao, "Guoshi kuoda mianyan de yige kanfa," *Yao Congwu*, 235–236.

109. Ibid., 240–258.

110. Ibid., 256–257.

111. Yao, "Cong lishi shang kan dongya rujia datong wenhua de liguo jingshen," 259–275.

112. Yao Congwu, "Qidan hanhua de fenxi" (An analysis of the sinicization of the Khitans), *Yao Congwu xiansheng quanji*, V, 33–64.

113. In her presidential address at the Association for Asian Studies in 1996, Evelyn Rawski challenges this viewpoint regarding sinicization, or sinicization, in the Qing Dynasty. She argues instead that Qing was quite a "multiethnic empire." "Re-envisioning the Qing: The Significance of the Qing Period in Chinese History," *Journal of Asian Studies*, 55:4 (November 1996), 829–850. But her argument was challenged by Ping-ti Ho in his "In Defense of Sinicization: A Rebuttal of Evelyn Rawski's 'Reenvisioning the Qing,'" *Journal of Asian Studies*, 57:1 (1998): 123–155.

114. Yao, "Nuzhen hanhua de fenxi" (An analysis of the sinicization of the Jurchens), ibid., V, 163–198.

115. In her monograph, *The Southern Ming*, 1644–1662 (New Haven: Yale University Press, 1984), Lynn Struve documents the resistance of the Han Chinese to the Manchu army. The issue regarding Manchu sinicization is also discussed in detail in Pamela Crossley's *A Translucent Mirror: History and Identity in Qing Ideology: The Manchus* (forthcoming) and *Orphan Warriors: Three Manchu Generations and the End of the Qing World* (Princeton: Princeton University Press, 1990).

116. Yao, "Chengji Sihan xinren Qiu Chuji yu zhejianshi duiyu baoquan zhongyuan chuantong wenhua de gongxian" (Chinggis Khan's trust in Qiu Chuji and the preservation of the mainland traditional culture), ibid., VI, 1–138.

117. Yao, "Hubilei Han yu Mengge Han zhili handi de qijian" (The differences between Khubilai Khan and Mangu Khan in their attitudes towards the Han inhabitants), ibid., VI, 379–398; "Yuan Shizu Hubilei Han, tade jiashi, tade shidai yu ta zaiwei qijian zhongyao sheshi" (Yuan Shizu Khubilai Khan: his family, his times, and the important policies in his reign), VI, 399–416; "Yuan Shizu chongxin kongxue de chenggong yu suo zaoyu de kunnan" (Yuan Shizu's admiration of Confucianism, its success and difficulty), VI, 417–448. Khubilai Khan's "benevolent" policy toward Han Chinese culture was noticed by many Western scholars, including Otto Franke.

118. Yao, "Yang Jiye baowei guotu" (Yang Jiye's defense of the country), ibid., V, 153–156. According to Song records, Yang's death was caused by factionalism in the Song army. His story later became widely circulated and a source for literary creations. Yang's name is thus known to Chinese people as Shakespeare's *King Lear* and *Othello* to the English-speaking people.

119. Yao, "Fu Bi," ibid., V, 157–162.

120. "Yu Jie pingzhuan" (A critical biography of Yu Jie), ibid., VI, 309–378. In the beginning of the book, Yao tells us that his purpose is to let both ordinary people and scholars know this national hero and superb strategist.

121. Besides the above two articles, Yao's important works on this subject are seen mostly in *Yao Congwu xiansheng quanji*, Vols. 5–7. Some of his articles deal with the Han Chinese who defended mainland culture, which suggests more clearly that he deemed the Han as the stalk of Chinese culture.

122. Gu Jiegang's multi-ethnic theory of Chinese civilization is discussed in Tze-ki Hon's article, "Ethnic and Cultural Pluralism: Gu Jiegang's Vision of a New China in His Studies of Ancient History," *Modern China*, 22:3 (July 1996), 315–340.

123. Chen's grandfather assisted Zeng Guofan in defeating the Taiping rebels, which led to his appointment as the governor of Hunan. He also advocated Zhang Zhidong's *ti-yong* idea. See Jiang Tianshu, *Chen Yinke xiansheng biannian shiji* (A chronological record of Chen Yinke) (Shanghai: Shanghai Guji Chubanshe, 1981), 5–21.

124. Chen Yinke, "*Zhongguo zhexueshi* shencha baogao" (A review of *History of Chinese Philosophy*), *Chen Yinke xiansheng quanji* (The complete works of Chen Yinke) (Taipei: Jiusi Publisher, 1977), II, 1365.

125. Wu Mi, Chen's lifelong friend, visited Chen in 1961 and later wrote in his diary that "Chen Yinke's opinions and ideas have never changed; he still follows the 'Chinese learning as the substance and Western learning the function' doctrine. Among our generation, Chen is probably the only one who did not adjust his ideas to the new social circumstances." Wu's comment was made after Chen had been exposed to CCP's political campaigns after 1949. See Wu's diary on August 30, 1961, in Jiang Tianshu, *Chen Yinke*, 158.

126. Chen, *Chen Yinke xiansheng quanji*, II, 1364–1365.

127. For the humanist origins of modern European historiography, see Donald Kelley, *Foundations of Modern Historical Scholarship* and Joseph M. Levine, *Humanism and History: Origins of Modern English Historiography* (Ithaca: Cornell University Press, 1987). Hans-Georg Gadamer gives a philosophical summary of the humanist tradition in his *Truth and Method*, 5–38.

128. Lately the study of the *Xueheng* group has become quite popular among PRC scholars. Wu Mi has received a tremendous attention, especially after the publication of his eight-volume diary. In addition to Richard Rosen's dissertation and Shen Songqiao's book quoted earlier, there is an anthology of the writings of the group, see *Guogu xinzhilun: xueheng pai wenhua lunzhu jiyao* (On national essence and new knowledge: essential

writings of the *Critical Review* group), eds. Sun Shangyang and Guo Lanfang (Beijing: Zhongguo guangbo dianshi chubanshe, 1995).

129. Yu Ying-shih has found evidence from Chen's writings that he was quite aware of the works of European thinkers such as Plato, Aristotle, Cicero, St. Augustine, and Pascal. See *Chen Yinke wannian shiwen shizheng* (Evidential interpretations of Chen Yinke's poems and essays in his later years) (Taipei: Shidai Wenhua Qiye Chuban Youxian Gongsi, 1986), 20–21.

130. Cf. Paul Demiéville, "Necrologie: Tch'en Yinko," *Toung Pao*, 26 (1971), 138. When Cambridge extended its invitation to Chen as the visiting professor in 1942, Pelliot wrote the recommendation for him. This suggests that they must have kept contact after Chen's return to China.

131. Chen left 64 notebooks which he used in Germany for his study. Each notebook has a topic, suggesting the course he took or the language he learned. From these notebooks, we find that Chen had a very broad and ambitious study plan; he learned Tibetan, Mongolian, Uighur, Turkish, Manchu, Korean, Hindi, Pali. Russian, Persian, and Hebrew. Besides these languages, he also studied different sects of Buddhism and Buddhist Sutras. Moreover, there was even a notebook titled "mathematics" in which many formulae of calculus were found. See Ji Xianlin, "Cong xuexi bijiben kan Chen Yinke xiansheng de zhixue fanwei he tujing" (From Chen Yinke's notebooks to see his study and method), *Jinian Chen Yinke jiaoshou guoji xueshu taolunhui wenji* (Proceedings of the international conference for Chen Yinke) (Guangzhou: Zhongshan University Press, 1989), 74–87.

132. See Yu Dawei, "Tan Chen Yinke xiansheng" (My memoir of Chen Yinke), *Tan Chen Yinke* 9 (Taipei: Zhuanji wenxue, 1969). Also Mao Zishui, "Ji Chen Yinke xiansheng" (My memory of Chen Yinke), ibid., 21. Chen's daughter remembers this also, in Jiang Tianshu *Chen Yinke*, 80.

133. Yu Ying-shih was told by a colleague of Chen Yinke at Qinghua that he was the only professor in the school who could write Latin. See Yu Ying-shih, *Chen Yinke wannian shiwen shizheng*, 20.

134. See Chen's letter to Luo Xianglin, in Wang Rongzu, *Shijia Chen Yinke zhuan*, 259.

135. Wu Mi, *Wu Yuseng shiwenji (Wu Mi's poems and writings)* (Taipei: Dipingxian, 1971), 438.

136. Mao Zishui, "Ji Chen Yinke xiansheng" (My memory of Chen Yinke), *Tan Chen Yinke*, 19.

137. Yang Buwei and Zhao Yuanren, "Yi Yinke" (In memory of Chen Yinke), ibid., 24–25. Chen's daughter also writes that though Chen was supposed to receive an official scholarship from Jiangxi Province, he did not receive it because of the domestic chaos in China. As a result, he had to bring bread to the library and stayed there for the whole day. In Jiang Tianshu, *Chen Yinke*, 53.

138. Chen, *Chen Yinke xiansheng quanji*, II, 1437.

139. See Jiang Tainshu, "Shimen wangshi zalu" (Some recollections of my study with Chen Yinke), *Jinian Chen Yinke xiansheng dancheng bainian xueshu lunwenji* (Studies in honor of Prof. Chen Yin-que), eds. Ji Xianlin et al. (Beijing: Beijing Daxue chubanshe, 1989), 15.

140. Chen Zhesan recalled that one day he and his classmates visited Chen and had some foreign wine in Chen's place. Chen told them the origin of the wine by telling a detailed story of the wine, which greatly impressed them. In Jiang Tianshu, *Chen Yinke*, 62. Tang Zhenchang told me on April 12, 1992, that he deemed Chen's death the end of a whole generation of Chinese scholars.

141. In the article, Chen gives two examples. One is found in the translation of Lotus Sutra where "Siddhanta" was first translated into "Xitan" according to the pronunciation. But later scholars gave another meaning to "Xitan." Another example is that Xuanzhuang, the great Tang Buddhist who actually visited India and learned Sanskrit, tried to translate some Buddhist terms by using words with similar sounds, because he found that many of terms translated earlier had caused some confusion. "Dacheng yizhang shuhou" (A study of Mahayana principles), *Chen Yinke xiansheng quanji*, II, 1387–1389.

142. Ibid., II, 1389–1390.

143. Chen, "*Xiyouji* Xuanzhuang dizi gushi zhi yanbian" (Evolutions of stories about Xuanzhuang and his disciples in *The Journey to the West*) and "*Sanguozhi* Cao Chong Hua Tuo zhuan yu fojiao gushi" (Biographies of Can Chong and Hua Tuo in *The Three Kingdoms* and Buddhist stories), ibid., II, 1113–1122.

144. Chen, *Suitang zhidu suyuan luelungao* (Manuscript of the origins of institutions in the Sui and Tang Dynasties), 1939, and *Tangdai zhengzhishi sulungao* (Manuscript of a political history of the Tang Dynasty), 1941.

145. During his stay in Hong Kong, Chen and his family suffered a great deal economically. In his letters to Fu Sinian, he described that his family often had meatless meals for over a month. Wu Han also wrote to Fu, asking him to offer help for Chen's escape from Hong Kong. After his escape, Chen thanked Fu and decided to stay in Guangxi for a brief rest. See "Fu Sinian dangan" (Fu Sinian's archive), I-1693, I-1688, I-1689, III-63.

146. In my talk with Tang Zhenchang, Chen's student, on April 12, 1992, Tang recalled that Chen once discussed in the classroom the question of whether Yang Guifei, Tang Xuanzong's famous concubine, was a virgin when she entered the palace. Through the discussion of this seemingly unimportant issue, Chen helped students to understand the marital system in the Tang Dynasty. Tang Zhenchang believed that this was a good example of Chen's historical method.

147. See Chen, *Tangdai zhengzhishi sulungao* (Manuscript of Tang political history), *Chen Yinke xiansheng quanji*, I, 151–199. About the origin of Li clan, Chen wrote three essays in 1931, 1933, and 1935. Ibid., I, 341–364, 475–480. Some of Chen's interpretations were challenged by some Chinese and Western scholars, see Wang Rongzu, *Shijia Chen Yinke zhuan*, 124–150.

148. Chen, *Tangdai zhengzhishi sulungao* (Manuscript of Tang political history), *Chen Yinke xiansheng quanji*, I, 200–273. Chen's geopolitical interpretation of Tang history was challenged by Howard Wechsler who pointed out that the Guanlong bloc was not based on a geographical connection. See his "Factionalism in Early Tang Government," in *Perspectives on the Tang*, eds. Arthur Wright and Denis Twitchett (New Haven: Yale University Press, 1973), 87–120. See also *Mirror to the Son of Heaven: Wei Cheng at the Court of T'ang T'ai-tsung* (New Haven: Yale University Press, 1974), 88–95.

149. Chen Yinke, "Ji tangdai zhi Li, Wu, Wei, Yang hunyin jituan" (A study of Li, Wu, Wei, and Yang marital groups in the Tang) and "Lun suimo tangchu suowei 'Shandong haojie'" (The so-called 'Shandong Heroes' at the end of the Sui and beginning of the Tang Dynasty), *Chen Yinke xiansheng quanji*, I, 619–638; 639–664. *Yuan Bai shijian zhenggao* (Manuscript of a study of Yuan Zhen and Bai Juyi poems), ibid., II, 689–1011. Besides poetry, Chen also studied fiction in the Tang. See his article, translated by J. R. Ware in English: "Han Yu and Tang Novel," *Harvard Journal of Asian Studies*, 1:1 (1936), 39–43.

150. Huang Xuan, "Huainian Chen Yinke jiaoshou" (My memoir of Prof. Chen Yinke), *Jinian Chen Yinke jiaoshou guoji xueshu taolunhui wenji*, 67–73. For a new and detailed account of Chen Yinke's later life, see Lu Jiandong, *Chen Yinke de zuihou ershi nian* (Chen Yinke's Last Twenty Years) (Hong Kong: Tiandi tushu, 1996).

151. Chen expressed his feelings in his poems. For his decision not to go to Taiwan, see Jiang Tianshu, *Chen Yinke*, 137. Also Wang Rongzu, *Shijia Chen Yinke zhuan*, 183–185. According to Tang Zhenchang, Chen had an antithetical couplet hanging in his study, which read "since one never knows what is to happen tomorrow, his life is unpredictable in reincarnation." His pessimistic view about the leadership of the GMD government accounted for his remaining on the mainland.

152. The CCP governor of the Guangdong Province and other CCP leaders called on him and provided with him some help. Even for the CCP, Chen was a respected scholar. See Jiang Tianshu, *Chen Yinke*, 151–153, 156, 159–160.

153. According to Lu Jiandong, Chen refused the offer from Beijing and stated that unless the institute under his leadership can be exempted from the study of Marxism, he would not join the Academy. *Chen Yinke de zuihou ershi nian*, 101–109.

154. Chen, *Liu Rushi beizhuan* (An informal biography of Liu Rushi), 3 vols. (Shanghai: Shanghai Guji Chubanshe, 1980).

155. Chen's confession later became an important source for his biographers. Jiang Tianshu's *Chen Yinke xiansheng biannian shiji* (A chronological record of Chen Yinke) utilizes in many places his confessions to reconstruct his life.

156. In Yang Liansheng, "Chen Yinke xiansheng suitangshi diyijiang biji" (My notes of the first class of Prof. Chen Yinke's course of Sui and Tang history), *Tan Chen Yinke*, 29. Yu Ying-shih, by studying Chen's poems, has done a penetrating analysis of Chen Yinke's mind and life during the period. Yu found that Chen often wrote his criticism of Communist rule into his enigmatic poems, which require painstaking effort to decipher. See *Chen Yinke wannian shiwen shizheng*.

Chapter Six

1. Chen Yinke's experience in the Cultural Revolution was indeed tragic, but not uncommon during those fierce years. In Gu Chao's (Gu Jiegang's daughter) biography of her father, *Lijie zhongjiao zhibuthui*, we have found that Gu suffered, along with his family and many intellectuals, from a similar experience, although they survived at last. In fact, even those intellectuals of a younger generation who had less exposure to Western cultural influence and had embraced the Communist revolution, hence the "establishment intellectuals," also faced similar, if not more, persecutions and life-threatening dangers. See *China's Establishment Intellectuals*, eds. Carol Lee Hamrin and Timothy Cheek (Armonk, NY: M. E. Sharpe, 1986) and Timothy Cheek, *Propaganda and Culture in Mao's China: Deng Tuo and the Intelligentsia* (Oxford: Clarendon Press, 1997).

2. For an early discussion of the rise of New-Confucianism, see Hao Chang, "New Confucianism and the Intellectual Crisis of Contemporary China." Furth, *The Limits of Change*, 276–302. Some of the main issues raised by these New-Confucians are also discussed by Thomas Metzger in his *Escape from Predicament: Neo-Confucianism and China's Evolving Political Culture* (New York: Columbia University Press, 1977).

3. Hu Shi's speech on scientific development and social reform is in *Zhuanji wenxue*, 55:1 (1989), 38–40. For how Hu was attacked by his critics and his death, see Hu Songping, *Hu Shizhi xiansheng wannian tanhua lu* (Conversations with Hu Shi in his later years) (Taipei: Lianjing chuban shiye gongsi, 1984), 284–322.

4. Hu Shi was involved in the magazine, which was an outlet of political criticisms in 1950s Taiwan and Hong Kong. In the late summer of 1960, however, Lei Zhen, the editor, was arrested for some circumstantial charges

and the magazine was banned subsequently. Hu Shi protested several times but to no avail. Lei received the sentence of ten years of imprisonment.

5. See Zhou Liangkai (Chow Liang-kai), "Shixueshi yanjiu de quxiang: yijiusiwu nian yilai Taiwan shijia de lunshu" (Tendencies in the history of historiography: an analysis on the works of Taiwan historians since 1945), 3–4, presented at the International Conference on Chinese Historiography, Heidelberg, Germany, March 29–April 2, 1995.

6. For the situation of historical studies in Taiwan during the period, see Xu Guansan, "sanshiwu nian (1950–1985) lai de Taiwan shijie bianqian" (Transformations in Taiwan historians' circle in the last thirty five years, 1950–1985), 243–273. Zhang Pengyuan's *Guo Yingyi, Fei Zhengqing, Wei Muting* (Guo Tingyi, John Fairbank, C. Martin Wilbur) recalls the founding of the Institute and its working relations with American China scholars and the Ford and Rockefeller Foundations in the 1950s and the 1960s.

7. See Fu's remarks: "We are not book readers. We go all the way to Heaven above and Yellow Spring below, using our hands and feet, to look for things." *Fu Sinian quanji*, IV, 256–260.

8. See my article on the changes in the historical studies in Taiwan, "Taiwan shixue de 'bian' yu 'bubian', 1949–99," (Tradition and Transformation: Historical Studies in Taiwan, 1949–1999), in *Taida lishi xuebao* (Historical journal of Taiwan University) 24 (Dec. 1999), 329–374.

9. Some American-educated historians, such as Xu Zhuoyun (Hsu Cho-yun) and Tao Jinsheng (Tao Chin-sheng) who teach at University of Pittsburgh and University of Arizona, respectively, were instrumental in pioneering the study of Chinese social history. But intellectuals historians like Yu Ying-shih (Princeton) and Lin Yu-sheng (Wisconsin) were also very popular among history students in Taiwan.

10. *Cultural Change in Postwar Taiwan*, eds. Stevan Harrell and Huang Chün-chieh (Boulder, CO: Westview Press, 1994). However, I have not hitherto seen any study of Taiwan historiography in English.

11. Quoted in Liu Danian, "How to Appraise the History of Asia?" *History in Communist China*, ed. Albert Feuerwerker (Cambridge, MA: MIT Press, 1958), 366. Liu was then the deputy director of the office in modern history in the Institute of Historical Research, Chinese Academy. Other works on Chinese Marxist historiography during the period are James P. Harrison, *The Communists and Chinese Peasant Rebellions: A Study in the Rewriting of Chinese History* (New York: Atheneum, 1969); Arif Dirlik, "Mirror to Revolution: Early Marxist Images of Chinese History," *Journal of Asian Studies*, 33 (2) (1974), 193–223, and "The Problem of Class Viewpoint versus Historicism in Chinese Historiography," *Modern China*, 3 (4) (Oct. 1977), 465–488; Dorothea Martin, *The Making of a Sino-Marxist World View* (Armonk, NY: M. E. Sharpe, 1990); and *Using the Past to*

Serve the Present: Historiography and Politics in Contemporary China, ed. Jonathan Unger (Armonk, NY: M. E. Sharpe, 1993).

12. See Q. Edward Wang, "Between Marxism and Nationalism: Chinese Historiography and the Soviet Influence, 1949–1963," *Journal of Contemporary China*, 9:23 (2000), 95–111.

13. Anthologies on these discussions are as follows. For the periodization question, see *Zhongguo de nulizhi yu fengjianzhi fenqi wenti lunwen xuanji* (Selected essays on the periodization of the slave and feudal eras in China) (Beijing: Sanlian shudian, 1956); *Zhongguo gushi fenqi wenti luncong* (Essays on the periodization question in ancient Chinese history) (Beijing: Zhonghua shuju, 1957); Lin Ganquan et al., eds. *Zhongguo gudaishi fenqi taolun wushinian* (Discussions on the periodization of ancient Chinese history in the last fifty years) (Shanghai: Shanghai renmin chubanshe, 1982). For the peasant wars, see *Zhongguo fengjian shehui nongmin zhanzheng wenti taolunji* (Collected articles on the problem of the peasant wars in Chinese feudal society), ed. Shi Shaobin, (Beijing: Sanlian shudian, 1962). For Chinese capitalism, see *Zhongguo zibenzhuyi mengya wenti taolunji* (Collected papers on the problem of the incipiency of capitalism in China), 2 vols. (Beijing: Sanlian shudian, 1957).

14. There have been a plenty of works on the "social history controversy," in addition to Arif Dirlik's *Revolution and History*. See Wang Lixi and Lu Qingqing, eds. *Zhongguo shehuishi di lunzhan* (Controversy on the Social History of China) (Shanghai: 1936); He Ganzhi, *Zhongguo shehui shi wenti lunzhan* (Controversy on the Problem of Chinese Social History) (Shanghai: 1937), Mechthild Leutner, *Geschichtsschreibung zwischen Politik und Wissenschaft: Zur Herausbildung der chinesischen marxistischen Geschichtswissenschaft in den 30er under 40er Jahren* (Wiesbaden: Otto Harrassowitz, 1982); and Wu An-chia, "Revolution and History: On the Causes of the Controversy over the Social History of China (1931–33)," *Chinese Studies in History*, XI:3 (Spring 1988), 77–96.

15. Albert Feverwerker, ed., "China's History in Marxian Dress," *History in Communist China* (Cambridge, MA: MIT Press, 1968), 28.

16. Karl Marx, "Preface to a Contribution to the Critique of Political Economy," *Early Writings* (New York: Vintage Books, 1975), 426.

17. For the discussion, see *Han minzu xingcheng wenti taolunji* (Discussions on the formation of the Han nation) (Beijing: Sanlian shudian, 1957). For Fan's historical career, see Xu Guansan, *Xinshixue jiushinian*, Vol. 2, 145–160.

18. Quoted in Xu, *Xinshixue jiushinian*, vol. 2, 150.

19. R. V. Vyatkin and S. L. Tikhvinsky, "Historical Science in the People's Republic," *History in Communist China*, 340.

20. Fan's words, quoted in Xu, *Xinshixue jiushinian*, vol. 2, 150–151.

21. This "culture fever" movement, especially the popular TV series *He Shang* (River Elegy) in which the new generation of Chinese intellectuals demonstrated a profound cultural and historical criticism that is equivalent, if not more, to the May Fourth iconoclasm, has attracted some attention in the West. See Xiaomei Chen, "Occidentalism as Counterdiscourse: '*He Shang*' in Post-Mao China, *Critical Inquiry*, 18:4 (Summer 1992), 686–712, and *Occidentalism* (New York: Oxford University Press, 1995); Selden Field, "*He Shang* and the Plateau of Ultrastability," Edward Gunn, "The Rhetoric of *He Shang*: From Cultural Criticism to Social Act," and Jing Wang, "*He Shang* and the Paradoxes of Chinese Enlightenment," *Bulletin of Concerned Asian Scholars*, 23:3 (July 1991), 4–33, and *High Culture Fever: Politics, Aesthetics, and Ideology in Deng's China* (Berkeley: University of California Press, 1996). These young scholars also showed enthusiasm for Western culture. For their introduction of Western historical practice, see Qingjia Wang, "Western Historiography in the People's Republic of China (1949 to the present)," *Storia della Storiografia*, 19 (1991), 23–46.

22. Chen Xulu (1918–1988), for example, a prominent historian in modern Chinese history, wrote a few articles during the 1980s for the *Lishi yanjiu* (Historical research), a leading historical journal in the PRC, analyzing the *ti-yong* idea and other relevant issues in modern China. See *Chen Xulu xueshu wencun* (Chen Xulu's scholarly essays) (Shanghai: Shanghai renmin chubanshe, 1990). Li Zehou also discusses similar questions in his "manshuo xiti zhongyong" (Remarks on Western substance and Chinese function), *Zhongguo xiandai sixiangshi lun* (Beijing: Renmin chubanshe 1986), 311–342.

23. I, for example, served on the editorial board for a translation series entitled "A translation Series of Modern Western Scholarly Trend" *(dangdai xifang xueshu sichao yicong)*, in the Shanghai Translation Publishing House *(Shanghai yiwen chubanshe)*. Each of the first ten books in the series sold between 50,000 and 100,000 copies. Of course, this series was just one of many translation series that appeared during the period. The most successful series was *(zouxiang weilai)* "Toward the Future," although it was not an exclusive translation series.

24. Craig Calhoun, a noted social theorist, has noticed the intrinsic linkage between the May Fourth Movement and the political culture of the 1980s. See his "Science, Democracy, and the Politics of Identity," *Popular Protest and Political Culture in Modern China*, eds. Jeffrey Wasserstrom and Elizabeth Perry (Boulder, CO: Westview Press, 1994), 93–124.

25. Cf. Xudong Zhang, "The Politics of Hermeneutics: Notes on the Re-Invention of Tradition in Post-Mao Chinese Cultural Discussions," paper presented at the International Conference on Chinese Hermeneutic Cultures, Rutgers University, October 10–12, 1996, 5–7 and his *Chinese Modernism in the Era of Reforms: Cultural Fever, Avant-Garde Fiction, and the New Chinese Cinema* (Durham, NC: Duke University Press, 1996),

33–100. Also, Edward Xin Gu, "Cultural Intellectuals and the Politics of Cultural Public Space in Communist China (1979–1989): A Case Study of the Three Intellectual Group," *Journal of Asian Studies*, 58:2 (1999), 389–431.

26. In his popular book, Jenner analyzes how China's past, ranging from law, government, and economics to family, ethics, and values, acting as the "tyranny of history," accounts for the difficulty of modernity in modern China. *The Tyranny of History: The Roots of China's Crisis* (New York: Penguin Books, 1992).

27. Bao, "Cong qimeng dao xin qimeng: dui wusi de fansi" (From the enlightenment to the new enlightenment: a May Fourth reflection), *Cong wusi dao xin wusi* (From the May Fourth to the new May Fourth) (Taipei: Shibao wenhua congshu, 1989), ed. Zhou Yangshan, 167–168.

28. Foucault, "Nietzsche, Genealogy, History," in *The Foucault Reader*, ed. Paul Rabinow (New York: Pantheon Books, 1984), 89.

29. "Chuantong wenhua yu wenhua chuantong" (Traditional culture and cultural tradition), in Zhu Weizheng, *Yindiao weiding de chuantong* (A tradition without definite tone) (Shenyang: Liaoning Jiaoyu chubanshe, 1995), 19–21.

30. Croce, *History as the Story of Liberty*, trans. Sylvia Sprigge (New York: Meridian Books, 1955), 15, also see Croce's *History: Its Theory and Practice*, trans. Douglas Ainslie (New York: Russell & Russell, 1960).

31. Lowenthal, *The Past Is a Foreign Country*, 356.

Selected Bibliography

Chinese Sources

Bai Ji'an. *Hu Shi zhuan* (Biography of Hu Shi) (Beijing: Renmin chubanshe, 1993).

Cai Shangsi, ed. *Zhongguo xiandai sixiangshi ziliao jianbian* (Selected sources for the study of modern Chinese intellectual history), 5 vols. (Hangzhou: Zhejiang Renmin Chubanshe, 1982).

Cang Xiuliang, et al. *Zhongguo gudai shixueshi jianbian* (A concise history of ancient Chinese historiography (Harbin: Heilongjiang Renmin Chubanshe, 1983).

Chen Chunsheng. *Xinwenhua de qishou—Luo Jialun zhuan* (The forerunner of the new culture—biography of Luo Jialun) (Taipei: Jindai Zhongguo Chubanshe, 1985).

Chen Yinke. *Chen Yinke xiansheng wenshi lunji* (Chen Yinke's essays on literature and history), 2 vols. (Hong Kong: Xianggang Wenshi Chubanshe, 1972–1973).

———. *Chen Yinke xiansheng quanji* (The complete works of Chen Yinke), 2 vols. (Taipei: Jiusi Chuban Youxian Gongsi, revised ed., 1977).

———. *Yu Xifang shijia lun zhongguo shixue* (Discussions with Western historians on Chinese historiography) (Taipei: Dongda tushu gongsi, 1981).

———. *Chen Yinke ziliao* (Sources on Chen Yinke), 2 vols., n.p, n.d, available at Yale University.

Chen Yishen. *Duli pinglun de minzhu sixiang* (The democratic ideas of the *Independent Critique*) (Taipei: Lianjing chuban shiye gongsi, 1989).

Du Weiyun. *Qingdai shixue yu shijia* (History and historians in the Qing) (Beijing: Zhonghua Shuju, 1988).

———. *Jinian Chen Yinke jiaoshou guoji xueshu taolunhui wenji* (Proceedings of the international conference for Chen Yinke) (Guangzhou: Zhongshan University Press, 1989).

Du Zhengsheng and Wang Fansen, eds. *Xinxueshu zhilu: zhongyang yanjiuyuan lishi yuyan yanjiusuo qishi zhounian jinian wenji* (Along new pathways of research: Essays in honor of the seventieth anniversary of the Institute of History and Philology) (Taipei: Institute of History and Philology, Academia Sinica, 1998).

Feng Aiqun, ed. *Hu Shizhi xiansheng jinianji* (Commemorative volume for Hu Shi) (Taipei: Xuesheng Shuju, 1962).

Fu Lecheng. *Fu Mengzhen xiansheng nianpu* (Chronological biography of Fu Sinian) (Taipei: Wenxin Shudian, 1964).

Fu Sinian. "Fu Sinian dangan" (Fu Sinian's archive), Fu Sinian Library, Institute of History and Philology, Academia Sinica.

———. *Dongbei shigang* (Outline history of Manchuria) (Beijing: the Institute of History and Philology, Academia Sinica, 1932).

———. *Fu guxiaozhang aiwuanlu* (In memory of former president Fu Sinian) (Taipei: National Taiwan University Press, 1951).

———. *Fu suozhang jinian tekan* (Special publication for Director Fu Sinian) (Taipei: the Institute of History and Philology, Academia Sinica, 1951).

———. *Fu Sinian ziliaoji* (Sources on Fu Sinian), n.p., n.d., available at Yale University.

———. *Fu Sinian quanji* (The complete works of Fu Sinian), 7 vols. (Taipei: Lianjing Chuban Shiye Gongsi, 1980).

Gong Zizhen. *Gongzizhen quanji* (The complete works of Gong Zizhen) (Shanghai: Shanghai renmin chubanshe, 1975).

Gu Chao. *Lijie zhongjiao zhibuhui: wode fuqin Gu Jiegang* (My father Gu Jiegang) (Shanghai: Huadong shifan daxue chubanshe, 1997).

Gu Xin. *Zhongguo qimeng de lishi tujing* (A History of the Chinese Enlightenment) (Hong Kong: Oxford University Press, 1992).

He Bingsong. *Lishi yanjiufa* (Historical methods) (Shanghai: Commerical Press, 1927).

———. *Zhedong xuepai suyuan* (A history of the eastern Zhejiang School) (Shanghai: Commerical Press, 1932).

———. *Cheng Zhu bianyi* (On the difference between Cheng Yi and Zhu Xi) (Hong Kong: Cuncui Xueshe, 1971).

———. *He Bingsong xiaozhang wenji* (Works of chancellor He Bingsong), ed. Si Qi (Taipei: Commercial Press, 1988).

———. *He Bingsong jinian wenji* (Commemorative volume for He Bingsong), eds. Liu Yinsheng et al. (Shanghai: East China Normal University Press, 1990).

———. *He Bingsong lunwenji* (Works of He Bingsong), eds. Liu Yinsheng et al. (Beijing: Commercial Press, 1990).

Hu Shi. *Hu Shi lunxue jinzhu* (Hu Shi's recent works) (Shanghai: Commercial Press, 1935).

———. *Hu Shi yanlunji* (Hu Shi's speeches) (Taipei: 1955).

———. *Hu Shi xuanji* (Selected works of Hu Shi), 10 vols. (Taipei: Wenxin Shudian, 1966).

———. *Hu Shi* (Taipei: Huaxin Cultural Center, 1979).

———. *Hu Shi zhexue sixiang ziliao xuan* (Selected works of Hu Shi's philosophical ideas), eds. Ge Maochun et al., 2 vols. (Shanghai: East China Normal University Press, 1979).

———. *Hu Shi laiwang shuxinxuan* (Selected correspondences of Hu Shi), 2 vols. (Beijing: Zhonghua Shuju, 1983).

Hu Songping, ed. *Hu Shizhi xiansheng wannian tanhualu* (Conversations with Hu Shi in his later years) (Taipei: Lianjing chuban shiye gongsi, 1984).

Jiang Tianshu. *Chen Yinke xiansheng biannian shiji* (A chronological record of Chen Yinke) (Shanghai: Shanghai Guji Chubanshe, 1981).

Liang Qichao. *Zhongguo jinsanbainian xueshushi* (Chinese intellectual history of the last three centuries) (Beijing: Zhonghua Shuju, 1936).

———. *Liang Qichao shixue lunzhu sanzhong* (Liang Qichao's three historical works) (Hong Kong: Sanlian Shudian, 1980).

———. *Zhongguo lishi yanjiufa* (Method for the study of Chinese history) (Shanghai: Shanghai Guji Chubanshe, 1987).

———. *Yinbingshi quanji* (The completed works of the ice drinker's studio) (Taipei: Wenhua tushu gongsi, 1989).

Liu Zhiji. *Shitong tongshi* (Perspectives in historiography), annotated. Pu Qilong, (Shanghai: Commerical Press, 1937).

Li Zehou. *Zhongguo jindai sixiangshi lun* (Essays on modern Chinese intellectual history) (Beijing: Renmin chubanshe, 1979).

———. *Zhongguo xiandai sixiangshi lun* (Essays on contemporary Chinese intellectual history) (Beijing: Dongfang chubanshe, 1987).

Li Zongye. *Zhongguo lishi yaoji jieshao* (An introduction to essential works in Chinese history) (Shanghai: Shanghai Guji Chubanshe, 1982).

Luo Jialun. *Shizhe rusi ji* (Recollections) (Taipei: Zhuanji Wenxue Chubanshe, 1967).

———. *Luo Zhixi xiansheng zhuanji ji zhusu ziliao* (Biography of Luo Jialun and his writings) (Taipei: 1969).

———. *Luo Jialun xiansheng wencun* (The complete works of Luo Jialun), 10 vols. (Taipei: Guoshiguan, 1976).

———. *Luo Jialun ziliaoji* (Sources on Luo Jialun), n.p., n.d., available at Yale University.

Lu Yaodong. *Qiezuo shenzhou xiushouren* (Taipei: Yunchen wenhua shiye gufen youxian gongsi, 1989).

Mao Zishui. *Shiyou ji* (About my friends) (Taipei: Zhuanji Wenxue Chubanshe, 1967).

Rao Yuyi. *Zhongguo lishi shang zhi zhengtonglun* (The legitimacy issue in Chinese historiography) (Hong Kong: Longmen Shudian, 1977).

Sima Qian. *Shiji* (Records of the grand historian) (Taipei: Zhonghua Shuju).

Tang Degang (Te-kang). *Hu Shi zaiyi* (Reminiscences of Hu Shi) (Beijing: Huawen chubanshe, 1992).

Wang Fansen. *Gushibian yundong de xinqi* (The rise of the National Studies

Movement—a study of intellectual history) (Taipei: Asian Culture Company, 1987).

Wang Rongzu. *Shijia Chen Yinke zhuan* (Chen Yinke: an historian) (Taipei: Lianjing Chuban Gongsi, 1984).

Wang Shumin. *Shibu yaoji jieti* (Studies of essential books in Chinese historiography) (Beijing: Zhonghua Shuju. 1981).

Wei Yuan. *Shengwu ji* (The military history of the Qing Dynasty) (Yangzhou: 1846).

———. *Haiguo tuzhi* (Illustrated treatise on the sea kingdoms) (Yangzhou: 1852).

———. *Wei Yuan ji* (The works of Wei Yuan), 2 vols. (Beijing: Zhonghua shuju, 1976).

Wu Ze, ed. *Zhongguo shixueshi lunwenji* (Essays on Chinese historiography), 2 vols. (Shanghai: Shanghai Renmin Chubanshe, 1980).

———, ed. *Zhongguo jindai shixueshi* (A history of modern Chinese historiography), 2 vols. (Nanjing: Jiangsu Guji Chubanshe, 1989).

Xin Ping. *Wang Tao pingzhuan* (A critical biography of Wang Tao) (Shanghai: Huadong shifan daxue chubanshe, 1990).

Xue Huayuan. *Wanqing zhongti xiyong sixiang lun, 1861–1900* (On the "*ti-yong*" ideology in the late Qing) (Taipei: Daoxiang chubanshe, 1991).

———. *Yao Congwu* (Taipei: Huaxin Cultural Center, 1979).

Xu Guansan. *Xinshixue jiushinian* (New history of the last ninety years), 2 vols. (Hong Kong: Chinese University Press, 1986).

Yao Congwu. *Lugouqiao shibian yilai zhongri zhanzheng shiliao souji jihuashu* (Proposal for source collection for the Sino-Japanese War after the Marco Polo Bridge incident) (Kunming, 1939), n.p., available at Harvard-Yenching Library.

———. *Dongbeishi luncong* (Essays on northeast Chinese history) (Taipei, 1955).

———. *Yao Congwu xiansheng aisilu* (Memories for Yao Congwu) (Taipei, 1971).

———. *Yaoshi Congwu xiansheng jinian lunwenji* (Commemorative volume for Yao Congwu), ed. History Department, Taiwan University (Taipei, 1971).

———. *Yaocongwu xiansheng quanji* (The complete works of Yao Congwu), 7 vols. (Taipei: Zhengzhong Shuju, 1971–1982).

Yu Naishu. *Xiandai zhongguo xinshixue* (New history in modern China) (Taizhong: 1969).

Yu Ying-shih. *Lun Dai Zhen he Zhang Xuecheng* (On Dai Zhen and Zhang Xuecheng) (Taipei: Lianjing Chuban shiye gongsi, 1975).

———. *Lishi yu sixiang* (History and ideas) (Taipei: Lianjing Chuban shiye gongsi, 1976).

———, et al. *Wusi xinlun: jifei wenyi fuxing, yifei qimeng yundong* (May Fourth reconsidered: neither Renaissance nor Enlightenment) (Taipei: Lianjing chuban shiye gongsi, 1999).

Zhang Nianshi, ed. *Zhang Taiyan shengping yu xueshu* (Zhang Taiyan's life and career) (Beijing: Sanlian Shudian, 1988).

Zhang Pengyuan. *Guo Tingyi, Fei Zhengqing, Wei Muting: Taiwan yu meiguo xueshu jiaoliu gean chutan* (Triangular Partnership: Guo Tingyi [Kuo Ting-yee], John Fairbank, and C. Martin Wilbur and their contribution to Taiwan-U.S. academic exchange) (Taipei: Institute of Modern History, Academia Sinica, 1997).

Zhang Qizhi et al. *Zhongguo jindai shixue xueshushi* (History of modern Chinese historiography) (Beijing: Zhongguo shehue kexue chubanshe, 1996).

Zhang Shunhui. *Zhongguo gudai shiji jiaodufa* (Methods of reading ancient Chinese books) (Beijing: Zhonghua Shuju, 1962).

Zhang Xuecheng. *Wenshi tongyi* (General meanings of literature and history) (Taipei: Zhonghua Shuju).

———. *Zhangshi yishu* (Literary remains of Zhang Xuecheng), ed. Liu Chengkan (Shanghai: Wuxin, 1922).

Zhou Yutong. "Wushinianlai zhongguo zhi xinshixue" (New history in China in the last fifty years," *Zhou Yutong jingxueshi lunzhu xuanji* (Zhou Yutong's selected works on classics and history), ed. Zhu Weizheng (Shanghai: Shanghai Renmin Chubanshe, 1983), pp. 513–573.

Western Language Sources

Barnes, Harry E. *A History of Historical Writing* (New York: Dover Publications, 1963).

Beasley, W. G. and E. G. Pulleyblank, eds. *Historians of China and Japan* (London: Oxford University Press, 1961).

Becker, Carl. *Everyman His Own Historian: Essays on History and Politics* (New York: Apppleton Century Crofts, 1935).

Blacker, Carmen. *The Japanese Enlightenment: A Study of the Writings of Fukuzawa Yukichi* (Cambridge: Cambridge University Press, 1964).

Bonner, Joey. *Wang Kuo-wei: An Intellectual Biography* (Cambridge, MA: Harvard University Press, 1986).

Breisach, Ernst A. *American Progressive History: An Experiment in Modernization* (Chicago: Chicago University Press, 1993).

———. *Historiography: Ancient, Medieval and Modern* (Chicago: University of Chicago Press, 1983).

Butterfield, Herbert. *Man on His Past* (Boston: Beacon Press, 1960).

Carr, Edward H. *What Is History?* (New York: Alfred A Knopf, 1965).

Chang Hao. *Liang Ch'i-ch'ao and Intellectual Transition in China, 1890–1907* (Cambridge, MA: Harvard University Press, 1971).

———. *Chinese Intellectuals in Crisis: Search for Order and Meaning (1890–1911)* (Berkeley: University of California Press, 1987).

Cheek, Timothy. *Propaganda and Culture in Mao's China: Deng Tuo and the Intelligentsia* (Oxford: Clarendon Press, 1997).

Chen Xiaomei. *Occidentalism* (New York: Oxford University Press, 1995).

Chou Min-chih. *Hu Shih and Intellectual Choice in Modern China* (Ann Arbor: University of Michigan Press, 1984).

Chow Tse-tsung. *The May Fourth Movement: Intellectual Revolution in Modern China* (Cambridge, MA: Harvard University Press, 1960).

Cohen, Paul A. *Between Tradition and Modernity: Wang T'ao and Reform in Late Ch'ing China* (Cambridge, MA: Harvard University Press, 1974).

———. *Discovering History in China: American Historical Writing on the Recent Chinese Past* (New York: Columbia University Press, 1984).

Cohen, Paul and Merle Goldman, eds. *Ideas across Cultures: Essays on Chinese Thought in Honor of Benjamin I. Schwartz* (Cambridge, MA: Harvard University Press, 1990).

Collingwood, R. G. *The Idea of History* (Oxford: Clarendon Press, 1946).

Dawson, Raywon, ed. *The Legacy of China* (Oxford: Clarendon Press, 1964).

De Bary, Wm. Theodore, et al., eds. *The Unfolding of Neo-Confucianism* (New York: Columbia University Press, 1975).

DeLaney, C. F. *Mind and Nature: A Study of the Naturalistic Philosohies of Cohen, Woodbridge and Sellars* (Notre Dame: University of Notre Dame Press, 1969).

Dennerlne, Jerry. *Qian Mu and the World of Seven Mansions* (New Haven: Yale University Press, 1988).

Dewey, John. *How We Think* (Boston: D. C. Heath & Co., Publishers, 1910).

Dirlik, Arif. *Revolution and History: The Origins of Marxist Historiography in China, 1919–1937* (Berkeley: University of California Press, 1978).

Dittmer, Lowell and Samuel Kim, eds. *China's Quest for National Identity* (Ithaca and London: Cornell University Press, 1993).

Duara, Prasenjit. *Rescuing History from the Nation: Questioning Narratives of Modern China* (Chicago: University of Chicago Press, 1995).

Eastman, Lloyd. *Seeds of Destruction: Nationalist China in War and Revolution, 1937–1949* (Stanford: Stanford University Press, 1984).

Egan, Susan Chan. *A Latterday Confucian: Reminiscences of William Hong (1893–1980)* (Cambridge, MA: Harvard University Press, 1987).

Eisenstadt, S. N. and S. R. Graubard, eds. *Intellectuals and Tradition* (New York: Humanities Press, 1973).

Elman, Benjamin. *From Philosophy to Philology: Intellectual and Social Aspects of Change in Late Imperial China* (Cambridge, MA: Harvard University Press, 1984).

Fairbank, John K, ed. *Chinese Thought and Institutions* (Chicago: University of Chicago Press, 1957).

———. *Chinabound: A Fifty-year Memoir* (New York: Harper & Row, 1982).

Feuerwerker, Albert, ed. *History in Communist China* (Cambridge, MA: MIT Press, 1968).

Fogel, Joshua A. *Politics and Sinology: The Case of Naito Konan* (Cambridge, MA: Harvard University Press, 1984).

Frykenberg, Robert E. *History and Belief: The Foundations of Historical Understanding* (Grand Rapids, MI: William B. Ferdmans Publishing Company, 1996).

Fueter, Eduard. *Geschichte der neueren Historiographie* (München & Berlin, 1911).

Fukuzawa Yukichi. *An Outline of a Theory of Civilization*, trans. David A Dilworth and G. Cameron Hurst (Tokyo: Sophia University, 1973).

Fung Yu-lan. *A Short History of Chinese Philosophy*, ed. Derk Bodde (New York: Free Press, 1948).

Furth, Charlotte. *Ting Wen-chiang: Science and China's New Culture* (Cambridge, MA: Harvard University Press, 1979).

———, ed. *The Limits of Change: Essays on Conservative Alternatives in Republican China* (Cambridge, MA: Harvard University Press, 1976).

Gadamer, Hans-Georg. *Truth and Method* (New York: Crossroad, 1984).

Gardner, Charles. *Chinese Traditional Historiography* (Cambridge, MA: Harvard University Press, 1961).

Gilbert, Felix. *History: Politics or Culture? Reflections on Ranke and Burckhardt* (Princeton: Princeton University Press, 1990).

Gluck, Carol. *Japan's Modern Myths: Ideology in the Late Meiji Period* (Princeton: Princeton University Press, 1985).

Goldman, Merle. *China's Intellectuals: Advise and Dissent* (Cambridge, MA: Harvard University Press, 1981).

Gooch, G. P. *History and Historians in the Nineteen Century* (Boston: Beacon Press, 1959).

Graham, Gordon. *The Shape of the Past: A Philosophical Approach to History* (Oxford: Oxford University Press, 1997).

Grieder, Jerome B. *Hu Shih and the Chinese Renaissance: Liberalism in the Chinese Revoution, 1917–1937* (Cambridge, MA: Harvard University Press, 1970).

———. *Intellectuals and the State in Modern China: A Narrative History* (New York: Free Press, 1981).

Gu, Edward X. "Cultural Intellectuals and the Politics of Cultural Public Space in Communist China (1979–1989): A Case Study of the Three Intellectual Group," *Journal of Asian Studies*, 58:2 (1999), 389–431.

Gu Jiegang (Ku Chieh-kang). *The Autobiography of a Chinese Historian*, trans. Arthur W. Hummel (Leyden: Late E. J. Brill Ltd., 1931).

Hamrin, Carol Lee and Timothy Cheek, eds. *China's Establishment Intellectuals* (Armonk, NY: M. E. Sharpe, 1986).

Han Yu-shan. *Elements of Chinese Historiography* (Hollywood, CA: W. M. Hawley, 1955).

Higham, John, Leonard Krieger, and Felix Gilbert. *History: the Development of Historical Studies in the United States* (Englewood Cliffs, NJ: Prentice-Hall, 1968).

Hirth, Friedrich. *The Ancient History of China to the End of the Chou Dynasty* (New York: Columbia University Press, 1908).

———. *China and the Roman Orient: Researches into Their Ancient and Medieval Relations as Presented in Old Chinese Records* (Shanghai: 1885; New York: Paragon Book Reprint Corp. 1966).

Hobsbawm, Eric and Terence Ranger, eds. *The Invention of Tradition* (Cambridge: Cambridge University Press, 1983).

Hofstadter, Richard. *The Progressive Historians: Turner, Beard, Parrington* (New York: A Vintage Book, 1970).

Hon Tze-ki. "Ethnic and Cultural Pluralism: Gu Jiegang's Vision of a New China in His Studies of Ancient History," *Modern China*, 22:3 (July 1996), 315–339.

Huang, Philip C. *Liang Ch'i-ch'ao and Modern Chinese Liberalism* (Seattle: University of Washington Press, 1972).

Hughes, H. Stuart. *Consciousness and Society: The Reorientation of European Social Thought, 1890–1930* (New York: Vintage Books, 1961).

Hung Chang-tai. *Going to the People: Chinese Intellectuals and Folk Literature, 1918–1937* (Cambridge, MA: Harvard University Press, 1985).

Hu Shih. *The Chinese Renaissance: the Haskell Lectures, 1933* (New York: Paragon Book Reprint Corp., 1963).

———. *The Development of the Logical Method in Ancient China* (New York: Paragon Book Reprint Corp., 1963).

Iggers, Georg G. "The Image of Ranke in American and German Historical Thought," *History and Theory*, 2 (1962), 17–40.

———. *The German Conception of History: The National Tradition of Historical Thought from Herder to the Present* (Wesleyan University Press, 1968, rep. 1983).

———. *Historiography in the Twentieth Century: From Scientific Objectivity to the Postmodern Challenge* (Hanover, NH: University Press of New England, 1997).

Israel, John. *Student Nationalism in China, 1927–37* (Stanford: Stanford University Press, 1966).

———. *Lianda: A Chinese University in War and Revolution* (Stanford: Stanford University Press, 1998).

Jenner, W. J. F. *The Tyranny of History: The Roots of China's Crisis* (New York: Penguin Books, 1992).

Jensen, Lionel M. *Manufacturing Confucianism: Chinese Tradition and Universal Civilization* (Durham, NC: Duke University Press, 1997).

Keenan, Barry. *The Dewey Experiment in China: Educational Reform and Political Power in the Early Republic* (Cambridge, MA: Harvard University Press, 1977).

Kelley, Donald R. *Foundations of Modern Historical Scholarship: Language, Law, and History in the French Renaissance* (New York: Columbia University Press, 1970).

Kemp, Anthony. *The Estrangement of the Past: A Study in the Origins of Modern Historical Consciousness* (New York: Oxford University Press, 1991).

Kohn, Hans. *A History of Nationalism in the East* (New York: Harcourt, Brace and Company, 1929).

Kwok, D. W. Y. *Scientism in Chinese Thought 1900–1950* (New Haven: Yale University Press, 1965).

Langlois, Charles and Charles Seignobos. *Introduction to the Study of History*, trans. G. G. Berry (New York: Henry Holt & Company, 1926).

Leonard, Jane Kate. *Wei Yuan and China's Rediscovery of the Maritime World* (Cambridge, MA: Harvard University Press, 1984).

Leslie, Donald D. et al., eds. *Essays on the Sources for Chinese History* (Canberra: Australian National University Press, 1973).

Levenson, Joseph R. *Liang Ch'i-ch'ao and the Mind of Modern China* (Cambridge, MA: Harvard University Press, 1959).

———. *Confucian China and Its Modern Fate: A Trilogy* (Berkeley: University of California Press, 1968).

Liang, Hsi-huey. *The Sino-German Connection: Alexander von Falkenhausen between China and Germany, 1900–41* (Amsterdam: Van Gorcum, Assen, 1978).

Liang, Qichao. *Intellectual Trends in the Ch'ing Period*, trans. Immanuel C. Y. Hsu (Cambridge, MA: Harvard University Press, 1959).

Lieberthal, Kenneth et al., eds. *Perspectives on Modern China: Four Anniversaries* (Armonk, NY: M. E. Sharpe, 1991).

Linde, Max. "Chinese Students in Germany," *Ostasiatische Rundschau*, 7:11 (1926).

Lin Yu-sheng. *The Crisis of Chinese Consciousness: Radical Antitraditionalsim in the May Fourth Era* (Madison: University of Wisconsin Press, 1979).

Liu, Lydia H. *Translingual Practice: Literature, National Culture, and Translated Modernity—China, 1900–1937* (Stanford: Stanford University Press, 1995).

Lowenthal, David. *The Past Is a Foreign Country* (Cambridge: Cambridge University Press, 1985).

Lubot, George. *Liberalism in an Illiberal Age: New Culture Liberals in Republican China, 1919–1937* (Westport, CT: Greenwood Press, 1982).

Martin, Dorothea. *The Making of a Sino-Marxist World View* (Armonk, NY: M. E. Sharpe, 1990).

Meinecke, Friedrich. *Historism: The Rise of a New Historical Outlook*, trans. J. E. Anderson (London: Routledge & Kegan Paul, 1972).

Meisner, Maurice. *Li Ta-chao and the Origins of Chinese Marxism* (Cambridge, MA: Harvard University Press, 1967).

Meisner, Maurice and Rhoads Murphey, eds. *The Mozartian Historian: Essays on the Works of Joseph R. Levenson* (Berkeley: University of California Press, 1976).

Meskill, John, ed. *The Pattern of Chinese History: Cycles, Development, or Stagnation?* (Boston: D. C. Heath and Company, 1965).

Momigliano, Arnaldo. *Studies in Historiography* (New York: Harper & Row, Publishers, 1966).

Moore, Charles, ed. *The Chinese Mind: Essentials of Chinese Philosophy and Culture* (Honolulu: University of Hawaii Press, 1967).

Needham, Joseph. *Science in Traditional China* (Cambridge, MA: Harvard University Press, 1981).

Nivison, David S. *The Life and Thought of Chang Hsueh-ch'eng* (Standford: Stanford University Press, 1966).

Novick, Peter. *That Noble Dream: the "Objectivity Question" and the American Historical Profession* (Cambridge: Cambridge University Press, 1988).

Ong Aihwa. *Flexible Citizenship: The Cultural Logics of Transnationality* (Durham, NC: Duke University Press, 1999).

Pagden, Anthony, ed. *The Languages of Political Theory in Early-Modern Europe* (Cambridge: Cambridge University Press, 1987).

Pocock, J. G. A. *Virtue, Commerce, and History: Essays on Political Thought and History, Chiefly in the Eighteenth Century* (Cambridge: Cambridge University Press, 1985).

Pusey, James. *China and Charles Darwin* (Cambridge, MA: Harvard University Press, 1983).

Pyle, Kenneth B. *The New Generation in Meiji Japan: Problems of Cultural Identity, 1885–1895* (Stanford: Stanford University Press, 1969).

Richter, Ursula. *Zweifel am Altertum: Gu Jiegang und die Diskussion ueber Chinas alte Geschichte als Konsequenz der "Neuen Kulturbewegung" ca. 1915–23* (Stuttgart: Franz Steiner Verlag, 1992).

Rosen, Richard. "The National Heritage Opposition to the New Culture and Literary Movements of China in the 1920s" (Ph.D. Dissertation, University of California/Berkeley, 1969).

Rüsen, Jörn and Friedrich Jaeger, *Geschichte des Historismus* (München, 1992).

Ryckmans, Pierre. *The Chinese Attitude toward the Past* (Canberra: Australian National University Press, 1986).

Said, Edward. *Orientalism* (New York: Vintage Books, 1978).

Sato Masayuki. "Historiographical Encounters: The Chinese and Western Traditions in Turn-of-the-century Japan," *Storia della Storiografia*, 19 (1991), 13–21.

Schneider, Axel. "Between Dao and History: Two Chinese Historians in Search of a Modern Identity for China," *History and Theory*, 35:4 (1996), 34–53.

Schneider, Laurence A. *Ku Chieh-kang and China's New History: Nationalsim and the Quest for Alternative Traditions* (Berkeley: University of California Press, 1971).

Schwarcz, Vera. *The Chinese Enlightenment: Intellectuals and the Legacy of the May Fourth Movement of 1919* (Berkeley: University of California Press, 1986).

Schwartz, Benjamin, ed. *Reflections on the May Fourth Movement: A Symposium* (Cambridge, MA: Harvard University Press, 1972).

———. *In Search of Wealth and Power: Yen Fu and the West* (Cambridge, MA: Harvard University Press, 1964).

Strout, Cushing. *The Pragmatic Revolt in American History: Carl Becker and Charles Beard* (New Haven: Yale University Press, 1958).

Tang Xiaobing. *Global Space and the Nationalist Discource of Modernity: The Historical Thinking of Liang Qichao* (Stanford: Stanford University Press, 1996).

Tu Wei-ming, ed. *The Living Tree: The Changing Meaning of Being Chinese Today* (Stanford: Stanford University Press, 1994).

Twitchett, Denis. *The Writing of Official History under the T'ang* (New York: Cambridge University Press, 1992).

Unger, Jonathan, ed. *Using the Past to Serve the Present: Historiography and Politics in Contemporary China* (Armonk, NY: M. E. Sharpe, 1993).

Wakeman, Frederic, Jr. *The Fall of Imperial China* (New York: Free Press, 1975).

Wang Fansen (Fan-shen). *Fu Ssu-nien (Sinian): An Intellectual Biography* (Ph.D. Dissertation, Princeton University, 1993).

Wang Jing. *High Culture Fever: Politics, Aesthetics, and Ideology in Deng's China* (Berkeley: University of California Press, 1996).

Wang, Qingjia Edward. "Western Historiography in the People's Republic China, 1949 to the present," *Storia della Storiografia*, 19 (1991), 23–46.

———. "Chinese Historians and the West: The Origins of Modern Chinese Historiography" (Ph.D. Dissertation, Syracuse University, 1992).

———. "History in Late Imperial China," *Storia della Storiografia*, 22 (1992), 3–22.

———. "Between Marxism and Nationalism: Chinese Historiography and the Soviet Influence, 1949–1963," *Journal of Contemporary China*, 9:23 (2000), 95–111.

Wang, Y. C. *Chinese Intellectuals and the West, 1872–1949* (Chapel Hill: University of North Carolina Press, 1966).

Wasserstrom, Jeffrey N. and Elizabeth J. Perry, eds. *Popular Protest and Political Culture in Modern China* (Boulder, CO: Westview Press, 1994).

Watson, Burton. *Ssu-ma Ch'ien, Grand Historian of China* (New York: Columbia University Press, 1958).

———. *Records of the Grand Historian of China*, 2 vols. (New York: Columbia University Press, 1961).

West, Philip. *Yenching University and Sino-Western Relations, 1916–1952* (Cambridge, MA: Harvard University Press, 1976).

White, Hayden. *Metahistory: The Historical Imagination in Nineteenth-Century Europe* (Baltimore and London: Johns Hopkins University Press, 1973).

Windelband, Wilhelm. *History of Ancient Philosophy*, trans. Herbert E. Cushman (New York: Charles Scribner's Sons, 1898).

Woodbridge, Frederick J. K. *The Purpose of History* (New York: Columbia University Press, 1916).

———. *Nature and Mind: Selected Essays of Frederick J. E. Woodbridge* (New York: Russell & Russell, 1965).

Wright, Arthur F., ed. *Studies in Chinese Thought* (Chicago: University of Chicago Press, 1953).

Xu Guansan (Hsu Kwan-san). "The Chinese Critical Tradition," *The Historical Journal*, 26:2 (1983), 431–446.

Yeh Wen-hsin. *The Alienated Academy: Culture and Politics in Republican China, 1919–1937* (Cambridge, MA: Harvard University Press, 1990).

Yu Ying-shih. "The Radicalization of China in the Twentieth Century," *Daedalus*, 122:2 (Spring 1993), 125–150.

———. "Changing Conceptions of National History in Twentieth-Century China," *Conceptions of National History*, eds. Erik Lönnroth, Karl Molin, and Ragnar Björk (Berlin: Walter de Gruyter, 1994), 155–174.

Zhang Longxi. *Mighty Opposites: From Dichotomies to Differences in the Comparative Study of China* (Stanford: Stanford University Press, 1998).

Zhang Xudong. *Chinese Modernism in the Era of Reforms: Cultural Fever, Avant-Garde Fiction, and the New Chinese Cinema* (Durham, NC: Duke University Press, 1996).

Index